LANDMARKS IN Rhetoric and Public Address

LANDMARKS IN Rhetoric and Public Address

David Potter, *General Editor*

SELECTED ESSAYS ON

Rhetoric

BY

THOMAS DE QUINCEY

EDITED BY

Frederick Burwick

FOREWORD BY

David Potter

Carbondale and Edwardsville

SOUTHERN ILLINOIS UNIVERSITY PRESS

FEFFER & SIMONS, INC.

London and Amsterdam

FOREWORD

By David Potter

IN LEGEND and in fact Thomas De Quincey is one of the most
fascinating of English writers. Born Thomas Quincey in 1785,
he managed to survive the imaginative forays of a vigorous
older brother, the discipline of an unbending mother, and the
stifling atmosphere of a series of preparatory schools. Escap-
ing from Manchester Grammar School with little more than a
copy of Wordsworth's poems and a volume of Euripides, he
wandered for several months in Wales and London. Finally,
in December, 1803, he allowed himself to be enrolled at
Worcester College, Oxford. But he left the university without a
degree, refusing to take the orals despite a successful written
examination. His marriage to Margaret Simpson after the
birth of their first child, offended a forgetful Wordsworth and
ruptured their friendship. In 1821 De Quincey submitted the
"Confessions of an Opium-Eater" to the *London Magazine*.
In 1822 the *Confessions* appeared in book form and brought
considerable notice and attendant discomfort to its author.
From this period until his death in 1859, he planned great
masterpieces and contributed an uneven flow of manuscripts
to popular magazines. The ministrations of his beloved daughters lightened his last ten years as did the appearance of his
collected works in America and England.

Much of De Quincey's career can be described, superficially,
as a series of paradoxes. Shy to an extreme, he was a willing
and brilliant conversationalist. Master of a musical and sensitive prose style, he resorted frequently to interminable digression. Attuned to the genius of Wordsworth and Coleridge
long before the Lake School was widely accepted and an early
popularizer of German literature and philosophy, he allowed a

wide assortment of political and social prejudices to blind him
to the talents of some of the more enduring writers of his time.
A childlike inability to comprehend his financial situations,
the consequent resort to hack journalism, loss of an enormous
and indispensable library, unbelievably littered quarters which
made the location of material an insurmountable chore, and
understandable break-downs in a prodigious memory contributed to lapses in scholarship. But despite these obstacles, the
sapping influence of drugs, chronic ill health, and the demands
of an alien and often antagonistic world, this strange and endearing little nocturnal wanderer attained, especially in the
cadences and crescendos of his dream-visions and bravura
pieces, pre-eminence as a prose-stylist. His careful attention
to the rhythm and harmony of sounds and ideas is also evident
in the essays on *Rhetoric, Style, Conversation, Language*, and
Greek Literature, which are contained in this volume.

Despite the importance of these essays, they remain among
the least available of De Quincey's writings. *Rhetoric* (1828)
and *Style* (1840 - 41) originally appeared in *Blackwood's*;
Greek Literature (1838 - 39) and *Conversation* (1847), in *Tait's
Magazine*. When De Quincey brought together his randomly
published essays in the fourteen volume *Selections Grave and
Gay* (1853 - 60), he introduced a few essays for which no previous publication is known, and omitted several essays altogether; thus the *Selections* include the first known printing
of the essay on *Language* (Vol. IX, 1858), while the *Brief
Appraisal of Greek Literature* is absent. A more complete edition, *The Collected Writings of Thomas De Quincey*, was edited
by David Masson in 1889 - 90. Here De Quincey's five important essays appeared together for the first and, with the
exception of this *Landmarks* edition, the only time. Just three
years after Masson's collection, Fred Newton Scott, recogniz-
ing the importance of De Quincey's rhetorical theory and the
need for a more generally available edition, reprinted a selection in *De Quincey's Essays on Style, Rhetoric, and Language*.
A representative selection also appeared in Helen Darbishire's
De Quincey's Literary Criticism (1909). Since then there has been
more concern for De Quincey's "impassioned prose" and for
his biographical and autobiographical sketches, and propor-
tionately less attention has been given to his rhetorical theory.

The present edition has been reproduced by offset from Volume X of the Masson edition of 1889 - 90, retaining the original pagination of Masson's volume. The type has been increased by 18 per cent to improve appearance and readability. Editor Frederick Burwick has contributed a comprehensive index, a selected bibliography, and a luminous introductory essay which traces the sources and development of a belletristic theory of rhetoric which "is one of the most original and, for a few critics, the most puzzling of the nineteenth century." Professor Burwick's scholarship, buttressed by his study of German literature and philosophy at the Universities of Göttingen and Würzburg, experience in computer analysis of rhetorical techniques of prose style at the Universities of Wisconsin and California, and four years of intensive preparation for this essay, should result in a clearer conception of and increased interest in De Quincey as a rhetorician and critic.

CONTENTS

INTRODUCTION

By Frederick Burwick

FROM THE *Confessions of an English Opium-Eater*, published in 1821 at the very beginning of his literary career, to the *English Mail-Coach*, composed in 1849 when that career was drawing to a close, Thomas De Quincey contributed to English literature some of the finest prose ever written in the language. The same sensitivity that made him such a master of "impassioned prose" also enabled him to discuss perceptively the problems of rhetoric and style. Following his own interests as a writer and critic, De Quincey's concern with rhetoric is belletristic rather than oratorical, and the theory which he developed is one of the most original and, for a few critics, the most puzzling of the nineteenth century.

In reading his essays, we must keep in mind that De Quincey attempted only an informal commentary and not a systematic treatise on rhetoric, for the very factors which have previously puzzled some of De Quincey's critics are those factors which arise from De Quincey's own concept of the nature and function of the informal essay. The essay itself, as De Quincey defines it, is a rhetorical act, based upon paradox and developed with polemic skill. "These specimens," De Quincey says of one volume of his essays, "are sufficient for the purpose of informing the reader that I do not write without a thoughtful consideration of my subject, and also that to think reasonably upon any question has never been allowed by me as a sufficient ground for writing upon it, unless I believed myself able to offer some considerable novelty." [1] A paradox, which counters the orthodox and "contradicts the popular opinion," provides

[1] *The Collected Writings of Thomas De Quincey*, ed. David Masson (Edinburgh, 1889-90), VI, 2.

the needed element of novelty. Rhetorically, the special function of paradoxes is that they "fix the public attention" by shouting " 'Here, reader, are some extraordinary truths, looking so very like falsehoods that you would never take them for anything else if you were not invited to give them special examination.' " [2] Polemics and paradox go hand-in-hand: a paradox is a truth at odds with general opinion; polemics is the art of debating a controversial issue. De Quincey explains his notion of the polemic method by contrasting "the good speaker" with "the good debater":

> The radical and characteristic idea concerned in this term *polemic* is found in our own Parliamentary distinction of *the good speaker* as contrasted with *the good debater*. The good speaker is he who unfolds the whole of a question in its affirmative aspects, who presents these aspects in their just proportions, and according to their orderly and symmetrical deductions from each other. But *the good debater* is he who faces the negative aspects of the question, who meets sudden objections, has an answer for any momentary summons of doubt or difficulty, dissipates seeming inconsistencies, and reconciles the geometrical smoothness of *a priori* abstractions with the coarse angularities of practical experience.[3]

With this combination of paradox and polemics, then, De Quincey's essays are written in the manner of "the good debater" in combat with prevailing error. Thus in *Rhetoric* (1828), we find De Quincey correcting the popular misconceptions of rhetoric and basing his own definition on an interpretation of Aristotle that counters much scholarly opinion. The essay on *Style* (1840 - 41) opens with an argument against the British notion that manner and matter are separate entities in composition. The same argument is continued in *Language* (n.d.), where he also discusses misconceptions concerning the national attributes of languages. In *Conversation* (1847), the paradox is that conversation as a fine art depends not upon brilliant speech, but upon a rhetoric of sympathy and association. And in *A Brief Appraisal of the Greek Literature* (1838 - 39), he examines the negative aspects of Greek poetry, prose, and oratory often ignored in the general veneration of Grecian culture.

[2] *Collected Writings*, VII, 206.   [3] *Collected Writings*, IX, 53–54.

These five essays, it will be noticed, appeared over a span of twenty years, and, because of the wide range in time, they are not without a few inconsistencies and contradictions. However, they also reveal a fundamental continuity of thought that springs in part from his prodigious memory, and in part from his underlying philosophic system: De Quincey's signal contribution to the history of rhetoric is that he brought together for the first time the principal elements of Scottish associationism and German aesthetics.

In addition to the German and Scottish backgrounds of his theory, De Quincey also claims at the beginning of his essay on *Rhetoric* that his view of rhetoric and its functions closely follows the Aristotelian system. This claim, of course, needs to be qualified in terms of his paradoxical argument, for several scholars have been at a loss to find much truth in it, excepting perhaps the truth of De Quincey's sly observation that "all parties may possibly fancy a confirmation of their views in Aristotle" (83). In editing the essays, David Masson, convinced that De Quincey suffered "an imperfect recollection" of Aristotle's *Rhetorica* and had only "a hazy conception" of the history of rhetorical theory, felt it necessary to append four full pages of notes explaining Aristotelian rhetoric. But Masson did not have the last word. In his *Ancient Rhetoric and Poetic*, Charles Sears Baldwin stated that the major distinction of Aristotelian rhetoric is "confirmed by De Quincey's distinction between literature of knowledge and literature of power." [4] Wilbur Samuel Howell rose with the rebuttal that not only is De Quincey's theory non-Aristotelian, but it is "so attenuated, so unreal, so far divorced from actual experience, so completely devoid of connections with the urgent issues of politics and law, that we can only wonder why De Quincey would think it worthwhile for Aristotle or any serious-minded person to bother with it in any theoretical or practical way." [5] On the same grounds, René Wellek concluded that De Quincey's concept of rhetoric is without value and best forgotten.[6]

[4] Charles Sears Baldwin, *Ancient Rhetoric and Poetic* (New York, 1924), p. 4.
[5] "De Quincey on Science, Rhetoric, and Poetry," *Speech Monographs*, XII, No. 1 (1946), p. 3.
[6] "Thomas De Quincey's Status in the History of Ideas," *PQ*, XXIII (July, 1944), 269.

Hoyt H. Hudson, on the other hand, is a much more sympathetic critic of De Quincey's theory, praising it especially for its astute description of rhetorical invention and amplification, but even Hudson is puzzled by De Quincey's claim that "amongst the greater orators of Greece there is not a solitary gleam of rhetoric" (94). The only explanation that Hudson can find is that "De Quincey is in a hurry to set down his own delightful ideas . . . so that he has not time enough to be wholly fair to his predecessors." [7]

Such critical comments make it clear that De Quincey's theory of rhetoric is Aristotelian only in a limited sense. Certainly Aristotle's distinction between the literature of statement (science, history, oratory) and the literature of representation (drama, poetry) suggests—as it no doubt suggested to De Quincey—the literature of knowledge and the literature of power, but Howell is quite correct in his assertion that the two distinctions are not at all the same.[8] The Aristotelian element in De Quincey's theory is most apparent in his emphasis on probabilities and enthymemic reasoning, but even here Masson has rightly pointed out that De Quincey's emphasis on probability is much stronger than Aristotle's.[9]

Why does De Quincey consider Greek oratory barren of rhetoric, why does his theory ignore "the urgent issues of politics and law"? The answer is to be found in the three major premises of De Quincey's belletristic approach:

1] Whatsoever is certain, or matter of fixed science, can be no subject for the rhetorician: where it is possible for the understanding to be convinced, no field is open for rhetorical persuasion. (90–91)

2] Rhetoric is the art of aggrandizing and bringing out into strong relief, by means of various and striking thoughts, some aspect of truth which of itself is supported by no spontaneous feelings, and therefore rests upon artificial aids. (92)

[7] "De Quincey on Rhetoric and Public Speaking," in *Historical Studies of Rhetoric and Rhetoricians*, ed. Raymond F. Howes (Ithaca, N. Y., 1961), p. 200.

[8] Howell, pp. 6–12.

[9] James H. McBurney, "Some Recent Interpretations of the Aristotelian Enthymeme," *Papers of the Michigan Academy of Science, Arts, and Letters*, XXI (1935), 485–500, affirms De Quincey's emphasis on probability and on enthymemic reasoning as accurately interpreting Aristotle's *Rhetorica*.

3] Rhetoric . . . aims at an elaborate form of beauty which shrinks from the strife of business, and could neither arise nor make itself felt in a tumultuous assembly. . . . All great rhetoricians in selecting their subject have shunned the determinate cases of real life. (93–94) [10]

The premises are purposefully one-sided, geared only to the appeal to the intellect through the Aristotelian mode of *logos*; the mode of *pathos*, the appeal to the passions, belongs to eloquence, which De Quincey defines in Wordsworthian terms as "the overflow of powerful feelings upon occasions fitted to excite them." The highest form of literature is a combination of both rhetoric and eloquence brought into play by the creative genius. As for the mode of *ethos*, the appeal through character, that De Quincey considers part of the matter of discourse rather than of the manner.

The mode of *logos* appeals to the intellect through its control over the logic of probabilities, and it is this area of logic that De Quincey considers the proper realm of rhetoric. As he interprets Aristotelian rhetoric, that theory, like his own, is addressed to a *ratio probabilis*, to a consideration "of plausible or colourable truth" (86). The Aristotelian *enthymeme*, he further argues, is not an abridged syllogism, rather it is a syllogism applied to probabilities instead of realities. The syllogism proper deals with what is certain and factual; the enthymeme, by contrast, deals with what is only opinion and probable. Although De Quincey summarizes Jacobi Facciolati's *De Enthymemate* in defense of his interpretation of Aristotle, he acknowledges primary indebtedness to his friend, Sir William Hamilton, as "the central authority" in the controversy concerning the place of the enthymeme in Aristotle's logic and rhetoric. The importance of probabilities and enthymemic reasoning in De Quincey's rhetoric is readily seen in the topics

[10] Hudson, pp. 202, 403–4, calls attention to De Quincey's inconsistency on this point. Although Hudson misquotes the phrase as "shunned the determinate causes of real life," he correctly identifies the contradiction in De Quincey's attributing "the fine, sonorous modulations" of Cicero to the advantages derived "from real campaigns, from unsimulated strife of actual stormy life" in contrast to the "torpid dreams of what the Romans called an *umbratic* experience" (*A Brief Appraisal of the Greek Literature*, p. 324). This observation hardly accords with De Quincey's earlier reference to rhetoric, "in its finest and most absolute burnish," as "an *eloquentia umbratica*" (*Rhetoric*, p. 93).

which he identifies as especially suited for rhetorical treatment,
for his principal criteria are either that there be "a *pro* and a
con, with the chance of right and wrong, true and false, distributed in varying proportions between them," or that there
be "no chances at all concerned, but the affirmative and
the negative are both true" (91). Thus rhetorical expression
assumes, as a matter of course, a paradoxical form where both
alternatives may be true. As examples of this order of paradox,
De Quincey lists: "the goodness of human nature and its
wickedness; the happiness of human life and its misery; the
charms of knowledge, and its hollowness; the fragility of human prosperity in the eye of religious meditation, and its security as estimated by worldly confidence and youthful hope"
(91). As an inexhaustible mine of paradoxes, human nature itself shall always be the rhetorician's most abundant as well as
his most popular subject. Thus there is no strain upon the
techniques of rhetorical *inventio*; not finding, but resolving the
paradoxes is the rhetorician's problem. In dealing with the
paradoxical probabilities of an argument such as "the goodness
of human nature and its wickedness," the rhetorician's trick is
to put the weight of his evidence on one of the alternatives:
"In all such cases the rhetorician exhibits his art by giving an
impulse to one side, and withdrawing the mind so steadily from
all thoughts or images which support the other as to leave it
practically under the possession of a one-sided estimate" (91).
This does not demand delusive sophistries, nor deceptive
eristics, nor deceitful obfuscations, for the truths at stake are
not absolute, not factual.

If nothing absolute or factual is at stake, what, then, is the
end of the rhetorical appeal? Intellectual pleasure, in De
Quincey's terms, is the primary end, and the "artifice and
machinery of rhetoric furnishes in its degree as legitimate a
basis for intellectual pleasure as any other" (101). But that
pleasure, he grants, is of an "inferior order." It is less than the
literature of power, which appeals to the whole man, to both
his reason and his passions, by combining the *logos* of rhetoric
and the *pathos* of eloquence. De Quincey's distinction between
rhetoric and eloquence, and his explanation of the interplay
between them, follows the reasoning of Schiller's *Kallias*
letters and his letters *On the Aesthetic Education of Man*.

Language itself opposes the ends of both rhetoric and eloquence, for it is purely mechanical in nature, a complexity of
sounds existing in an arbitrary and changing network of meaning, and meaning is further modified by grammatical inflec-
tions and syntactical order. The success of rhetoric and eloquence impinges on the extent to which they can surmount the
resistive nature of language and make its machinery organic.
Schiller's premise that language is resistive grows out of the
Aristotelian concept of resistive opposition as the initiating
principle.[11] De Quincey not only accepts this premise, but he
also follows Schiller's reasoning from this premise toward the
final resolution of form and content through the facility of
creative play. Schiller formulates his idea of resistive language
several times, but always he sees the difficulties of style as
militating against an easy and accurate expression of individual
sensibility. This resistive tendency is the unavoidable result
of mechanical and general language, for the writer or speaker
must use words which communicate only in terms of the restrictions of grammar and syntax. The crux of the problem
is in transforming what is mechanical and general in language
into a style that is organic and individual.[12] In his essay on
Style, De Quincey acknowledges the same problem: "Every
man who has studied and meditated the difficulties of style
must have had a sub-conscious sense of a bar in his way at a
particular point of the road thwarting his free movement"
(191). Because the necessities of language stand in opposition
to the freedom of expression, De Quincey addresses his theory
to the difficulties of language "which apply to the mechanology
of style" (191). That language is mechanical but may also become organic affords no paradox, for every organism functions
according to mechanical principles (164). Since language as
the "raw material" of literature is merely mechanical, the
challenge to the creative genius is to instill his medium with
life. This can never be performed by the discursive reason
(*Verstand*) but requires the imaginative and intuitive reason
(*Vernunft*) (103). This is the point of De Quincey's criticism of
the rhetoric of *Paradise Lost*, and it is also the point of Schiller's

[11] See *Metaphysica*, Book IX.
[12] *Friedrich Schiller, Sämtliche Werke*, ed. Gerhard Fricke and Herbert
G. Göpfert (Munich, 1960), V, 431–32.

objections to the "language of discursive reason" which can educate but can never inspire.[13] There are, then, two modes of language: the discursive mode which remains mechanical, and the intuitive mode which becomes organic. This organic style, the only true literary style, may, as Schiller postulates, address either the higher reason or the sensibilities.[14] De Quincey identifies the same ends of literary style when he says that it may serve either "to brighten the *intelligibility* of a subject" or "to regenerate the normal *power* and impressiveness of a subject which has become dormant to the sensibilities (260–61). Schiller's influence on this dualistic approach is especially apparent when De Quincey develops at length the contrast between mechanic and organic style (163–64).

In Schiller's theory, the mechanic and the organic are respectively distinguished by necessity and freedom. In the last two *Kallias* letters, Schiller discusses first the idea of necessity and freedom as they apply to art in general, and then as they apply to literary composition in particular. Nature, because it is autonomous, determined by its own laws and obeying an inner necessity, is free; and to the extent that art follows the rules of its own forms, art, too, appears free. Nature is true freedom; art is freedom in appearance ("Freiheit in der Erscheinung"). Necessity is mechanical if it is imposed upon the subject to make it adhere to some ulterior purpose. Necessity, however, is organic if it expresses a harmony between the essence of the subject and the form, that is, if the form appears to be given by the subject itself. Thus the stipulation that art must reveal an inner necessity of form does not restrict its freedom, because it is duty determined by the very nature of the object. An object is free and beautiful when it accomplishes this duty; when it does not, it is mechanical.[15]

De Quincey gives a perfect example of this principle in that anecdote in *Rhetoric* where he argues that it is "the duty of a golden coin to be as florid as it can." The same duty, he says, must be expressed by rhetoric (130). Restraint, the restriction of duty, does not render freedom impossible; it provides the very opposition that makes freedom possible. On the other hand, neither does necessity assure freedom in the arts, for

---

[13] "Verstand," *Tabulae Votivae*, in Schiller, *Werke*, I, 310.
[14] *Werke*, V, 732.   [15] *Werke*, V, 416.

De Quincey agrees with Schiller that art is free only when necessity is not directed by some exterior means to some ulterior end. When the means "pre-exist in the end," they must then be "unfolded by the understanding, gradually and tentatively as respects the individual artist, but with severest necessity as respects the object." [16] Thus when De Quincey states that freedom in fine art results from the conflict with restraint, he refers, with Schiller, to an inner conflict. What, the question at this point must be, are the conditions of such a conflict, and what determines that freedom, not necessity, will triumph?

The solution is derived from Schiller's idea of the inner necessity of form. Art appears free to the extent that necessity seems self-determined. Style, in Schiller's definition, is the complete elevation of language beyond the accidental to the general and necessary. [17] The accidental is subsumed in the necessary and the mechanic in the organic. In the next step of the argument, Schiller postulates the unity of matter (*Stoff*) and manner (*Behandlung*), but he attributes the effects of art to manner alone. [18] The matter and manner appear, as they must, confluent and harmonious, but manner elevates the base to the beautiful, transforms natural beauty into artistic beauty, or — where it fails — renders natural beauty base. [19]

De Quincey is not altogether consistent in following this argument. Within the three essays, *Rhetoric*, *Style*, and *Language*, De Quincey leans now toward an emphasis on the inseparability of form and content, and now toward a belief that form may provide a pleasure completely apart from content. But the main line of his discussion conforms to Schiller's idea of the twofold relationship between form and content: literary style attains unity and harmony in total appearance, but only through the conditioning of manner upon matter.

The problems of language in strictly discursive topics can be solved mechanically by overcoming "the *friction* of style, the needless joltings and retardations of our fluent motion." But a mechanical facility can go no further; it cannot affect "the motion itself in all that is positive in its derivation, in its exciting impulses, in its speed, and in its characteristic varieties" (193). The real problem of language is not concerned

---

[16] *Collected Writings*, XI, 194–95.   [17] *Werke*, V, 429–30.
[18] *Werke*, V, 993.   [19] *Werke*, V, 639.

with merely presenting objective concepts clearly to others—
this is only a mechanical problem. The real problem, rather, is
expressing both the soul and body of style in an objective-
subjective synthesis—this is the organic problem. Schiller
expresses the problem in these words: "I do not desire merely
to make my thoughts clear to another, rather I wish at the
same time to give him my entire soul and to affect his sensual
as well as his intellectual powers." [20] What is desired is the
complete confluence of the externalities of the matter with the
internal sensibilities of the writer. As De Quincey describes it
in his essay on *Style*, "the more closely any exercise of mind is
connected with what is internal and individual in the sensibilities,—that is, with what is philosophically termed *subjective*,—precisely in that degree . . . does the manner, . . .
become confluent with the matter" (229). This confluence De
Quincey compares to Wordsworth's definition of style as "the
incarnation of thoughts," as opposed to "the *dress* of thoughts."
Whereas the latter suggests style and content are separable,
the former makes them "soul and body . . . each co-existing
not merely *with* the other, but each *in* and *through* the other"
(230). Although style is thus confluent with content, De
Quincey elsewhere states that the two may be analyzed and
valued separately. Earlier in the same essay, for example, he
undertakes a consideration of the *"form of style"* apart from
the *"form of logic"* (185). De Quincey's ideas on the varying
degrees of relationship between form and content are most
carefully delineated in three points at the end of his essay on
Language: 1] De Quincey affirms that while the matter may
stimulate interest, the pleasure in language as a fine art is
induced exclusively by the manner. Style, defined here as "the
management of language," De Quincey places "amongst the
fine arts" because of its ability "to yield a separate intellectual
pleasure quite apart from the interest of the subject treated."
Style as a fine art is not "necessarily a secondary or subordinate
thing," for it has *"absolute* value" in its independent ability,
"irrelatively to the subject," to evoke an aesthetic response.
2] De Quincey next affirms that style must not be at odds
with content, but must harmoniously condition it. This aspect
of style, however, he considers of less aesthetic merit, for he

[20] *Schillers Briefe, Kritische Gesamtausgabe*, ed. Fritz Jonas (Stuttgart,
1892 - 96), IV, 221.

refers to it as "this narrow valuation of style, founded on the interest of the subject to which it is ministerial." The manner conditions the matter by bringing to it the light of intelligibility and the power of action; "under this idea of ministeriality," style functions, through matter, "as a mode *per se* of the beautiful and a fountain of intellectual pleasure." 3] De Quincey also affirms that style and content may be completely confluent in cases "where style cannot be regarded as a *dress* or alien covering, but where style becomes the *incarnation* of the thoughts." This statement obviously echoes the passage quoted above from the essay on *Style*, with the notable exception that here he insists that style deserves a separate valuation, a valuation that it seldom receives merely because it is seldom recognized. Much of the inconsistency and contradiction that has been attributed to De Quincey's pronouncements on style is clearly resolved by this comprehensive definition which embraces first the independent value, second the ministerial relations, and third "the metaphysical relations of style" (260–62). There is no more a contradiction here than in Schiller's notion that form and content are united, but that the aesthetic value of their union is achieved only through form.

The interactions of form and content as conceived by Schiller and De Quincey are directly linked to the artistic endeavor. De Quincey's idea of *play* is an application of Schiller's *Formtrieb*, *Stofftrieb*, and *Spieltrieb* to the creative process in prose art.

The terms *rhetoric* and *eloquence* were used interchangeably throughout the eighteenth century. The importance of De Quincey's theory lies in his explanation of the antithetical contrast between them. Previous critics have seen that the exercise of the two as "manipulation" or "mind-play" is the prime thesis of De Quincey's theory,[21] but the indebtedness of his theory to Schiller's aesthetics has never before been examined. In light of Schiller's aesthetics, it is obvious that the philosophical rationale of the antithesis and synthesis of rhetoric and eloquence is the logical culmination of the interrelated series of opposing factors we have just reviewed: organic *vs.*

[21] Sigmund Proctor, *Thomas De Quincey's Theory of Literature* (Ann Arbor, 1943), pp. 228–68; John E. Jordan, *Thomas De Quincey, Literary Critic* (Berkeley, 1952), pp. 215–26.

mechanical, freedom *vs.* necessity, form *vs.* content. The subsumption in each case of the latter into the former is achieved in literature through creative play.

Schiller's aesthetics, as his theory progresses from this point, provides the following grounds for De Quincey's rhetoric. Confronted with the opposition between the subjective individuality of the artist's imagination and the objective generality of the language, Schiller proposes the possibility of a resolution: the nature of language, its tendency to generality, must be subordinated, so that the matter to be represented may appear before the imagination in its total truth, vivacity, and personality, in spite of all the chains of language.[22] This possibility of resolution, however, is contingent upon the subsumption of content in form, of language in idea. Since the language is general and formless and the idea is abstract and lifeless, the resolution can only be realized through the intermediating action of a third factor, which Schiller calls *play*. Man possesses three mental powers: the physically perceptual *Stofftrieb*, which is concerned with matter, change, and manifold reality; the metaphysically conceptual *Formtrieb*, which is concerned with essence, permanence, and generic formality; the emergent intermediating *Spieltrieb*, which combines the concerns of the other two drives. The purpose of the *Spieltrieb* is to bring both aspects of human nature into balance; aesthetically, the effect of this balance in human nature is beauty, the union of form and content as living form: "Ideale Schönheit heißt lebende Gestalt." Corollary to this end, Schiller provides the following observations: first, "man should only *play* with beauty, and he should play *only with beauty*," that is, in aesthetic play no interfering concerns (political, moral, etc.) should be introduced or permitted to detract; second, man "is only then completely man, when he plays," otherwise human nature is only partially fulfilled — either his physical or his intellectual nature dominates, or both strive on disparate disharmony. Out of the harmonizing principle of play, man has constructed "the entire edifice of aesthetic art." [23]

Play is also the harmonizing principle in De Quincey's theory, the means whereby rhetoric and eloquence are ulti-

[22] *Werke*, V, 432–33.
[23] *Über die ästhetische Erziehung des Menschen.* Nos. 11–15, *Werke*, V, 601–19.

mately synthesized in style. When De Quincey defines eloquence as "the overflow of powerful feelings" and rhetoric as "aggrandizing and bringing out into strong relief, by means of various and striking thoughts, some aspect of truth," David Masson adds a note which suggests that De Quincey's unique conception "may be translated as meaning the art of intellectual and fantastic play with any subject to its utmost capabilities" (92). Masson's interpretation is essentially correct, for the idea of "intellectual or fantastic play," translated from Schiller's general aesthetic into the particular terms of rhetoric, does indeed govern the ensuing commentary. Just a few pages following, De Quincey gives us a description of the subtle intellectual activity of play: "To hang upon one's own thoughts as an object of conscious interest, to play with them, to watch and pursue them through a maze of inversions, evolutions, and harlequin changes" (97). Rhetoric brought into play with eloquence becomes organic; De Quincey quotes extensively from Jeremy Taylor to illustrate how this interplay of rhetoric and eloquence quickens his prose with the pulsations of life: "the everlasting strife and fluctuation between his rhetoric and his eloquence, which maintain their alternations with force and inevitable recurrence, like the systole and diastole (the contraction and expansion, of some living organ" (108). By itself, however, rhetoric is merely mechanical, "laying the principal stress upon the management of the thoughts, and only a secondary one upon the ornaments of style" (101). The mechanical display of rhetoric may provide pleasure, but it is a lesser pleasure than that afforded by the balanced play of rhetoric and eloquence. Thus John Donne is a master of play, really a rhetorical poet rather than a metaphysical poet, because he has surpassed all others in combining "the last sublimation of dialectical subtlety and address with the most impassioned majesty" (101). In paying similar tribute to Jeremy Taylor and Sir Thomas Browne, De Quincey says they "were undoubtedly the richest, the most dazzling, and, with reference to their matter, the most captivating, of all rhetoricians"; in their prose rhetoric and eloquence, together with matter and manner, interact in stylistic play:

> In them first, and perhaps (if we except occasional passages in
> the German John Paul Richter) in them only, are the two op-
> posite forces of eloquent passion and rhetorical fancy brought

into an exquisite equilibrium,—approaching, receding,—attracting, repelling,—blending, separating,—chasing and chased, as in
a fugue,—and again lost in a delightful interfusion, so as to create
a middle species of composition, more various and stimulating
to the understanding than pure eloquence, more gratifying to the
affections than naked rhetoric. (106–7)

Donne, Browne, Taylor, and Richter have utilized the facility
of play in their writings; De Quincey discusses, as well, certain
French "sentimentalists" who have not. Florian and Chateaubriand, since their art lacks play, have only half fulfilled their
artistic purpose. They are "semi-poetic . . . eloquent, but
never rhetorical" (121). Where the "strains of feeling" are not
balanced by the "flux and reflux of thought, half meditative,
half capricious," where, in short, there is no play, the writer
may achieve a conceptual clarity, but he inevitably falls short
of that "middle species of composition" which, simultaneously,
is "stimulating to the understanding" and "gratifying to the
senses."

Schiller wrote that his own goal as a writer was to create of
language an "Ensemble der Gemütskräfte" which would not
merely express his thoughts clearly but also affect the sensual
and intellectual powers of the reader;[24] as a philosopher, he
predicted play as the source of balance and harmony between
the sensual and intellectual facilities. In De Quincey's terms,
stylistic play—the interaction of rhetoric and eloquence—
achieves both intelligibility and power. Since images may not
be translated into concepts any more than concepts may be
translated into images, Schiller reasoned, the only possibility
is to make the two merge in a harmonious literary style.[25]
De Quincey comes to the same conclusion. Imagery, he says, is
not always an alien and separable element merely superim-
posed upon thought, sometimes it is "the coefficient that, being superadded to something else, absolutely *makes* the thought
as a *third* and separate existence" (262). Conceptual clarity of
thought and sensual clarity of image, as they coincide in this
"third" or "middle species of composition," are not simply in
static juxtaposition. They interact dynamically. There is a
constant tension between the *Formtrieb* and *Stofftrieb* that is
sustained by the *Spieltrieb* as the *anspannende* and *auflösende*,

---

[24] *Schillers Briefe*, IV, 221.   [25] *Werke*, V, 639.

the tensing and relaxing, effects of art.[26] De Quincey's affirmation of this dynamic interaction of play is apparent especially in the essays on *Style* and *Rhetoric*, where the *auflösende* and *anspannende* effects of play are described, for example, as "approaching, receding, — attracting, repelling, — blending, separating, — chasing and chased, as in a fugue" (106–7). Play, as the manipulation of matter and manner, brings all the aspects of style into a sensible relation to one another — the logical qualities of thought in harmony with the sensuous qualities of rhythm and metaphor. In terms of syntactic structure, stylistic play gives vitality and meaning to the internal relations of a sentence. Where the tension of modification — "of colour, of outline, or of expression" — between two figures is strained by too remote a juxtaposition, the synthesis through play is interrupted. "A chasm between them, so vast as to prevent the synthesis of the two objects in one coexisting field of vision, interrupts the play of all genial comparison" (259).

Although the basic tenets of his theory are clearly borrowed from the German, De Quincey did more than merely introduce a foreign theory to his countrymen. Not only did he bring the tenets of Schiller's aesthetics to an extensive analysis of the problems of composition and style, he also adapted those tenets to the major assumptions of Scottish associationist rhetoric. Concerning the backgrounds of De Quincey's theory, a little has been said of the controversy over the extent of De Quincey's adaptations from Aristotle. Some of his notions, specifically those on probability and enthymemic reasoning, are borrowed directly. Others, such as his acceptance of the idea of resistance as the initiating principle and the division of *logos* as the controlling mode of rhetoric and *pathos* as the mode of eloquence, came to him through Schiller's aesthetics. Still another, the description in *De Memoria* of the operations of mind as proceeding in a series of recollections "from something either similar, or contrary, to what we seek, or else from that which is contiguous with it," [27] De Quincey incorporated not directly from Aristotle but from the Scottish associationists.

[26] *Werke*, V, 619.
[27] *The Basic Works of Aristotle*, ed. Richard McKeon (New York, 1941), p. 612.

The old faculty psychology was no distant kin of the old rhetoric with its system of *inventio* carefully atomized in topics, places, and predicaments. When the new associationist psychology was introduced, corresponding changes in rhetorical *inventio* were soon to follow. Here was a psychology, as David Hartley proclaimed, that described the physiology of the sensory system, that accurately explained the natural processes of thought. The rhetoricians were quick to see the significance of this theory: the most effective writing and speech must be that which conforms to those processes, which appeals to those processes through the medium of language. The result was a shifting of the five Ciceronian divisions: *inventio, dipositio, elocutio, memoria,* and *pronunciatio.*[28] In Ciceronian rhetoric *memoria* comprised those mnemonic tricks and devices which enabled the orator to memorize quickly and to recall correctly his complex array of arguments. Since memory was to the associationists the very source of all knowledge and the basis of all thinking, it is not surprising that in associationist rhetoric the classical divisions of *inventio* and *memoria* were compounded. When Lord Kames states that rhetorical invention and arrangement are the result of memory, he means by memory the mental process of evoking an image or a sequence of ideas; memory, he says, is the natural power by which "a thing formerly seen may be recalled to the mind with different degrees of accuracy." The proper end of invention and arrangement is to elicit an "ideal presence" which is more universal than the "real presence" of experience, and more vivid than mere "reflective remembrance." [29] In his rhetoric as well as his aesthetic Lord Kames draws his "fundamental principles . . . from human nature." [30]

Lord Kames' *Elements of Criticism* (1762) provides the earliest statement on natural style and rhetorical invention as they were affirmed by the other members of the Scottish school, and as they were ultimately employed by Thomas De Quincey. The most explicit statement of the potentialities of Hartley's psychology for a system of rhetoric was provided by

[28] Cicero, *De Inventione,* trans. H. M. Hubbell (Cambridge, Mass., and London, 1949), pp. 19–21.
[29] Henry Home, Lord Kames, *Elements of Criticism* (seventh ed., Edinburgh, 1788), I, 90–91.
[30] Kames, I, 13.

a man outside the Scottish school, that universal scholar,
Joseph Priestley. In the opening pages of *A Course of Lectures
on Oratory and Criticism* (1777) [31] Priestley announces his indebtedness to both Lord Kames and David Hartley. The twofold purpose of these lectures is to illustrate the association of
ideas and to relate "the influence of Oratory, and the striking
effect of Excellencies in Composition, upon the genuine principles of human nature." [32] Rhetoric is founded upon the
knowledge of human nature and must work through it; every
poet and orator must "be well acquainted with *human nature*;
that knowing the passions, prejudices, interests, and views of
those he hath to do with, he may address them accordingly."
Style should not be imposed artificially but should be based
upon the "principles of human nature" derived from man's
attention to "the emotions of his own heart." [33] Compounding
the divisions *inventio* and *memoria*, Priestley calls his division
"Recollection"; one does not invent "things with which the
mind was wholly unacquainted," rather, one engages in "recol-
lecting, and judiciously selecting, what is proper for his
purpose, out of the materials with which the mind was previously furnished." [34] The place of the artifices of language
within a natural style is defended in associationist terms.
Priestley claims that interest is stirred by elements of discourse which excite "those gross and more sensible feelings we
call *passions*" or "awaken those more delicate sensations,
which are generally called the *pleasures of the imagination*." The
feelings or sensations, "according to Dr. Hartley's theory, . . .
consist of nothing more than a congeries or combination of
ideas and sensations, separately indistinguishable, but which
were formerly associated either with the idea itself that excites
them, or with some other idea or circumstance, attending the
introduction of them." [35] Proposing "to throw some new light
on this curious subject," Priestley constructs his rhetoric upon
the psychology of "those *finer feelings*, which constitute the

[31] Written from the series of lectures originally delivered in the Academy at Warrington, where Priestley was Tutor in Language and Belles
Lettres in 1762. Edited by Vincent Bevilacqua and Richard Murphy in
the "Landmarks in Rhetoric and Public Address" series (Carbondale,
Ill., 1965).
[32] Priestley, pp. i–iii.   [33] Priestley, pp. 3–4.   [34] Priestley, p. 5.
[35] Priestley, pp. 72–73.

pleasures of the imagination." First, he defines the passions and emotions evoked by literature; these belong to corresponding *"critical situations of mind"* which, through association, may be excited by the ornaments of thought or diction. Second, he explains "those *forms of address* which are *adapted to gain assent"*; these are general devices which arouse associations by appealing to the common experiences of men. Third, he distinguishes between the imaginative and logical application of the ornaments of style; both, however, are considered modes of natural style, "for style the most highly ornamented, and enlivened with the strongest figures is as natural as the plain style, and occurs as naturally, without the precepts of art, and even without design, in proper circumstances." [36] The difference lies in the imaginative extension of literal fact which accompanies the figurative style, while the plain style conveys its meaning with deliberate rhetorical restraint through the order of grammar and logic alone.[37]

The term "natural style" as used by Priestley, by the members of the Scottish school, and by De Quincey, is perhaps misleading: it does *not* mean the humble or the rustic, the plain or the simple, as opposed to the flowery, ornamental, highly figurative style of impassioned prose. Natural style may express itself with severe restraint or with ornate flourish, so long as it truly reflects human nature and the natural processes of human mind. The "artificial style," by contrast, is an affected and unnatural style — the result of trying to impose an impression of passion or reserve, of sublimity or dignity, that the author has never felt. Invention, arrangement, and style are not isolated divisions of composition: they progress one out of the other in accordance with the associational sequence of images and ideas.

The interpretation of rhetorical invention and natural style on associationist principles is shared not only by Lord Kames and Joseph Priestley, but also by George Campbell, James Beattie, and Hugh Blair [38] — it is an interpretation common to

[36] Priestley, p. 75.   [37] Priestley, pp. 74–76.

[38] See George Campbell, *The Philosophy of Rhetoric*, ed. Lloyd Bitzer (Carbondale, Ill., 1963), pp. xlviii–xlix, 119; James Beattie, "An Essay on Poetry and Music, as they Affect the Mind," *Essays* (London, 1779; first published in 1776), pp. 205–7; and Hugh Blair, *Lectures on Rhetoric and Belles Lettres*, ed. Harold F. Harding (Carbondale, Ill., 1965), I, 1–12.

members of the Scottish school and one of those frequently echoed in the essays of De Quincey.

Memory, for De Quincey, is "the *vis imaginatrix* of the mind . . . the true *fundus* from which the understanding draws." [39] Vivacity of memory is essential in all invention, and De Quincey knew his own memory stimulated the most vivid of associations:

> And, as regards myself, touch but some particular key of laughter and of echoing music, sound but for a moment one bar of preparation, and immediately the pomps and glory of all that has composed for me the delirious vision of life re-awaken for torment; the orchestras of the earth open simultaneously to my inner ear; and in a moment I behold, forming themselves into solemn groups and processions, and passing over sad phantom stages all, that chiefly I have loved, or in whose behalf chiefly I have abhorred and cursed the grave—all that should *not* have died, yet died the soonest—the brilliant, the noble, the wise, the innocent, the brave, the beautiful.[40]

Such are the intricate associations upon which is built the world of dream and memory in De Quincey's own prose artistry; it is in terms of his own habits of memory, then, that he especially favors the analogical method of associational recall. "Rarely do things perish from my memory that are worth remembering," he writes in his *Confessions*, "due to the higher faculty of an electric aptitude for seizing analogies, and by means of those aërial pontoons passing over like lightning from one topic to another." [41] It is this "electric aptitude for seizing analogies" that De Quincey analyzes in his essay on *Conversation*. The rhetorical art of conversation rests less upon talking and more upon timing. Again, De Quincey draws introspectively from his own experience to affirm this electric sensation present in free analogical discourse but absent in formal exposition: "in the electric kindling of life between two minds . . . the kindling through sympathy with the object discussed in its momentary coruscation of shifting phases," conversation may evoke "glimpses and shy revelations of affinity, suggestion, relation, analogy, that could not have been approached through any avenues of methodical study"

[39] *Collected Writings*, X, 445.   [40] *Collected Writings*, V, 305.
[41] *Confessions of an English Opium-Eater* (London, 1822), p. 192.

(268–69). When he attributes the "magic" of conversation not to "the brilliancy, the ease, or the adroitness of the expounder" but to "the absolute interests of the thing expounded," De Quincey is not praising the matter and dismissing the manner, for the manner *is* the matter, that is, free analogical discourse has no matter other than what is "kindled" by the analogical manner (268).

The memory, De Quincey believed, "strengthens as you lay burdens upon it," and as a result of his own studies he found his "abstracting and condensing powers sensibly enlarged." [42] When he speaks of his "prodigious memory," it is in conjunction with the "logical instinct for feeling in a moment the secret analogies or parallelisms that connected things else apparently remote." [43] The relevance of the analogical method is suggested here in the phrase "logical instinct for feeling," for the Scottish rhetoricians agreed that it was the instinctive feelings which responded to the analogical effects of discourse. Beattie, for instance, in a chapter on analogical reasoning, identifies the perception of analogies as an "instinctive propensity"; instinctive, because it adduces causal relationships beyond experience.[44] Like the logical method, the analogical method is subject to error, but it is not confined to factual similarities. Analogy serves the aesthetic function of presenting fanciful and metaphorical truths, in addition to its rational function of proceeding "from a fact or thing experienced to something similar not experienced." [45] Further, analogy is the facility which communicates the universal associations of the particular, the facility through which an indirect sequence of resemblances joins and supplements the direct responses of mind. It is this same facility of analogy which De Quincey observes in *Conversation* when he says the "*direct* approaches to knowledge" are severely limited and "a wise man should turn to account any INDIRECT and supplementary means" (276). When not regimented by formal and direct demands of exposition, conversation acquires the special advantages of "the natural *excursiveness* of colloquial intercourse, its tendency to

---

[42] *Collected Writings*, III, 240.   [43] *Collected Writings*, III, 332.
[44] Beattie, *Essay on the Nature and Immutability of Truth, in Opposition to Sophistry and Scepticism* (Edinburgh, 1771), pp. 131–35.
[45] Beattie, *Essay on Truth*, p. 133.

advance by subtle links of association" (287). Not all men, however, have the ability to utilize these associational advantages of informal discourse. Samuel Johnson, who had nothing to say about David Hartley and David Hume "beyond a personal sneer, founded on some popular slander" (272), is De Quincey's example of a man so handicapped in the discursive and analogical constitution of mind that he "never, in any instance, GROWS a truth before your eyes whilst in the act of delivering it or moving towards it" (270).

By associating the experiences of sensibility and rationality, the analogical method may involve the whole spectrum of *logos* and *pathos*. Yet analogy is but one method of rhetorical invention, one method of ordering the ideas of language.

In his effort to explain the nature of invention and style, De Quincey calls up from childhood memory two ingenious similes. Invention, he tells us, is like boys teasing passers-by with the sunlight reflected from a mirror, for "you must shift your lights and vibrate your reflections at every possible angle, if you would agitate the popular mind extensively" (139). And style, he says, is like boys skipping flat stones across a river, for altering the structure of a sentence may provide "that power by which a sequence of words that naturally is directly consecutive commences, intermits, and reappears at a remote part of the sentence, like what is called drake-stone on the surface of a river" (130). Hoyt Hudson has pointed out that De Quincey does not consider invention and style as separate processes in composition, but as "an inner and an outer phase — of the same process." [46] As a concise statement of the operations of invention and style, Hudson cites the following passage from De Quincey's essay on *Style*:

> Time must be given for the intellect to eddy about a truth, and to appropriate its bearings. There is a sort of previous lubrication, such as the boa-constrictor applies to any subject of digestion, which is requisite to familiarize the mind with a startling or a complex novelty. And this is obtained for the intellect by varying the modes of presenting it, — now putting it directly before the eye, now obliquely, now in an abstract shape, now in the concrete; all which, being the proper technical discipline for dealing with such cases, ought no longer to be viewed as a licen-

[46] Hudson, p. 203.

tious mode of style, but as the just style in respect of those
licentious circumstances. And the true art for such popular display is to contrive the best forms for appearing to say something
new when in reality you are but echoing yourself; to break up
massy chords into running variations; and to mask, by slight
differences in the manner, a virtual identity in the substance.
(140)

This description of invention and style is, of course, an extension of the idea expressed in the mirror-simile. Skilled prose-
stylists have the ability of "eddying about their own thoughts"
(121), of letting their intellect "eddy about a truth." This
creative process is related both to the association of ideas and,
as we have already seen, to Schiller's play-theory of art. Although De Quincey considers rhetorical amplification, the art
of "appearing to say something new when in reality you are but
echoing yourself," an essential part of invention, he agrees
with the Scottish rhetoricians in justifying repetitions and
amplifications not for their own sake, but in accordance with
the effects they are capable of producing in the minds of the
readers.[47] De Quincey advocates in theory and in practice the
amplified style, but he also insists that only functional and
effective repetition is to be tolerated. Good prose style should
be "cleansed from *verbiage*, from elaborate parenthesis, and
from circumlocution, as the only style fitted for a purpose
which is one of pure enjoyment." There is a point where amplification trespasses the limits of interest and begins to bore.
Anticipation and intellectual tension are among the pleasures
of good prose, but, as De Quincey recognized, "suspense is
anxiety," and the sin of circumlocution and parenthesis is that
"they keep the attention in a painful condition of suspense"
(287). Because the free flow of associations and analogies are
essential to the genial movement of the mind, they are a
necessary aspect of the natural style, but these "running variations" are to be distinguished from empty verbosity, bookish
bombast, and a "diarrhœa of garrulity" (155). De Quincey
follows the Scottish rhetoricians in discussing the natural style
in contrast with artificial style, rather than in contrast with
figurative style.

The natural style, as is evident in the foregoing discussion of

[47] Hudson, p. 203.

Kames and Priestley, is based upon the immediate relation between words and the corresponding association of thoughts and feelings. De Quincey is quite explicit in contrasting this extensive freedom of natural style with the limitations of artificial style. Whereas the range of artifice is restricted by the mechanical conventions of literature, "the modes of human feeling are inexhaustible." Furthermore, the appeal to artificial conventions is unnecessary, since "the forms by which feeling connects itself with thought are indefeasibly natural," and since "the channels through which both impress themselves upon language are infinite." Because these natural modes are "imperturbable by human art" and "past the reach of mechanism," the movements of style — natural style — are free and will remain free (193).

Even though natural style may in this sense be considered as inexhaustible as human thoughts and feeling, De Quincey also saw that expression is inevitably frustrated by the mechanical finitude of language itself. The trains of association are far too complex ever to be unravelled through the narrower media of words. Here, in different terms, is a principle that clearly corresponds to Schiller's concept of the resistive nature of language. Despite the insurmountable constraints of language, however, natural style remains the freest mode of communication because it is the closest to the free movement of thought. By definition, natural style is the natural medium of expression, but, because he is engulfed by the mechanisms of civilization and by the artifices of social intercourse, it is no easy matter for an author to maintain control of a natural style. In *Style*, De Quincey cautions against the infringements of pedantry, which, as they influence the tendencies of thought and expression, "could not but stiffen the natural graces of composition, and weave fetters about the free movement of human thought" (152). But here De Quincey recognizes a paradox that grows out of the progressive changes in language: just as in music the discords of one generation become the harmonies of another, so do the verbal pedantries and affectations of one age often become the natural expressions of the next. "Every one of us would have felt, sixty years ago, that the general tone and colouring of a style was stiff, bookish, pedantic, which, from the habituation of our organs, we now feel to be natural and within the privilege of learned art" (153).

Hugh Blair was probably more adamant than the other Scottish rhetoricians in stressing the merits of style derived from the "science of human nature" over an "artificial and scholastic rhetoric." [48] If "the invention of the schools . . . the mere product of study" was accounted less than "that language which nature dictates to men," [49] Blair nevertheless saw that artificial graces had their place and may be used to advantage where the involvement of natural graces is impossible.[50] De Quincey's case for the artificial style is more liberal, although based on the same assumptions. De Quincey believed composition "under a law of artificial style far more difficult to manage" (199). He also argued that "the artifice and machinery of rhetoric furnishes in its degree as legitimate a basis for intellectual pleasure as any other"; however the artificial style must not be judged by the same criteria as the natural style: "that the pleasure is of an inferior order, can no more attaint the idea or model of the composition than it can impeach the excellence of an epigram that it is not a tragedy. Every species of composition is to be tried by its own laws" (101).

The ideal of natural style is besieged left and right by the extremes "of coarseness, of carelessness, of imperfect art, on the one hand; of spurious refinement and fantastic ambition on the other" (144). Natural style is a conservative norm amidst the "novelties" of popular taste. Although De Quincey scorned the sycophantic appeal to the tides of public whim, he was no archreactionary on matters of style and diction. Changes in vocabulary, he knew, are constantly operative in language, and he begins his essay on *Language* by acknowledging the principles of change. Moderate coinages based upon accurate "associations" and "known analogies" he considered rhetorically justifiable, but he strongly objected to rampant neologizing as "an infirmity of caprice" that can do no more than "gratify the mere appetite for innovation" (246–47). Thus, too, in *Style*, he condemns those authors "seeking distinction through novelties of diction." "Hopeless of any audience through mere weight of matter, they will turn for their last resource to such tricks of innovation as they can

[48] Blair, I, 3.   [49] Blair, I, 274.   [50] Blair, I, 285–89.

bring to bear upon language. What care they for purity or simplicity of diction, if at any cost of either they can win a special attention to themselves?" (144).

The strongest objection against the artificial style is, of course, its use as a substitute for the expression of real feelings, a stylistic pretension that Blair called "ostentatious and deceitful." [51] The classical concept of decorum is redefined in terms of psychological veracity: the expression of genuine conviction or genuine passion. The parallel between De Quincey and the Scottish rhetoricians on this point is especially close. "Let nature and passion always speak their own language," is Blair's precept, and he specifically stipulates that an author must adhere to a natural manner in matter of emotion or passion, and "above all, that he never affect the style of a passion which he does not feel." No artifice can mask the lack of natural expression: "when we seek to counterfeit a warmth which we do not feel, no Figures will either supply the defect, or conceal the imposture." [52] De Quincey affirms the same precept in almost the same words: "Now, there is not in the world so certain a guarantee for pure idiomatic diction, without tricks or affectation, as a case of genuine excitement. Real situations are always pledges of a real natural language." In agreement with Blair, De Quincey criticizes the "counterfeit passion" and "mimical situations" in poems and novels which "are efforts of ingenuity and no ebullitions of absolute unsimulated feeling" and obvious attempts "to reinforce the languishing interest of their readers by extravagances of language." De Quincey offers a simple remedy for such impostures of style: "strength of real feeling shuts out all temptation to the affectation of false feeling" (145).

When he finally gets around to discussing the book which had prompted his essay on *Rhetoric*, De Quincey states that Richard Whately's *Elements of Rhetoric* "somewhat disappoints us" in treating the subject of style, and he accuses Whately of delivering his remarks in a "desultory way" (126). And when, in his essay on *Style*, he objects to the same casual manner in the theory of "the elegant but desultory Blair" (192), we may be deluded into anticipating a systematic discussion of the problems of arrangement. But De Quincey

[51] Blair, I, 3.   [52] Blair, I, 357–60.

remains the elegant but desultory De Quincey, and his comments on diction, syntax, connectives, and prose rhythms, although they benefit from his own added insights as a practicing prose-master, reveal no great departure from the precepts of the Scottish rhetoricians.

De Quincey defines style in a narrow sense as "the mere *synthesis onomaton*, the syntaxis or combination of words into sentences," and in a broad sense which embraces "all possible relations that can arise between thoughts and words—the total effect of a writer as derived from manner" (163). These two aspects working in harmony, as organic style, become, through the synthesizing activity of play, the sum of the variable activities of the higher understanding balanced by the passions and effective mechanically through the musical arrangement of syntax and connections. The art of rhetoric is addressed to the ends of intellectual pleasure through the management of language. The emphasis is upon effect. The writer must try "the effect upon his ear of his periods as musical wholes" (108). Following from his insistence upon "natural grace" not "biassed by bookish connexions," and on "free natural movement of thought" unaffected by "artificial standards" (146), De Quincey objects, as did the Scottish rhetoricians, to the symmetrical balances (*isocolon, parison, paromoion*) and sustained periods (*hirmus*) of the Ciceronian style. Periodic involution, to De Quincey, is a symptom of the "contagion of bookishness" (150). The moderate use of periodic structure has given way to a monotonous frequency which De Quincey finds the "extensive evil . . . of popular style." Periodic syntax is the "single vice" which has "counterbalanced all possible vices of any other order." By disrupting the proper habits of mind, periodic syntax has created a "vast sphere" of evil. Perhaps it seems rather extreme to cast such a curse upon something as apparently innocent as the pedantic affectation of periodic involution. But anything less, De Quincey says, would be disproportionate to the crime. He justifies his extreme condemnation on two counts: 1] the enormity of the problem which convinced him that the "characteristic defect of this age lies in the tumid and tumultuary structure of our sentences" (153); 2] because his theory of style was based upon psychological effect, he believed that the violence which periodic involution wrought upon the natural modes of thought would either encourage an abnormal mental response or enforce a desultory habit of reading (162–63).

Because periodic involution is a studied device, it makes the style ponderous. Simple syntactic inversion (*anastrophe*), on the other hand, is accepted by De Quincey as a natural part of colloquial style, not only contributing to the rhythmic variations of syntax but also permitting prime emphasis on a key word or phrase. De Quincey's opinion here is for the most part in line with the Scottish rhetoricians, but there is some variance among the comments of Lord Kames, Hugh Blair, and George Campbell. Lord Kames distinguishes between logical and illogical inversion, but classes both as departures from natural style.[53] Hugh Blair's statement accords with De Quincey's on the functions of inversion, but Blair nevertheless considers it an artificial device.[54] George Campbell, however, supplies a very good argument for inversion as psychologically natural and logically necessary.[55] Concerning the possible artificiality of inversion, De Quincey concludes that "It is not mere power of inversion, but of self-intrication, and of self-dislocation, which marks the extremity of the artificial structure" (130). The forms of language as well as the patterns of thought and personal expression are relevant to the functions of inversion in colloquial speech. De Quincey, of course, gives praise to the "natural *excursiveness* of colloquial intercourse" (287), but he notes that not all languages are suited to the colloquial mode of expression. Greek, for instance, is so grammatically formal that such informality of style would appear incongruous. Yet this is precisely the fault that De Quincey finds abounding in Greek prose. The undignified garrulity of "all those forms of lively colloquialism" appealed to a people who possessed an excess of "demonstrative energy" and were "unduly excited by bodily presence and by ocular appeals to their sensibility." Inversion, as well as pictorial similitude and other aspects of colloquial vigor, are always to be governed by the rules of decorum; colloquial expression has vitality and energy, "but what man in his senses," De Quincey

[53] Kames, II, 51–52.   [54] Blair, I, 232–36.   [55] Campbell, pp. 355–56.

asks, "would employ it in a grave work, and speaking in his
own person?" (188).

Another reaction against "the plethoric form of cumulation
and 'periodic' writing" (162) is the clipped or aphoristic style.
Although De Quincey himself favored the rhythmic extensions
of Sir Thomas Browne over the succinct concision of Francis
Bacon, he defended the propriety of the aphoristic style. He
felt, in regard to Bacon's essays, that "the short-hand style of
his composition, in which connexions are seldom fully developed," is an "unfavourable circumstance," but it must be
attributed to "the plethoric fulness of Lord B.'s mind" (109).
And in response to a critical review objecting to the clipped
manner of Coleridge's prose composition, De Quincey launches
a more detailed commentary on the aphoristic style. The objection is that the "detached and insulated form" of Coleridge's "Aphorisms" evades "all the difficulties connected
with composition." This, De Quincey replies, is true of any-
one "who adopts the same aphoristic form of expression for
his thoughts"; and, while he agrees that "the labour of composition begins when you have put your separate threads of
thought into a loom, to weave them into a continuous whole;
to connect, to introduce them; to blow them out or to expand
them; to carry them to a close," De Quincey also points out
that the same argument might be given in behalf of the style
which evades all these evils. In addition to the aesthetic objection to the incompleteness of the aphoristic style, De
Quincey also recognizes psychological objections, for the
verbal connections of style are required to facilitate the re-
sponding mental connections (181). Blair explains the fault
of the clipped style in these terms: "there may be an excess in
too many short Sentences also; by which the sense is split and
broken, the connexion of thought weakened, and the memory
burdened, by presenting to it a long succession of minute
objects." [56]

Also in contrast to the "bookish" style of periodic involutions and studied balances, is the journalistic style, which De
Quincey condemns as typically disfigured by carelessness. In
the arrangement of words and in sentence structure, this style
"has laboured with two faults that might have been thought

[56] Blair, I, 205–6.

incompatible": not only is it ridden with the latinate artifices of the "bookish" style, but it is also ravaged of all order and continuity. The journalist, then, is frequently an unlearned pedant who substitutes "teasing *surplusage*" for Ciceronian prose (162). Newspaper style, "in spite of its artificial bias," is characteristically "*unorganized.*" The "elaborate and artificial" structure of periodic prose, and this is part of its vice, requires careful organization; "to be viewed as not having received it, such periods must be hyperbolically careless" (153–54).

Despite the rather latinate tendency of his own vocabulary, De Quincey speaks out against latinate diction in his essays on *Rhetoric* and *Style.* In *Rhetoric*, De Quincey identifies three faults among the latinate affectations: one is the "elliptic brevity of connexion and transition"; another is the "wealth of abstractions"; and the third is a capacity for "the long-tailed words in *osity* and *ation*" (130). In *Style*, De Quincey repeats his proscription of the "bookish air" of "Latinized and artificial phraseology" which is "impressed upon composition . . . by 'long-tailed words in *osity* and *ation*' " (153).[57] His cautions concerning "artificial vocabulary," however, must not be exaggerated out of context. Latinate words and phrasings are an omnipresent aspect of his own style. What he objects to is pedantic pretension—those *osity* and *ation* words that reflect the writer's pomposity and affectation. In fact, De Quincey counters Whately's maxim that " 'elaborate stateliness is always to be regarded as a worse fault than the slovenliness and languor which accompanies a very loose style.' " De Quincey answers here, as he has elsewhere, that decorum is the final arbiter in questions of style. Considered in isolation, elaborate stateliness of style and diction can have "no fault at all"; merit or lack of it becomes evident only "in relation to a given subject, or to any subject under given circumstances." If those circumstances happen to involve a royal feast, say, or a coronation, then a rhetoric of elaborate stateliness becomes an indispensable virtue while an

[57] De Quincey echoes himself a third time in commenting on Wordsworth's theory of poetic diction: The Saxon part of the language, he says, is the language of the nursery – "in which great philological academy no toleration is given to words in '*osity*' or '*ation*,' " *Collected Writings*, XI, 297.

"elegant simplicity" would offend the taste. Further, "at a coronation, what can be more displeasing to a philosophic taste than a pretended chastity of ornament, at war with the very purposes of a solemnity essentially magnificent?" (130). When De Quincey praises "purity or simplicity of diction," "a fidelity to the idiom," "pure idiomatic diction," and "idiomatic propriety," (144–45), his precepts are to be understood within the context of rhetorical decorum.

Decorum governs the level of style; logic controls the interrelations of style. "True rhetoric and sound logic," as Blair wrote on the problem of invention, "are very nearly allied." [58] The same may be said on the problem of disposition, for it is logic in its formative role that brings the various elements of style into a relationship and gives them form. In associationist terms, De Quincey says that the parts of discourse "coalesce" in a "joint or complex impression" (259). Because of this process, the connections of style gain a special importance for De Quincey and the Scottish rhetoricians.

The verbal logic of connection, juncture, or juxtaposition is the author's means of communicating a sequential train of images or ideas. Connection gives the parts "a sensible relation to each other." It expresses the relation of the *"sensuous* qualities — rhythmus, for instance, or the continuity of metaphor." Connection permits the "synthesis" of stylistic elements and promotes "the play of all genial comparison." Particular attention to the devices of "transition and connection," wrote Blair, is the requisite "for promoting the Strength of a Sentence." [59] De Quincey wholeheartedly agrees:

> it is in the *relation* of sentences, in what Horace terms their *"junctura,"* that the true life of composition resides. The mode of their *nexus,* the way in which one sentence is made to arise out of another, and to prepare the opening for a third: this is the great loom in which the textile process of the moving intellect reveals itself and prospers. Here the separate clauses of a period become architectural parts, aiding, relieving, supporting each other. (258–59)

Not only are the modifications of word with word, clause with clause, and period with period communicated, but even the

[58] Blair, I, 6–7.   [59] Blair, I, 227.

subtleties of ideas and images are revealed or concealed through transition and connection; "the parts," De Quincey writes, "are shown *as* parts, cohering and conspiring to a common result" (259). Connection is, in this sense, the linguistic correlative of the associationist process of coalescence. In actual experience objects are perceived in total: size, shape, color, motion, all the attributes impress themselves on the mind at once and form natural patterns of coalescence. Words can communicate these attributes only separately. Thus connection serves to overcome the disparity between language and experience. In natural style, verbal connections reproduce the natural sequence of impressions; following the natural tendency of mind to respond more keenly to certain attributes, to give them a relative emphasis, and to link them to associated attributes, the writer uses verbal connections to translate the association of ideas into language.[60]

Although in the essay on *Language* De Quincey places "the true life of composition" in the *"relation,"* the *"junctura,"* the *"nexus"* of sentences, he is careful not to push the point to an absurd extreme. In the association of ideas, the immediate sensations have the most force and liveliness, the ideas of memory retain some of the vivacity of the sensations, and the ideas of imagination are the furthest removed from the vivacity of sensual experience. Vivacity in language, in George Campbell's theory, depends upon the ability to stimulate the lively sensations and the ideas of memory; because they communicate no ideas, the connections and transitions are, of all the elements of syntax, "the most unfriendly to vivacity." Campbell explains that since the vivacity lies in the sensations and ideas, the connectives, "which are not themselves the signs of things, of operations, or of attributes," can serve only the secondary function of providing the logic which links together the significant parts of discourse. But the logic must serve, not dominate the ideas; the connectives must not obtrude: a cabinet or piece of furniture, in Campbell's analogy, is the more admired the less we see of "the pegs and tacks" that hold it together. Without "the pegs and tacks," of course, we see only the lumber and no cabinet at all.[61] This is the point of the similar analogy in De Quincey's *Language:* no temple

[60] Cf. Kames, II, 51.   [61] Campbell, pp. 365, 384–99.

exists merely "because the materials of the temple—the stone, the lime, the iron, the timber—had been carted to the ground" (258). A subtle artistry of "connexions and transitions," De Quincey agrees with Campbell, is necessary to bring the parts together in effective arrangement.

As accurate and as illuminating as De Quincey's adaptations from Campbell and Blair and the other Scottish rhetoricians may appear to be, these adaptations draw only from individual details and there is no attempt to consolidate the details in a systematic whole. To be sure, there are a few obvious points of corroboration between De Quincey's application of the play-theory to the problem of literary composition and the many ideas on style borrowed from the Scottish school. But De Quincey merely relies on his sense of the coherency between the two aspects of his theory, rather than attempting a formal account of their philosophical relationship. A similar lack of systematic development is evident in his account of the history of rhetoric. He proceeds in a digressionary, not to say erratic, manner, tarrying where he finds a paradoxical argument that may disturb the complacent orthodoxy, and throughout he ignores the general conception of oratory in favor of his own belletristic view of rhetoric and eloquence.

De Quincey follows the usual fourfold division of rhetorical history into the Greek, the Roman, the Medieval, and the Modern (with British distinguished from Continental) periods. Three factors, however, make this pattern of organization somewhat difficult to delineate: first, because his approach is belletristic, his comments on rhetorical history confound oratory with literature; second, because his method is often analogical, many aspects of rhetorical history are developed comparatively, that is, the Greek and Roman or the Classic and Modern periods are sometimes treated simultaneously rather than chronologically; third, because each of the essays was intended as an autonomous commentary, there is some repetition and some variation of opinion. But for the purpose of introduction, it is easy enough to reassemble De Quincey's examination of rhetorical history in accordance with the basic fourfold division.

De Quincey's qualifications as a scholar of Greek are admirable. Among the greatest distinctions of his student days, a matter of pride in his own autobiography and a fact amply supported by his academic record, was his mastery of Greek. His ability to debate extemporaneously in Greek astounded his examiners at Worcester College, Oxford. His knowledge of Greek literature and history commanded respect and, when he came to write for the literary magazines, permitted him the license of authoritarian appraisal. But lest it be thought that De Quincey abused that license with his faultfinding criticism, it should be remembered that ancient and pagan Greece suffered a general *disapprobrium* in romantic criticism, especially in the criticism of the influential Schlegels in Germany.

In the essay *Rhetoric*, De Quincey acclaims Greece "the birthplace of Rhetoric," as it was of all the fine arts. The notable contribution of the Greeks was in rhetorical theory, the *ars docens*, not in rhetorical practice, the *ars utens* (93; also 217). The theory that arose in Greece, from the general probability or *eikos* stressed by Corax to the enthymemic arguments on probability emphasized by Aristotle, is a theory that always avoids factual issues and focuses exclusively on areas of irresolvable *pros* and *cons*. Greece, as an emerging democratic state, provided a stage for vigorous oratory; eloquence flourished; but no room was left for the intellectual subtleties of rhetoric. Extemporaneous response was a requisite to the oratory of the senate, the courtroom, the marketplace, but, De Quincey says, while "Extemporaneousness" is "a favourable circumstance to impassioned eloquence," it "is death to Rhetoric." This is the reasoning behind De Quincey's often misunderstood contention that "amongst the greater orators of Greece there is not a solitary gleam of rhetoric" (93–94).

Even considering all three of De Quincey's brief sketches on Isocrates—in *Rhetoric* (94), *Style* (210–12), and *Greek Literature* (323–24)—the appraisal we find is disappointing, and the information scant. In supporting his view of Isocrates as a teacher and theorist but no orator, as a "chamber rhetorician" but no public debater, De Quincey does, however, give praise to the rhythmic skill of his style and mentions his influence on Cicero. The humorous account of Isocrates' longevity is entertaining enough, but it seems to have been at the expense of any serious account of Isocrates' theory of persuasion or the training of the orator.

The discussion of Demosthenes, which concentrates on that

great orator's stress upon delivery, is more thorough and more just. Of course, in De Quincey's sense, he was not a rhetorician, but still he was a debater *par excellence*, a master of forensic eloquence, on "questions of elementary justice, large and diffusive, apprehensible even to the uninstructed, and connecting themselves at every step with powerful and tempestuous feelings." Such was the affective eloquence of Demosthenes' invocation of the dead warriors of Marathon and Salamais. Demosthenes was the most eloquent of Grecian orators, not because " 'he thunders and lightens,' " not because of his "naked quality of vehemence"—for in this respect he does not surpass the precedence of Pericles—but because his oratorical skills were of a range beyond all his rivals. Neither Demosthenes nor Cicero held pre-eminence in the "native and fervent vigour" of their oratory, but in their "large and comprehensive harmony of gifts," in a range of skill capable of "adapting itself to a far larger variety of situations" than the "*mere* son of thunder" who is lost when without a passionate cause, a theme of strife, or a tempestuous audience. Eloquence, De Quincey says, commands more than the combustible passions. Rhetoric was available to Isocrates because he chose the more reflective medium of the written word over the extemporaneity of public address, but, for this very reason, his rhythms and cadences are too obviously studied and without the eloquent sonority that a confrontation with "the unstimulated strife of actual gloomy life" was able to elicit from the oratory of Cicero. Like Isocrates, Demosthenes achieved none of the rhythmic sweep of Cicero; his strength is in his emotive appeal; his weakness is his rude style. But that rudeness was forced upon him, not by any shortcomings of his language, but by his audience: ignorant and impatient, high-spirited and "always on the fret. "Since the achievement of the orator is conditioned by his audience, Demosthenes had no opportunity for "the long, voluminous sweeps of beautiful rhythmus which we find in Cicero." Instead, we find in Demosthenes an array of short sentences and "the animated form of apostrophe and crowded interrogations addressed to the audience." Here then is the application to Greek oratory which De Quincey draws from his dichotomy of rhetoric and eloquence: "the necessity of rousing attention, or of sustaining it," demands a relentless emphasis upon "the *immediate*" and denies, *ipso facto*, any attention to a "purpose of beauty, dignity, instruction, or even of *ultimate* effect." No occasion arose for the interplay of rhetoric and eloquence, nor even for the intellectual pleasure of naked rhetoric. All that was possible, Demosthenes accomplished: a forceful but unelaborated eloquence (325–33).

In addition to the extensive commentary on Greek oratory and belles lettres in *A Brief Appraisal of Greek Literature*, De Quincey devotes much of his essay on *Style* to the problems of Greek style: the whole of Part II (168–89) is ostensibly dedicated to the examination of style in Greek literature, but the digressions are numerous; in Part III De Quincey devotes two sections exclusively to Greek style (194–98, 203–16), and in the second he develops the interesting contrast between the creative Age of Pericles and the reflective Age of Alexander; in Part IV (216–44) he surveys Greek literature with an attention to the drama not present in *A Brief Appraisal of Greek Literature*, and he concludes with a contrast of Athenian and Modern literature in terms of the impact of publication upon the generic nature and essential quality of literature (231–35, 244–45). The short survey of rhetorical history in *Rhetoric*, as we have seen, opens with a few comments on ancient Greece (173–74); in *Language* De Quincey describes the peculiarities and literary potentialities inherent in the Greek language; and in *Conversation* he mentions the dictatorial function of the Symposiarch in moderating an Athenian Symposium.

As Greece was the "birthplace of Rhetoric," so was Rome its "true El Dorado." The historical significance of Roman literature and oratory is touched upon three times in the essays: in *Rhetoric* (95), in *Style* (198–200), and in *Language* (253–55). Cicero is discussed more as a master of the *utens* than of the *docens* of rhetoric, as an orator who manfully supported "the pretensions of his mother-tongue" (255). Even his *De Oratore* De Quincey praises more as an artistic accomplishment than as a philosophic exposition, for here, he says, Cicero translates the "demonic powers" of Crassus and Antony into the perfected artistry of his own "splendid dialogues" (199). Of Quintilian's *Institutiones Oratoriæ*, De Quincey says that "for a triumph over the difficulties of the subject, and as a lesson on the possibility of imparting grace to the treatment of scholastic topics as intractable as that of Grammar and Prosody there is no such *chef-d'œuvre* to this hour in any literature as the Institutions of Quintilian" (95). Again, it is apparent that De Quincey is concerned more with the belletristic manner of the work than with the matter, nor does he give any attention to the splendid oratory of the law courts which won Quintilian the chair of rhetoric in Rome under Vespasian. That third great work of Latin rhetorical theory, the *Rhetorica ad Herennium* is not discussed at all. The belletristic direction of De Quincey's interest is once more evident in the names of the other figures whom he nominates as Rome's leading rhetoricians: Livy, Ovid, Lucan, Petronius Arbiter, the Plinys, and the Senecas (95).

With the exception of his discussion of the Church Fathers, De Quincey devotes no attention to the ecclesiastical developments in the rhetorical tradition during the Middle Ages. The Latin Fathers occasionally surpassed even the Senecas in their rhetorical *bravuras*; the greatest among them, says De Quincey, were Tertullian, Arnobius, and St. Augustine, then with an ironic indication of the importance he grants to the period he adds, "and some writer whose name we cannot at this moment recall." As for the Greek Fathers, De Quincey dismisses them, "one and all," as "Birmingham rhetoricians," making no exception even for Gregory Nazianzen, who had "a turgid style of mouthy grandiloquence" but no talent for "polished rhetoric." St. Augustine's *Confessions* remains the first and greatest triumph of rhetoric in the Medieval period. All else from the sixth century A.D. to the birth of the Modern period in the Renaissance is, in De Quincey's estimation, not worth considering. During that "*crepusculum* between Ancient and Modern History all Rhetoric (as the professional pretension of a class) seems to have finally expired" (96). Nevertheless De Quincey recognizes that rhetoric as the *ars utens* became during this period an *ars dictaminis* and an *ars prædicandis*, thus establishing many of the generic norms of epistle and sermon which persisted into the Modern period.

The great trends of rhetorical theory that have arisen in the Modern period are not analyzed by De Quincey. In his

Life of Milton, he discusses Milton's adaptation of Ramistic logic,[62] but nowhere does he consider the impact of Ramus on rhetorical theory. In his *Rhetoric*, he scoffs at the "Messieurs of the Port Royal and other bigoted critics" (96), but again the influence of the Port Royalist rhetoric is virtually ignored. What De Quincey does analyze is the progression of rhetoric and eloquence in literature. Sidney and Fulke Greville "(in whose prose there are some bursts of pathetic eloquence, as there is of rhetoric in his verse, though too often harsh and cloudy)" are nominated, but "the first very eminent rhetorician in the English Literature is Donne" (100). As we have noted before, Donne, Sir Thomas Browne, and Jeremy Taylor are all praised by De Quincey for their effective play of eloquence and rhetoric. Burton in his *Anatomy of Melancholy* and Milton in his prose works are acclaimed as powerful rhetoricians. Francis Bacon does not make the list, for, De Quincey says, excepting a few letters and parts of speeches, Bacon never comes forward as a rhetorician—his was a philosophic fancy, resting upon real analogies, rather than a rhetorical fancy, resting on probabilities and seeming resemblances (109). A few other names are considered and dismissed. From David Hume's *On Oratory* and *Rise and Progress of the Arts*, De Quincey accepts the speculations on "the declension of eloquence in our deliberative assemblies" (97). There has grown with the complexities of society too much concern with technical points and details to permit rhetorical or eloquent oratory in an English Parliament: what rhetoric or eloquence is possible in a debate over a cabbage tariff or a road bill? "The object of Hume," De Quincey concludes, "remains unimpeached as to the fact that eloquence is a rarer growth of modern than of ancient civil polity" (99). The last of the great orators recognized by De Quincey is Edmund Burke, and in him rhetoric and eloquence are once more brought together (114–17). The historical survey in *Rhetoric* concludes with an appraisal of the contributions of France, Germany, Italy, and Spain (121–24); there are similar appraisals in *Style* (154–61,

---

[62] *Collected Writings*, IV, 101. De Quincey refers to the Ramistic logic of Milton's *De Doctrina Christiana* (1672) which stirred considerable controversy when it was discovered in 1823. Masson notes that an English translation was published along with the Latin original in 1825.

200–203) and *Language* (255–58). The only objections which might be raised against De Quincey's critical judgment here are resolved if we tolerate his unquestioning confidence in the superiority of his native English, and if we disregard his exaggerations of the faults of the other European languages. Beyond these pardonable distortions, De Quincey provides many insights into the prevailing problems of style in European literature.

Clearly, De Quincey was not a critic free from prejudices. His national bias, for example, led him to ridicule the bulky syntax of Kant and the immorality of Goethe. Similarly, the belletristic bias of his rhetorical theory led him to subordinate the general issues of oratory, from the cumulation of evidence to the moral objectives, and to concentrate, instead, upon the creative process and the problems of style. He was, foremost, an eclectic thinker, and through his combination of Schiller's aesthetics and Scottish associationism he has created a means to examine the interrelationships of thought and emotion and of form and content in more perceptive detail than had previously been possible. What he sacrificed by not presenting his ideas in the organized manner of a systematic treatise, he has compensated by presenting them in the more discursive yet more entertaining medium of the informal essay. The merit of his theory is substantiated by the accomplishments of the man himself. As a critic of prose style, De Quincey surpassed even the great critics who were his contemporaries — Coleridge, Hazlitt, and Lamb. And as a practicing master, his control of the cadences and harmonies of prose has earned him an enduring reputation in English literature.

RHETORIC[1]

No art cultivated by man has suffered more in the revolutions of taste and opinion than the art of Rhetoric. There was a time when, by an undue extension of this term, it designated the whole cycle of accomplishments which prepared a man for public affairs. From that height it has descended to a level with the arts of alchemy and astrology, as holding out promises which consist in a mixed degree of impostures wherever its pretensions happened to be weighty, and of trifles wherever they happened to be true. If we look into the prevailing theory of Rhetoric, under which it meets with so degrading an estimate, we shall find that it fluctuates between two different conceptions, according to one of which it is an art of ostentatious ornament, and according to the other an art of sophistry. A man is held to play the rhetorician when he treats a subject with more than usual gaiety of ornament, and, perhaps we may add, as an essential element in the idea, with *conscious* ornament. This is one view of Rhetoric ; and under this what it accomplishes is not so much to persuade as to delight, not so much to win

[1] Suggested as an excursive review by Whately's *Elements of Rhetoric*. [Such is De Quincey's brief footnote to the title of the paper in his reprint of it in 1859 in vol. xi of his Collective Edition of his Writings. It had appeared originally in *Blackwood's Magazine* for December 1828, in the form of a review of Whately's well-known "Rhetoric," then a new book with the title " *Elements of Rhetoric. By Richard Whately, D.D., Principal of St. Albans Hall, and late Fellow of Oriel College, Oxford.*" In the magazine the paper itself bore the title " Elements of Rhetoric " ; but this title was shortened in the reprint.—M.]

the assent as to stimulate the attention and captivate the taste. And even this purpose is attached to something separable and accidental in the *manner*. But the other idea of Rhetoric lays its foundation in something essential to the *matter*. This is that rhetoric of which Milton spoke as able " to dash maturest counsels and to make the worse appear the better reason." Now, it is clear that *argument* of some quality or other must be taken as the principle of this rhetoric ; for those must be immature counsels indeed that could be dashed by mere embellishments of manner, or by artifices of diction and arrangement.

Here then we have in popular use two separate ideas of Rhetoric : one of which is occupied with the general end of the fine arts—that is to say, intellectual pleasure ; the other applies itself more specifically to a definite purpose of utility, viz. fraud.

Such is the popular idea of Rhetoric ; which wants both unity and precision. If we seek these from the formal teachers of Rhetoric, our embarrassment is not much relieved. All of them agree that Rhetoric may be defined *the art of persuasion*. But, if we inquire what *is* persuasion, we find them vague and indefinite or even contradictory. To waive a thousand of others, Dr. Whately, in the work before us, insists upon the *conviction* of the understanding as " an essential part of persuasion " ; and, on the other hand, the author of the *Philosophy of Rhetoric* is equally satisfied that there is no persuasion without an appeal to the *passions*.[1] Here are two views. We, for our parts, have a third which excludes both. Where conviction begins, the field of Rhetoric ends ; that is our opinion : and, as to the passions, we contend that they are not within the province of Rhetoric, but of Eloquence.[2]

[1] The Scottish theologian and critic, Dr. George Campbell, Principal of Marischal College and University, Aberdeen (1719-1796); whose *Philosophy of Rhetoric*, published in 1776, is one of the shrewdest books on the Principles of Style and Literature produced in Great Britain in the course of the eighteenth century.—M.

[2] As these opening paragraphs of the paper seem to imply an imperfect recollection of the contents and substance of Aristotle's Treatise on Rhetoric, and a hazy conception of the causes of the change of meaning which the word " Rhetoric " has undergone in its

In this view of Rhetoric and its functions we coincide
with Aristotle ; as indeed originally we took it up on a
suggestion derived from him.   But, as all parties may
possibly fancy a confirmation of their views in Aristotle, we
will say a word or two in support of our own interpretation

descent from the Greek and Roman world into modern times, a few
words may here be interposed by way of elucidation and addition :—
Rhetoric, as understood by Aristotle, and by all his Greek and Roman
successors, was the Science and Art of Oratory.   It was the Science
and Art of persuasion by means of speech,—whether by that actual
method of direct address to an audience face to face which we usually
call "public speaking," or, more obliquely, by written pleadings
which might be read in private.   Now, as there were three recognised
kinds of oratory in the ancient world,—the oratory of political
assemblies, the oratory of law-courts, and that third and rarer kind of
oratory the sole purpose of which was some immediate moral effect
upon the hearers,—the distribution of the Ancient Rhetoric corre-
sponded.   The oratory of political assemblies, or all oratory of what
we should now call the Parliamentary type, was distinguished by
Aristotle as *Symbouleutic Oratory*, the Latin equivalent of which was
Deliberative Oratory ; the oratory of law-courts was called *Dikanic
Oratory* by the Greeks, and *Judicial or Forensic Oratory* by the
Latins ; and the third kind of oratory, or such oratory as most nearly
resembled our oratory of the pulpit, was called *Epideictic Oratory* by
the Greeks, and *Demonstrative Oratory* by the Latins.   The ancient
orators having to practise all the three kinds as occasion offered, and
the functions of the orator or public speaker having been far more
extensive and continual in the system of ancient society than they are
now, it happened naturally that Rhetoric assumed a most important
place in the business of education among the ancients.   It was, in
fact, all but co-extensive with the *whole* business of education ; for, as
De Quincey remarks, "it designated the whole cycle of accomplishments which prepared a man for public affairs."   Philosophy, on the
one hand, it is true, and Poetry on the other, were recognised as high
forms of private intellectual activity for those who were at leisure ;
but it was by oratory that a man exerted public influence, and rose to
eminence and statesmanship.   Hence the extraordinary elaborateness
of the Science and Art of Rhetoric as set forth in Aristotle's treatise,
and subsequently expounded and developed by such Roman masters
as Cicero and Quintilian.   The instruction of a young man in Rhetoric
included, or presupposed, in their view, in the first place, instruction in
all the kinds of *matter* or *doctrine* required in oratory.   An orator must
come to his special work adequately instructed in History, in Jurisprudence, in Political Economy, in Politics, in Ethics or Moral
Philosophy, and in whatever other sort of knowledge might be
necessary to him in his deliberative, forensic, or epideictic speeches.
Thus Rhetoric included or presupposed much that may be described as
the ancient equivalent to the teaching of our modern Universities.

of that author which will surprise our Oxford friends. Our explanation involves a very remarkable detection, which will tax many thousands of books with error in a particular point supposed to be as well established as the hills. We question, indeed, whether any fulminating powder, descending upon the schools of Oxford, would cause more consterna-

But it was in the theory of the ways of applying this acquired knowledge of all varieties to the special purposes of the orator's art that the Ancient Rhetoric reached its perfection. The following is a summary under that head :—The success of a speech on any particular occasion depends, according to Aristotle, on three things : viz. (1) the PISTIS, or combined strength of the *persuasives* found out for the occasion, the nature and amount of the means employed for getting the hearers to agree with the speaker and go along with him ; (2) the TAXIS, or right and orderly arrangement of the discourse ; (3) the LEXIS, or Style and Diction. In Aristotle's treatise each of these three subjects—PISTIS, TAXIS, LEXIS—is treated systematically ; but it is the part on the PISTIS that occupies most space, and that alone presents any points of difficulty. The PISTEIS or "means of persuasion" available for an orator on any occasion, but in greater or less proportion according to the circumstances, are classed by Aristotle as of these three varieties :—(1) *The Ethical Pistis*, consisting in those persuasives which are derived from the character, antecedents, and demeanour of the speaker himself,—his reputation for ability and integrity, his evident or seeming earnestness, &c. ; (2) *The Pathetic Pistis*, consisting in the orator's power to sway the passions of his audience,—to move them to pity, anger, &c.—and so to compel them to a different view of a case from that which would have recommended itself to their cool judgment ; (3) *The Logical Pistis*, consisting in the actual reasoning or argumentation, the address to the pure understanding.—Under this last head there was further subdivision ; to which we shall have to advert in another note ; but from the preceding sketch so far of the Ancient or Aristotelian Rhetoric it will be seen how the term "Rhetoric" has gradually lost its original meaning and acquired a new one. Aristotle, as has been said, does discuss the subject of Style or Diction as belonging properly to Rhetoric. He devotes twelve short chapters to this subject—containing remarks on the different kinds of style, on figures of speech, &c. ; and admirable little chapters they are, with hints and suggestions good to this day. Now, it is on these chapters, as the easiest and most popular portion of his treatise, to the neglect, or comparative neglect, of all the more abstruse and difficult parts, that modern taste has fastened. After training in oratory had ceased to be the main object or form of education, and especially after there had been devolved on the printing-press many of those oratorical functions which had formerly belonged to the living voice with some aid from annexed manuscript, people recollected but vaguely the more scientific solidities of the Ancient Rhetoric, and became interested chiefly in

tion than the explosion of that novelty which we are going to discharge.

Many years ago, when studying the Aristotelian Rhetoric at Oxford, it struck us that, by whatever name Aristotle might describe the main purpose of Rhetoric, practically, at least, in his own treatment of it, he threw the whole stress upon finding such arguments for any given thesis as, without positively proving or disproving it, should give it a

---

what it had taught on the special subject of Style or Literary Expression. So far there was a narrowing of the old idea or definition of Rhetoric. But the narrowing was compensated by a curious accompanying extension. Although what Aristotle had said on the subject of style had been said most directly for the behoof of the orator and with relation to *his* craft, did not most of it hold good for practitioners of the literary art in any form whatever,—for historians, or poets, or philosophers, as well as orators ? Had not all these to employ *language* for their purposes ; and would not any body of precepts for the use of language that served for the orator serve pretty well also, though with some necessary modifications perhaps, for the historical writer, the philosopher, or the poet ? Thus all kinds of literature,— narrative literature in all its forms, poetry in all its forms, and all forms of expository or speculative literature,—were taken within the field of Rhetoric, so far as there might be principles of *diction* or literary expression common to them all ; and, this having been done, it was easy to generalise still more by assuming for Rhetoric not only the charge of the *diction* in all kinds of literature, but also to some extent the charge of the *matter* or *intrinsic psychological substance* in each kind,—allowing Rhetoric to discuss, for example, such questions as the difference between wit and humour, the nature of the poetic imagination, the laws of tragic poetry or of any other species of poetry, and so in fact to annex to itself all that had been treated independently and separately by Aristotle in his POETICS, and by Horace in his DE ARTE POETICA.—Three definitions of Rhetoric have thus come down in competition with each other, or more or less in confusion : viz. I. The Ancient or Aristotelian definition, which made Rhetoric strictly the Art and Science of Oratory, spoken or written. II. That middle kind of definition which makes Rhetoric the Art and Science of Style or Diction for any literary purpose. III. A definition which would stretch Rhetoric into the Science of Literature, or of Literary Theory and Literary Criticism universally, and make it treat of the principles of Historical Writing, Poetry, and Expository Writing, as well as of Oratory. Whately endeavoured, on the whole, to revert to the old or Aristotelian definition ; but the general modern drift has favoured one or other of the two other definitions, or perhaps a compromise between the second and the third. This in the main is De Quincey's position, though, as we shall see, he attempts a difference.—M.

colourable support. It could not be by accident that the topics, or general heads of argument, were never in an absolute and unconditional sense true, but contained so much of plausible or colourable truth as is expressed in the original meaning of the word *probable*. A *ratio probabilis*, in the Latin use of the word *probabilis*, is that ground of assent— not which the understanding can solemnly approve and abide by—but the very opposite to this ; one which it can submit to for a moment, and countenance as within the limits of the plausible.[1] That this was the real governing law of Aristotle's procedure it was not possible to doubt : but was it consciously known to himself ? If so, how was it to be reconciled with his own formal account of the office of Rhetoric, so often repeated, that it consisted in finding enthymemes ?[2] What then was an Enthymeme ?

[1] It is ludicrous to see the perplexity of some translators and commentators of the Rhetoric, who, having read it under a false point of view, labour to defend it on that footing. On its real footing it needs no defence.

[2] This is an exaggeration of the proportions assigned to the Enthymeme in the Aristotelian Rhetoric. The Enthymeme is certainly of importance there ; but it is by no means the all-in-all there that one might infer it to have been from De Quincey's words. It came in more particularly at that point of Aristotle's survey of Rhetoric where he discussed the *Logical Pistis*,—*i.e.* that means of persuasion which consists in the actual ratiocination, the logical address to the pure understanding, which an orator may employ in support of his case (see footnote, *ante*, p. 84).—All Rhetorical reasoning, all the reasoning of common life, Aristotle explained, is, and can only be, of one or other of two kinds, corresponding severally to *induction* and *deduction* in Logic. Now, inductive reasoning in rhetoric, as in common life, is always in the form of *Paradigm* or *Example*, whereas deductive reasoning in rhetoric, as in common life, is always in the form of *Enthymeme* (i.e. *thought* or *maxim*). If an orator in any Greek city, observing that one of the leading citizens had been going about for some time attended by an armed body-guard, were to argue in the public assembly that this looked suspicious and indicated a design of forcibly seizing the tyranny or single and personal sovereignty in the state, and if that orator were to try to gain over his fellow-citizens to this view by reminding them of this and that well-remembered instance in previous Grecian history where a tyrant had prepared the way for his assumption of the tyranny by surrounding himself with a body-guard,—that would be *inductive reasoning* or reasoning by *Paradigm*. This kind of reasoning, in short, consists in the production of examples or like cases, which may shed probability on

Oxford ! thou wilt think us mad to ask.[1] Certainly we knew, what all the world knows, that an enthymeme was understood to be a syllogism of which one proposition is suppressed—major, minor, or conclusion. But what possible relation had *that* to rhetoric ? Nature sufficiently prompts all men to that sort of ellipsis ; and what impertinence in a teacher to build his whole system upon a solemn precept to do this or that, when the rack would not have forced any man to do otherwise ! Besides, Aristotle had represented it as the fault of former systems that they applied themselves exclusively to the treatment of the passions — an object

the view argued for. Reasoning by *Enthymeme*, or *deductive reasoning*, on the other hand, consists in first putting forth some general proposition or maxim likely to be assented to, and then bringing the particular case on hand under the cover of that proposition or maxim so as to partake of its plausibility. If, by way of fastening a charge of murder on the accused person at the bar, an advocate, in default of more direct evidence, were to advance the proposition that the murderer in any case of murder is likely to be some one who had an interest in the death of the murdered person, and were then to show that the prisoner was remarkably in this predicament with respect to the man whose murderer had to be discovered,—that, along with other arguments, might have some weight with the jury, and would at all events be an instance of *deductive reasoning* or *Enthymeme*.—So far it is not difficult to grasp the distinction ; but the toughest and most obscure bit in all Aristotle's Rhetoric is undoubtedly that in which he defines the *Enthymeme* more minutely and specifies the varieties into which it may break itself. It is at this point that De Quincey comes in with his proposed correction of the traditional notion of the *Enthymeme*. It is acute and interesting, and will probably be more intelligible to the reader after this general explanation.—M.

[1] Whatever validity there may be in that correction of the traditional doctrine of the *Enthymeme* to which De Quincey now proceeds, he is certainly wrong in some of these introductory remarks. Not only, as has been shown in the preceding note, does he greatly exaggerate the place and proportions of the Enthymeme in Aristotle's Rhetoric ; but he is wrong, utterly wrong, in the statement that Aristotle excluded from his Rhetoric all appeal to the passions. On the contrary, the PATHETIC PISTIS, or that means of persuasion to which an orator might help himself by powerful playing upon the feelings of his audience, was distinctly recognised by Aristotle and discussed by him at large (see footnote, *ante*, p. 84). One of the most curious and interesting portions of his Rhetoric, indeed, is a little Natural History of the Passions, or inventory of the ruling feelings of men, in youth, middle life, old age, &c., which he introduces in illustration of the PATHETIC PISTIS.—M.

foreign to the purpose of the rhetorician, who, in some situations, is absolutely forbidden by law to use any such arts : whereas, says he, his true and universal weapon is the enthymeme, which is open to him everywhere. Now, what opposition, or what relation of any kind, can be imagined between the system which he rejects and the one he adopts, if the enthymeme is to be understood as it usually has been ? The rhetorician is not to address the passions, but—what ? to mind that in all his arguments he suppresses one of his propositions ! And these follies are put into the mouth of Aristotle !

In this perplexity a learned Scottish friend [1] communicated to us an Essay of Facciolati's, read publicly about a century ago (Nov. 1724), and entitled De Enthymemate,[2] in which he maintains that the received idea of the enthymeme is a total blunder, and triumphantly restores the lost idea. " Nego," says he, " nego enthymema esse syllogismum mutilum, ut vulgo dialectici docent. Nego, inquam, et pernego enthymema enunciatione una et conclusione constare, quamvis ita in scholis omnibus finiatur, et a nobis ipsis finitum sit aliquando, nolentibus extra locum lites suscipere." I deny, says he, that the enthymeme properly understood is a truncated syllogism, as commonly is taught by dialecticians. I deny, let me repeat, peremptorily and furiously I deny, that the enthymeme consists of one premiss and the conclusion: although that doctrine has been laid down universally in the schools, and upon one occasion even by myself, as unwilling to move the question prematurely or out of its natural place.

Facciolati is not the least accurate of logicians because he may chance to be the most elegant. Yet, we apprehend, that at such innovations Smiglecius will stir in his grave, Keckermannus will groan, " Dutch [3] Burgersdyk " will snort,

---

[1] This "learned Scottish friend" was the late Sir William Hamilton. It was in the summer before Waterloo, viz. in the summer of 1814, that I first became acquainted with him—in fact forty-five years ago on this 20th day of March 1859, from which I date my hurried revision of this paper entitled Rhetoric. [See ante, Vol. V, pp. 338-340.—M.]

[2] It stands at p. 227 of Jacobi Facciolati Orationes XII, Acroases, &c.   Patavii, 1729.—This is the second Italian edition, and was printed at the University Press. [See ante, Vol. V, p. 340.—M.]

[3] " Dutch Burgersdyk " :—Pope in the Dunciad.   The other names,

and English Crackenthorpius (who has the honour to be an ancestor of Mr. Wordsworth), though buried for two centuries, will revisit the glimpses of the moon. And really, if the question were for a name, Heaven forbid that we should disturb the peace of logicians : they might have leave to say, as of the Strid in Wharfdale,

> "It has borne that name a thousand years,
> And shall a thousand more."

But, whilst the name is abused, the idea perishes. Facciolati undoubtedly is right : nor is he the first who has observed the error. Julius Pacius, who understood Aristotle better than any man that ever lived, had long before remarked it.[1] The arguments of Facciolati we will give below [2] ; it may be

---

if qualified apparently to frighten a horse, are all real names of men who did business in logic some 250 and 200 years ago, and were really no pretenders, though unhappily both grim and grimy in the impertinent estimates of contemporary women. [Martin Smigletius, Polish theologian and logician, 1562-1618 ; Bartholomew Keckermann, German writer, 1573-1609 ; Francis Burgersdyk (Burgersdicius), Dutch logician, 1590-1629 ; Richard Crakanthorpe, English controversialist, 1567-1624.—M.]

[1] Giulio Pacio, Venetian scholar, jurist, editor of Aristotle, &c., 1550-1635.—M.

[2] Upon an innovation of such magnitude, and which will be so startling to scholars, it is but fair that Facciolati should have the benefit of all his own arguments : and we have therefore resolved to condense them. 1. He begins with that very passage (or one of them) on which the received idea of the Enthymeme most relies ; and from this he derives an argument for the new idea. The passage is to this effect, that the enthymeme is composed ἐκ πολλάκις ἐλαττόνων ἢ ἐξ ὧν ὁ συλλογισμος — i.e. frequently consists of fewer parts than the syllogism. Frequently! What logic is there in that? Can it be imagined that so rigorous a logician as Aristotle would notice, as a circumstance of frequent occurrence in an enthymeme, what, by the received doctrine, should be its mere essence and differential principle? To say that this happens frequently is to say, by implication, that sometimes it does not happen—i.e. that it is an accident, and no part of the definition, since it may thus confessedly be absent, salva ratione conceptus. 2. Waiving this argument, and supposing the suppression of one proposition to be even universal in the enthymeme, still it would be an impertinent circumstance, and (philosophically speaking) an accident. Could it be tolerated that a great systematic distinction (for such it is in Aristotle) should rest upon a mere abbreviation of convenience, "quasi vero argumentandi ratio et natura varietur cum brevius effertur," whereas Aristotle himself tells us, that " οὐ προς τον

sufficient here to state the result. An enthymeme differs from a syllogism, not in the accident of suppressing one of its propositions; either may do this, or neither; the difference is essential, and in the nature of the *matter* : that of the syllogism proper being certain and apodeictic; that of the enthymeme simply probable, and drawn from the province of opinion.

This theory tallies exactly with our own previous construction of Aristotle's Rhetoric, and explains the stress which he had laid at the outset upon enthymemes. Whatsoever is certain, or matter of fixed science, can be no subject

ἔξω λογον ἡ ἀποδειξις, ἀλλα προς τον ἐν τῃ ψυχῃ" ? 3. From a particular passage in the 2d book of the Prior Analytics (chap. 27), generally interpreted in a way to favour the existing account of the enthymeme, after first of all showing that under a more accurate construction it is incompatible with that account, whilst it is in perfect harmony with the new one, Facciolati deduces an explanation of that accidental peculiarity in the enthymeme which has attracted such undue attention as to eclipse its true characteristic : the peculiarity, we mean, of being entitled (though not, as the common idea is, required) to suppress one proposition. So much we shall here anticipate as to say that this privilege arises out of the peculiar *matter* of the enthymeme, which fitted it for the purposes of the rhetorician ; and these purposes, being loose and popular, brought with them proportionable indulgences ; whereas the syllogism, technically so called, employing a severer matter, belonged peculiarly to the dialectician, or philosophic disputant, whose purposes, being rigorous and scientific, imposed much closer restrictions ; and one of these was that he should in no case suppress any proposition, however obvious, but should formally enunciate all : just as in the debating schools of later ages it has always been the rule that, before urging his objection, the opponent should repeat the respondent's syllogism. Hence, although the rhetorician naturally used his privilege, and enthymemes were in fact generally shorn of one proposition (and *vice versa* with respect to syllogisms in the strict philosophic sense), yet was all this a mere effect of usage and accident ; and it was very possible for an enthymeme to have its full complement of parts, whilst a syllogism might be defective in the very way which is falsely supposed to be of the essence of an enthymeme. 4. He derives an argument from an inconsistency with which Aristotle has been thought chargeable under the old idea of the enthymeme, and with which Gassendi has in fact charged him.[1] 5. He meets and

---

[1] However, as in reality the whole case was one of mere misapprehension on the part of Gassendi, and has, in fact, nothing at all to do with the nature of the enthymeme, well or ill understood, Facciolati takes nothing by this particular argument ; which, however, we have retained, to make our analysis complete.

for the rhetorician: where it is possible for the understanding to be convinced, no field is open for rhetorical persuasion. Absolute certainty and fixed science transcend opinion, and exclude the probable. The province of Rhetoric, whether meant for an influence upon the actions, or simply upon the belief, lies amongst that vast field of cases where there is a *pro* and a *con*, with the chance of right and wrong, true and false, distributed in varying proportions between them. There is also an immense range of truths where there are no chances at all concerned, but the affirmative and the negative are both true : as, for example, the goodness of human nature and its wickedness ; the happiness of human life and its misery ; the charms of knowledge, and its hollowness ; the fragility of human prosperity in the eye of religious meditation, and its security as estimated by worldly confidence and youthful hope. In all such cases the rhetorician exhibits his art by giving an impulse to one side, and by withdrawing the mind so steadily from all thoughts or images which support the other as to leave it practically under the possession of a one-sided estimate.

rebuts the force of a principal argument in favour of the enthymeme as commonly understood, viz. that in a particular part of the Prior Analytics the enthymeme is called συλλογισμος ἀτελης, an *imperfect* syllogism, — which word the commentators generally expound by "*mutilus atque imminutus.*" Here he uses the assistance of the excellent J. Pace, whom he justly describes as "virum Græcarum litterarum peritissimum, philosophum in primis bonum, et Aristotelis interpretum, quot sunt, quotque fuerunt, quotque futuri sunt, longe præstantissimum." This admirable commentator, so indispensable to all who would study the *Organon* and the Περι Ψυχης, had himself originally started that hypothesis which we are now reporting as long afterwards adopted and improved by Facciolati. Considering the unrivalled qualifications of Pace, this of itself is a great argument on our side. The objection before us, from the word ἀτελης, Pace disposes of briefly and conclusively. *First*, he says that the word is wanting in four MSS. ; and he has no doubt himself "quin ex glossemate irrepserit in contextum." *Secondly*, the Latin translators and school-men, as Agricola and many others, take no notice of this word in their versions and commentaries. *Thirdly*, the Greek commentators, such as Joannes Grammaticus and Alexander Aphrodisiensis, clearly had no knowledge of any such use of the word *enthymeme* as that which has prevailed in later times ; which is plain from this,—that, wherever they have occasion to speak of a syllogism wanting one of its members, they do not in any instance call it an enthymeme, but a συλλογισμον μονολημματον.

Upon this theory, what relation to Rhetoric shall we assign to style and the ornamental arts of composition ? In some respects they seem liable to the same objection as that which Aristotle has urged against appeals to the passions.[1] Both are extra-essential, or ἐξω του πραγματος; they are subjective arts, not objective ; that is, they do not affect the thing which is to be surveyed, but the eye of him who is to survey. Yet, at a banquet, the epicure holds himself not more obliged to the cook for the venison than to the physician who braces his stomach to enjoy. And any arts which conciliate regard to the speaker indirectly promote the effect of his arguments. On this account, and because (under the severest limitation of Rhetoric) they are in many cases indispensable to the perfect interpretation of the thoughts, we may admit arts of style and ornamental composition as the ministerial part of Rhetoric. But with regard to the passions, as contended for by Dr. Campbell, it is a sufficient answer that they are already preoccupied by what is called *Eloquence*.

Coleridge, as we have often heard, is in the habit of drawing the line with much philosophical beauty between Rhetoric and Eloquence. On this topic we were never so fortunate as to hear him : but, if we are here called upon for a distinction, we shall satisfy our immediate purpose by a very plain and brief one. By Eloquence we understand the overflow of powerful feelings upon occasions fitted to excite them. But Rhetoric is the art of aggrandizing and bringing out into strong relief, by means of various and striking thoughts, some aspect of truth which of itself is supported by no spontaneous feelings, and therefore rests upon artificial aids.[2]

Greece, as may well be imagined, was the birthplace of Rhetoric : to which of the Fine Arts was it not ? and here, in one sense of the word Rhetoric, the art had its consum-

---

[1] See footnote, *ante*, p. 87.—M.

[2] Is this to be taken as De Quincey's own special conception of Rhetoric ? If so, it may be translated as meaning the art of intellectual and fantastic play with any subject to its utmost capabilities, or the art of enriching any main truth or idea by inweaving with it the largest possible amount of subsidiary and illustrative thought and fancy. I do not think that he keeps very strictly to this conception

mation : for the theory, or *ars docens*, was taught with a fulness and an accuracy by the Grecian masters not afterwards approached. In particular, it was so taught by Aristotle : whose system we are disposed to agree with Dr. Whately in pronouncing the best as regards the primary purpose of a teacher ; though otherwise, for elegance and as a practical model in the art he was expounding, neither Aristotle, nor any less austere among the Greek rhetoricians, has any pretensions to measure himself with Quintilian. In reality, for a triumph over the difficulties of the subject, and as a lesson on the possibility of imparting grace to the treatment of scholastic topics naturally as intractable as that of Grammar or Prosody there is no such *chef-d'œuvre* to this hour in any literature as the Institutions of Quintilian.[1] Laying this one case out of the comparison, however, the Greek superiority was indisputable.

Yet how is it to be explained that, with these advantages on the side of the Greek Rhetoric as an *ars docens*, Rhetoric as a practical art (the *ars utens*) never made any advances amongst the Greeks to the brilliancy which it attained in Rome ? Up to a certain period, and throughout the palmy state of the Greek republics, we may account for it thus :— Rhetoric, in its finest and most absolute burnish, may be called an *eloquentia umbratica* ; that is, it aims at an elaborate form of beauty which shrinks from the strife of business, and could neither arise nor make itself felt in a tumultuous assembly. Certain features, it is well known, and peculiar styles of countenance, which are impressive in a drawing-room become ineffective on a public stage. The fine tooling and delicate tracery of the cabinet artist is lost upon a building of colossal proportions. Extemporaneousness, again,—a favourable circumstance to impassioned eloquence,—is death to Rhetoric. Two characteristics indeed there were of a Greek popular assembly which must have operated fatally on the

of Rhetoric,—which does not accord perfectly with any of the traditional definitions already mentioned, *ante*, p. 85, footnote ; but it does accompany him through a good deal of what follows, and regulates to some extent his selection of authors to represent the rhetorical style. —M.

[1] Quintilian, A.D. 42-118, author of *Institutiones Oratoriæ* or *Institutes of Oratory.*—M

rhetorician : its fervour, in the first place ; and, secondly, the coarseness of a real interest. All great rhetoricians in selecting their subject have shunned the determinate cases of real life : and even in the single instance of a deviation from the rule—that of the author (whoever he be) of the Declamations attributed to Quintilian—the cases are shaped with so romantic a generality, and so slightly circumstantiated, as to allow him all the benefit of pure abstractions.

We can readily understand, therefore, why the fervid oratory of the Athenian assemblies, and the intense reality of its interest, should stifle the growth of rhetoric : the smoke, tarnish, and demoniac glare of Vesuvius easily eclipse the pallid coruscations of the aurora borealis. And, in fact, amongst the greater orators of Greece there is not a solitary gleam of rhetoric. Isocrates may have a little, being (to say the truth) neither orator nor rhetorician in any eminent sense ; Demosthenes has none. But, when those great thunders had subsided which reached "to Macedon and Artaxerxes' throne," when the "fierce democracy" itself had perished, and Greece had fallen under the common circumstances of the Roman Empire, how came it that Greek Rhetoric did not blossom concurrently with Roman ? Vegetate it did ; and a rank crop of weeds grew up under the name of Rhetoric, down to the times of the Emperor Julian and his friend Libanius (both of whom, by the way, were as worthless writers as have ever abused the Greek language).[1] But this part of Greek Literature is a desert with no oasis. The fact is, if it were required to assign the two bodies of writers who have exhibited the human understanding in the most abject poverty, and whose works by no possibility emit a casual scintillation of wit, fancy, just thinking, or good writing, we should certainly fix upon Greek rhetoricians and Italian critics. Amongst the whole mass there is not a page that any judicious friend to literature would wish to reprieve from destruction. And in both cases we apprehend that the possibility of so much inanity is due in part to the quality of the two languages. The diffuseness and loose structure of Greek style unfit it for the closeness, condensa-

[1] The Emperor Julian, A.D. 331-363 ; Libanius, Greek rhetorician, A.D. 314-391.—M.

tion, and το ἀγχίστροφον of rhetoric ; the melodious beauty
of the mere sounds, which both in the Italian and in the
Greek are combined with much majesty, dwells upon the
ear so delightfully that in no other language is it so easy as
in these two to write with little or no meaning, and to flow
along through a whole wilderness of inanity without parti·
cularly rousing the reader's disgust.

In the literature of Rome it is that we find the true El
Dorado of rhetoric, as we might expect from the sinewy
compactness of the language. Livy, and, above all preceding writers, Ovid, display the greatest powers of rhetoric in
forms of composition which were not particularly adapted to
favour that talent. The contest of Ajax and Ulysses for the
arms of Achilles in one of the latter books of the *Metamor-
phoses* is a *chef-d'œuvre* of rhetoric, considering its metrical
form ; for metre, and especially the flowing heroic hexameter,
is no advantage to the rhetorician.[1]   The two Plinys, Lucan
(though again under the disadvantage of verse), Petronius
Arbiter, and Quintilian, but above all the Senecas[2] (for a
Spanish cross appears to improve the quality of the rhetorician), have left a body of rhetorical composition such as no
modern nation has rivalled. Even the most brilliant of
these writers, however, were occasionally surpassed in particular *bravuras* of rhetoric by several of the Latin Fathers,
particularly Tertullian, Arnobius, St Austin,[3] and a writer
whose name we cannot at this moment recall. In fact, a
little African blood operated as genially in this respect as
Spanish, whilst an Asiatic cross was inevitably fatal, by
prompting a diffusion and inflation of style radically hostile

---

[1] This, added to the style and quality of his poems, makes it the
more remarkable that Virgil should have been deemed a rhetorician.
Yet so it was. Walsh notices, in the Life of Virgil which he furnished
for his friend Dryden's Translation, that "his (Virgil's) rhetoric was
in such general esteem that lectures were read upon it in the reign of
Tiberius, and the subject of declamations taken out of him."

[2] Pliny the elder, A.D. 23-79 ; Pliny the younger, A.D. 61-106 ;
Lucan, A.D. 39-65 ; Petronius Arbiter, died A.D. 66 ; Quintilian, A.D.
42-118 ; Seneca the elder, died about A.D. 32 ; Seneca the younger,
died A.D. 65.—M.

[3] Tertullian died *circa* A.D. 240 ; Arnobius lived about A.D. 290 ;
St. Augustine, A.D. 354-430.—M.

to the condensation of keen, arrowy rhetoric. Partly from this cause, and partly because they wrote in an unfavourable language, the Greek Fathers are, one and all, Birmingham rhetoricians. Even Gregory Nazianzen is so, with submission to Messieurs of the Port Royal and other bigoted critics who have pronounced him at the very top of the tree among the fine writers of antiquity.[1] Undoubtedly he has a turgid style of mouthy grandiloquence (though often the merest bombast); but for polished rhetoric he is singularly unfitted, by inflated habits of thinking, by loitering diffuseness, and a dreadful trick of calling names. The spirit of personal invective is peculiarly adverse to the coolness of rhetoric. As to Chrysostom and Basil, with less of pomp and swagger than Gregory, they have not at all more of rhetorical burnish and compression.[2] Upon the whole, looking back through the dazzling files of the ancient rhetoricians, we are disposed to rank the Senecas and Tertullian as the leaders of the band; for St. Austin, in his Confessions, and wherever he becomes peculiarly interesting, is apt to be impassioned and fervent in a degree which makes him break out of the proper pace of rhetoric. He is matched to trot, and is continually breaking into a gallop. Indeed, his Confessions have in parts,—particularly in those which relate to the death of his young friend and his own frenzy of grief,—all that real passion which is only imagined in the Confessions of Rousseau under a preconception derived from his known character and unhappy life. By the time of the Emperor Justinian (say A.D. 530), or in the interval between that time and the era of Mahomet (A.D. 620),—which interval we regard as the common *crepusculum* between Ancient and Modern History, all Rhetoric (as the professional pretension of a class) seems to have finally expired.

In the Literature of Modern Europe Rhetoric has been cultivated with success. But this remark applies only with any force to a period which is now long past; and it is probable, upon various considerations, that such another

[1] Gregory Nazianzen, bishop of Constantinople about A D. 380 —M.

[2] John Chrysostom, bishop of Constantinople from 397 to 407; St. Basil, bishop of Cæsarea from 371 to 380.—M.

period will never revolve. The rhetorician's art in its glory and power has silently faded away before the stern tendencies of the age; and, if, by any peculiarity of taste or strong determination of the intellect, a rhetorician *en grande costume* were again to appear amongst us, it is certain that he would have no better welcome than a stare of surprise as a posture-maker or balancer, not more elevated in the general estimate, but far less amusing, than the acrobat, or funambulist, or equestrian gymnast. No; the age of Rhetoric, like that of Chivalry, has passed amongst forgotten things; and the rhetorician can have no more chance for returning than the rhapsodist of early Greece or the troubadour of romance. So multiplied are the modes of intellectual enjoyment in modern times that the choice is absolutely distracted; and in a boundless theatre of pleasures, to be had at little or no cost of intellectual activity, it would be marvellous indeed if any considerable audience could be found for an exhibition which presupposes a state of tense exertion on the part both of auditor and performer. To hang upon one's own thoughts as an object of conscious interest, to play with them, to watch and pursue them through a maze of inversions, evolutions, and harlequin changes, implies a condition of society either, like that in the monastic ages, forced to introvert its energies from mere defect of books (whence arose the scholastic meta-physics, admirable for its subtlety, but famishing the mind whilst it sharpened its edge in one exclusive direction); or, if it implies no absolute starvation of intellect, as in the case of the Roman rhetoric, which arose upon a considerable (though not very various) literature, it proclaims at least a quiescent state of the public mind, unoccupied with daily novelties, and at leisure from the agitations of eternal change.

Growing out of the same condition of society, there is another cause at work which will for ever prevent the resurrection of rhetoric : viz. the necessities of public business, its vast extent, complexity, fulness of details, and consequent vulgarity, as compared with that of the ancients. The very same cause, by the way, furnishes an answer to the question moved by Hume, in one of his essays, with regard to the declension of eloquence in our deliberative assemblies. Eloquence, or at least that which is senatorial and forensic, has languished under the same changes of society which have proved fatal to Rhetoric. The political economy of the ancient republics, and their commerce, were simple and unelaborate ; the system of their public services, both martial and civil, was arranged on the most naked and manageable principles ; for we must not confound the perplexity in our modern explanations of these things with a perplexity in the things themselves. The foundation of these differences was in the differences of domestic life. Personal wants being few, both from climate and from habit, and, in the great majority of the citizens, limited almost to the pure necessities of nature,—hence arose, for the mass of the population, the possibility of surrendering themselves, much more than with us, either to the one paramount business of the state, war, or to a state of Indian idleness. Rome, in particular, during the ages of her growing luxury, must be regarded as a nation supported by other nations ; by largesses, in effect ; that is to say, by the plunder of conquest. Living, therefore, upon foreign alms, or upon corn purchased by the product of tribute or of spoils, a nation could readily dispense with that expansive development of her internal resources upon which Modern Europe has been forced by the more equal distribution of power amongst the civilized world.

The changes which have followed in the functions of our popular assemblies correspond to the great revolution here described. Suppose yourself an ancient Athenian at some customary display of Athenian oratory, what will be the topics ? Peace or war, vengeance for public wrongs, or mercy to prostrate submission, national honour and national gratitude, glory and shame, and every aspect of open appeal to the primal sensibilities of man. On the other hand, enter an English Parliament, having the most of a popular character in its constitution and practice that is anywhere to be found in the Christendom of this day, and the subject of debate will probably be a road bill, a bill for enabling a coal-gas company to assume certain privileges against a competitor in oil-gas,[1] a bill for disfranchising a corrupt borough, or perhaps some technical point of form in the Exchequer Bills bill. So much is the face of public business vulgarized by details.

[1] Written thirty years ago [*i.e.* in 1828.—M.]

The same spirit of differences extends to forensic eloquence. Grecian and Roman pleadings are occupied with questions of elementary justice, large and diffusive, apprehensible even to the uninstructed, and connecting themselves at every step with powerful and tempestuous feelings.[1] In British trials, on the contrary, the field is foreclosed against any interest of so elevating a nature, because the rights and wrongs of the case are almost inevitably absorbed to an unlearned eye by the technicalities of the law, or by the intricacy of the facts.

But this is not always the case ! Doubtless not : subjects for eloquence, and therefore eloquence, will sometimes arise in our senate and our courts of justice. And in one respect our British displays are more advantageously circumstanced than the ancient, being more conspicuously brought forward into effect by their contrast to the ordinary course of business.

> "Therefore are feasts so solemn and so rare,
> Since, seldom coming, in the long year set,
> Like stones of worth they thinly placèd are,
> Or captain jewels in the carcanet." [2]

But still the objection of Hume remains unimpeached as to the fact that eloquence is a rarer growth of modern than of ancient civil polity, even in those countries which have the advantage of free institutions. Now, why is this ? The letter of this objection is sustained, but substantially it is disarmed, so far as its purpose was to argue any declension on the part of Christian nations, by this explanation of ours, which traces the impoverished condition of civil eloquence to the complexity of public business.

But eloquence in one form or other is immortal, and will never perish so long as there are human hearts moving under the agitations of hope and fear, love and passionate hatred. And, in particular to us of the modern world, as an endless source of indemnification for what we have lost in the simplicity of our social systems, we have received a new dowry of eloquence, and *that* of the highest order, in the sanctities of our religion : a field unknown to antiquity, for

[1] There were speeches of Demosthenes and others on intricate civil cases of debt, &c.—M.

[2] Shakspere, *Sonnet 52.*

the pagan religions did not produce much poetry, and of oratory none at all.

On the other hand, that cause which, operating upon eloquence, has but extinguished it under a single direction, to rhetoric has been unconditionally fatal. Eloquence is not banished from the public business of this country as useless, but as difficult, and as not spontaneously arising from topics such as generally furnish the staple of debate. But rhetoric, if attempted on a formal scale, would be summarily exploded as pure foppery and trifling with time. Falstaff on the field of battle presenting his bottle of sack for a pistol, or Polonius with his quibbles, could not appear a more unseasonable *plaisanteur* than a rhetorician alighting from the clouds upon a public assembly in Great Britain met for the despatch of business.

Under these malign aspects of the modern structure of society, a structure to which the whole world will be moulded as it becomes civilized, there can be no room for any revival of rhetoric in public speaking, and, from the same and other causes, acting upon the standard of public taste, quite as little room in written composition. In spite, however, of the tendencies to this consummation, which have been long ripening, it is a fact that, next after Rome, England is the country in which rhetoric prospered most at a time when science was unborn as a popular interest, and the commercial activities of aftertimes were yet sleeping in their rudiments. This was in the period from the latter end of the sixteenth to the middle of the seventeenth century ; and, though the English Rhetoric was less rigorously true to its own ideal than the Roman, and often modulated into a higher key of impassioned eloquence, yet unquestionably in some of its qualities it remains a monument of the very finest rhetorical powers.

Omitting Sir Philip Sidney, and omitting his friend, Fulke Greville, Lord Brooke (in whose prose there are some bursts of pathetic eloquence, as there is of rhetoric in his verse, though too often harsh and cloudy), the first very eminent rhetorician in the English Literature is Donne.[1]

[1] Sir Philip Sidney, 1554-1586 ; Lord Brooke, 1554-1628 ; Dr. John Donne, 1573-1631.—M.

Dr. Johnson inconsiderately classes him in company with Cowley, &c., under the title of *Metaphysical* Poets [1] : metaphysical they were not ; *Rhetorical* would have been a more accurate designation. In saying *that*, however, we must remind our readers that we revert to the original use of the word *Rhetoric*, as laying the principal stress upon the management of the thoughts, and only a secondary one upon the ornaments of style. Few writers have shown a more extraordinary compass of powers than Donne ; for he combined—what no other man has ever done—the last sublimation of dialectical subtlety and address with the most impassioned majesty. Massy diamonds compose the very substance of his poem on the Metempsychosis, thoughts and descriptions which have the fervent and gloomy sublimity of Ezekiel or Æschylus, whilst a diamond dust of rhetorical brilliancies is strewed over the whole of his occasional verses and his prose. No criticism was ever more unhappy than that of Dr. Johnson's which denounces all this artificial display as so much perversion of taste. There cannot be a falser thought than this ; for upon that principle a whole class of compositions might be vicious by conforming to its own ideal. The artifice and machinery of rhetoric furnishes in its degree as legitimate a basis for intellectual pleasure as any other ; that the pleasure is of an inferior order, can no more attaint the idea or model of the composition than it can impeach the excellence of an epigram that it is not a tragedy. Every species of composition is to be tried by its own laws ; and, if Dr. Johnson had urged explicitly (what was evidently moving in his thoughts) that a metrical structure, by holding forth the promise of poetry, defrauds the mind of its just expectations, he would have said what is notoriously false. Metre is open to any form of composition, provided it will aid the expression of the thoughts ; and the only sound objection to it is that it has *not* done so. Weak criticism, indeed, is that which condemns a copy of verses under the ideal of poetry, when the mere substitution of another name and classification suffices to evade the sentence, and to reinstate the composition in its rights as rhetoric. It

---

[1] Abraham Cowley, 1618 - 1667 : Johnson's dissertation on the " Metaphysical Poets " occurs in his Life of Cowley.—M.

may be very true that the age of Donne gave too much encouragement to his particular vein of composition. That, however, argues no depravity of taste, but a taste erring only in being too limited and exclusive.

The next writers of distinction who came forward as rhetoricians were Burton in his *Anatomy of Melancholy*[1] and Milton in many of his prose works. They labour under opposite defects. Burton is too quaint, fantastic, and disjointed ; Milton too slow, solemn, and continuous. In the one we see the flutter of a parachute ; in the other the stately and voluminous gyrations of an ascending balloon. Agile movement, and a certain degree of fancifulness, are indispensable to rhetoric. But Burton is not so much fanciful as capricious ; his motion is not the motion of freedom, but of lawlessness ; he does not dance, but caper. Milton, on the other hand, *polonaises* with a grand Castilian air, in paces too sequacious and processional ; even in his passages of merriment, and when stung into a quicker motion by personal disdain for an unworthy antagonist, his thoughts and his imagery still appear to move to the music of the organ.

In some measure it is a consequence of these peculiarities, and so far it is the more a duty to allow for them, that the rhetoric of Milton, though wanting in animation, is unusually superb in its colouring ; its very monotony is derived from the sublime unity of the presiding impulse ; and hence it sometimes ascends into eloquence of the highest kind, and sometimes even into the raptures of lyric poetry. The main thing, indeed, wanting to Milton was to have fallen upon happier subjects : for, with the exception of the "Areopagitica," there is not one of his prose works upon a theme of universal interest, or perhaps fitted to be the ground-work of a rhetorical display.

But, as it has happened to Milton sometimes to give us poetry for rhetoric, in one instance he has unfortunately given us rhetoric for poetry. This occurs in the *Paradise Lost*, where the debates of the fallen angels are carried on by a degrading process of gladiatorial rhetoric. Nay, even the counsels of God, though not debated to and fro, are, however,

---

[1] Robert Burton, 1576-1640. His *Anatomy of Melancholy* was first published in 1621.—M.

expounded rhetorically. This is astonishing ; for no one was better aware than Milton[1] of the distinction between the *discursive* and *intuitive* acts of the mind as apprehended by the old metaphysicians, and the incompatibility of the former with any but a limitary intellect. This indeed was familiar to all the writers of his day ; but, as Mr. Gifford has shown, by a most idle note upon a passage in Massinger,[2] that it is a distinction which has now perished (except indeed in Germany), we shall recall it to the reader's attention. An *intuition* is any knowledge whatsoever, sensuous or intellectual, which is apprehended *immediately* : a notion, on the other hand, or product of the discursive faculty, is any knowledge whatsoever which is apprehended *mediately*. All reasoning is carried on discursively ; that is, *discurrendo*,—by running about to the right and the left, laying the separate notices together, and thence mediately deriving some third apprehension. Now, this process, however grand a characteristic of the human species as distinguished from the brute, is degrading to any supra-human intelligence, divine or angelic, by arguing limitation. God must not proceed by steps and the fragmentary knowledge of accretion ; in which case at starting he has all the intermediate notices as so many bars between himself and the conclusion, and even at the penultimate or antepenultimate act he is still short of the truth. God must *see* ; he must *intuit*, so to speak ; and all truth must reach him simultaneously, first and last, without succession of time or partition of acts : just as light, before that theory had been refuted by the Satellites of Jupiter, was held not to be propagated in time, but to be here and there at one and the same indivisible instant. Paley, from mere rudeness of metaphysical skill, has talked of the *judgment* and the *judiciousness* of God : but this is profaneness, and a language unworthily applied even to an angelic being. To judge, that is to subsume one proposition under another,— to be judicious, that is, to collate the means with the end,— are acts impossible in the Divine nature, and not to be ascribed, even under the licence of a figure, to any being

[1] See the Fifth Book of the *Paradise Lost*, and passages in his prose writings.

[2] Gifford's edition of Massinger, published 1813.—M.

which transcends the limitations of humanity.   Many other instances there are in which Milton is taxed with having too grossly sensualized his supernatural agents ; some of which, however, the necessities of the action may excuse ; and at the worst they are readily submitted to as having an intelligible purpose—that of bringing so mysterious a thing as a spiritual nature or agency within the limits of the representable.   But the intellectual degradation fixed on his spiritual beings by the rhetorical debates is purely gratuitous, neither resulting from the course of the action nor at all promoting it.   Making allowances, however, for the original error in the conception, it must be granted that the execution is in the best style.   The mere logic of the debate, indeed, is not better managed than it would have been by the House of Commons.   But the colours of style are grave and suitable to afflicted angels.   In the *Paradise Regained* this is still more conspicuously true : the oratory there, on the part of Satan in the Wilderness, is no longer of a rhetorical cast, but in the grandest style of impassioned eloquence that can be imagined as the fit expression for the movements of an angelic despair ; and in particular the speech, on being first challenged by our Saviour, beginning

" 'Tis true, I *am* that spirit unfortunate "

is not excelled in sublimity by any passage in the poem.

Milton, however, was not destined to gather the *spolia opima* of English rhetoric.   Two contemporaries of his own, and whose literary course pretty nearly coincided with his own in point of time, surmounted all competition, and in that amphitheatre became the Protagonistæ.   These were Jeremy Taylor and Sir Thomas Browne ; who, if not absolutely the foremost in the accomplishments of art, were undoubtedly the richest, the most dazzling, and, with reference to their matter, the most captivating, of all rhetoricians.[1]   In them first, and perhaps (if we except occasional passages in the German John Paul Richter) in them only, are the two opposite forces of eloquent passion and rhetorical fancy brought into an exquisite equilibrium,—approaching, receding,

---

[1] Jeremy Taylor, 1613-1667 ; Sir Thomas Browne of Norwich, 1605-1682.—M.

—attracting, repelling,—blending, separating,—chasing and chased, as in a fugue,—and again lost in a delightful inter-fusion, so as to create a middle species of composition, more various and stimulating to the understanding than pure eloquence, more gratifying to the affections than naked rhetoric.   Under this one circumstance of coincidence, in other respects their minds were of the most opposite tempera-ment : Sir Thomas Browne, deep, tranquil, and majestic as Milton, silently premeditating and "disclosing his golden couplets," as under some genial instinct of incubation ; Jeremy Taylor, restless, fervid, aspiring, scattering abroad a prodigality of life, not unfolding but creating, with the energy and the "myriad-mindedness" of Shakspere.   Where but in Sir T. B. shall one hope to find music so Miltonic, an intonation of such solemn chords as are struck in the follow-ing opening bar of a passage in the *Urn-Burial*—"Now, since these bones have rested quietly in the grave under the drums and tramplings of three conquests," &c.[1]   What a melodious ascent as of a prelude to some impassioned requiem breathing from the pomps of earth, and from the sanctities of the grave !   What a *fluctus decumanus* of rhetoric !   Time expounded, not by generations or centuries, but by the vast periods of conquests and dynasties ; by cycles of Pharaohs and Ptolemies, Antiochi and Arsacides !   And these vast successions of time distinguished and figured by the uproars which revolve at their inaugurations ; by the drums and tramplings rolling overhead upon the chambers of forgotten dead — the trepidations of time and mortality vexing, at secular intervals, the everlasting sabbaths of the grave ! Show us, O pedant, such another strain from the oratory of Greece or Rome !   For it is not an Οὐ μα τους ἐν Μαραθωνι τεθνηκοτας,[2] or any such bravura, that will make a fit

---

[1] Browne's *Urn-Burial* was published originally in 1658 ; and the splendid passage in it to which De Quincey refers is the whole of the concluding chapter.   His quotation of the opening words is not quite accurate.   The real words are :—"Now, since these dead bones have already outlasted the living ones of Methuselah, and in a yard under-ground, and thin walls of clay, outworn all the strong and spacious buildings above it, and quietly rested under the drums and tramplings of three conquests."—M.

[2] A famous passage in Demosthenes's great speech "Concerning the

antiphony to this sublime rapture.   We will not, however, attempt a descant upon the merits of Sir T. Browne after the admirable one by Coleridge : and, as to Jeremy Taylor, we would as readily undertake to put a belt about the ocean as to characterize him adequately within the space at our command.   It will please the reader better that he should characterize himself, however imperfectly, by a few specimens selected from some of his rarest works : a method which will, at the same time, have the collateral advantage of illustrating an important truth in reference to this florid or Corinthian order of rhetoric which we shall have occasion to notice a little further on :—

" It was observed by a Spanish confessor that, in persons not very religious, the confessions which they made upon their deathbeds were the coldest, the most imperfect, and with less contrition than all which he had observed them to make in many years before.   For, as the canes of Egypt, when they newly arise from their bed of mud and slime of Nilus, start up into an equal and continual length, and uninterrupted but with few knots, and are strong and beauteous, with great distances and intervals, but, when they are grown to their full length, they lessen into the point of a pyramid, and multiply their knots and joints, interrupting the fineness and smoothness of its body : so are the steps and declensions of him that does not grow in grace.   At first, when he springs up from his impurity by the waters of baptism and repentance, he grows straight and strong, and suffers but few interruptions of piety ; and his constant courses of religion are but rarely intermitted, till they ascend up to a full age, or towards the ends of their life ; then they are weak, and their devotions often intermitted, and their breaks are frequent, and they seek excuses, and labour for dispensations, and love God and religion less and less, till their old age, instead of a crown of their virtue and perseverance, ends in levity and unprofitable courses, light and useless as the tufted feathers upon the cane : every wind can play with it and abuse it, but no man can make it useful."

" If we consider the price that the Son of God paid for the redemption of a soul, we shall better estimate of it than from the weak discourses of our imperfect and unlearned philosophy.   Not the spoil of rich provinces—not the estimate of kingdoms—not the price of Cleopatra's draught—not anything that was corruptible or perishing ; for that which could not one minute retard the term of its own natural dissolution could not be a price for the redemption of one perishing soul.   When God *made* a soul, it was only *faciamus hominem ad*

Crown," in which he invokes the memories of the illustrious dead at Marathon, Salamis, &c.—M.

imaginem nostram ; he spake the word, and it was done. But, when man had lost his soul, which the spirit of God had breathed into him, it was not so soon *recovered.* It is like the Resurrection, which hath troubled the faith of many, who are more apt to believe that God made a man from nothing than that he can return a man from dust and corruption. But for this resurrection of the soul, for the re-implacing of the Divine image, for the re-entitling it to the kingdoms of grace and glory, God did a greater work than the creation. He was fain to contract Divinity to a span ; to send a person to die for us who of himself could not die, and was constrained to use rare and mysterious arts to make him capable of dying : He prepared a person instrumental to his purpose by sending his Son from his own bosom—a person both God and Man, an enigma to all nations and to all sciences ; one that ruled over all the angels, that walked on the pavements of heaven ; whose feet were clothed with stars ; whose understanding is larger than that infinite space which we imagine in the uncircumscribed distance beyond the first orb of heaven ; a person to whom felicity was as essential as life to God. This was the only person that was designed in the eternal decrees to pay the price of a soul ; less than this person could not do it. Nothing less than an infinite excellence could satisfy for a soul lost to infinite ages, who was to bear the load of an infinite anger from the provocation of an eternal God. And yet, if it be possible that Infinite can receive degrees, this is but one-half of the abyss, and I think the lesser."

"It was a strange variety of natural efficacies that manna should corrupt in twenty-four hours if gathered upon Wednesday or Thursday, and that it should last till forty-eight hours if gathered upon the even of the Sabbath, and that it should last many hundreds of years when placed in the sanctuary by the ministry of the high priest. But so it was in the Jews' religion ; and manna pleased every palate, and it filled all appetites ; and the same measure was a different proportion, —it was much, and it was little ; as if nature, that it might serve religion, had been taught some measures of infinity, which is everywhere and nowhere, filling all things, and circumscribed with nothing, measured by one omer, and doing the work of two ; like the crowns of kings, fitting the brows of Nimrod and the most mighty warrior, and yet not too large for the temples of an infant prince."

"His mercies are more than we can tell, and they are more than we can feel : for all the world, in the abyss of the Divine mercies, is like a man diving into the bottom of the sea, over whose head the waters run insensibly and unperceived, and yet the weight is vast, and the sum of them immeasurable : and the man is not pressed with the burden, nor confounded with numbers : and no observation is able to recount, no sense sufficient to perceive, no memory large enough to retain, no understanding great enough to apprehend, this infinity."

These passages are not cited with so vain a purpose as that of furnishing a sea-line for measuring the " soundless deeps " of Jeremy Taylor, but to illustrate that one remarkable characteristic of his style which we have already noticed. viz. the everlasting strife and fluctuation between his rhetoric and his eloquence, which maintain their alternations with force and inevitable recurrence, like the systole and diastole, the contraction and expansion, of some living organ. For this characteristic he was indebted in mixed proportions to his own peculiar style of understanding and the nature of his subject. Where the understanding is not active and teeming, but possessed and filled by a few vast ideas (which was the case of Milton), there the funds of a varied rhetoric are wanting. On the other hand, where the understanding is all alive with the subtlety of distinctions, and nourished (as Jeremy Taylor's was) by casuistical divinity, the variety and opulence of the rhetoric is apt to be oppressive. But this tendency, in the case of Taylor, was happily checked and balanced by the commanding passion, intensity, and solemnity of his exalted theme, which gave a final unity to the tumultuous motions of his intellect. The only very obvious defects of Taylor were in the mechanical part of his art, in the mere *technique*. He writes like one who never revises, nor tries the effect upon his ear of his periods as musical wholes, and in the syntax and connexion of the parts seems to have been habitually careless of slight blemishes.

Jeremy Taylor [1] died in a few years after the Restoration.

[1] In retracing the history of English rhetoric, it may strike the reader that we have made some capital omissions. But in these he will find we have been governed by sufficient reasons. Shakspere is no doubt a rhetorician *majorum gentium* ; but he is so much more that scarcely an instance is to be found of his rhetoric which does not pass by fits into a higher element of eloquence or poetry. The first and the last acts, for instance, of the *Two Noble Kinsmen*,—which, in point of composition, is perhaps the most superb work in the language, and beyond all doubt from the loom of Shakspere,—would have been the most gorgeous rhetoric, had they not happened to be something far better. The supplications of the widowed Queens to Theseus, the invocations of their tutelar divinities by Palamon and Arcite, the death of Arcite, &c., are finished in a more elaborate style of excellence than any other almost of Shakspere's most felicitous scenes. In their first intention they were perhaps merely rhetorical ; but the furnace of composition has transmuted their substance. Indeed, specimens of mere rhetoric would be better sought in some of the other great dramatists, who are under a less fatal necessity of

Sir Thomas Browne, though at that time nearly thirty years removed from the first surreptitious edition of his *Religio Medici*, lingered a little longer. But, when both were gone, it may be truly affirmed that the great oracles of rhetoric were finally silenced. South and Barrow, indeed, were brilliant dialecticians in different styles ; but, after Tillotson, with his meagre intellect, his low key of feeling, and the smug and scanty draperies of his style, had announced a new era, English divinity ceased to be the racy vineyard that it had been in the ages of ferment and struggle.[1] Like the soil of Sicily (*vide* Sir H. Davy's *Agricultural Chemistry*), it was exhausted for ever by the tilth and rank fertility of its golden youth.

Since then great passions and high thinking have either

turning everything they touch into the pure gold of poetry. Two other writers, with great original capacities for rhetoric, we have omitted in our list from separate considerations : we mean Sir Walter Raleigh and Lord Bacon. The first will hardly have been missed by the general reader ; for his finest passages are dispersed through the body of his bulky history, and are touched with a sadness too pathetic, and of too personal a growth, to fulfil the conditions of a gay rhetoric as an art rejoicing in its own energies. With regard to Lord Bacon the case is different. He had great advantages for rhetoric, being figurative and sensuous (as great thinkers must always be), and having no feelings too profound, or of a nature to disturb the balance of a pleasurable activity; but yet, if we except a few letters, and parts of a few speeches, he never comes forward as a rhetorician. The reason is that, being always in quest of absolute truth, he contemplates all subjects, not through the rhetorical fancy, which is most excited by mere seeming resemblances, and such as can only sustain themselves under a single phasis, but through the philosophic fancy, or that which rests upon real analogies. Another unfavourable circumstance, arising in fact out of the plethoric fulness of Lord B.'s mind, is the short-hand style of his composition, in which the connexions are seldom fully developed. It was the lively *mot* of a great modern poet, speaking of Lord B.'s Essays, " that they are not plants, but seeds ; not oaks, but acorns."

[1] Dr. Robert South, 1633-1716; Dr. Isaac Barrow, 1630-1677 ; Archbishop John Tillotson, 1630-1694.—As De Quincey's list of the finest representatives of English Prose Rhetoric in the sixteenth and seventeenth centuries ends here, we may note with some surprise the omission of John Lyly, the author of *Euphues* (died about 1601), and Drummond of Hawthornden (1585 - 1649), whose prose - tract entitled *A Cypress Grove* rivals for beauty and music of style the best of Browne of Norwich.—M.

disappeared from literature altogether, or thrown themselves into poetic forms which, with the privilege of a masquerade, are allowed to assume the spirit of past ages, and to speak in a key unknown to the general literature. At all events, no pulpit oratory of a rhetorical cast for upwards of a century has been able to support itself when stripped of the aids of voice and action. Robert Hall and Edward Irving, when printed, exhibit only the spasms of weakness.[1] Nor do we remember one memorable burst of rhetoric in the pulpit eloquence of the last one hundred and fifty years, with the exception of a fine oath ejaculated by a dissenting minister of Cambridge, who, when appealing for the confirmation of his words to the grandeur of man's nature, swore,—By this and by the other, and at length, " By the Iliad, by the Odyssey," as the climax in a long bead-roll of *speciosa miracula* which he had apostrophized as monuments of human power. As to Foster, he has been prevented from preaching by a complaint affecting the throat ; but, judging from the quality of his celebrated Essays, he could never have figured as a truly splendid rhetorician ; for the imagery and ornamental parts of his Essays have evidently not grown up in the loom, and concurrently with the texture of the thoughts, but have been separately added afterwards, as so much embroidery or fringe.[2]

Politics, meantime, however inferior in any shape to religion as an ally of real eloquence, might yet, either when barbed by an interest of intense personality, or on the very opposite footing of an interest *not* personal but comprehensively national, have irritated the growth of rhetoric such as the spirit of the times allowed. In one conspicuous instance it did so ; but generally it had little effect, as a cursory glance over the two last centuries will show.

In the reign of James I. the House of Commons first became the theatre of struggles truly national. The relations of the People and the Crown were then brought to issue, and, under shifting names, continued *sub judice* from that time to

---

[1] Robert Hall, Baptist preacher, 1764-1831 ; Edward Irving, 1792-1834. Strange that Chalmers is left unmentioned !—M.

[2] John Foster, essayist, 1770-1846 ; not to be confounded with John Forster, biographer of Dickens, &c.—M.

1688 ; and from that time, in fact, a corresponding interest was directed to the proceedings of Parliament. But it was not until 1642 that any free communication was made of what passed in debate. During the whole of the Civil War the speeches of the leading members upon all great questions were freely published in occasional pamphlets. Naturally they were very much compressed ; but enough survives to show that, from the agitations of the times and the religious gravity of the House, no rhetoric was sought or would have been tolerated. In the reign of Charles II, judging from such records as we have of the most critical debates (that preserved by Locke, for instance, through the assistance of his patron Lord Shaftesbury), the general tone and standard of Parliamentary eloquence had taken pretty nearly its present form and level. The religious gravity had then given way ; and the pedantic tone, stiffness, and formality of punctual divisions, had been abandoned for the freedom of polite conversation. It was not, however, until the reign of Queen Anne that the qualities and style of parliamentary eloquence were submitted to public judgment ; this was on occasion of the trial of Dr. Sacheverell,[1] which was managed by members of the House of Commons. The Whigs, however, of that era had no distinguished speakers. On the Tory side, St. John (Lord Bolingbroke) was the most accomplished person in the House. His style may be easily collected from his writings, which have all the air of having been dictated without premeditation ; and the effect of so much showy and fluent declamation, combined with the graces of his manner and person, may be inferred from the deep impression which they seem to have left upon Lord Chesterfield, himself so accomplished a judge, and so familiar with the highest efforts of the next age in Pulteney and Lord Chatham. With two exceptions, indeed, to be noticed presently, Lord Bolingbroke came the nearest of all parliamentary orators who have been particularly recorded to the

---

[1] Henry Sacheverell, Tory divine, tried before the House of Lords in 1710 for sermons attacking the Revolution Settlement, the Act of Toleration, &c. He was suspended from the clerical office for three years, and the sermons were ordered to be burnt by the hangman. —M.

ideal of a fine rhetorician. It was no disadvantage to him that
he was shallow, being so luminous and transparent ; and
the splendour of his periodic diction, with his fine delivery,
compensated his defect in imagery. Sir Robert Walpole was
another Lord Londonderry ; like him, an excellent statesman, and a first-rate leader of the House of Commons, but in
other respects a plain unpretending man ; and, like Lord
Londonderry, he had the reputation of a blockhead with all
eminent blockheads, and of a man of talents with those who
were themselves truly such. " When I was very young,"
says Burke, " a general fashion told me I was to admire
some of the writings against that minister ; a little more
maturity taught me as much to despise them." Lord Mansfield, " the fluent Murray," was, or would have been but for
the counteraction of law, another Bolingbroke. " How sweet
an Ovid was in Murray lost ! " says Pope ; and, if the comparison were suggested with any thoughtful propriety, it
ascribes to Lord Mansfield the talents of a first-rate rhetorician. Lord Chatham had no rhetoric at all, any more than
Charles Fox of the next generation : both were too fervent,
too Demosthenic, and threw themselves too ardently upon
the graces of nature. Mr. Pitt came nearer to the idea of a
rhetorician, in so far as he seemed to have more artifice ;
but this was only in the sonorous rotundity of his periods,
which were cast in a monotonous mould,—for in other respects
he would have been keenly alive to the ridicule of rhetoric
in a First Lord of the Treasury.

All these persons, whatever might be their other differences, agreed in this,—that they were no jugglers, but really
were that which they appeared to be, and never struggled for
distinctions which did not naturally belong to them. But
next upon the roll comes forward an absolute *charlatan* : a
charlatan the most accomplished that can ever have figured
upon so intellectual a stage. This was Sheridan, a mocking-
bird through the entire scale, from the highest to the lowest
note of the gamut ; in fact, to borrow a coarse word, the
mere impersonation of humbug. Even as a wit, he has been
long known to be a wholesale plagiarist ; and the exposures
of his kind biographer, Mr. Moore,[1] exhibit him in that line

---

[1] Moore's *Life of Sheridan*, published in 1825.—M.

as the most hide-bound and sterile of performers, lying *perdu*
through a whole evening for a natural opportunity, or by
miserable stratagem creating an artificial one, for exploding
some poor starveling jest ; and in fact sacrificing to this
petty ambition, in a degree never before heard of, the ease
and dignity of his life.   But it is in the character of a
rhetorical orator that he, and his friends on his behalf, have
put forward the hollowest pretensions.   In the course of the
Hastings trial, upon the concerns of paralytic *Begums*, and
mouldering queens—hags that, if ever actually existing, were
no more to us and our British sympathies than we to
Hecuba—did Mr. Sheridan make his capital exhibition.
The real value of his speech was never at any time mis-
appreciated by the judicious ; for his attempts at the grand,
the pathetic, and the sentimental had been continually in
the same tone of falsetto and horrible fustian.   Burke, however, who was the most double-minded person in the world,
cloaked his contempt in hyperbolical flattery ; and all the
unhappy people who have since written lives of Burke adopt
the whole for gospel truth.   Exactly in the same vein of
tumid inanity is the speech which Mr. Sheridan puts into
the mouth of Rolla the Peruvian.   This the reader may
chance to have heard upon the stage ; or, in default of that
good luck, we present him with the following fragrant
twaddle from one of the Begummiads, which has been
enshrined in the praises (*si quid sua carmina possunt*) of
many worthy critics.   The subject is *Filial Piety*.

"Filial piety," Mr. Sheridan said, "it was impossible by words to
describe, but description by words was unnecessary.   It was that
duty which they all felt and understood, and which required not the
powers of language to explain.   It was in truth more properly to be
called a *principle* than a duty.   It required not the aid of memory; it
needed not the exercise of the understanding ; it awaited not the slow
deliberations of reason : it flowed spontaneously from the fountain of
our feelings ; it was involuntary in our natures ; it was a quality of
our being, innate and coeval with life, which, though afterwards
cherished as a passion, was independent of our mental powers ; it was
earlier than all intelligence in our souls ; it displayed itself in the
earliest impulses of the heart, and was an emotion of fondness that
returned in smiles of gratitude the affectionate solicitudes, the tender
anxieties, the endearing attentions experienced before memory began,
but which were not less dear for not being remembered.   It was the

sacrament of nature in our hearts, by which the union of the parent
and child was sealed and rendered perfect in the community of love;
and which, strengthening and ripening with life, acquired vigour from
the understanding, and was most lively and active when most wanted."

Now, we put it to any candid reader whether the above
Birmingham ware might not be vastly improved by one
slight alteration, viz. omitting the two first words, and reading it as a conundrum.   Considered as rhetoric, it is
evidently fitted "to make a horse sick"; but, as a conundrum in the *Lady's Magazine*, we contend that it would have
great success.

How it aggravates the disgust with which these paste-
diamonds are now viewed to remember that they were
paraded in the presence of Edmund Burke; nay—*credite
posteri*!—in jealous rivalry of his genuine and priceless
jewels!   Irresistibly, one is reminded of the dancing efforts
of Lady Blarney and Miss Carolina Wilhelmina Skeggs
against the native grace of the Vicar of Wakefield's family:
—"The ladies of the town strove hard to be equally easy,
" but without success. *They swam, sprawled, languished, and*
" *frisked*; but all would not do.   The gazers, indeed, owned
" that it was fine; but neighbour Flamborough observed
" that Miss Livy's feet seemed as pat to the music as its
" echo."   Of Goldsmith it was said in his epitaph,—*Nil
tetigit quod non ornavit*: of the Drury Lane rhetorician it
might be said with equal truth,—*Nil tetigit quod non fuco
adulteravit*.[1]   But avaunt, Birmingham!   Let us speak of a
great man.

All hail to Edmund Burke, the supreme writer of his
century, the man of the largest and finest understanding!
Upon that word, *understanding*, we lay a stress: for, oh! ye
immortal donkeys who have written "about him and about
him," with what an obstinate stupidity have ye brayed

---

[1] Johnson's epitaph on Goldsmith is here incorrectly quoted, as
usual. The words were not *Nil tetigit quod non ornavit*—which would
be incorrect Latin for "He touched nothing that he did not adorn"—
but "*nullum fere scribendi genus non tetigit, nullum quod tetigit non
ornavit*." "No kind of writing almost but he touched, none that he
touched but he adorned." De Quincey's parody of this for Sheridan
is "He touched nothing that he did not corrupt and discolour."—M.

away for one third of a century about that which ye are
pleased to call his "fancy." Fancy in your throats, ye
miserable twaddlers ! As if Edmund Burke were the man to
play with his fancy for the purpose of separable ornament !
He was a man of fancy in no other sense than as Lord Bacon
was so, and Jeremy Taylor, and as all large and discursive
thinkers are and must be: that is to say, the fancy which
he had in common with all mankind, and very probably in
no eminent degree, in him was urged into unusual activity
under the necessities of his capacious understanding.   His
great and peculiar distinction was that he viewed all objects
of the understanding under more relations than other men,
and under more complex relations.   According to the multi-
plicity of these relations, a man is said to have a *large* understanding ; according to their subtlety, a *fine* one ; and in an
angelic understanding all things would appear to be related
to all.   Now, to apprehend and detect more relations, or to
pursue them steadily, is a process absolutely impossible without the intervention of physical analogies.   To say, therefore,
that a man is a great thinker, or a fine thinker, is but
another expression for saying that he has a *schematizing* (or,
to use a plainer but less accurate expression, a figurative)
understanding.   In that sense, and for that purpose, Burke
is figurative : but, understood, as he *has* been understood by
the long-eared race of his critics, not as thinking in and by
his figures, but as deliberately laying them on by way of
enamel or after-ornament,—not as *incarnating*, but simply
as *dressing* his thoughts in imagery,—so understood, he is
not the Burke of reality, but a poor fictitious Burke,
modelled after the poverty of conception which belongs to
his critics.

It is true, however, that in some rare cases Burke *did*
indulge himself in a pure rhetorician's use of fancy ; consciously and profusely lavishing his ornaments for mere
purposes of effect.   Such a case occurs, for instance, in that
admirable picture of the degradation of Europe where he
represents the different crowned heads as bidding against
each other at Basle for the favour and countenance of Regi-
cide.   Others of the same kind there are in his ever-memor-
able letter on the Duke of Bedford's attack upon him in the

House of Lords [1] ; and one of these we shall here cite, disregarding its greater chance for being already familiar to the reader, upon two considerations : first, that it has all the appearance of being finished with the most studied regard to effect ; and, secondly, for an interesting anecdote connected with it which we have never seen in print, but for which we have better authority than could be produced perhaps for most of those which are. The anecdote is that Burke, conversing with Dr. Lawrence and another gentleman on the *literary* value of his own writings, declared that the particular passage in the entire range of his works which had cost him the most labour, and upon which, as tried by a certain canon of his own, his labour seemed to himself to have been the most successful, was the following :—

After an introductory paragraph, which may be thus abridged,—" The Crown has considered *me* after long service. " The Crown has paid the Duke of Bedford by advance. " He has had a long credit for any service which he may " perform hereafter. He is secure, and long may he be " secure in his advance, whether he performs any services or " not. His grants are engrafted on the public law of Europe, " covered with the awful hoar of innumerable ages. They " are guarded by the sacred rule of prescription. The " learned professors of the *rights of man*, however, regard " prescription not as a title to bar all other claim, but as a " bar against the possessor and proprietor. They hold an " immemorial possession to be no more than an aggravated " injustice,"—there follows the passage in question :—

"Such are *their* ideas, such *their* religion, and such *their* law. But, as to *our* country and *our* race, as long as the well-compacted structure of our Church and State, the sanctuary, the holy of holies, of that ancient law, defended by reverence, defended by power, a fortress at once and a temple (*templum in modum arcis* [2]), shall stand inviolate on the brow of the British Sion ; as long as the British monarchy, not more limited than fenced by the orders of the State, shall, like the

---

[1] *A Letter to a noble Lord on the attacks made upon Mr. Burke and his Pension in the House of Lords by the Duke of Bedford and the Earl of Lauderdale early in the present Sessions of Parliament, 1796.*—M.

[2] Tacitus of the Temple of Jerusalem.

proud Keep of Windsor, rising in the majesty of proportion, and girt with the double belt of its kindred and coeval towers ; as long as this awful structure shall oversee and guard the subjected land : so long the mounds and dykes of the low fat Bedford Level [1] will have nothing to fear from all the pickaxes of all the levellers of France. As long as our sovereign lord the king, and his faithful subjects the lords and commons of this realm,—the triple cord which no man can break; the solemn, sworn, constitutional frank-pledge of this nation ; the firm guarantees of each other's being and each other's rights ; the joint and several securities, each in its place and order, for every kind and every quality of property and of dignity,—as long as these endure, so long the Duke of Bedford is safe, and we are all safe together : the high from the blights of envy and the spoliation of rapacity ; the low from the iron hand of oppression and the insolent spurn of contempt. Amen ! and so be it : and so it will be

> ' Dum Domus Æneæ Capitoli immobile saxum
> Accolet, imperiumque Pater Romanus habebit.' "

This was the sounding passage which Burke alleged as the *chef-d'œuvre* of his rhetoric ; and the argument upon which he justified his choice is specious, if not convincing. He laid it down as a maxim of composition that every passage in a rhetorical performance which was brought forward prominently, and relied upon as a *key* (to use the language of war) in sustaining the main position of the writer, ought to involve a thought, an image, and a sentiment ; and such a synthesis he found in the passage which we have quoted. This criticism, over and above the pleasure which it always gives to hear a great man's opinion of himself, is valuable as showing that Burke, because negligent of trivial inaccuracies, was not at all the less anxious about the larger proprieties and decorums (for this passage, confessedly so laboured, has several instances of slovenliness in trifles), and that in the midst of his apparent hurry he carried out a jealous vigilance upon what he wrote, and the eye of a person practised in artificial effects.

An ally of Burke's upon East Indian politics ought to have a few words of notice, not so much for any power that he actually had as a rhetorician, but because he is sometimes reputed such. This was Sir Philip Francis, who, under his early disguise of Junius, had such a success as no writer of

---

[1] "*Bedford Level*" :—A rich tract of land so called in Bedfordshire.

libels ever will have again.[1]   It is our private opinion that
this success rested upon a great delusion which has never
been exposed.   The general belief is that Junius was read
for his elegance ; we believe no such thing.   The pen of an
angel would not, upon such a theme as personal politics,
have upheld the interest attached to Junius, had there been
no other cause in co-operation.   Language, after all, is a
limited instrument ; and it must be remembered that Junius,
by the extreme narrowness of his range, which went entirely
upon matters of fact and personal interests, still further
limited the compass of that limited instrument.   For it is
only in the expression and management of general ideas
that any room arises for conspicuous elegance.   The real
truth is this : the interest in Junius travelled downwards ;
he was read in the lower ranks, because in London it speedily
became known that he was read with peculiar interest in the
highest.   This was already a marvel ; for newspaper patriots,
under the signatures of Publicola, Brutus, and so forth, had
become a jest and a byword to the real practical statesman ;
and any man at leisure to write for so disinterested a purpose
as " his country's good " was presumed of course to write in
a garret.   But here for the first time a pretended patriot, a
Junius Brutus, was read even by statesmen, and read with
agitation.   Is any man simple enough to believe that such a
contagion could extend to cabinet ministers and official persons
overladen with public business on so feeble an excitement as
a little reputation in the art of constructing sentences with
elegance,—an elegance which, after all, excluded eloquence
and every other *positive* quality of excellence ?   That this
can have been believed shows the readiness with which men
swallow marvels.   The real secret was this :—Junius was
read with the profoundest interest by members of the
cabinet, who would not have paid half-a-crown for all the
wit and elegance of this world, simply because it was most
evident that some traitor was amongst them, and that, either
directly by one of themselves, or through some abuse of his
confidence by a servant, the secrets of office were betrayed.
The circumstances of this breach of trust are now fully

[1] For De Quincey on Sir Philip Francis and the authorship of the
Junius Letters see *ante*, Vol. III, pp. 132-143.—M.

known ; and it is readily understood why letters which
were the channel for those perfidies should interest the
ministry of that day in the deepest degree. The existence
of such an interest, but not its cause, had immediately become known ; it descended, as might be expected, amongst
all classes ; once excited, it seemed to be justified by the
real merits of the letters ; which merit again, illustrated by
its effects, appeared a thousand times greater than it was ;
and, finally, this interest was heightened and sustained by
the mystery which invested the author. How much that
mystery availed in keeping alive the public interest in
Junius is clear from this fact,—that since the detection of
Junius as Sir Philip Francis the Letters have suddenly
declined in popularity, and are no longer the saleable article
which once they were.

In fact, upon any other principle, the continued triumph
of Junius, and his establishment as a classical author, is a
standing enigma.   One talent, undoubtedly, he had in a rare
perfection—the talent of sarcasm.   He stung like a scorpion.
But, besides that such a talent has a narrow application, an
interest of personality cannot be other than fugitive, take
what direction it may ; and malignity cannot embalm itself
in materials that are themselves perishable.   Such were the
materials of Junius.   His vaunted elegance was, in a great
measure, the gift of his subject ; general terseness, short
sentences, and a careful avoiding of all awkward construction—these were his advantages.   And from these he would
have been dislodged by a higher subject, or one that would
have forced him out into a wider compass of thought.
Rhetorician he was none, though he has often been treated
as such ; for, without sentiment, without imagery, without
generalization, how should it be possible for rhetoric to
subsist ? It is an absolute fact that Junius has not one
principle, aphorism, or remark of a general nature in his
whole armoury ; not in a solitary instance did his barren
understanding ascend to an abstraction or general idea, but
lingered for ever in the dust and rubbish of individuality,
amongst the tangible realities of things and persons.
Hence the peculiar absurdity of that hypothesis which
discovered Junius in the person of Burke.   The opposi-

tion was here too pointedly ludicrous between Burke,
who exalted the merest personal themes into the dignity
of philosophic speculations, and Junius, in whose hands
the very loftiest dwindled into questions of person and
party.

Last of the family of rhetoricians, and in a form of
rhetoric as florid as the age could bear, came Mr. Canning.
"*Sufficit,*" says a Roman author, "*in una civitate esse unum
rhetorem.*" But, if more were in his age unnecessary, in ours
they would have been intolerable. Three or four Mr.
Cannings would have been found a nuisance ; indeed, the
very admiration which crowned his great displays manifested
of itself the unsuitableness of his style to the atmosphere of
public affairs ; for it was of that kind which is offered to a
young lady rising from a brilliant performance on the piano-
forte. Something, undoubtedly, there was of too juvenile
an air, too gaudy a flutter of plumage, in Mr. Canning's
more solemn exhibitions ; but much indulgence was reasonably extended to a man who in his class was so complete.
He was formed for winning a favourable attention by every
species of popular fascination. To the eye he recommended
himself almost as much as the Bolingbroke of a century
before ; his voice, and his management of it, were no less
pleasing ; and upon him, as upon St. John, the air of a
gentleman sat with a native grace. Scholarship and literature, as far as they belong to the accomplishments of a
gentleman, he too brought forward in the most graceful
manner ; and, above all, there was an impression of honour,
generosity, and candour, stamped upon his manner, agree-
able rather to his original character than to the wrench
which it had received from an ambition resting too much on
mere personal merits. What a pity that this "gay creature
of the elements" had not taken his place contentedly, where
nature had assigned it, as one of the ornamental performers of
the time ! His station was with the lilies of the field, which
toil not, neither do they spin. He should have thrown
himself upon the admiring sympathies of the world as the
most dazzling of rhetorical artists, rather than have challenged their angry passions in a vulgar scuffle for power.
In that case he would have been alive at this hour [1828] ;

he would have had a perpetuity of that admiration which to
him was as the breath of his nostrils; and would not, by
forcing the character of rhetorician into an incongruous alliance
with that of trading politician, have run the risk of making
both ridiculous.

In thus running over the modern history of Rhetoric, we
have confined ourselves to the Literature of England : the
Rhetoric of the Continent would demand a separate notice,
and chiefly on account of the French pulpit orators.   For,
laying *them* aside, we are not aware of any distinct body of
rhetoric, properly so called, in Modern Literature.   Four
continental languages may be said to have a literature
regularly mounted in all departments, viz. the French,
Italian, Spanish, and German ; but each of these has stood
under separate disadvantages for the cultivation of an ornamented rhetoric.   In France, whatever rhetoric they have
(for Montaigne, though lively, is too gossiping for a rhetorician) arose in the age of Louis XIV ; since which time the
very same development of science and public business
operated there as in England to stifle the rhetorical impulses, and all those analogous tendencies in arts and in
manners which support it.   Generally it may be assumed
that rhetoric will not survive the age of the ceremonious in
manners and the gorgeous in costume.   An unconscious
sympathy binds together the various forms of the elaborate
and the fanciful, under every manifestation.   Hence it is
that the national convulsions by which modern France has
been shaken produced orators,—Mirabeau, Isnard, the Abbé
Maury,—but no rhetoricians.   Florian, Chateaubriand, and
others, who have written the most florid prose that the
modern taste can bear, are elegant sentimentalists, sometimes maudlin and semi-poetic, sometimes even eloquent,
but never rhetorical.   There is no eddying about their own
thoughts ; no motion of fancy self-sustained from its own
activities ; no flux and reflux of thought, half meditative,
half capricious ; but strains of feeling, genuine or not, supported at every step from the excitement of independent
external objects.

With respect to the German Literature the case is very
peculiar. A chapter upon German Rhetoric would be in

the same ludicrous predicament as Van Troil's chapter on
the snakes of Iceland, which delivers its business in one
summary sentence, announcing that—snakes in Iceland there
are none. Rhetoric, in fact, or any form of ornamented
prose, could not possibly arise in a literature in which prose
itself had no proper existence till within these seventy years.
Lessing was the first German who wrote prose with elegance ;
and even at this day a decent prose style is the rarest of
accomplishments in Germany. We doubt, indeed, whether
any German has written prose with grace unless he had
lived abroad (like Jacobi, who composed indifferently in
French and German), or had at least cultivated a very long
acquaintance with English and French models. Frederick
Schlegel was led by his comprehensive knowledge of other
literatures to observe this singular defect in that of his own
country. Even he, however, must have fixed his standard
very low, when he could praise, as elsewhere he does, the
style of Kant. Certainly in any literature where good
models of prose existed Kant would be deemed a monster
of vicious diction, so far as regards the construction of his
sentences. He does not, it is true, write in the hybrid
dialect which prevailed up to the time of our George the
First, when every other word was Latin with a German
inflexion ; but he has in perfection that obtuseness which
renders a German taste insensible to all beauty in the
balancing and structure of periods, and to the art by which
a succession of periods modify each other. Every German
regards a sentence in the light of a package, and a package
not for the mail-coach but for the waggon, into which his
privilege is to crowd as much as he possibly can. Having
framed a sentence, therefore, he next proceeds to *pack* it,
which is effected partly by unwieldy tails and codicils, but
chiefly by enormous parenthetic involutions. All qualifications, limitations, exceptions, illustrations, are stuffed and
violently rammed into the bowels of the principal proposition. That all this equipage of accessaries is not so arranged
as to assist its own orderly development no more occurs to a
German as any fault than that in a package of shawls or of
carpets the colours and patterns are not fully displayed.
To him it is sufficient that they are *there*. And Mr. Kant,

when he has succeeded in packing up a sentence which covers three close-printed octavo pages, stops to draw his breath with the air of one who looks back upon some brilliant and meritorious performance. Under these disadvantages it may be presumed that German rhetoric is a nonentity ; but these disadvantages would not have arisen had there been a German bar or a German senate with any public existence. In the absence of all forensic and senatorial eloquence no standard of good prose style—nay, which is more important, no example of ambition directed to such an object—has been at any time held up to the public mind in Germany ; and the pulpit style has been always either rustically negligent or bristling with pedantry.

These disadvantages with regard to public models of civil eloquence have in part affected the Italians. The few good prose writers of Italy have been historians ; and it is observable that no writers exist in the department of what are called *Moral Essayists*,—a class which, with us and the French, were the last depositaries of the rhetorical faculty when depressed to its lowest key. Two other circumstances may be noticed as unfavourable to an Italian rhetoric : one, to which we have adverted before, in the language itself, which is too loitering for the agile motion and the το ἀγχιστροφον of rhetoric ; and the other in the constitution of the national mind, which is not reflective nor remarkably fanciful, the two qualities most indispensable to rhetoric. As a proof of the little turn for reflection which there is in the Italian mind, we may remind the reader that they have no meditative or philosophic poetry,[1] such as that of our Young, Cowper, Wordsworth, &c.,—a class of poetry which existed very early indeed in the English Literature (*e.g.*, Sir J. Davies, Lord Brooke, Henry More, &c.), and which in some shape has arisen at some stage of almost every European literature.

Of the Spanish rhetoric, *a priori*, we should have augured well ; but the rhetoric of their pulpit in past times,

---

[1] The nearest approach to reflective poetry which we ourselves remember in Italian literature lies amongst the works of Salvator Rosa (the great painter)—where, however, it assumes too much the character of satire.

which is all that we know of it, is vicious and unnatural ; whilst, on the other hand, for eloquence profound and heartfelt, measuring it by those heart-stirring proclamations issued in all quarters of Spain during 1808-9, the national capacity must be presumed to be of the very highest order.

We are thus thrown back upon the French pulpit orators as the only considerable body of modern rhetoricians out of our own language. No writers are more uniformly praised ; none are more entirely neglected. This is one of those numerous hypocrisies so common in matters of taste, where the critic is always ready with his good word as the readiest way of getting rid of the subject. To blame might be hazardous ; for blame demands reasons ; but praise enjoys a ready dispensation from all reasons and from all discrimination. Superstition, however, as it is under which the French rhetoricians hold their reputation, we have no thought of attempting any disturbance to it in so slight and incidental a notice as this. Let critics by all means continue to invest them with every kind of imaginary splendour. Meantime let us suggest, as a judicious caution, that French rhetoric should be praised with a reference only to its own narrow standard ; for it would be a most unfortunate trial of its pretensions to bring so meagre a style of composition into a close comparison with the gorgeous opulence of the English rhetoric of the same century. Under such a comparison two capital points of weakness would force themselves upon the least observant of critics : first, the defect of striking imagery ; and, secondly, the slenderness of the thoughts. The rhetorical manner is supported in the French writers chiefly by an abundance of *ohs* and *ahs* ; by interrogatories, apostrophes, and startling exclamations ; all which are mere mechanical devices for raising the style ; but in the substance of the composition, apart from its dress, there is nothing properly rhetorical. The leading thoughts in all pulpit eloquence, being derived from religion, and in fact the common inheritance of human nature, if they cannot be novel, for that very reason cannot be undignified ; but for the same reason they are apt to become unaffecting and trite unless varied and individualized by new infusions of thought and feeling. The smooth monotony of the leading religious topics, as managed by the French orators, receives under the treatment of Jeremy Taylor at each turn of the sentence a new flexure, or what may be called a separate *articulation* [1] ; old thoughts are surveyed from novel stations and under various angles ; and a field absolutely exhausted throws up eternally fresh verdure under the fructifying lava of burning imagery. *Human life*, for example, *is short; human happiness is frail* ; how trite, how obvious a thesis ! Yet, in the beginning of the *Holy Dying*, upon that simplest of themes how magnificent a descant ! Variations the most original upon a ground the most universal, and a sense of novelty diffused over truths coeval with human life ! Finally, it may be remarked of the imagery in the French rhetoric that it is thinly sown, commonplace, deficient in splendour, and above all merely ornamental ; that is to say, it does no more than echo and repeat what is already said in the thought which it is brought to illustrate ; whereas in Jeremy Taylor and in Burke it will be found usually to extend and amplify the thought, or to fortify it by some indirect argument of its truth. Thus, for instance, in the passage above quoted from Taylor upon the insensibility of man to the continual mercies of God, at first view the mind is staggered by the apparent impossibility that so infinite a reality, and of so continual a recurrence, should escape our notice ; but the illus-

[1] We may take the opportunity of noticing what it is that constitutes the peculiar and characterizing circumstances in Burke's manner of composition. It is this : that under his treatment every truth, be it what it may, every thesis of a sentence, *grows* in the very act of unfolding it. Take any sentence you please from Dr. Johnson, suppose, and it will be found to contain a thought, good or bad, fully preconceived. Whereas in Burke, whatever may have been the preconception, it receives a new determination or inflexion at every clause of the sentence. Some collateral adjunct of the main proposition, some temperament or restraint, some oblique glance at its remote affinities, will invariably be found to attend the progress of his sentences, like the spray from a waterfall, or the scintillations from the iron under the blacksmith's hammer. Hence, whilst a writer of Dr. Johnson's class seems only to look back upon his thoughts, Burke looks forward, and does in fact advance and change his own station concurrently with the advance of the sentences. This peculiarity is no doubt in some degree due to the habit of extempore speaking, but not to that only.

trative image, drawn from the case of a man standing at the bottom of the ocean, and yet insensible to that world of waters above him, from the uniformity and equality of its pressure, flashes upon us with a sense of something equally marvellous in a case which we know to be a physical fact. We are thus reconciled to the proposition by the same image which illustrates it.

In a single mechanical quality of good writing, that is in the structure of their sentences, the French rhetoricians, in common with French writers generally of that age, are superior to ours. This is what in common parlance is expressed (though inaccurately) by the word *style*, and is the subject of the third part of the work before us. Dr. Whately, however, somewhat disappoints us by his mode of treating it. He alleges, indeed, with some plausibility, that his subject bound him to consider style no further than as it was related to the purpose of persuasion. But, besides that it is impossible to treat it with effect in that mutilated section, even within the limits assumed we are not able to trace any outline of the law or system by which Dr. Whately has been governed in the choice of his topics. We find many very acute remarks delivered, but all in a desultory way, which leave the reader no means of judging how much of the ground has been surveyed and how much omitted. We regret also that he has not addressed himself more specifically to the question of English style,—a subject which has not yet received the comprehensive discussion which it merits. In the age of our great rhetoricians it is remarkable that the English language had never been made an object of conscious attention. No man seems to have reflected that there was a wrong and a right in the choice of words, in the choice of phrases, in the mechanism of sentences, or even in the grammar.[1] Men wrote eloquently, because they wrote feelingly; they wrote idiomatically, because they wrote naturally and without affectation ; but, if a false or acephalous structure of sentence, if a barbarous idiom or an exotic word happened to present itself, no writer of the seventeenth century seems to have had any such scrupulous sense of the dignity belonging to his own language

[1] Hardly true !—M.

as should make it a duty to reject it or worth his while to remodel a line. The fact is that verbal criticism had not as yet been very extensively applied even to the classical languages ; the Scaligers, Casaubon, and Salmasius, were much more critics on things than critics philologically. However, even in that age the French writers were more attentive to the cultivation of their mother tongue than any other people. It is justly remarked by Schlegel that the most worthless writers amongst the French as to matter generally take pains with their diction ; or perhaps it is more true to say that with equal pains in their language it is more easy to write well than in one of greater compass. It is also true that the French are indebted for their greater purity from foreign idioms to their much more limited acquaintance with foreign literature. Still, with every deduction from the merit, the fact is as we have said ; and it is apparent not only by innumerable evidences in the *concrete*, but by the superiority of all their *abstract* auxiliaries in the art of writing. We English even at this day have no learned grammar of our language ; nay, we have allowed the blundering attempt in that department of an imbecile stranger (Lindley Murray) to supersede the learned (however imperfect) works of our own Wallis, Lowth, &c. ; we have also no sufficient dictionary ; and we have no work at all, sufficient or insufficient, on the phrases and idiomatic niceties of our language, corresponding to the works of Vaugelas and others for the French.[1]

Hence an anomaly not found perhaps in any literature but ours,—that the most eminent English writers do not write their mother tongue without continual violations of propriety. With the single exception of William Wordsworth, who has paid an honourable attention to the purity and accuracy of his English, we believe that there is not one celebrated author of this day who has written two pages consecutively without some flagrant impropriety in the grammar (such as the eternal confusion of the preterite with the past participle, confusion of verbs transitive with intransitive, &c.), or some

---

[1] Claude Favre de Vaugelas (1585-1650), author of *Sur la Langue Françoise.*—M.

violation more or less of the vernacular idiom.[1]   If this last sort of blemish does not occur so frequently in modern books, the reason is that since Dr. Johnson's time the freshness of the idiomatic style has been too frequently abandoned for the lifeless mechanism of a style purely bookish and artificial.

The practical judgments of Dr. Whately are such as will seldom be disputed.   Dr. Johnson, for his triads and his antithetic balances, he taxes more than once with a plethoric and tautologic tympany of sentence, and in the following passage with a very happy illustration :—" Sentences which " might have been expressed as simple ones are expanded " into complex ones by the addition of clauses which add " little or nothing to the sense, and which have been com- " pared to the false handles and key-holes with which furniture " is decorated, that serve no other purpose than to *correspond* " *to the real ones.*   Much of Dr. Johnson's writings is charge- " able with this fault."

We recollect a little biographic sketch of Dr. Johnson, published immediately after his death, in which, amongst other instances of desperate tautology, the author quotes the well-known lines from the Doctor's imitation of Juvenal—

> " Let observation, with extensive view,
> Survey mankind from China to Peru,"

and contends with some reason that this is saying in effect,— " *Let observation with extensive observation observe mankind* " *extensively.*"   Certainly Dr. Johnson was the most faulty writer in this kind of inanity that ever has played tricks with language.[2]   On the other hand, Burke was the least so ;

---

[1] For ample verification of this remark, see the late Professor Hodgson's admirable little book entitled *Errors in the Use of English*,— a wonderful collection of examples of bad English from recent or still living English writers of celebrity.   No one escapes.—M.

[2] The following illustration, however, from Dr. Johnson's critique on Prior's *Solomon*, is far from a happy one : " He had infused into it " much knowledge and much thought ; had often *polished* it to *elegance*, " *dignified* it with *splendour*, and sometimes *heightened* it to *sublimity* ; " he perceived in it many excellences, and did not perceive that it " wanted that without which all others are of small avail, the power " of *engaging attention* and *alluring curiosity.*"   The parts marked in italics are those to which Dr Whately would object as tautologic.

and we are petrified to find him described by Dr. Whately as a writer "*qui variare cupit rem prodigialiter unam,*" and as on that account offensive to good taste. The understanding of Burke was even morbidly impatient of tautology ; progress and motion, everlasting motion, was a mere necessity of his intellect. We will venture to offer a king's ransom for one unequivocal case of tautology from the whole circle of Burke's writings. The *principium indiscernibilium,* upon which Leibnitz affirmed the impossibility of finding any two leaves of a tree that should be mere duplicates of each other in what we might call the *palmistry* of their natural markings, may be applied to Burke as safely as to nature : no two propositions, we are satisfied, can be found in *him* which do not contain a larger variety than is requisite to their sharp discrimination.

Speaking of the advantages for energy and effect in the licence of arrangement open to the ancient languages, especially to the Latin, Dr. Whately cites the following sentence from the opening of the 4th Book of Q. Curtius :—*Darius, tanti modo exercitus rex, qui, triumphantis magis quam dimicantis more, curru sublimis inierat prælium, per loca quæ prope immensis agminibus compleverat, jam inania et ingenti solitudine vasta, fugiebat.* "The effect," says he, "of the concluding verb, placed where it is, is most striking." [1] The sentence is far enough from a good one ; but, confining ourselves to the sort of merit for which it is here cited as a merit peculiar to the Latin, we must say that the very same position of the verb, with a finer effect, is attainable, and in fact often attained, in English sentences ; see, for instance, the passage in Richard's soliloquy beginning—*Now is the winter of our discontent,* and ending, *In the deep bosom of the ocean buried.* See also another at the beginning of Hooker's *Ecclesiastical Polity,* on the thanklessness of the labour employed upon the *foundations* of truth ; which, says he, like those of

Yet this objection can hardly be sustained ; the ideas are all sufficiently discriminated ; the fault is that they are applied to no real corresponding differences in Prior.

[1] We wish that, in so critical a notice of an effect derived from the fortunate position of a single word, Dr. Whately had not shocked our ears by this hideous collision of a double "*is,*"—"where it *is, is.*" Dreadful !

buildings, "are in the bosom of the earth concealed." The
fact is that the common cases of inversion, such as the
suspension of the verb to the end, and the anticipation of the
objective case at the beginning, are not sufficient illustrations
of the Latin structure.   All this can be done as well by the
English.   It is not mere power of inversion, but of self-
intrication, and of self-dislocation, which marks the extremity
of the artificial structure ; that power by which a sequence
of words that naturally is directly consecutive commences,
intermits, and reappears at a remote part of the sentence,
like what is called drake-stone on the surface of a river.   In
this power the Greek is almost as much below the Latin as
all modern languages ; and in this, added to its elliptic
brevity of connexion and transition, and to its wealth in
abstractions, " the long-tailed words in *osity* and *ation*," lie the
peculiar capacities of the Latin for rhetoric.

Dr. Whately lays it down as a maxim in rhetoric that
" elaborate stateliness is always to be regarded as a worse
" fault than the slovenliness and languor which accompany a
" very loose style."   But surely this is a rash position.
Stateliness the most elaborate, in an *absolute* sense, is no fault
at all ; though it may happen to be so in relation to a given
subject, or to any subject under given circumstances.
" Belshazzar the king made a great feast for a thousand of
his lords."   Reading these words, who would not be justly
offended in point of taste had his feast been characterized
by elegant simplicity ?   Again, at a coronation, what can
be more displeasing to a philosophic taste than a pretended
chastity of ornament, at war with the very purposes of a
solemnity essentially magnificent ?   An imbecile friend of
ours, in 1825, brought us a sovereign of a new coinage :
" Which," said he, " I admire, because it is so elegantly
simple."   This, he flattered himself, was thinking like a man
of taste.   But mark how we sent him to the right about :
" And *that*, weak-minded friend, is exactly the thing which a
coin ought not to be : the duty of a golden coin is to be as
florid as it can, rich with Corinthian ornaments, and as
gorgeous as a peacock's tail."   So of rhetoric.   Imagine that
you read these words of introduction, " *And on a set day
Tullius Cicero returned thanks to Cæsar on behalf of Marcus*

Marcellus," what sort of a speech is reasonably to be expected ? The whole purpose being a festal and ceremonial one, thanksgiving its sole burden first and last, what else than the most "elaborate stateliness"? If it were not stately, and to the very verge of the pompous, Mr. Wolf would have had one argument more than he had, and a better than any he has produced, for suspecting the authenticity of that thrice famous oration.[1]

In the course of his dissertation on style, Dr. Whately very needlessly enters upon the thorny question of the *quiddity*, or characteristic difference, of poetry as distinguished from prose.[2] We could much have wished that he had forborne to meddle with a *quæstio vexata* of this nature, both because in so incidental and cursory a discussion it could not receive a proper investigation, and because Dr. Whately is apparently not familiar with much of what has been written on that subject. On a matter so slightly discussed we shall not trouble ourselves to enter farther than to express our astonishment that a logician like Dr. Whately should have allowed himself to deliver so nugatory an argument as this which follows :—" Any composition in *verse* (and none that " is not) is always called, whether good or bad, a poem, by " all who have no favourite hypothesis to maintain." And the inference manifestly is that it is rightly so called. Now, if a man has taken up any fixed opinion on the subject, no matter whether wrong or right, and has reasons to give for

---

[1] The substance of all this is found elsewhere in De Quincey. See *ante*, Vol. V, pp. 230-236.—M.

[2] "*As distinguished from prose*" :—Here is one of the many instances in which a false answer is prepared beforehand by falsely shaping the question. The accessary circumstance, as "*distinguished from prose*," already prepares a false answer by the very terms of the problem. Poetry *cannot* be distinguished from prose without presupposing the whole question at issue. Those who deny that metre is the characteristic distinction of poetry deny, by implication, that prose *can* be truly opposed to poetry. Some have imagined that the proper opposition was between poetry and science ; but, suppose that this is an imperfect opposition, and suppose even that there is no adequate opposition, or counterpole, this is no more than happens in many other cases. One of two poles is often without a name, even where the idea is fully assignable in analysis. But at all events the expression, as "distinguished from prose" is a subtle instance of a *petitio principii*.

his opinion, this man comes under the description of those who have a favourite hypothesis to maintain. It follows, therefore, that the only class of people whom Dr. Whately will allow as unbiassed judges on this question—a question not of fact, but of opinion—are those who have, and who profess to have, no opinion at all upon the subject, or, having one, have no reasons for it. But, apart from this contradiction, how is it possible that Dr. Whately should, in *any* case, plead a popular usage of speech as of any weight in a philosophic argument ? Still more, how is it possible in *this* case, where the accuracy of the popular usage is the very thing in debate, so that, if pleaded at all, it must be pleaded as its own justification ? Alms-giving, and nothing but alms-giving, is universally called *charity*, and mistaken for the charity of the Scriptures, by all who have no favourite hypothesis to maintain,—*i.e.* by all the inconsiderate. But Dr. Whately will hardly draw any argument from this usage in defence of that popular notion.

In speaking thus freely of particular passages in Dr. Whately's book, we are so far from meaning any disrespect to him that, on the contrary, if we had not been impressed with the very highest respect for his talents by the acuteness and originality which illuminate every part of his book, we could not have allowed ourselves to spend as much time upon the whole as we have in fact spent upon single paragraphs. In reality, there is not a section of his work which has not furnished us with occasion for some profitable speculations; and we are, in consequence, most anxious to see his *Logic*,—which treats a subject so much more important than *Rhetoric*, and so obstinately misrepresented that it would delight us much to anticipate a radical exposure of the errors on this subject taken up from the days of Lord Bacon. It has not fallen in our way to quote much from Dr. Whately *totidem verbis*; our apology for which will be found in the broken and discontinuous method of treatment by short sections and paragraphs which a subject of this nature has necessarily imposed upon him. Had it coincided with our purpose to go more into detail, we could have delighted our readers with some brilliant examples of philosophical penetration, applied to questions interesting from their importance or difficulty with the happiest effect. As it is, we shall content ourselves with saying that in any elementary work it has not been our fortune to witness a rarer combination of analytical acuteness with severity of judgment ; and, when we add that these qualities are recommended by a scholarlike elegance of manner, we suppose it hardly necessary to add that Dr. Whately's is incomparably the best book of its class since Campbell's *Philosophy of Rhetoric*.

NOTE.—In what is said at the beginning of this paper of the true meaning of the Enthymeme, as determined by Facciolati, we must be understood with an exclusive reference to Rhetoric. In Logic the old acceptation cannot be disturbed.

STYLE [1]

PART I

AMONGST the never-ending arguments for thankfulness in the privilege of a British birth—arguments more solemn even than numerous, and telling more when weighed than when counted, *pondere quam numero*—three aspects there are of our national character which trouble the uniformity of our feelings. A good son, even in such a case, is not at liberty to describe himself as "ashamed." Some gentler word must be found to express the character of his distress. And, whatever grounds of blame may appear against his venerated mother, it is one of his filial duties to suppose either that the blame applies but partially, or, if it should seem painfully universal, that it is one of those excesses to which energetic natures are liable through the very strength of their constitutional characteristics. Such things do happen. It is certain, for instance, that to the deep sincerity of British nature, and to that shyness or principle of reserve which is inseparable from self-respect, must be traced philosophically the churlishness and unsocial bearing for which, at one time, we were so angrily arraigned by the smooth south of Europe. That facile obsequiousness which attracts the inconsiderate in Belgians, Frenchmen, and Italians, is too generally a mixed product from impudence and insincerity. Want of principle

---

[1] Published first in four successive parts in *Blackwood* for July, September, and October 1840, and February 1841 : reprinted by De Quincey in 1859 in vol. xi of his Collective Edition of his Writings,— the same volume which contained the preceding paper.—M.

and want of moral sensibility compose the original *fundus* of southern manners ; and the natural product, in a specious hollowness of demeanour, has been afterwards propagated by imitation through innumerable people who may have partaken less deeply, or not at all, in the original moral qualities that have moulded such a manner.

Great faults, therefore—such is my inference—may grow out of great virtues in excess. And this consideration should make us cautious even towards an enemy ; much more when approaching so holy a question as the merits of our maternal land. Else, and supposing that a strange nation had been concerned in our judgment, we should declare ourselves mortified and humiliated by three expressions of the British character, too public to have escaped the notice of Europe. First, we writhe with shame when we hear of semi-delirious lords and ladies, sometimes theatrically costumed in caftans and turbans—Lord Byrons, for instance, and Lady Hester Stanhopes—proclaiming to the whole world, as the law of their households, that all nations and languages are free to enter their gates, with one sole exception directed against their British compatriots ; that is to say, abjuring by sound of trumpet the very land through which only they themselves have risen into consideration ; spurning those for countrymen " without whom " (as M. Gourville had the boldness to tell Charles II)—" without whom, by G—, sir, you yourself are nothing." We all know who *they* are that have done this thing : we *may* know, if we inquire, how many conceited coxcombs are at this moment acting upon that precedent ; in which, we scruple not to avow, are contained funds for everlasting satire more crying than any which Juvenal found in the worst days of Rome. And we may ask calmly, Would not death, judicial death, have visited such an act amongst the ancient republics ? Next, but with that indulgence which belongs to an infirmity rather than an error of the will, we feel ashamed for the obstinate obtuseness of our country in regard to one and the most effective of the Fine Arts. It will be understood that we speak of Music. In Painting and in Sculpture it is now past disputing that, if we are destined to inferiority at all, it is an inferiority only to the Italians of the fifteenth century— an inferiority which, if

it were even sure to be permanent, we share with all the
other malicious nations around us.   On that head we are
safe.   And in the most majestic of the Fine Arts,—in Poetry,
—we have a clear and vast pre-eminence as regards all nations.
No nation but ourselves has equally succeeded in both forms
of the higher poetry, epic and tragic ; whilst of meditative or
philosophic poetry (Young's, Cowper's, Wordsworth's)—to say
nothing of lyric—we may affirm what Quintilian says justly
of Roman satire : " *tota quidem nostra est.*"   If, therefore, in
every mode of composition through which the impassioned
mind speaks a nation has excelled its rivals, we cannot be
allowed to suppose any general defect of sensibility as a cause
of obtuseness with regard to music.   So little, however, is
the grandeur of this divine art suspected amongst us generally that a man will write an essay deliberately for the
purpose of putting on record his own preference of a song to
the most elaborate music of Mozart : he will glory in his
shame, and, though speaking in the character of one seemingly confessing to a weakness, will evidently view himself
in the light of a candid man, laying bare a state of feeling
which is natural and sound, opposed to a class of false pretenders who, whilst servile to rules of artists, in reality
contradict their own musical instincts, and feel little or
nothing of what they profess.   Strange that even the analogy
of other arts should not open his eyes to the delusion he is
encouraging !   A song, an air, a tune,—that is, a short
succession of notes revolving rapidly upon itself,—how could
that, by possibility, offer a field of compass sufficient for the
development of great musical effects ?   The preparation
pregnant with the future ; the remote correspondence ; the
questions, as it were, which to a deep musical sense are asked
in one passage and answered in another ; the iteration and
ingemination of a given effect, moving through subtle variations that sometimes disguise the theme, sometimes fitfully
reveal it, sometimes throw it out tumultuously to the blaze
of daylight : these and ten thousand forms of self-conflicting
musical passion,—what room could they find, what opening,
what utterance, in so limited a field as an air or song ?   A
hunting-box, a park-lodge, may have a forest grace and the
beauty of appropriateness ; but what if a man should match

such a bauble against the Pantheon, or against the minsters of York and Cologne ? A repartee may by accident be practically effective : it has been known to crush a party scheme, and an oration of Cicero's or of Burke's could have done no more ; but what judgment would match the two against each other as developments of power ? Let him who finds the *maximum* of his musical gratification in a song be assured, by that one fact, that his sensibility is rude and undeveloped. Yet exactly upon this level is the ordinary state of musical feeling throughout Great Britain ; and the howling wilderness of the psalmody in most parish churches of the land countersigns the statement. There is, however, accumulated in London more musical science than in any capital of the world. This, gradually diffused, will improve the feeling of the country. And, if it should fail to do so, in the worst case we have the satisfaction of knowing, through Jean Jacques Rousseau, and by later evidences, that, sink as we may below Italy and Germany in the sensibility to this divine art, we cannot go lower than France. Here, however, and in this cherished obtuseness as regards a pleasure so important for human life and at the head of the physico-intellectual pleasures, we find a second reason for quarrelling with the civilisation of our country. At the summit of civilisation in other points, she is here yet uncultivated and savage.

A third point is larger. Here (properly speaking) our quarrel is co-extensive with that general principle in England which tends in all things to set the matter above the manner, the substance above the external show,—a principle noble in itself, but inevitably wrong wherever the manner blends inseparably with the substance.

This general tendency operates in many ways : but our own immediate purpose is concerned with it only so far as it operates upon Style. In no country upon earth, were it possible to carry such a maxim into practical effect, is it a more determinate tendency of the national mind to value the *matter* of a book not only as paramount to the *manner*, but even as distinct from it, and as capable of a separate insulation. What first gave a shock to such a tendency must have been the unwilling and mysterious sense that in some

cases the matter and the manner were so inextricably inter-
woven as not to admit of this coarse bisection. The one was
embedded, entangled, and interfused through the other, in a
way which bade defiance to such gross mechanical separations.
But the tendency to view the two elements as in a separate
relation still predominates, and, as a consequence, the tendency to undervalue the accomplishment of style. Do we
mean that the English, as a literary nation, are practically
less sensible of the effects of a beautiful style ? Not at all.
Nobody can be insensible to these effects. And, upon a
known fact of history,—viz. the *exclusive* cultivation of
popular oratory in England throughout the seventeenth and
eighteenth centuries,—we might presume a peculiar and
exalted sense of style amongst ourselves. Until the French
Revolution no nation of Christendom except England had
any practical experience of popular rhetoric : any deliberative
eloquence, for instance ; any forensic eloquence that was
made public ; any democratic eloquence of the hustings ; or
any form whatever of public rhetoric beyond that of the
pulpit. Through two centuries at least, no nation could
have been so constantly reminded of the powers for good and
evil which belong to style. Often it must have happened,
to the mortification or joy of multitudes, that one man out
of windy nothings has constructed an overwhelming appeal
to the passions of his hearers, whilst another has thrown
away the weightiest cause by his manner of treating it.
Neither let it be said that this might not arise from differences of style, but because the triumphant demagogue made
use of fictions, and therefore that his triumph was still
obtained by means of his matter, however hollow that matter
might have proved upon investigation. That case, also, is a
possible case ; but often enough two orators have relied upon
the same identical matter—the facts, for instance, of the
slave-trade—and one has turned this to such good account
by his arrangements, by his modes of vivifying dry statements, by his arts of illustration, by his science of connecting
things with human feeling, that he has left his hearers in
convulsions of passion ; whilst the other shall have used
every tittle of the same matter without eliciting one scintillation of sympathy, without leaving behind one distinct

impression in the memory or planting one murmur in the heart.

In proportion, therefore, as the English people have been placed for two centuries and a quarter (*i.e.* since the latter decennium of James the First's reign) under a constant experience of popular eloquence thrown into all channels of social life, they must have had peculiar occasion to feel the effects of style. But to feel is not to feel consciously. Many a man is charmed by one cause who ascribes the effect to another. Many a man is fascinated by the artifices of composition who fancies that it is the subject which has operated so potently. And even for the subtlest of philosophers who keeps in mind the interpenetration of the style and the matter it would be as difficult to distribute the true proportions of their joint action as, with regard to the earliest rays of the dawn, it would be to say how much of the beauty lay in the heavenly light which chased away the darkness, how much in the rosy colour which that light entangled.

Easily, therefore, it may have happened that, under the constant action and practical effects of style, a nation may have failed to notice the cause *as* the cause. And, besides the disturbing forces which mislead the judgment of the auditor in such a case, there are other distuibing forces which modify the practice of the speaker. That is good rhetoric for the hustings which is bad for a book. Even for the highest forms of popular eloquence the laws of style vary much from the general standard. In the senate, and for the same reason in a newspaper, it is a virtue to reiterate your meaning : tautology becomes a merit : variation of the words, with a substantial identity of the sense and dilution of the truth, is oftentimes a necessity. A man who should content himself with a single condensed enunciation of a perplexed doctrine would be a madman and a *felo-de-se* as respected his reliance upon that doctrine. Like boys who are throwing the sun's rays into the eyes of a mob by means of a mirror, you must shift your lights and vibrate your reflections at every possible angle, if you would agitate the popular mind extensively. Every mode of intellectual communication has its separate strength and separate weakness,—its peculiar embarrassments, compensated by peculiar resources. It is

the advantage of a book that you can return to the past page
if anything in the present depends upon it. But, return
being impossible in the case of a spoken harangue, where
each sentence perishes as it is born, both the speaker and the
hearer become aware of a mutual interest in a much looser
style, and a perpetual dispensation from the severities of
abstract discussion. It is for the benefit of both that the
weightier propositions should be detained before the eye a
good deal longer than the chastity of taste or the austerity
of logic would tolerate in a book. Time must be given for
the intellect to eddy about a truth, and to appropriate its
bearings. There is a sort of previous lubrication, such as the
boa-constrictor applies to any subject of digestion, which is
requisite to familiarize the mind with a startling or a complex
novelty. And this is obtained for the intellect by varying
the modes of presenting it,—now putting it directly before
the eye, now obliquely, now in an abstract shape, now in
the concrete ; all which, being the proper technical discipline
for dealing with such cases, ought no longer to be viewed as
a licentious mode of style, but as the just style in respect of
those licentious circumstances. And the true art for such
popular display is to contrive the best forms for appearing to
say something new when in reality you are but echoing
yourself ; to break up massy chords into running variations;
and to mask, by slight differences in the manner, a virtual
identity in the substance.

　We have been illustrating a twofold neutralizing effect
applied to the advantages otherwise enjoyed by the English
people for appreciating the forms of style. What was it
that made the populace of Athens and of Rome so sensible to
the force of rhetoric and to the magic of language ? It was
the habit of hearing these two great engines daily worked for
purposes interesting to themselves as citizens, and sufficiently
intelligible to command their willing attention. The English
amongst modern nations have had the same advantages,
allowance being made for the much less intense concentration
of the audience. In the ancient republics it was always the
same city, and, therefore, the same audience, except in so far
as it was spread through many generations. This has been
otherwise in England ; and yet, by newspaper reports, any

great effect in one assize town, or electoral town, has been
propagated to the rest of the empire, through the eighteenth
and the present century. But all this, and the continual
exemplification of style as a great agency for democratic
effect, have not availed to win a sufficient *practical* respect
in England for the arts of composition as essential to authorship. And the reason is because, in the first place, from the
intertexture of style and matter, from the *impossibility that
the one should affect them otherwise than in connexion with the
other*, it has been natural for an audience to charge on the
superior agent what often belonged to the lower. This in
the first place ; and, secondly, because, *the modes of style
appropriate to popular eloquence being essentially different from
those of written composition*, any possible experience on the
hustings, or in the senate, would *pro tanto* tend rather to
disqualify the mind for appreciating the more chaste and
more elaborate qualities of style fitted for books ; and thus
a real advantage of the English in one direction has been
neutralized by two causes in another.

Generally and ultimately it is certain that our British
disregard or inadequate appreciation of style, though a very
lamentable fault, has had its origin in the manliness of the
British character ; in the sincerity and directness of the
British taste ; in the principle of " *esse quam videri*," which
might be taken as the key to much in our manner, much in
the philosophy of our lives ; and, finally, has had some part
of its origin in that same love for the practical and the
tangible which has so memorably governed the course of our
higher speculations from Bacon to Newton. But, whatever
may have been the origin of this most faulty habit, whatever
mixed causes now support it, beyond all question it is that
such a habit of disregard or of slight regard applied to all
the arts of composition does exist in the most painful extent,
and is detected by a practised eye in every page of almost
every book that is published.

If you could look anywhere with a right to expect continual illustrations of what is good in the manifold qualities
of style, it should reasonably be amongst our professional
authors ; but, as a body, they are distinguished by the most
absolute carelessness in this respect. Whether in the choice

of words and idioms, or in the construction of their sentences, it is not possible to conceive the principle of lazy indifference carried to a more revolting extremity. Proof lies before you, spread out upon every page, that no excess of awkwardness, or of inelegance, or of unrhythmical cadence, is so rated in the tariff of faults as to balance in the writer's estimate the trouble of remoulding a clause, of interpolating a phrase, or even of striking the pen through a superfluous word. In our own experience it has happened that we have known an author so laudably fastidious in this subtle art as to have recast one chapter of a series no less than seventeen times : so difficult was the ideal or model of excellence which he kept before his mind ; so indefatigable was his labour for mounting to the level of that ideal. Whereas, on the other hand, with regard to a large majority of the writers now carrying forward the literature of the country from the last generation to the next, the evidence is perpetual not so much that they rest satisfied with their own random preconceptions of each clause or sentence as that they never trouble themselves to form any such preconceptions. Whatever words tumble out under the blindest accidents of the moment, those are the words retained ; whatever sweep is impressed by chance upon the motion of a period, that is the arrangement ratified. To fancy that men thus determinately careless as to the grosser elements of style would pause to survey distant proportions, or to adjust any more delicate symmetries of good composition, would be visionary. As to the links of connexion, the transitions, and the many other functions of logic in good writing, things are come to such a pass that what was held true of Rome in two separate ages by two great rhetoricians, and of Constantinople in an age long posterior, may now be affirmed of England : the idiom of our language, the mother tongue, survives only amongst our women and children ; not, Heaven knows, amongst our women who write books — they are often painfully conspicuous for all that disfigures authorship — but amongst well-educated women not professionally given to literature. Cicero and Quintilian, each for his own generation, ascribed something of the same pre-eminence to the noble matrons of Rome ; and more than one writer of the Lower Empire has

recorded of Byzantium that in the nurseries of that city was
found the last home for the purity of the ancient Greek. No
doubt it might have been found also amongst the innumerable mob of that haughty metropolis, but stained with
corruptions and vulgar abbreviations ; or, wherever it might
lurk, assuredly it was not amongst the noble, the officials, or
the courtiers, — else it was impossible that such a master
of affectation as Nicetas Choniates,[1] for instance, should have
found toleration. But the rationale of this matter lies in
a small compass : why are the local names, whenever they
have resulted from the general good sense of a country,
faithful to the local truth, grave, and unaffected ? Simply
because they are not inventions of any active faculty, but
mere passive depositions from a real impression upon the
mind. On the other hand, wherever there is an ambitious
principle set in motion for name-inventing, there it is sure
to terminate in something monstrous and fanciful. Women
offend in such cases even more than men, because more of
sentiment or romance will mingle with the names they
impose. Sailors again err in an opposite spirit ; there is no
affectation in their names, but there is too painful an effort
after ludicrous allusions to the gravities of their native land
—" Big Wig Island," or " the Bishop and his Clerks "—or
the name becomes a memento of real incidents, but too
casual and personal to merit this lasting record of a name,
such as *Point Farewell*, or *Cape Turn - again*. This fault
applies to many of the Yankee[2] names, and to many more
in the southern and western States of North America, where
the earliest population has usually been of a less religious
character ; and most of all it applies to the names of the
back settlements. These people live under influences the
most opposite to those of false refinement : coarse necessities,
elementary features of peril or embarrassment, primary

[1] Nicetas Acominatus Choniates, a Byzantine historian, died about
1216.—M.

[2] " *Yankee names* " :—Foreigners in America subject themselves
to a perpetual misinterpretation by misapplying this term. " *Yankee*,"
in the American use, does not mean a citizen of the United States as
opposed to a foreigner, but a citizen of the Northern New England
States (Massachusetts, Connecticut, &c.) opposed to a Virginian, a
Kentuckian, &c.

aspects of savage nature, compose the scenery of their thoughts, and these are reflected by their names. *Dismal Swamp* expresses a condition of unreclaimed nature, which must disappear with growing civilisation. *Big Bone Lick* tells a tale of cruelty that cannot often be repeated. Buffaloes, like all cattle, derive medicinal benefit from salt ; they come in droves for a thousand miles to lick the masses of rock salt. The new settlers, observing this, lie in ambush to surprise them : 25,000 noble animals in one instance were massacred for their hides. In the following year the usual crowds advanced, but the first who snuffed the tainted air wheeled round, bellowed, and " recoiled " far into his native woods. Meantime the large bones remain to attest the extent of the merciless massacre. Here, as in all cases, there is a truth expressed, but again too casual and special. Besides that, from contempt of elegance, or from defect of art, the names resemble the seafaring nomenclature in being too rudely compounded.

As with the imposition of names, so with the use of the existing language, most classes stand between the pressure of two extremes : of coarseness, of carelessness, of imperfect art, on the one hand ; of spurious refinement and fantastic ambition upon the other. Authors have always been a dangerous class for any language. Amongst the myriads who are prompted to authorship by the coarse love of reputation, or by the nobler craving for sympathy, there will always be thousands seeking distinction through novelties of diction. Hopeless of any audience through mere weight of matter, they will turn for their last resource to such tricks of innovation as they can bring to bear upon language. What care they for purity or simplicity of diction, if at any cost of either they can win a special attention to themselves ? Now, the great body of women are under no such unhappy bias. If they happen to move in polished circles, or have received a tolerable education, they will speak their native language of necessity with truth and simplicity. And, supposing them not to be professional writers (as so small a proportion *can* be, even in France or England), there is always something in the situation of women which secures a fidelity to the idiom. From the greater excitability of females, and the superior vivacity of their feelings, they will be liable to far more irritations from wounded sensibilities. It is for such occasions chiefly that they seek to be effective in their language. Now, there is not in the world so certain a guarantee for pure idiomatic diction, without tricks or affectation, as a case of genuine excitement. Real situations are always pledges of a real natural language. It is in counterfeit passion, in the mimical situations of novels, or in poems that are efforts of ingenuity and no ebullitions of absolute unsimulated feeling, that female writers endeavour to sustain their own jaded sensibility, or to reinforce the languishing interest of their readers by extravagances of language. No woman in this world, under a movement of resentment from a false accusation, or from jealousy, or from confidence betrayed, ever was at leisure to practise vagaries of caprice in the management of her mother tongue : strength of real feeling shuts out all temptation to the affectation of false feeling.

Hence the purity of the female Byzantine Greek. Such caprices as they might have took some other course, and found some other vent than through their mother tongue. Hence, also, the purity of female English. Would you desire at this day to read our noble language in its native beauty, picturesque from idiomatic propriety, racy in its phraseology, delicate yet sinewy in its composition, steal the mail-bags, and break open all the letters in female hand-writing. Three out of four will have been written by that class of women who have the most leisure and the most interest in a correspondence by the post : that class who combine more of intelligence, cultivation, and of thoughtfulness, than any other in Europe—the class of unmarried women above twenty-five—an increasing class[1] ; women who, from mere dignity of character, have renounced all prospects of conjugal and parental life, rather than descend into habits unsuitable to their birth. Women capable of

[1] "*An increasing class*" :—But not in France. It is a most remarkable moral phenomenon in the social condition of that nation, and one which speaks a volume as to the lower tone of female dignity, that unmarried women at the age which amongst us obtains the insulting name of *old maids* are almost unknown. What shocking sacrifices of sexual honour does this one fact argue !

such sacrifices, and marked by such strength of mind, may be expected to think with deep feeling, and to express themselves (unless where they have been too much biassed by bookish connexions) with natural grace. Not impossibly these same women, if required to come forward in some public character, might write ill and affectedly. They would then have their free natural movement of thought distorted into some accommodation to artificial standards, amongst which they might happen to select a bad one for imitation. But in their letters they write under the benefit of their natural advantages ; not warped, on the one hand, into that constraint or awkwardness which is the inevitable effect of conscious exposure to public gaze ; yet, on the other, not left to vacancy or the chills of apathy, but sustained by some deep sympathy between themselves and their correspondents.

So far as concerns idiomatic English, we are satisfied, from the many beautiful female letters which we have heard upon chance occasions from every quarter of the empire, that they, the educated women of Great Britain—above all, the interesting class of women unmarried upon scruples of sexual honour—and also (as in Constantinople of old) the nurseries of Great Britain,—are the true and best depositaries of the old mother idiom. But we must not forget that, though this is another term for what is good in English when we are talking of a human and a popular interest, there is a separate use of the language, as in the higher forms of history or philosophy, which ought *not* to be idiomatic. As respects that which *is*, it is remarkable that the same orders cling to the ancient purity of diction amongst ourselves who did so in Pagan Rome : viz. *women*, for the reasons just noticed, *and people of rank.* So much has this been the tendency in England that we know a person of great powers, but who has in all things a one-sided taste, and is so much a lover of idiomatic English as to endure none else, who professes to read no writer since Lord Chesterfield. It is certain that this accomplished nobleman, who has been most unjustly treated from his unfortunate collision with a national favourite, and in part also from the laxity of his moral principles,—where, however, he spoke

worse than he thought —wrote with the ease and careless
grace of a high-bred gentleman. But his style is not peculiar : it has always been the style of his order. After
making the proper allowance for the continual new infusions
into our peerage from the bookish class of lawyers, and for
some modifications derived from the learned class of spiritual
peers, the tone of Lord Chesterfield has always been the tone
of our old aristocracy,—a tone of elegance and propriety,
above all things free from the stiffness of pedantry or
academic rigour, and obeying Cæsar's rule of shunning
tanquam scopulum any *insolens verbum.* It is, indeed,
through this channel that the solicitudes of our British
nobility have always flowed : other qualities might come
and go according to the temperament of the individual ; but
what in all generations constituted an object of horror for
that class was bookish precision and professional peculiarity.
From the free popular form of our great public schools, to
which nine out of ten amongst our old nobility resorted, it
happened unavoidably that they were not equally clear of
popular vulgarities ; indeed, from another cause, *that* could
not have been avoided : for it is remarkable that a connexion,
as close as through an umbilical cord, has always been maintained between the very highest orders of our aristocracy
and the lowest of our democracy, by means of nurses. The
nurses and immediate personal attendants of all classes come
from the same sources, most commonly from the peasantry of
the land ; they import into all families alike, into the highest and lowest, the coarsest expressions from the vernacular
language of anger and contempt. Whence, for example, it
was that about five or six years ago, when a new novel
circulated in London, with a private understanding that it
was a juvenile effort from two very young ladies, daughters
of a ducal house, nobody who reflected at all could feel much
surprise that one of the characters should express her self-
esteem by the popular phrase that she did not "think small
beer of herself." Naturally, papa, the duke, had not so
much modified the diction of the two young ladies as Nurse
Bridget. Equally in its faults and its merits, the language
of high life has always tended to simplicity and the vernacular ideal, recoiling from every mode of bookishness. And in

this, as in so many other instances, it is singular to note the close resemblance between polished England and polished Rome.   Augustus Cæsar was so little able to enter into any artificial forms or tortuous obscurities of ambitious rhetoric that he could not so much as understand them.   Even the old antique forms of language, where it happened that they had become obsolete, were to him disgusting.   Indeed, as regarded the choice and colouring of diction, Augustus was much of a blockhead : a truth which we utter boldly, now that none of his thirty legions can get at us.   And probably the main bond of connexion between himself and Horace was their common and excessive hatred of obscurity; from which quality, indeed, the very intellectual defects of both, equally with their good taste, alienated them to intensity.

The pure racy idiom of colloquial or household English, we have insisted, must be looked for in the circles of well-educated women not too closely connected with books.   It is certain that books, in any language, will tend to encourage a diction too remote from the style of spoken idiom ; whilst the greater solemnity and the more ceremonial costume of regular literature must often demand such a non-idiomatic diction upon mere principles of good taste.   But why is it that in our day literature has taken so determinate a swing towards this professional language of books as to justify some fears that the other extreme of the free colloquial idiom will perish as a living dialect?   The apparent cause lies in a phenomenon of modern life which on other accounts also is entitled to anxious consideration.   It is in newspapers that we must look for the main reading of this generation ; and in newspapers, therefore, we must seek for the causes operating upon the style of the age.   Seventy years ago this tendency in political journals to usurp upon the practice of books, and to mould the style of writers, was noticed by a most acute observer, himself one of the most brilliant writers in the class of satiric sketchers and personal historians that any nation has produced.   Already before 1770 the late Lord Orford, then simply Horace Walpole, was in the habit of saying to any man who consulted him on the cultivation of style,—" Style is it that you want?   Oh, go and look into the newspapers for a style."   This was said half contemptuously and half seriously. But the evil has now become overwhelming. One single number of a London morning paper,—which in half a century has expanded from the size of a dinner napkin to that of a breakfast tablecloth, from that to a carpet, and will soon be forced, by the expansions of public business, into something resembling the mainsail of a frigate,—already is equal in printed matter to a very large octavo volume. Every old woman in the nation now reads daily a vast miscellany in one volume royal octavo. The evil of this, as regards the quality of knowledge communicated, admits of no remedy. Public business, in its whole unwieldy compass, must always form the subject of these daily chronicles. Nor is there much room to expect any change in the style. The evil effect of this upon the style of the age may be reduced to two forms. Formerly the natural impulse of every man was spontaneously to use the language of life ; the language of books was a secondary attainment, not made without effort. Now, on the contrary, the daily composers of newspapers have so long dealt in the professional idiom of books as to have brought it home to every reader in the nation who does not violently resist it by some domestic advantages. Time was, within our own remembrance, that, if you should have heard, in passing along the street, from any old apple-woman such a phrase as " I will *avail myself* of your kindness," forthwith you would have shied like a skittish horse ; you would have run away in as much terror as any old Roman upon those occasions when *bos loquebatur*. At present you swallow such marvels as matters of course. The whole artificial dialect of books has come into play as the dialect of ordinary life. This is one form of the evil impressed upon our style by journalism : a dire monotony of bookish idiom has encrusted and stiffened all native freedom of expression, like some scaly leprosy or elephantiasis, barking and hide-binding the fine natural pulses of the elastic flesh. Another and almost a worse evil has established itself in the prevailing structure of sentences. Every man who has had any experience in writing knows how natural it is for hurry and fulness of matter to discharge itself by vast sentences, involving clause within clause *ad infinitum* ; how difficult it is, and how much a work of art, to break up this huge fasciculus of cycle and epicycle into a graceful succession of sentences, long intermingled with short, each modifying the other, and arising musically by links of spontaneous connexion. Now, the plethoric form of period, this monster model of sentence, bloated with decomplex intercalations, and exactly repeating the form of syntax which distinguishes an act of Parliament, is the prevailing model in newspaper eloquence. Crude undigested masses of suggestion, furnishing rather raw materials for composition and jottings for the memory than any formal developments of the ideas, describe the quality of writing which *must* prevail in journalism : not from defect of talents,—which are at this day of that superior class which may be presumed from the superior importance of the function itself,—but from the necessities of hurry and of instant compliance with an instant emergency, granting no possibility for revision or opening for amended thought, which are evils attached to the flying velocities of public business.

As to structure of sentence and the periodic involution, *that* scarcely admits of being exemplified in the conversation of those who do not write. But the choice of phraseology is naturally and easily echoed in the colloquial forms of those who surrender themselves to such an influence. To mark in what degree this contagion of bookishness has spread, and how deeply it has moulded the habits of expression in classes naturally the least likely to have been reached by a revolution so artificial in its character, we will report a single record from the memorials of our own experience. Some eight years ago, we had occasion to look for lodgings in a newly-built suburb of London to the south of the Thames.[1] The mistress of the house (with respect to whom we have nothing to report more than that she was in the worst sense a vulgar woman : that is, not merely a low-bred person—so much might have been expected from her occupation—but morally vulgar by the evidence of her own complex precautions against fraud, reasonable enough in so dangerous a capital, but not calling for the very ostentatious display of

[1] This, if taken literally, records a visit of De Quincey to London in 1832.—M.

them which she obtruded upon us) was in regular training, it appeared, as a student of newspapers. She had no children ; the newspapers were her children. There lay her studies ; that branch of learning constituted her occupation from morning to night ; and the following were amongst the words which she—this semi-barbarian—poured from her cornucopia during the very few minutes of our interview; which interview was brought to an abrupt issue by mere nervous agitation upon our part. The words, as noted down within an hour of the occasion, and after allowing a fair time for our recovery, were these :—first, "category"; secondly, "predicament" (where, by the way, from the twofold iteration of the idea—Greek and Roman—it appears that the old lady was "twice armed"); thirdly, "individuality"; fourthly, "procrastination"; fifthly, "speaking diplomatically, would not wish to *commit* herself,"—who knew but that "inadvertently she might even *compromise* both herself and her husband"? sixthly, "would spontaneously adapt the several modes of domestication to the reciprocal interests," &c. ; and, finally—(which word it was that settled us : we heard it as we reached the topmost stair on the second floor, and, without further struggle against our instincts, round we wheeled, rushed down forty-five stairs, and exploded from the house with a fury causing us to impinge against an obese or protuberant gentleman, and calling for mutual explanations : a result which nothing *could* account for but a steel bow, or mustachios on the lip of an elderly woman : meantime the fatal word was),—seventhly, "anteriorly." Concerning which word we solemnly depose and make affidavit that neither from man, woman, nor book, had we ever heard it before this unique rencontre with this abominable woman on the staircase. The occasion which furnished the excuse for such a word was this :—From the staircase-window we saw a large shed in the rear of the house ; apprehending some nuisance of "manufacturing industry" in our neighbourhood,—"What's that ?" we demanded. Mark the answer : "A shed ; that's what it is ; *videlicet* a shed ; and anteriorly to the existing shed there was——" ; *what* there was posterity must consent to have wrapt in darkness, for there came on our nervous

seizure, which intercepted further communication. But
observe, as a point which took away any gleam of consolation
from the case, the total absence of all *malaprop* picturesqueness that might have defeated its deadly action upon the
nervous system. No ; it is due to the integrity of *her*
disease, and to the completeness of *our* suffering, that we
should attest the unimpeachable correctness of her words,
and of the syntax by which she connected them.

Now, if we could suppose the case that the old household
idiom of the land were generally so extinguished amongst us
as it was in this particular instance ; if we could imagine, as
a *universal* result of journalism, that a coarse unlettered
woman, having occasion to say "this or that stood in such
a place before the present shed," should take as a natural
or current formula "anteriorly to the existing shed there
stood," &c., what would be the final effect upon our literature ?   Pedantry, though it were unconscious pedantry, once
steadily diffused through a nation as to the very moulds of
its thinking, and the general tendencies of its expression,
could not but stiffen the natural graces of composition, and
weave fetters about the free movement of human thought.
This would interfere as effectually with our power of enjoying much that is excellent in our past literature as it would
with our future powers of producing.   And such an agency
has been too long at work amongst us not to have already
accomplished some part of these separate evils.   Amongst
women of education, as we have argued above, standing
aloof from literature, and less uniformly drawing their intellectual sustenance from newspapers, the deadening effects
have been partially counteracted.   Here and there, amongst
individuals alive to the particular evils of the age, and watching the very set of the current, there may have been even a
more systematic counteraction applied to the mischief.   But
the great evil in such cases is this, that we cannot see the
extent of the changes wrought or being wrought, from having ourselves partaken in them.   *Tempora mutantur* ; and
naturally, if we could review them with the neutral eye of
a stranger, it would be impossible for us not to see the
extent of those changes.   But our eye is *not* neutral ; we
also have partaken in the changes ; *nos et mutamur in illis.*

And this fact disturbs the power of appreciating those changes. Every one of us would have felt, sixty years ago, that the general tone and colouring of a style was stiff, bookish, pedantic, which, from the habituation of our organs, we now feel to be natural and within the privilege of learned art. Direct objective qualities it is always by comparison easy to measure ; but the difficulty commences when we have to combine with this outer measurement of the object another corresponding measurement of the subjective or inner qualities by which we apply the measure ; that is, when besides the objects projected to a distance from the spectator, we have to allow for variations or disturbances in the very eye which surveys them.   The eye cannot see itself ; we cannot project from ourselves, and contemplate as an object, our own contemplating faculty, or appreciate our own appreciating power. Biasses, therefore, or gradual warpings, that have occurred in our critical faculty as applied to style, we cannot allow for : and these biasses will unconsciously mask to our perceptions an amount of change in the quality of popular style such as we could not easily credit.

Separately from this change for the worse in the drooping idiomatic freshness of our diction, which is a change that has been going on for a century, the other characteristic defect of this age lies in the tumid and tumultuary structure of our sentences.   The one change has partly grown out of the other.   Ever since a more bookish air was impressed upon composition without much effort by the Latinized and artificial phraseology, by forms of expression consecrated to books, and by "long-tailed words in *osity* and *ation*,"— either because writers felt that already, in this one act of preference shown to the artificial vocabulary, they had done enough to establish a differential character of regular composition, and on that consideration thought themselves entitled to neglect the combination of their words into sentences or periods ; or because there is a real natural sympathy between the Latin phraseology and a Latin structure of sentence,—certain it is and remarkable that our popular style, in the common limited sense of arrangement applied to words or the syntax of sentences, has laboured with two faults that might have been thought incompatible :

it has been artificial, by artifices peculiarly adapted to the powers of the Latin language, and yet at the very same time careless and disordinate. There is a strong idea expressed by the Latin word *inconditus, disorganized,* or rather *unorganized.* Now, in spite of its artificial bias, that is the very epithet which will best characterize our newspaper style. To be viewed as susceptible of organization, such periods must already be elaborate and artificial; to be viewed as not having received it, such periods must be hyperbolically careless.

But perhaps the very best illustration of all this will be found in putting the case of English style into close juxtaposition with the style of the French and Germans, our only very important neighbours. As leaders of civilisation, as *powers* in an intellectual sense, there are but three nations in Europe—England, Germany, France. As to Spain and Italy, outlying extremities, they are not moving bodies ; they rest upon the past. Russia and North America are the two bulwarks of Christendom east and west. But the three powers *at the centre* are in all senses the motive forces of civilisation. In all things they have the initiation, and they preside.

By this comparison we shall have the advantage of doing what the French express by *s'orienter,* the Germans by *sich orientiren.* Learning one of our bearings on the compass, we shall be able to deduce the rest, and we shall be able to conjecture our valuation as respects the art by finding our place amongst the artists.

With respect to French style, we can imagine the astonishment of an English author practised in composition, and with no previous knowledge of French literature, who should first find himself ranging freely amongst a French library. That particular fault of style which in English books is all but universal absolutely has not an existence in the French. Speaking rigorously and to the very letter of the case, we, upon a large experience in French literature, affirm that it would be nearly impossible (perhaps strictly so) to cite an instance of that cumbrous and unwieldy style which disfigures English composition so extensively. Enough could not be adduced to satisfy the purpose of illustration. And,

to make a Frenchman sensible of the fault as a possibility,
you must appeal to some *translated* model.

But why? The cause of this national immunity from a
fault so common everywhere else, and so natural when we
look into the producing occasions, is as much entitled to our
notice as the immunity itself. The fault is inevitable, as
one might fancy, to two conditions of mind : hurry in the
first place ; want of art in the second. The French must be
liable to these disadvantages as much as their neighbours ;
by what magic is it that they evade them or neutralize them
in the result? The secret lies here ; beyond all nations, by
constitutional vivacity, the French are a nation of talkers,
and the model of their sentences is moulded by that fact.
Conversation, which is a luxury for other nations, is for
them a necessity ; by the very law of their peculiar intellect
and of its social training they are colloquial. Hence it
happens that there are no such people endured or ever heard
of in France as *al*loquial wits,—people who talk *to* but not
with a circle : the very finest of their *beaux esprits* must submit to the equities of conversation, and would be crushed
summarily as monsters if they were to seek a selfish mode of
display or a privilege of lecturing any audience of a *salon*
who had met for purposes of *social* pleasure. " *De Monologue*,"
as Madame de Staël, in her broken English, described this
mode of display when speaking of Coleridge, is so far from
being tolerated in France as an accomplishment that it is not
even understood as a disease. This kind of what may be
called irresponsible talk, when a man runs on *perpetuo
tenore*, not accountable for any opinion to his auditors, open
to no contradiction, liable to no competition, has sometimes
procured for a man in England the affix of *River* to his
name : *Labitur et labetur in omne volubilis ævum.* In Dryden's happy version,—

" He flows, and, as he flows, for ever will flow on."

But that has been in cases where the talking impulse was
sustained by mere vivacity of animal spirits, without knowledge
to support it, and liable to the full weight of Archbishop
Huet's sarcasm, that it was a diarrhœa of garrulity, a *fluxe de
bouche.* But in cases like that of Coleridge, where the

solitary display, if selfish, is still dignified by a pomp of
knowledge, and a knowledge which you feel to have been
fused and combined by the genial circumstances of the
speaker's position in the centre of an admiring circle, we
English do still recognise the *métier* of a professional talker
as a privileged mode of social display. People are asked to
come and hear such a performer, as you form a select party
to hear Thalberg or Paganini. The thing is understood at
least with us ; right or wrong there is an understanding
amongst the company that you are not to interrupt the great
man of the night. You may prompt him by a question ;
you may set him in motion ; but to begin arguing against
him would be felt as not less unseasonable than to insist on
whistling Jim Crow during the *bravuras* and *tours de force* of
great musical artists.

In France, therefore, from the intense adaptation of the
national mind to real colloquial intercourse, for which
reciprocation is indispensable, the form of sentence in use is
adjusted to that primary condition ; brief, terse, simple ;
shaped to avoid misunderstanding, and to meet the impatience of those who are waiting for their turn. People who
write rapidly everywhere write as they talk ; it is impossible
to do otherwise. Taking a pen into his hand, a man frames
his periods exactly as he would do if addressing a companion.
So far the Englishman and the Frenchman are upon the
same level. Suppose them, therefore, both preparing to
speak : an Englishman in such a situation has no urgent
motive for turning his thoughts to any other object than the
prevailing one of the moment, viz. how best to convey his
meaning. That object weighs also with the Frenchman ;
but he has a previous, a paramount, object to watch—the
necessity of avoiding *des longueurs*. The rights, the equities
of conversation are but dimly present to the mind of the
Englishman. From the mind of a Frenchman they are
never absent. To an Englishman, the right of occupying
the attention of the company seems to inhere in *things* rather
than in persons ; if the particular subject under discussion
should happen to be a grave one, then, in right of *that*, and
not by any right of his own, a speaker will seem to an
Englishman invested with the privilege of drawing largely

upon the attention of a company. But to a Frenchman this right of participation in the talk is a *personal* right, which cannot be set aside by any possible claims in the subject; it passes by necessity to and fro, backwards and forwards, between the several persons who are present ; and, as in the games of battledore and shuttlecock, or of "hunt the slipper," the momentary subject of interest never *can* settle or linger for any length of time in any one individual without violating the rules of the sport, or suspending its movement. Inevitably, therefore, the structure of sentence must for ever be adapted to this primary function of the French national intellect, the function of communicativeness, and to the necessities (for to the French they *are* necessities) of social intercourse, and (speaking plainly) of interminable garrulity.

Hence it is that in French authors, whatever may otherwise be the differences of their minds, or the differences of their themes, uniformly we find the periods short, rapid, unelaborate : Pascal or Helvetius, Condillac or Rousseau, Montesquieu or Voltaire, Buffon or Duclos,—all alike are terse, perspicuous, brief. Even Mirabeau or Chateaubriand, so much modified by foreign intercourse, in this point adhere to their national models. Even Bossuet or Bourdaloue, where the diffusiveness and amplitude of oratory might have been pleaded as a dispensation, are not more licentious in this respect than their compatriots. One rise in every sentence, one gentle descent, that is the law for French composition ; even too monotonously so ; and thus it happens that such a thing as a long or an involved sentence can hardly be produced from French literature, though a sultan were to offer his daughter in marriage to the man who should find it. Whereas now, amongst us English, not only is the too general tendency of our sentences towards hyperbolical length, but it will be found continually that, instead of one rise and one corresponding fall—one *arsis* and one *thesis*—there are many. Flux and reflux, swell and cadence, that is the movement for a sentence ; but our modern sentences agitate us by rolling fires after the fashion of those internal earthquakes that, not content with one throe, run along spasmodically in a long succession of intermitting convulsions.

It is not often that a single fault can produce any vast

amount of evil.   But there are cases where it does ; and this
is one : the effect of weariness and of repulsion which may
arise from this single vice of unwieldly comprehensiveness in
the structure of sentences cannot better be illustrated than
by a frank exposure of what often happens to ourselves, and
(as we differ as to this case only by consciously noticing what
all feel) must often happen to others.   In the evening, when
it is natural that we should feel a craving for rest, some book
lies near us which is written in a style clear, tranquil, easy
to follow.   Just at that moment comes in the wet newspaper, dripping with the dewy freshness of its news ; and
even in its parliamentary memorials promising so much
interest that, let them be treated in what manner they may,
merely for the subjects they are often commandingly attractive.   The attraction indeed is but too potent ; the interest
but too exciting.   Yet, after all, many times we lay aside
the journal, and we acquiesce in the gentler stimulation of
the book.   Simply the news we may read ; but the discussions, whether direct from the editor, or reported from the
Parliament, we refuse or we delay.   And why ?   It is the
subject, perhaps you think ; it is the great political question,
too agitating by the consequences it may happen to involve.
No.   All this, if treated in a winning style, we could bear.
It is the effort, the toil, the exertion of mind requisite to
follow the discussion through endless and labyrinthine sentences ; this it is that compels us to forgo the journal or to
lay it aside until the next morning.

Those who are not accustomed to watch the effects of
composition upon the feelings, or have had little experience
in voluminous reading pursued for weeks, would scarcely
imagine how much of downright physical exhaustion is produced by what is technically called the *periodic* style of
writing : it is not the length, the ἀπεραντολογια, the paralytic flux of words,—it is not even the cumbrous involution
of parts within parts,—separately considered, that bears so
heavily upon the attention.   It is the suspense, the holding-
on of the mind until what is called the ἀποδοσις, or coming
round of the sentence commences ; this it is which wears out
the faculty of attention.   A sentence, for example, begins
with a series of *ifs* ; perhaps a dozen lines are occupied with

expanding the conditions under which something is affirmed or denied : here you cannot dismiss and have done with the ideas as you go along, for as yet all is hypothetic; all is suspended in air. The conditions are not fully to be understood until you are acquainted with the dependency ; you must give a separate attention to each clause of this complex hypothesis, and yet, having done *that* by a painful effort, you have done nothing at all ; for you must exercise a reacting attention through the corresponding latter section, in order to follow out its relations to all parts of the hypothesis which sustains it. In fact, under the rude yet also artificial character of newspaper style, each separate monster period is a vast arch, which, not receiving its keystone, not being locked into self-supporting cohesion, until you nearly reach its close, imposes of necessity upon the unhappy reader all the *onus* of its ponderous weight through the main process of its construction. The continued repetition of so Atlantean an effort soon overwhelms your patience, and establishes at length that habitual feeling which causes you to shrink from the speculations of journalists, or (which is more likely) to adopt a worse habit than absolute neglect, which we shall notice immediately.

Meantime, as we have compared ourselves on this important point with the French, let us now complete our promise by noticing our relation in the same point to the Germans. Even on its own account, and without any view to our present purpose, the character of German prose is an object of legitimate astonishment. Whatever is bad in our own ideal of prose style, whatever is repulsive in our own practice, we see there carried to the most outrageous excess. Herod is out-Heroded, Sternhold is out-Sternholded, with a zealotry of extravagance that really seems like wilful burlesque. Lessing, Herder, Paul Richter, and Lichtenberg, with some few beside, either prompted by nature or trained upon foreign models, have avoided the besetting sin of German prose. Any man of distinguished talent, whose attention has been once called steadily to this subject, cannot fail to avoid it The misfortune of most writers has been that, once occupied with the interest of *things*, and overwhelmed by the embarrassments of disputed *doctrines*, they never advert to any question affecting what they view, by comparison, as a trifle. The το *docendum*, the thing to be taught, has availed to obscure or even to annihilate for their eyes every anxiety as to the mode of teaching. And, as one conspicuous example of careless style acts by its authority to create many more, we need not wonder at the results, even when they reach a point of what may be called monstrous. Among ten thousand offenders, who carry their neglect of style even to that point, we would single out Immanuel Kant. Such is the value of his philosophy in some sections, and partially it is so very capable of a lucid treatment, intelligible to the plainest man of reflective habits, that within no long interval we shall certainly see him naturalised amongst ourselves : there are particular applications of his philosophy, not contemplated by himself, for which we venture to predict that even the religious student will ultimately be thankful, when the cardinal principles have been brought under a clear light of interpretation. Attention will then be forced upon his style, and facts will come forward not credible without experimental proof. For instance, we have lying before us at this moment his *Critik der Practischen Vernunft* in the unpirated edition of Hartknoch, the respectable publisher of all Kant's great works. The text is therefore authentic, and, being a fourth edition (Riga, 1797), must be presumed to have benefited by the author's careful revision. We have no time for search ; but, on barely throwing open the book, we see a sentence at pp. 70, 71, exactly covering one whole octavo page of thirty-one lines (each line averaging forty-five to forty-eight letters). Sentences of the same calibre, some even of far larger *bore*, we have observed in this and other works of the same author. And it is not the fact taken as an occasional possibility, it is the prevailing character of his style, that we insist on as the most formidable barrier to the study of his writings, and to the progress of what will soon be acknowledged as important in his principles. A sentence is viewed by him, and by most of his countrymen, as a rude mould or elastic form admitting of expansion to any possible extent : it is laid down as a rough outline, and then by superstruction and *epi*-superstruction it is gradually reared to a giddy altitude which no eye can follow. Yielding to his natural impulse of subjoining all additions, or exceptions, or modifications, not in the shape of separate consecutive sentences, but as intercalations and stuffings of one original sentence, Kant might naturally enough have written a book from beginning to end in one vast hyperbolical sentence. We sometimes see an English Act of Parliament which does literally accomplish that end, by an artifice which in law has a purpose and a use. Instead of laying down a general proposition, which is partially false until it has received its proper restraints, the framer of the act endeavours to evade even this momentary falsehood by coupling the limitations with the very primary enunciation of the truth : *e.g.* A shall be entitled, provided always that he is under the circumstances of *e*, or *i*, or *o*, to the right of X. Thus, even a momentary compliance with the false notion of an absolute unconditional claim to X is evaded ; a truth which is only a conditional truth is stated as such from the first. There is, therefore, a theoretic use. But what is the practical result ? Why, that, when you attempt to read an Act of Parliament where the exceptions, the secondary exceptions to the exceptions, the limitations and the sublimitations, descend, *seriatim*, by a vast scale of dependencies, the mind finds itself overtasked ; the energy of the most energetic begins to droop ; and so inevitable is that result that Mr. Pitt, a minister unusually accomplished for such process by constitution of mind and by practice, publicly avowed his inability to follow so trying a conflict with technical embarrassments. He declared himself to be lost in the labyrinth of clauses : the Ariadne's clue was wanting for his final extrication : and he described his situation at the end with the simplicity natural to one who was no charlatan, and sought for no reputation by the tricks of a funambulist : " In the crowd of things excepted and counter-excepted, he really ceased to understand the main point—what it was that the law allowed, and what it was that it disallowed."

We might have made our readers merry with the picture of German prose ; but we must not linger. It is enough to say that it offers the counterpole to the French style. Our own popular style, and (what is worse) the *tendency* of our own, is to the German extreme. To those who read German, indeed, German prose, as written by the mob of authors, presents, as in a Brobdignagian and exaggerating mirror, the most offensive faults of our own.

But these faults—are they in practice so wearisome and exhausting as we have described them ? Possibly not ; and, where that happens to be the case, let the reader ask himself if it is not by means of an evasion worse in its effects than any fault of style could ever prove in its most overcharged form. Shrinking, through long experience, from the plethoric form of cumulation and "periodic" writing in which the journalist supports or explains his views, every man who puts a business value upon his time slips naturally into a trick of shorthand reading. It is more even by the effort and tension of mind in *holding on* than by the mere loss of time that most readers are repelled from the habit of careful reading. An evil of modern growth is met by a modern remedy. Every man gradually learns an art of catching at the leading words, and the cardinal or hinge joints of transition, which proclaim the general course of a writer's speculation. Now, it is very true, and is sure to be objected, that, where so much is certain to prove mere iteration and teasing *surplusage*, little can be lost by this or any other process of abridgment. Certainly, as regards the particular subject concerned, there may be no room to apprehend a serious injury. Not there, not in any direct interest, but in a far larger interest— indirect for the moment, but the most direct and absolute of all interests for an intellectual being,—the reader suffers a permanent debilitation. He acquires a factitious propensity ; he forms an incorrigible habit of desultory reading. Now, to say of a man's knowledge, that it will be shallow, or (which is worse than shallow) will be erroneous and insecure in its foundations, is vastly to underrate the evil of such a habit : it is by reaction upon a man's faculties, it is by the effects reflected upon his judging and reasoning powers, that loose habits of reading tell eventually. And these are durable effects. Even as respects the minor purpose of information, better it is, by a thousandfold, to have read threescore of books (chosen judiciously) with severe attention than to have raced through the library of the Vatican at a newspaper pace. But, as respects the final habits acquired, habits of thinking coherently and of judging soundly, better that a man should have not read one line throughout his life than have travelled through the journals of Europe by this random process of "reading short."

Yet, by this Parthian habit of aiming at full gallop,—of taking flying shots at conspicuous marks, and, like Parthians also, directing their chance arrows whilst retreating, and revolting with horror from a direct approach to the object,—thus it is that the young and the flexible are trained amongst us under the increasing tyranny of journalism. A large part of the evil, therefore, belongs to style ; for it is this which repels readers, and enforces the shorthand process of desultory reading. A large part of the evil, therefore, is of a nature to receive a remedy.

It is with a view to that practical part of the extensive evil that we have shaped our present notice of popular style, as made operative amongst ourselves. One single vice of periodic syntax,—a vice unknown to the literature of Greece, and, until Paterculus,[1] even of Rome (although the language of Rome was so naturally adapted to that vice),—has with us counterbalanced all possible vices of any other order. Simply by the vast sphere of its agency for evil, in the habits of mind which it produces and supports, such a vice merits a consideration which would else be disproportionate. Yet, at the same time, it must not be forgotten that, if the most operative of all vices, after all it is but one. What are the others ?

It is a fault, amongst many faults, of such works' as we have on this subject of style, that they collect the list of qualities, good or bad, to which composition is liable, not under any principle from which they might be deduced *a priori*, so as to be assured that all had been enumerated, but by a tentative groping, a mere conjectural estimate. The word *style* has with us a twofold meaning : one, the narrow meaning, expressing the mere *synthesis onomaton*, the syntaxis or combination of words into sentences ; the other of far wider extent, and expressing all possible relations that can arise between thoughts and words—the total effect of a writer as derived from manner. Style may be viewed as an *organic* thing and as a *mechanic* thing. By organic, we mean that

---

[1] Velleius Paterculus, Roman historian, born about B.C. 19, died about A.D. 31.—M.

which, being acted upon, reacts, and which propagates the communicated power without loss. By mechanic, that which, being impressed with motion, cannot throw it back without loss, and therefore soon comes to an end. The human body is an elaborate system of organs ; it is sustained by organs. But the human body is exercised as a machine, and as such may be viewed in the arts of riding, dancing, leaping, &c., subject to the laws of motion and equilibrium. Now, the use of words is an organic thing, in so far as language is connected with thoughts, and modified by thoughts. It is a mechanic thing, in so far as words in combination determine or modify each other. The science of style as an organ of thought, of style in relation to the ideas and feelings, might be called the *organology* of style. The science of style considered as a machine, in which words act upon words, and through a particular grammar, might be called the *mechanology* of style. It is of little importance by what name these two functions of composition are expressed. But it is of great importance not to confound the functions : that function by which style maintains a commerce with thought, and that by which it chiefly communicates with grammar and with words. A pedant only will insist upon the names ; but the distinction in the ideas, under some name, can be neglected only by the man who is careless of logic.

We know not how far we may be ever called upon to proceed with this discussion. If it should happen that we were, an interesting field of questions would lie before us for the first part (the organology). It would lead us over the ground trodden by the Greek and Roman rhetoricians, and over those particular questions which have arisen by the contrast between the circumstances of the ancients and our own since the origin of printing. Punctuation,[1] trivial as such an innovation may seem, was the product of typo-

---

[1] This is a most instructive fact ; and it is another fact not less instructive that lawyers in most parts of Christendom, I believe, certainly wherever they are wide-awake professionally, tolerate no punctuation. But why ? Are lawyers not sensible to the luminous effect from a point happily placed ? Yes, they *are* sensible ; but also they are sensible of the false prejudicating effect from a punctuation managed (as too generally it is) carelessly and illogically. Here is the brief abstract of the case. All punctuation narrows the path,

graphy ; and it is interesting to trace the effects upon style even of that one slight addition to the resources of logic. Previously a man was driven to depend for his security against misunderstanding upon the pure virtue of his syntax. Miscollocation or dislocation of related words disturbed the whole sense ; its least effect was to give *no* sense,—often it gave a dangerous sense. Now, punctuation was an artificial machinery for maintaining the integrity of the sense against all mistakes of the writer ; and, as one consequence, it withdrew the energy of men's anxieties from the natural machinery, which lay in just and careful arrangement. Another and still greater machinery of art for the purpose of maintaining the sense, and with the effect of relaxing the care of the writer, lay in the exquisitely artificial structure of the Latin language, which by means of its terminal forms indicated the arrangement, and referred the proper predicate to the proper subject, spite of all that affectation or negligence could do to disturb the series of the logic or the succession of the syntax. Greek, of course, had the same advantage in kind, but not in degree ; and thence rose some differences which have escaped all notice of rhetoricians. Here also would properly arise the question, started by Charles Fox (but probably due originally to the conversation of some far subtler friend, such as Edmund Burke), how far the practice of footnotes—a practice purely modern in its *form*—is reconcilable with the laws of just composition : and whether in virtue, though not in form, such footnotes did not exist for the ancients, by an evasion we could point out. The question is clearly one which grows out of style in its relations to thought : how far, viz., such an excrescence as a note argues that the sentence to which it is attached has not received the benefit of a full development for the conception involved ; whether, if thrown into the furnace again and

which is else unlimited ; and (*by* narrowing it) may chance to guide the reader into the right groove amongst several that are *not* right. But also punctuation has the effect very often (and almost always has the power) of biassing and predetermining the reader to an erroneous choice of meaning. Better, therefore, no guide at all than one which is likely enough to lead astray, and which must always be suspected and mistrusted, inasmuch as very nearly always it has the *power* to lead astray.

re-melted, it might not be so recast as to absorb the redundancy which had previously flowed over into a note.   Under this head would fall not only all the differential questions of style and composition between us and the ancients, but also the questions of merit as fairly distributed amongst the moderns compared with each other.   The French, as we recently insisted, undoubtedly possess one vast advantage over all other nations in the good taste which governs the arrangement of their sentences ; in the simplicity (a strange pretension to make for anything French) of the modulation under which their thoughts flow ; in the absence of all cumbrous involution, and in the quick succession of their periods.   In reality this invaluable merit tends to an excess ; and the *style coupé* as opposed to the *style soutenu*, flippancy opposed to solemnity, the subsultory to the continuous, these are the too frequent extremities to which the French manner betrays men. Better, however, to be flippant than by a revolting form of tumour and perplexity to lead men into habits of intellect such as result from the modern vice of English style.   Still, with all its practical value, it is evident that the intellectual merits of the French style are but small.   They are chiefly negative, in the first place ; and, secondly, founded in the accident of their colloquial necessities.   The law of conversation has prescribed the model of their sentences, and in that law there is quite as much of self-interest at work as of respect for equity.   *Hanc veniam petimusque damusque vicissim.*   Give and take is the rule ; and he who expects to be heard must condescend to listen ; which necessity for both parties binds over both to be brief.   Brevity so won could at any rate have little merit, and it is certain that for profound thinking it must sometimes be a hindrance.   In order to be brief a man must take a short sweep of view ; his range of thought cannot be extensive ; and such a rule, applied to a general method of thinking, is fitted rather to aphorisms and maxims, as upon a known subject, than to any process of investigation as upon a subject yet to be fathomed.   Advancing still further into the examination of style as the organ of thinking, we should find occasion to see the prodigious defects of the French in all the higher qualities of prose composition.   One advantage, for a practical purpose of life, is sadly counterbalanced by numerous faults, many of which are faults of *stamina*, lying not in any corrigible defects, but in such as imply penury of thinking from radical inaptitude in the thinking faculty to connect itself with the feeling and with the creative faculty of the imagination.   There are many other researches belonging to this subtlest of subjects, affecting both the logic and the ornaments of style, which would fall under the head of organology.   But for instant practical use, though far less difficult for investigation, yet for that reason far more tangible and appreciable, would be all the suggestions proper to the other head of mechanology.   Half a dozen rules for evading the most frequently recurring forms of awkwardness, of obscurity, of misproportion, and of double meaning, would do more to assist a writer in practice, laid under some necessity of hurry, than volumes of general disquisition. It makes us blush to add that even grammar is so little of a perfect attainment amongst us that, with two or three exceptions (one being Shakspere, whom some affect to consider as belonging to a semi-barbarous age), we have never seen the writer, through a circuit of prodigious reading, who has not sometimes violated the accidence or the syntax of English grammar.

Whatever becomes of our own possible speculations, we shall conclude with insisting on the growing necessity of style as a practical interest of daily life.   Upon subjects of public concern, and in proportion to that concern, there will always be a suitable (and as letters extend a growing) competition.   Other things being equal, or appearing to be equal, the determining principle for the public choice will lie in the style.   Of a German book, otherwise entitled to respect, it was said—*er lässt sich nicht lesen*—it does not permit itself to be read, such and so repulsive was the style.   Among ourselves this has long been true of newspapers.   They do not suffer themselves to be read *in extenso* ; and they are read short, with what injury to the mind we have noticed.   The same style of reading, once largely practised, is applied universally.   To this special evil an improvement of style would apply a special redress.   The same improvement is otherwise clamorously called for by each man's interest of competition.

Public luxury, which is gradually consulted by everything else, must at length be consulted in style.

Part II

It is a natural resource that whatsoever we find it difficult to investigate as a result we endeavour to follow as a growth. Failing analytically to probe its nature, historically we seek relief to our perplexities by tracing its origin. Not able to assign the elements of its theory, we endeavour to detect them in the stages of its development. Thus, for instance, when any feudal institution (be it Gothic, Norman, or Anglo-Saxon) eludes our deciphering faculty from the imperfect records of its use and operation, then we endeavour conjecturally to amend our knowledge by watching the circumstances in which that institution arose ; and, from the necessities of the age, as indicated by facts which have survived, we are sometimes able to trace, through all their corresponding stages of growth, the natural succession of arrangements which such necessities would be likely to prescribe.

This mode of oblique research, where a more direct one is denied, we find to be the only one in our power. And, with respect to the liberal arts, it is even more true than with respect to laws or institutions, because remote ages widely separated differ much more in their pleasures than they can ever do in their social necessities. To make property safe and life sacred,—that is everywhere a primary purpose of law. But the intellectual amusements of men are so different that the very purposes and elementary functions of these amusements are different. They point to different ends as well as different means. The Drama, for instance, in Greece, connects itself with Religion ; in other ages, Religion is the power most in resistance to the Drama. Hence, and because the elder and ruder ages are most favourable to a ceremonial and mythological religion, we find the tragedy of Greece defunct before the literary age arose. Aristotle's era may be taken as the earliest era of refinement and literary development. But Aristotle wrote his Essay on the Greek Tragedy just a century after the *chefs-d'œuvre* of that tragedy had been published.

If, therefore, it is sometimes requisite for the proper
explanation even of a law or legal usage that we should go
to its history, not looking for a sufficient key to its meaning
in the mere analogies of our own social necessities, much more
will that be requisite in explaining an art or a mode of intellectual pleasure.   Why it was that the ancients had no
landscape painting, is a question deep almost as the mystery
of life, and harder of solution than all the problems of jurisprudence combined.   What causes moulded the Tragedy of
the ancients could hardly be guessed if we did not happen to
know its history and mythologic origin.   And, with respect
to what is called *Style*, not so much as a sketch, as an outline, as a hint, could be furnished towards the earliest speculations upon this subject, if we should overlook the historical
facts connected with its earliest development.

What was it that first produced into this world that
celebrated thing called *Prose*?   It was the bar, it was the
hustings, it was the *Bema* (το βημα).   What Gibbon and
most historians of the Mussulmans have rather absurdly
called the pulpit of the Caliphs should rather be called the
rostrum, the Roman military *suggestus*, or Athenian *bema*.
The fierce and generally illiterate Mohammedan harangued
his troops ; preach he could not ; he had no subject for
preaching.[1]   Now, this function of man in almost all states

---

[1] *" No subject "* :—If he had a subject, what was it ?   As to the
sole doctrines of Islam—the unity of God, and the mission of Mahomet
as his chief prophet (*i.e.* not predictor or foreseer, but interpreter)—
that must be presumed known to every man in a Mussulman army,
since otherwise he could not have been admitted into the army.   But
these doctrines might require expansion, or at least evidence?   Not at
all : the Mussulman believes them incapable of either.   But at least
the Caliph might mount the pulpit in order to urge the primary duty
of propagating the true faith ?   No ; it was *not* the primary duty, it
was a secondary duty ; else there would have been no option allowed
—tribute, death, or conversion.   Well then, the Caliph might ascend
the pulpit for the purpose of enforcing a secondary duty ?   No, he
could not, because that was no duty of time or place ; it was a postu-
late of the conscience at all times alike, and needed no argument or
illustration.   Why, then, what *was* it that the Caliph talked about ?
It was this : He praised the man who had cut most throats ; he pronounced the funeral panegyric of him who had his own throat cut
under the banners of the Prophet; he explained the prudential merits
of the next movement or of the next campaign.   In fact, he did pre-

of society, the function of public haranguing, was, for the
Pagan man who had no printing-press, more of a mere
necessity through every mode of public life than it is for the
modern man of Christian light ; for, as to the modern man
of Mohammedan twilight, his perfect bigotry denies him this
characteristic resource of Christian energies.   Just four
centuries have we of the Cross propagated our light by this
memorable invention ; just four centuries have the slaves
of the Crescent clung to their darkness by rejecting it.
Christianity signs her name ; Islamism makes her mark.
And the great doctors of the Mussulmans take their stand
precisely where Jack Cade took *his* a few years after printing had been discovered.   Jack and they both made it
felony to be found with a spelling-book, and sorcery to deal
with syntax.

Yet, with these differences, all of us alike, Pagan, Mussulman, Christian, have practised the arts of public speaking
as the most indispensable resource of public administration
and of private intrigue.   Whether the purpose were to
pursue the interests of legislation, or to conduct the business
of jurisprudence, or to bring the merits of great citizens
pathetically before their countrymen ; or (if the state were
democratic enough) oftentimes to explain the conduct of the
executive government; oftentimes also to prosecute a scheme
of personal ambition : whether the audience were a mob, a

cisely what Pericles did, what Scipio did, what Cæsar did, what it was a
regular part of the Roman Imperator's commission to do, both before a
battle and after a battle, and universally under any circumstances
which make an explanation necessary.   What is now done in "general
orders" was then committed to a *viva voce* communication.   Trifling
communications probably devolved on the six centurions of each
cohort (or regiment) ; graver communications were reserved to the
Imperator, surrounded by his staff.   Why we should mislead the
student by calling this solemnity of addressing an army from a
tribunal or *suggestus* by the irrelevant name of preaching from a
pulpit can only be understood by those who perceive the false view
taken of the Mohammedan faith and its relation to the human mind.
It was certainly a poor plagiarism from the Judaic and the Christian
creeds ; but it did not rise so high as to conceive of any truth that
needed or that admitted intellectual development, or that was susceptible of exposition and argument.   However, if we will have it that
the Caliph preached, then did his lieutenant say *Amen.*   If Omar was
a parson, then certainly Caled was his clerk.

senate, a judicial tribunal, or an army : equally (though
not in equal degrees) for the Pagan of 2500 years back, and
for us moderns, the arts of public speaking, and consequently of prose as opposed to metrical composition, have
been the capital engine, the one great intellectual machine of
civil life.

This to some people may seem a matter of course.
" Would you have men speak in rhyme ? " We answer that,
when society comes into a state of refinement, the total uses
of language are developed in common with other arts ; but
originally, and whilst man was in his primitive condition of
simplicity, it must have seemed an unnatural, nay an
absurd, thing to speak in prose. For in those elder days
the sole justifying or exciting cases for a public harangue
would be cases connected with impassioned motives. Rare
they would be, as they had need to be, where both the " hon.
gentleman " who moves, and his " hon. friend " who seconds,
are required to speak in Trimeter Iambic. Hence the
necessity that the oracles should be delivered in verse. Who
ever heard of a prose oracle ? And hence, as Grecian taste
expanded, the disagreeable criticisms whispered about in
Athens as to the coarse quality of the verses that proceeded
from Delphi. It was like bad Latin from Oxford. Apollo
himself to turn out of his own temple, in the very age of
Sophocles, such Birmingham hexameters as sometimes
astonished Greece, was like our English court keeping a
Stephen Duck, the thresher, for the national poet-laureate,
at a time when Pope was fixing an era in the literature.
Metre fell to a discount in such learned times. But in itself
metre must always have been the earliest vehicle for public
enunciations of truth among men, for these obvious reasons :
—1. That, if metre rises above the standard of ordinary
household life, so must any truth of importance and singu-
larity enough to challenge a public utterance ; 2. That,
because religious communications will always have taken a
metrical form by a natural association of feeling, whatsoever
is invested with a privileged character will seek something
of a religious sanction by assuming the same external shape ;
and, 3. That expressions, or emphatic verbal forms, which
are naturally courted for the sake of pointed effect, receive a

justification from metre, as being already a departure from common usage to begin with, whereas in plain prose they would appear so many affectations. Metre is naturally and necessarily adopted in cases of impassioned themes, for the very obvious reason that rhythmus is both a cause of impassioned feeling, an ally of such feeling, and a natural effect of it; but upon other subjects, *not* impassioned, metre is also a subtle ally, because it serves to introduce and to reconcile with our sense of propriety various arts of condensation, of antithesis, and other rhetorical effects, which, without the metre (as a key for harmonizing them) would strike the feelings as unnatural or as full of affectation. Interrogations, for example, passionate ejaculations, &c., seem no more than natural when metre (acting as a key) has attuned and prepared the mind for such effects. The metre raises the tone of colouring so as to introduce richer tints without shocking or harshly jarring upon the presiding key, when without this semi-conscious pitching of the expectations the sensibility would have been revolted. Hence, for the very earliest stages of society, it will be mere nature that prompts men to metre ; it is a mode of inspiration, it is a promise of something preternatural ; and less than preternatural cannot be any possible emergency that should call for a public address. Only great truths could require a man to come forward as a spokesman ; he is then a sort of interpreter between God and man.

At first, therefore, it is mere nature which prompts metre. Afterwards, as truth begins to enlarge itself—as truth loses something of its sanctity by descending amongst human details—that mode of exalting it, and of courting attention, is dictated by artifice, which originally was a mere necessity of nature raised above herself. For these reasons, it is certain that men challenging high authentic character will continue to speak by metre for many generations after it has ceased to be a mere voice of habitual impulse. Whatsoever claims an oracular authority will take the ordinary external form of an oracle. And, after it has ceased to be a badge of inspiration, metre will be retained as a badge of professional distinction. Pythagoras, for instance, within five centuries of Christ, Thales or Theognis, will adopt metre out of a

secondary prudence ; Orpheus and the elder Sibyl, out of an
original necessity.

Those people are, therefore, mistaken who imagine that
prose is either a natural or a possible form of composition in
early states of society. It is such truth only as ascends from
the earth, not such as descends from heaven, which can ever
assume an unmetrical form. Now, in the earliest states of
society, all truth that has any interest or importance for
man will connect itself with heaven. If it does not originally come forward in that sacred character, if it does
not borrow its importance from its sanctity, then, by an
inverse order, it will borrow a sanctity from its importance.
Even agricultural truth, even the homeliest truths of rural
industry, brought into connexion with religious inspiration,
will be exalted (like the common culinary utensils in the
great vision of the Jewish prophet) and transfigured into
vessels of glorious consecration. All things in this early
stage of social man are meant mysteriously, have allegoric
values ; and week-day man moves amongst glorified objects.
So that, if any doctrine, principle, or system of truth, should
call for communication at all, infallibly the communication
will take the tone of a revelation ; and the holiness of a
revelation will express itself in the most impassioned form,
perhaps with accompaniments of music, but certainly with
metre.

Prose, therefore, strange as it may seem to say so, was something of a discovery. If not great invention, at least great
courage, would be required for the man who should first
swim without the bladders of metre. It is all very easy
talking when you and your ancestors for fifty generations
back have talked prose. But that man must have had
triplex œs about his *præcordia* who first dared to come forward
with pure prose as the vehicle for any impassioned form of
truth. Even the first physician who dared to lay aside the
ample wig and gold-headed cane needed *extra* courage. All
the Jovian terrors of his traditional costume laid aside, he
was thrown upon his mere natural resources of skill and good
sense. Who was the first lion-hearted man that ventured to
make sail in this frail boat of prose ? We believe the man's
name is reputed to have been Pherecydes. But, as nothing

is less worth remembering than the mere hollow shell of a
name where all the pulp and the kernel is gone, we shall
presume Herodotus to have been the first respectable artist
in prose.   And what was this worthy man's view of prose ?
From the way in which he connected his several books or
" fyttes " with the names of the muses, and from the romantic style of his narratives, as well as from his using a dialect
which had certainly become a poetic dialect in literary
Greece, it is pretty clear that Herodotus stood, and meant to
stand, on that isthmus between the regions of poetry and
blank unimpassioned prose which in modern literature is
occupied by such works as *Mort d'Arthur*.   In Thucydides, we
see the first exhibition of stern philosophic prose.   And, considering the very brief interval between the two writers,—
who stand related to each other, in point of time, pretty
much as Dryden and Pope,—it is quite impossible to look for
the solution of their characteristic differences in the mere
graduations of social development.   Pericles, as a young
man, would most certainly ask Herodotus to dinner, if business or curiosity ever drew that amiable writer to Athens.
As an elderly man, Pericles must often have seen Thucydides
at his levees ; although by that time the sacrifice of his
" social pleasure ill exchanged for power " may have abridged
his opportunity of giving "feeds" to literary men.   But
will anybody believe that the mere advance of social refinement, within the narrow period of one man's public life,
could bring about so marvellous a change as that the friend
of his youth should naturally write very much in the spirit
of Sir John Mandeville,[1] and the friend of his old age like
Machiavel or Gibbon ?   No, no : the difference between
these two writers does not reflect the different aspects of
literary Greece at two eras so slightly removed, too great to
be measured by that scale, as though those of the picturesque Herodotus were a splendid semi-barbarous generation, those of the meditative Thucydides, speculative,
political, experimental ; but we must look to subjective
differences of taste and temperament in the men.   The men,
by nature, and by powerful determination of original

[1] Reputed date of Mandeville's travels about the middle of the
fourteenth century. — M.

sensibility, belong to different orders of intellect. Herodotus was the Froissart of antiquity. He was the man that should have lived to record the crusades. Thucydides, on the other hand, was obviously the Tacitus of Greece, who (had he been privileged to benefit by some metempsychosis dropping him into congenial scenes of modern history) would have made his election for the wars of the French League, or for our Parliamentary war, or for the colossal conflicts which grew out of the French Revolution. The one was the son of nature, fascinated by the mighty powers of chance or of tragic destiny, as they are seen in elder times moulding the form of empires, or training the currents of revolutions. The other was the son of political speculation, delighting to trace the darker agencies which brood in the mind of man— the subtle motives, the combinations, the plots which gather in the brain of " dark viziers " when intrusted with the fate of millions, and the nation-wielding tempests which move at the bidding of the orator.

But these subjective differences were not all. They led to objective differences, by determining each writer's mind to a separate object. Does any man fancy that these two writers imagined, each for himself, the same audience ? Or, again, that each represented his own audience as addressed from the same station ? The earlier of the two, full of those qualities which fit a man for producing an effect as an artist, manifestly comes forward in a theatrical character, and addresses his audience from a theatrical station. Is it readers whom he courts ? No, but auditors. Is it the literary body whom he addresses—a small body everywhere ? No, but the public without limitation. Public ! but what public ? Not the public of Lacedæmon, drunk with the gloomy insolence of self-conceit ; not the public of Athens, amiably vain, courteous, affable, refined ! No : it is the public of universal Hellas, an august congress representing the total civilisation of the earth,—so that of any man not known at Olympia, prince, emperor, whatever he might call himself, if he were not present in person or by proxy, you might warrantably affirm that he was *homo ignorabilis*—a person of whose existence nobody was bound to take notice ; a man to be *ignored* by a grand jury. This representative

champ de Mai Herodotus addressed.   And in what character
did he address it?   What character did he ascribe to the
audience ?   What character did he assume to himself?   Them
he addressed sometimes in their general character of human
beings, but still having a common interest in a central network of civilisation, investing a certain ring-fence, beginning
in Sicily and Carthage, whence it ran round through Libya,
Egypt, Syria, Persia, the Ionian belt or zone, and terminating
in the majestic region of *Men* — the home of liberty, the
Pharos of truth and intellectual power, the very region in
which they were all at that moment assembled.   There was
such a collective body, dimly recognised at times by the
ancients, as corresponds to our modern Christendom, and
having some unity of possible interest by comparison with
the unknown regions of Scythias, Indias, and Ethiopias,
lying in a far wider circle beyond—regions that, from their
very obscurity, and from the utter darkness of their exterior
relations, must at times have been looked to with eyes of
anxiety as permanently harbouring that possible deluge of
savage eruption which, about one hundred and fifty years
after, did actually swallow up the Grecian colony of Bactria
(or Bokhara), as founded by Alexander ; swallowed it so
suddenly and so effectually that merely the blank fact of its
tragical catastrophe has reached posterity.   It was surprised
probably in one night, like Pompeii by Vesuvius, or like the
planet itself by Noah's flood ; or more nearly its fate
resembled those starry bodies which have been seen, traced,
recorded, fixed in longitude and latitude for generations, and
then suddenly are observed to be *missing* by some of our
wandering telescopes that keep watch and ward over the
starry heavens.   The agonies of a perishing world have been
going on, but all is bright and silent in the heavenly host.
Infinite space has swallowed up the infinite agonies.   Perhaps
the only record of Bactria was the sullen report of some
courier from Susa, who would come back with his letters
undelivered, simply reporting that, on reaching such a ferry
on some nameless river, or such an outpost upon a heath, he
found it in possession of a fierce, unknown race, the ancestors
of future Affghans or Tartars.

Such a catastrophe, as menacing by possibility the whole

of civilisation, and under that hypothetical peril as giving
even to Greece herself an interest in the stability even of
Persia, her sole enemy,—a great resisting mass interjacent
between Greece and the unknown enemies to the far north-
east or east,—could not but have mixed occasionally with
Greek anticipations for the future, and in a degree quite
inappreciable by us who know the geographical limits of
Asia. To the ancients, these were by possibility, in a strict
sense, infinite. The terror from the unknown Scythians of
the world was certainly vague and indistinct; but, if that
disarmed the terror or broke its sting, assuredly the very
same cause would keep it alive, for the peril would often
swell upon the eye merely from its uncertain limits. Far
oftener, however, those glorious certainties revolved upon
the Grecian imagination which presented Persia in the
character of her enemy than those remote possibilities which
might connect her as a common friend against some horrid
enemy from the infinite deserts of Asia. In this character
it was that Herodotus at times addressed the assembled
Greece, at whose bar he stood. That the intensity of this
patriotic idea intermitted at times; that it was suffered to
slumber through entire books: this was but an artist's
management which caused it to swell upon the ear all the
more sonorously, more clamorously, more terrifically, when
the lungs of the organ filled once more with breath, when
the trumpet-stop was opened, and the "foudroyant" style of
the organist commenced the hailstone chorus from Marathon.
Here came out the character in which Herodotus appeared.
The *Iliad* had taken Greece as she was during the building
of the first temple at Jerusalem—in the era of David and
Solomon — a thousand years before Christ. The eagle's
plume in her cap at that era was derived from Asia. It was
the Troad, it was Asia, that in those days constituted the
great enemy of Greece. Greece universal had been con-
federated against the Asia of that day, and, after an Iliad of
woes, had triumphed. But now another era of five hundred
years has passed since Troy. Again there has been a universal
war raging between Greece and a great foreign potentate;
again this enemy of Greece is called Asia. But what Asia?
The Asia of the *Iliad* was a petty maritime Asia. But Asia

now means Persia ; and Persia, taken in combination with
its dependencies of Syria and Egypt, means the world, ἡ
οἰκουμένη. The frontier line of the Persian Empire "marched"
or confined with the Grecian ; but now so vast was the revolution effected by Cyrus that, had not the Persians been withheld
by their dismal bigotry from cultivating maritime facilities,
the Greeks must have sunk under the enormous power now
brought to bear upon them. At one blow, the whole territory
of what is now Turkey in Asia,—viz. the whole of Anatolia
and of Armenia,—had been extinguished as a neutral and interjacent force for Greece. At one blow, by the battle of
Thymbra, the Persian armies had been brought nearer by
much more than a thousand miles to the gates of Greece.

That danger it is necessary to conceive, in order to conceive that subsequent triumph. Herodotus—whose family
and nearest generation of predecessors must have trembled,
after the thoughtless insult offered to Sardis, under the
expectation of the vast revenge prepared by the Great King
—must have had his young imagination filled and dilated
with the enormous display of Oriental power, and been thus
prepared to understand the terrific collisions of the Persian
forces with those of Greece. He had heard in his travels
how the glorious result was appreciated in foreign lands.
He came back to Greece with a twofold freight of treasures.
He had two messages for his country. One was a report
of all that was wonderful in foreign lands : all that was
interesting from its novelty or its vast antiquity ; all that was
regarded by the natives for its sanctity, or by foreigners with
amazement as a measure of colossal power in mechanics.
And these foreign lands, we must remember, constituted the
total world to a Greek. Rome was yet in her infant days,
unheard of beyond Italy. Egypt and the other dependencies
of Persia composed the total map south of Greece. Greece,
with the Mediterranean islands, and the eastern side of the
Adriatic, together with Macedon and Thrace, made up the
world of Europe. Asia, which had not yet received the
narrow limitation imposed upon that word by Rome, was
co-extensive with Persia ; and it might be divided into Asia
cis-Tigritana, and Asia trans-Tigritana : the Euxine and the
Caspian were the boundaries to the north ; and to one

advancing further the Oxus was the northern boundary, and the Indus the eastern. The Punjab, as far as the river Sutlege,—that is, up to our present British cantonments at Loodiana,—was indistinctly supposed to be within the jurisdiction of the Great King. Probably he held the whole intervening territory of the late Runjeet Singh, as now possessed by the Sikhs. And beyond these limits all was a mere zodiac of visionary splendour, or a dull repetition of monotonous barbarism.

The report which personal travels enabled Herodotus to make of this extensive region, composing neither more nor less than the total map of the terraqueous globe as it was then supposed to exist (all the rest being a mere Nova Zembla in their eyes), was one of two revelations which the great traveller had to lay at the feet of Greece. The other was a connected narrative of their great struggle with the King of Persia. The earth bisected itself into two parts— Persia and Greece. All that was not Persia was Greece : all that was not Greece was Persia. The Greek traveller was prepared to describe the one section to the other section, and, having done this, to relate in a connected shape the recent tremendous struggle of the one section with the other. Here was Captain Cook fresh from his triple circumnavigation of the world : here was Mungo Park fresh from the Niger and Timbuctoo : here was Bruce fresh from the coy fountains of the Nile : here were Phipps, Franklin, Parry, from the Arctic circle : here was Leo Africanus from Moorish palaces : here was Mandeville from Prester John, and from the Cham of Tartary, and

"From Agra and Lahore of Great Mogul."

This was one side of the medal ; and on the other was the patriotic historian who recorded what all had heard by fractions, but none in a continuous series. Now, if we consider how rare was either character in ancient times, how difficult it was to travel where no passport made it safe, where no preparations in roads, inns, carriages, made it convenient ; that, even five centuries in advance of this era, little knowledge was generally circulated of any region unless so far as it had been traversed by the Roman legions ;

considering the vast credulity of the audience assembled, a
gulf capable of swallowing mountains, and, on the other
hand, that here was a man fresh from the Pyramids and the
Nile, from Tyre, from Babylon and the temple of Belus, a
traveller who had gone in with his sickle to a harvest yet
untouched ; that this same man, considered as a historian,
spoke of a struggle with which the earth was still agitated ;
that the people who had triumphed so memorably in this
war happened to be the same people who were then listening;
that the leaders in this glorious war, whose names had
already passed into spiritual powers, were the fathers of the
present audience: combining into one picture all these circumstances, one must admit that no such meeting between giddy
expectation and the very excess of power to meet its most
clamorous calls is likely to have occurred before or since
upon this earth. Hither had assembled people from the
most inland and most illiterate parts of Greece,—people that
would have settled a pension for life upon any man who
would have described to them so much as a crocodile or
ichneumon. To these people the year of his public recitation
would be the meridian year of their lives. He saw that the
whole scene would become almost a dramatic work of art :
in the mere gratification of their curiosity, the audience
might be passive and neutral ; but in the history of the war
they became almost actors, as in a dramatic scene. This
scenical position could not escape the traveller - historian.
His work was recited with the exaggeration that belongs to
scenic art. It was read probably with gesticulations by one
of those thundering voices which Aristophanes calls a " dam-
nable " voice, from its ear-piercing violence.

Prose is a thing so well known to all of us,—most of our
" little accounts " from shoemakers, dressmakers, &c., being
made out in prose ; most of our sorrows and of our joys
having been communicated to us through prose, and very
few indeed through metre (unless on St. Valentine's day), —
that its further history, after leaving its original Olympic
cradle, must be interesting to everybody. Who were they
that next took up the literary use of Prose ? Confining our
notice to people of celebrity, we may say that the House of
Socrates (*Domus Socratica* is the expression of Horace) were

those who next attempted to popularize Greek prose,—viz. the old gentleman himself, the founder of the concern, and his two apprentices, Plato and Xenophon. We acknowledge a sneaking hatred towards the whole household, founded chiefly on the intense feeling we entertain that all three were humbugs.[1] We own the stony impeachment. Aristotle, who may be looked upon as literary grandson to Socrates, is quite a different person. But for the rest we cherish a sentimental (may we call it a Platonic?) disgust. As relates to the style, however, in which they have communicated their philosophy, one feature of peculiarity is too remarkable to pass without comment. Some years ago, in one of our four or five Quarterly Reviews (*Theological* it was, *Foreign*, or else *Westminster*), a critical opinion was delivered with respect to a work of Coleridge's which opens a glimpse into the true philosophy of prose composition. It was not a very good-natured opinion in that situation, since it was no more true of Coleridge than it is of every other man who adopts the same aphoristic form of expression for his thoughts ; but it was eminently just. Speaking of Coleridge's " Aphorisms," the reviewer observed that this detached and insulated form of delivering thoughts was, in effect, an evasion of all the difficulties connected with composition. Every man, as he walks through the streets, may contrive to jot down an independent thought, a shorthand memorandum of a great truth. So far as that purpose is concerned, even in tumultuous London,

" Puræ sunt plateæ, nihil ut meditantibus obstet."

Standing on one leg you may accomplish this. The labour of composition begins when you have to put your separate threads of thought into a loom ; to weave them into a continuous whole ; to connect, to introduce them ; to blow them out or expand them ; to carry them to a close. All this evil is evaded by the aphoristic form. This one remark, we repeat, lifts up a corner of that curtain which hangs over the difficult subjects of style and composition. Indicating what is *not* in one form, it points to what *is* in others. It was an original remark, we doubt not, to the reviewer.

[1] See *ante*, Vol. VIII, pp. 2-3, and p. 202.—M.

But it is' too weighty and just to have escaped meditative men in former times; and accordingly the very same remark will be found 150 years ago expanded in the *Huetiana*.[1]

But what relation had this remark to the House of Socrates? Did *they* write by aphorisms? No, certainly; but they did what labours with the same radical defect, considered in relation to the true difficulties of composition. Let us dedicate a paragraph to these great dons of literature. If we have any merely English scholars amongst our readers. it may be requisite first to inform them that Socrates himself wrote nothing. He was too much occupied with his talking—" *ambitiosa loquela.*" In this respect Socrates differed, as in some others that we could mention, from the late Mr. Coleridge, who found time both for talking and for writing at the least 25 volumes octavo. From the pupils of Socrates it is that we collect his pretended philosophy; and, as there were only two of these pupils who published, and as one of them intensely contradicts the other, it would be found a hard matter at *Nisi Prius* to extract any verdict as to what it was that constituted the true staple of the Socratic philosophy. We fear that any jury who undertook that question would finally be carted to the bounds of the county, and shot into the adjacent county like a ton of coals. For Xenophon uniformly introduces the worthy henpecked philosopher as prattling innocent nothings, more limpid than small beer; whilst Plato never lets him condescend to any theme less remote from humanity than those of Hermes Trismegistus. One or other must be a liar. And the manner of the philosopher, under these two Boswellian reporters, is not less different than his matter. With Xenophon, he reminds us much of an elderly hen, superannuated a little, pirouetting to " the hen's march," and clucking vociferously; with Plato, he seems much like a deep-mouthed hound in a chase after some unknown but perilous game,—much as such a hound is described by Wordsworth, ranging over the aerial heights of Mount Righi, his voice at times muffled by mighty forests, and then again swelling as he emerges upon the Alpine

---

[1] *Huetiana*, title of a volume published in 1722, containing relics of Peter Daniel Huet (1630-1721), editor of the Delphin classics, &c. —M.

breezes, whilst the vast intervals between the local points from which the intermitting voice ascends proclaim the storm pace at which he travels. In Plato there is a gloomy grandeur at times from the elementary mysteries of man's situation and origin, snatches of music from some older and Orphic philosophy, which impress a vague feeling of solemnity towards the patriarch of the school, though you can seldom trace *his* movement through all this high and vapoury region. You would be happy, therefore, to believe that there had been one word of truth in ascribing such colloquies to Socrates ; but how that can be, when you recollect the philosophic *vappa* of Xenophon, seems to pass the deciphering power of Œdipus.

Now, this body of inexplicable discord between the two evangelists of Socrates, as to the whole sources from which he drew his philosophy, as to the very wells from which he raised it, and the mode of medicating the draught, makes it the more worthy of remark that both should have obstinately adopted the same disagreeable form of composition. Both exhibit the whole of their separate speculations under the form of dialogue. It is always Socrates and Crito, or Socrates and Phædrus, or Socrates and Ischomachus,—in fact, Socrates and some man of straw or good-humoured nine-pin set up to be bowled down as a matter of course. How inevitably the reader feels his fingers itching to take up the cudgels instead of Crito for one ten minutes ! Had *we* been favoured with an interview, we can answer for it that the philosopher should not have had it all his own way ; there should have been a " scratch " at least between us ; and, instead of waiting to see Crito punished without delivering one blow that would "have made a dint in a pound of butter," [1] posterity should have formed a ring about us, crying out " Pull baker, pull devil," according as the accidents of the struggle went this way or that. If dialogue must be the form, at least it should not have been collusive dialogue. Whereas, with Crito and the rest of the men who were in training for the part of disputants, it was a matter of notoriety that, if they presumed to put in a sly thrust under the ribs of the philosopher, the Socratic partisans, οἱ αμφι τον Σωκρατην,

[1] See *ante*, Vol. VII, p. 71, footnote.—M.

would kick them into the kennel. It was a permanent
"cross" that was fought throughout life between Socrates
and his obsequious antagonists.

As Plato and Xenophon must have hated each other with
a theological hatred, it is a clear case that they would not
have harmonized in anything if they had supposed it open to
evasion. They would have got another atmosphere had it
been possible. Diverging from each other in all points
beside, beyond doubt they would have diverged as to this
form of dialogue, had they not conceived that it was essential
to the business of philosophy. It is plain from this one fact
how narrow was the range of conception which the Socratic
school applied to the possible modes of dealing with polemic
truth. They represented the case thus :—Truth, they
fancied, offered itself by separate units, by moments (to
borrow a word from dynamics), by what Cicero calls "apices
rerum" and "punctiunculæ." Each of these must be separately examined. It was like the *items* in a disputed account.
There must be an auditor to check and revise each severally
for itself. This process of auditing could only be carried on
through a brisk dialogue. The philosopher in monologue
was like a champion at a tournament with nobody to face
him. He was a chess-player with no opponent. The game
could not proceed. But how mean and limited a conception
this was, which lay as a basis for the whole Socratic philosophy,
becomes apparent to any man who considers any ample body
of truth, whether polemic truth or not, in all its proportions.
Yet, in all this, we repeat, the Socratic weakness is not
adequately exposed. There is a far larger and subtler class
of cases where the arguments for and against are not susceptible of this separate valuation. One is valid only through
and by a second, which second again is involved in a third ;
and so on. Thus, by way of a brief instance, take all the
systems of Political Economy which have grown up since
Turgot and Quesnel. They are all polemic : that is, all
have moulded themselves in hostility to some other systems ;
all had their birth in opposition. But it would be impossible to proceed Socratically with any one of them. If
you should attempt to examine Ricardo sentence by sentence,
or even chapter for chapter, his apologist would loudly resist

such a process as inapplicable. You must *hold on* ; you must keep fast hold of certain principles until you have time to catch hold of certain others—seven or eight, suppose ; and then from the whole taken in continuation, but not from any one as an insulated principle, you come into a power of adjudicating upon the pretensions of the whole theory. The Doctrine of Value, for example, could you understand that taken apart ? could you value it apart ? As a Socratic logician, could you say of it either *affirmatur* or *negatur*, until you see it coming round and revolving in the doctrines of rent, profits, machinery, &c., which are so many functions of value ; and which doctrines first react with a weight of verification upon the other ?

These, unless parried, are knock-down blows to the Socratic, and therefore to the Platonic, philosophy, if treated as a *modus philosophandi* ; and, if that philosophy is treated as a body of doctrines apart from any *modus* or *ratio docendi*, we should be glad to hear what they are,—for we never could find any whatever in Plato or Xenophon which are insisted on as essential. Accidental hints and casual suggestions cannot be viewed as doctrines in that sense which is necessary to establish a separate school. And all the German Tiedemanns and Tennemanns, the tedious men and the tenpenny-men, that have written their twelve or their eighteen volumes *viritim* upon Plato, will find it hard to satisfy their readers unless they make head against these little objections, because these objections seem to impeach the very *method* of the " Socraticæ Chartæ," and, except as the authors or illustrators of a method, the Socratici are no school at all.

But are not we travelling a little out of our proper field in attacking this method? Our business was with this method considered as a *form of style*, not considered as a *form of logic*. True, O rigorous reader ! Yet digressions and moderate excursions have a licence.[1] Besides which, on strict consideration, doubts arise whether we *have* been digressing ; for whatsoever acted as a power on Greek prose

---

[1] De Quincey betrays his consciousness here that his paper on "Style" has hitherto been rather digressive for a while, and begins to gird himself for more direct effort.—M.

through many ages, whatsoever gave it a bias towards any one characteristic excess, becomes important in virtue of its relations to our subject.   Now, the form of dialogue so obstinately maintained by the earliest philosophers who used prose as the vehicle of their teaching had the unhappy effect of impressing, from the earliest era of Attic literature, a colloquial taint upon the prose literature of that country. The great authority of Socrates, maintained for ages by the windiest of fables, naturally did much to strengthen this original twist in the prose style.   About fifty years after the death of Socrates, the writings of Aristotle were beginning to occupy the attention of Greece ; and in them we see as resolute a departure from the dialogue form as in his elders of the same house the adherence to that form had been servile and bigoted.   His style, though arid from causes that will hereafter be noticed, was much more dignified, or at least more grave and suitable to philosophic speculation, than that of any man before him.   Contemporary with the early life of Socrates was a truly great man, Anaxagoras, the friend and reputed preceptor of Pericles.   It is probable he may have written in the style of Aristotle.   Having great systematic truths to teach, such as solved existing phenomena, and not such as raised fresh phenomena for future solution, he would naturally adopt the form of continuous exposition.   Nor do we at this moment remember a case of any very great man who had any real and novel truth to communicate having adopted the form of dialogue, excepting only the case of Galileo.[1]   Plato, indeed, is *reputed*, and Galileo is known, to have exacted geometry as a qualification in his students,—that is, in those who paid him a δίδακτρον or fee for the privilege of personally attending his conversations ; but he demanded no such qualification in his readers, or else we can assure him that very few copies of his *Opera Omnia* would have been sold in Athens.   This low qualification it was for the readers of Plato, and still more for those of Xenophon, which operated to diffuse the reputation of Socrates.   Besides, it was a rare thing in Greece to see two men sounding the trumpet on behalf of a third ;

[1] Refers to Galileo's Dialogue on the Ptolemaic and Copernican Systems of Astronomy, completed 1632.—M.

and we hope it is not ungenerous to suspect that each
dallied with the same purpose as our Chatterton and
Macpherson,—viz. to turn round on the public when once
committed and compromised by some unequivocal applause
saying "Gentlemen of Athens, this idol Socrates is a phantom
of my brain : as respects the philosophy ascribed to him, *I*
am Socrates,"—or, as Handel (who, in consideration of his
own preternatural appetite, had ordered dinner for six) said
to the astonished waiter when pleading, as his excuse for not
bringing up the dishes, that he waited for the company,—
"Yong man, *I* am de gombany."

But in what mode does the conversational taint which
we trace to the writings of the Socratici, enforced by the
imaginary martyrdom of Socrates, express itself ? In what
forms of language ? By what peculiarities ? By what defects of style ? We will endeavour to explain. One of the
Scaligers (if we remember, it was the elder), speaking of the
Greek article ὁ, ἡ, το, called it *loquacissimæ gentis flabellum.*
Now, *pace superbissimi viri*, this seems nonsense, because the
use of the article was not capricious, but grounded in the
very structure and necessities of the Greek language. Garrulous or not, the poor men were obliged, by the philosophy
of their tongue, to use the article in certain situations ; and,
to say the truth, these situations were very much the same
as in English. Allowing for a few cases of proper names,
participles, or adjectives postponed to their substantives, &c.,
the two general functions of the article definite, equally in
Greek and in English, are : 1*st,* to individualize, as, *e.g.,* "It
is not any sword that will do, I will have *the* sword of my
father"; and, 2*d*, the very opposite function, viz. to generalize
in the highest degree—a use which our best English gram-
mars wholly overlook : as, *e.g.,* "Let *the* sword give way to
the gown"—not that particular sword, but every sword
(where each is used as a representative symbol of the corresponding professions) ; "*The* peasant presses on the kibes
of the courtier" (where the class is indicated by the individual). In speaking again of diseases and the organs
affected, we usually accomplish this generalization by means
of the definite article. We say "He suffered from *a*
headache" ; but also we say "from *the* headache"; and in·

variably we say, " He died of *the* stone," &c. And, though
we fancy it a peculiarity of the French language to say " *Le*
cœur lui était navré de douleur," yet we ourselves say " The
heart was affected in his case." In all these uses of the
definite article there is little real difference between the
Greek language and our own. The main difference is in the
negative use ; in the meaning implied by the absence of the
article, which, with the Greeks, expresses our article *a*, but
with us is a form of generalization. In all this there was
nothing left free to the choice ; and Scaliger had no right to
find any illustration of Greek levity in what was unavoidable.

But what *we* tax as undignified in the Greek prose style,
as a badge of garrulity, as a taint from which the Greek
prose never cleansed itself, are all those forms of lively
colloquialism, with the fretfulness and hurry and demonstrative energy of people unduly excited by bodily presence
and by ocular appeals to their sensibility. Such a style is
picturesque, no doubt. So is the Scottish dialect of low
life as first employed in novels by Sir Walter Scott ; that
dialect greatly assisted the characteristic expression ; it furnished the benefit of a Doric dialect : but what man in his
senses would employ it in a grave work, and speaking in
his own person ? Now, the colloquial expletives so profusely employed by Plato more than anybody, the forms
of his sentences, the forms of his transitions, and other
intense peculiarities of the chattering man as opposed to
the meditating man, have crept over the face of Greek
literature ; and, though some people think everything holy
which is printed in Greek characters, we must be allowed
to rank these forms of expression as mere vulgarities. Sometimes, in Westmoreland, if you chance to meet an ancient
father of his valley,—one who is thoroughly vernacular in
his talk, being unsinged by the modern furnace of revolution,
—you may have a fancy for asking him how far it is to the
next town. In which case you will receive for answer
pretty nearly the following words :—" Why like, it's gaily
nigh like to four mile like." Now, if the pruriency of your
curiosity should carry you to torment and vex this aged
man by pressing a special investigation into this word *like*,
the only result is likely to be that you will kill *him*, and do

yourself no good.   Call it an expletive indeed ! a filling up !
Why to him it is the only indispensable part of the sentence ;
the sole fixture.   It is the balustrade which enables him to
descend the stairs of conversation without falling overboard ;
and, if the word were proscribed by Parliament, he would
have no resource but in everlasting silence.   Now, the expletives of Plato are as gross, and must have been to the
Athenian as unintelligible, as those of the Westmoreland
peasant.   It is true, the value, the effect to the feelings,
was secured by daily use and by the position in the sentence.
But so it is to the English peasant.   *Like* in his use is a
modifying, a restraining, particle, which forbids you to
understand anything in a dangerous unconditional sense.
But then, again, the Greek particle of transition, that eternal
δε, and the introductory formula of μεν and δε !   However
earnestly people may fight for them, because Greek is now
past mending, in fact the δε is strictly equivalent to the
whereby of a sailor : " whereby I went to London ; whereby
I was robbed ; whereby I found the man that robbed me "!
All relations, all modes of succession or transition, are indicated by one and the same particle.   This could arise, even
as a licence, only in the laxity of conversation.   But the
most offensive indication of the conversational spirit as
presiding in Greek prose is to be found in the morbid energy
of oaths scattered over the face of every prose composition
which aims at rhetorical effect.   The literature is deformed
with a constant roulade of " by Jove," " by Minerva," &c.,
as much as the conversation of high-bred Englishmen in the
reign of Charles II.   In both cases this habit belonged to a
state of transition ; and, if the prose literature of Greece had
been cultivated by a succession of authors as extended as
that of England, it would certainly have outworn this badge
of spurious energy.   That it did not is a proof that the Greek
Literature never reached the consummation of art.

PART III

   Reader, you are beginning to suspect us.   " How long
do we purpose to detain people ?"   For anything that

appears we may be designing to write on to the twentieth century,—for twice thirty years. "And *whither* are we going? towards what object?"—which is as urgent a quære as *how far.* Perhaps we may be leading you into treason, or (which indeed is pretty much the same thing) we may be paving the way to "Repeal." You feel symptoms of doubt and restiveness; and, like Hamlet with his father's ghost, you will follow us no further, unless we explain what it is that we are in quest of.[1]

Our course, then, for the rest of our progress,—the outline of our method,—will pursue the following objects. We shall detain you a little longer on the Grecian Prose Literature ; and we shall pursue that Literature within the gates of Latium. What was the Grecian idea of *style*, what the Roman, will appear as a deduction from this review. With respect to the Greeks, we shall endeavour to show that they had not arrived at a full expanded consciousness of the separate idea expressed by *style*; and, in order to account for this failure, we shall point out the deflexion, the bias, which was impressed upon the Greek speculations in this particular by the tendency of their civil life. *That* was made important in the eyes of the speculative critic which was indispensable for the actual practitioner ; *that* was indispensable for the actual practitioner which was exacted by the course of public ambition. The political aspirant, who needed a command of fluent eloquence, sought for so much knowledge (and no more) as promised to be available in his own particular mode of competition. The speculative critic or professional master of rhetoric offered just so much inform-ation (and no more) as was likely to be sought by his clients. Each alike cultivated no more than experience showed him would be demanded. But in Rome, and for a reason perhaps which will appear worth pausing upon, a subtler conception of style was formed, though still far from being perfectly developed. The Romans, whether worse orators or not than the Grecians, were certainly better rhetoricians. And Cicero, the mighty master of language for the Pagan world, whom we shall summon as our wit-ness, will satisfy us that in this research at least the Roman

[1] See previous footnote, p. 185.—M.

intellect was more searching, and pressed nearer to the undiscovered truth, than the Grecian.

From a particular pasage in the *De Oratore*, which will be cited for the general purpose here indicated of proving a closer approximation on the part of Roman thinkers than had previously been made to the very heart of this difficult subject, we shall take occasion to make a still nearer approach for ourselves. We shall endeavour to bring up our reader to the fence, and persuade him, if possible, to take the leap which still remains to be taken in this field of style. But, as we have reason to fear that he will "refuse" it, we shall wheel him round and bring him up to it from another quarter. A gentle touch of the spur may then perhaps carry him over. Let not the reader take it to heart that we here represent him under the figure of a horse, and ourselves in a nobler character as riding him, and that we even take the liberty of proposing to spur him. Anything may be borne in metaphor. Figuratively, one may kick a man without offence. There are no limits to allegoric patience. But no matter who takes the leap, or how ; a leap there is which must be taken in the course of these speculations on style before the ground will be open for absolute advance. Every man who has studied and meditated the difficulties of style must have had a sub-conscious sense of a bar in his way at a particular point of the road thwarting his free movement ; he could not have evaded such a sense but by benefit of extreme shallowness. That bar which we shall indicate must be cleared away, thrown down, or surmounted. And then the prospect will lie open to a new map, and a perfect map, of the whole region. It will then become possible for the first time to overlook the whole geography of the adjacencies. An entire theory of the difficulties being before the student, it will at length be possible to aid his efforts by ample *practical* suggestions. Of these we shall ourselves offer the very plainest, viz. those which apply to the mechanology of style. For these there will be an easy opening ; they will not go beyond the reasonable limits disposable for a single subject in a literary journal. As to the rest, which would (Germanly speaking) require a "strong" octavo for their full exposition, we shall hold ourselves to have done enough in fulfilling the large promise we have made—the promise of marking out for subsequent cultivation and development all the possible subdivisions and sections amongst the resources of the rhetorician, all the powers which he can employ, and therefore all the difficulties which he needs to study,—the arts by which he can profit, and, in correspondence with them, the obstacles by which he will be resisted. Were this done, we should no longer see those incoherent sketches which are now circulating in the world upon questions of taste, of science, of practical address, as applied to the management of style and rhetoric ; the public ear would no longer be occupied by feeble Frenchmen— Rollin, Rapin, Batteux, Bouhours, Du Bos,[1] and *id genus omne* ; nor by the elegant but desultory Blair[2] ; nor by scores of others who bring an occasional acuteness or casual information to this or that subsection of their duty, whilst (taken as general guides) they are universally insufficient. No ; but the business of rhetoric, the management of our mother-tongue in all offices to which it can be applied, would become as much a matter of systematic art, as regular a subject for training and mechanic discipline, as the science of discrete quantity in Arithmetic, or of continuous quantity in Geometry. But will not *that* be likely to impress a character of mechanic monotony upon style, like the miserable attempts at reforming handwriting ? Look at them, touch them, or, if you are afraid of soiling your fingers, hold them up with the tongs ; they reduce all characteristic varieties of writing to one form of blank identity, and *that* the very vilest form of scribbling which exists in Europe— viz. to the wooden scratch (as if traced with a skewer) universally prevailing amongst French people. Vainly would Aldorisius apply his famous art (viz. the art of deciphering a man's character from handwriting) to the villainous scrawls which issue from this modern laboratory of pseudo-caligraphy. All pupils under *these* systems write

[1] Rollin, 1661-1741 ; Rapin, 1661-1725 ; Batteux, 1713-1780 ; Bouhours, 1628-1702 ; Du Bos, 1670-1740.—M.

[2] Dr. Hugh Blair, of the University of Edinburgh ; whose Lectures on Rhetoric and Belles Lettres were published in 1783. He died in 1800.—M.

alike ; the predestined thief is confounded with the patriot
or martyr ; the innocent young girl with the old hag that
watches country waggons for victims.   In the same indistinguishable character, so far as this reforming process is
concerned, would Joseph Hume sign a motion for retrenching
three half-crowns per annum from the orphan daughter of a
man who had died in battle, and Queen Adelaide write a
subscription towards a fresh church for carrying on war,
from generation to generation, upon sin and misery.

Now, if a mechanic system of training for style would
have the same levelling effects as these false caligraphies,
better by far that we should retain our old ignorance.   If
art is to terminate in a killing monotony, welcome the old
condition of inartificial simplicity !   So say you, reader ; ay,
but so say we.   This does not touch *us* : the mechanism *we*
speak of will apply to no meritorious qualities of style, but
to its faults, and, above all, to its awkwardness ; in fact, to
all that now constitutes the *friction* of style, the needless
joltings and retardations of our fluent motion.   As to the
motion itself in all that is positive in its derivation, in its
exciting impulses, in its speed, and its characteristic varieties,
it will remain unaffected.   The modes of human feeling are
inexhaustible ; the forms by which feeling connects itself
with thought are indefeasibly natural ; the channels through
which both impress themselves upon language are infinite.
All these are imperturbable by human art ; they are past
the reach of mechanism ; you might as well be afraid that
some steam-engine—Atlas, suppose, or Samson (whom the
Germans call Simpson)—should perfidiously hook himself to
the earth's axis, and run away with us to Jupiter.   Let
Simpson do his worst ; we defy him.   And so of style : in
that sense under which we all have an interest in its free
movements it will for ever remain free.   It will defy art
to control it.   In that sense under which it ever *can* be
mechanized we have all an interest in wishing that it should
be so.   Our final object therefore is a meritorious one, with
no intermixture of evil.   This being explained, and our
course onwards having been mapped out, let us now proceed
with our work, first recapitulating in direct juxtaposition
with each other the points of our future movement :—

1. Greek and Latin Literature we shall touch on only for the sake of appraising or deducing the sort of ideas which they had upon the subject of style. It will appear that these ideas were insufficient. At the best they were tentative. 2. From them, however, may be derived a hint, a dim suggestion, of the true question in arrear ; and, universally, that goes a great way towards the true answer. *" Dimidium facti,"* says the Roman proverb, *" qui bene cœpit, habet "* : to have made a good beginning is one half of the work. *Prudens interrogatio,* says a wise modern,—to have shaped your question skilfully,—is, in that sense, and with a view to the answer, a good beginning. 3. Having laid this foundation towards an answer, we shall then attempt the answer itself. 4. After which,—that is, after removing to the best of our power such difficulties to the *higher understanding* as beset the subject of style, rhetoric, composition,—having (if we do not greatly delude ourselves) removed the one great bar to a right theory of style, or a practical discipline of style, —we shall leave to some future work of more suitable dimensions the filling up of our outline. Ourselves we shall confine to such instant suggestions—practical, popular, broadly intelligible—as require no extensive preparation to introduce them on the author's part ; no serious effort to understand them on the reader's. Whatever is more than this will better suit with the variable and elastic proportions of a separate book than with the more rigid proportions of a miscellaneous journal.

Coming back, then, for hasty purposes, to Greek Literature, we wish to direct the reader's eye upon a remarkable phenomenon in the history of that literature, and subsequently of all human genius ; not *so* remarkable but that multitudes must have noticed it, and yet remarkable enough to task a man's ingenuity in accounting for it. The earliest known occasion on which this phenomenon drew a direct and strong gaze upon itself was in a little historical sketch composed by a Roman officer during the very opening era of Christianity. We speak of the *Historia Romana*, written and published about the very year of the crucifixion by Velleius Paterculus, in the court of Tiberius Cæsar, the introduction to which presents us with a very interesting

outline of general history.[1]   The style is sometimes clumsy
and unwieldy, but nervous, masculine, and such as became
a soldier.   In higher qualities, in thoughtfulness, and the
spirit of finer observation, it is far beyond the standard of a
mere soldier ; and it shows, in common with many other
indications lying on the face of Roman society at that era,
how profoundly the great struggles that had recently con-
vulsed the world must have terminated in that effect which
followed in the wake of the French Revolution,—viz. in a
vast stimulation to the meditative faculties of man.   The
agitation, the frenzy, the sorrow of the times, reacted upon
the human intellect, and forced men into meditation.   Their
own nature was held up before them in a sterner form.
They were compelled to contemplate an ideal of man far
more colossal than is brought forward in the tranquil aspects
of society ; and they were often engaged, whether they would
or not, with the elementary problems of social philosophy.
Mere danger forced a man into thoughts which else were
foreign to his habits.   Mere necessity of action forced him
to decide.   Such changes went along with the Reformation ;
such changes went along with the French Revolution ; such
changes went along with the great recasting of Roman society
under the two earliest Cæsars.   In every page of Paterculus
we read the swell and agitation of waters subsiding from a
deluge.   Though a small book, it is tumid with revolutionary
life.   And something also is due, no doubt, to the example
of the mighty leader in the Roman Revolution, to the intellectual and literary tastes diffused by him—

"The foremost man of all this world"—

who had first shown the possibility of uniting the military
leader's truncheon with the most brilliant *stylus* of the
rhetorician.   How wonderful and pleasing to find such
accomplishments of accurate knowledge, comprehensive reading and study, combined with so searching an intellect, in
a man situated as Paterculus, reared amongst camps, amidst

[1] C. Velleius Paterculus, born about B.C. 19, died about A.D. 31.
See *ante*, p. 163.   His *Historia Romana*, a brief compendium in two
books, comes down to A.D. 30.—M.

the hurry of forced marches, and under the privations of solitary outposts ! The old race of hirsute centurions how changed, how perfectly regenerated, by the influence of three Cæsars in succession applying a paternal encouragement to Literature !

Admiring this man so much, we have paused to review the position in which he stood. Now, recurring to that remark (amongst so many original remarks) by which, in particular, he connects himself with our subject, we may venture to say that, if it were a very just remark for *his* experience, it is far more so for ours. What he remarked, what he founded upon a review of two nations and two literatures, we may now countersign by an experience of eight or nine. His remark was upon the tendency of intellectual power to gather in clusters,—its unaccountable propensity (he thought it such) to form into separate insulated groups. This tendency he illustrates first in two cases of Grecian literature. Perhaps that might have been an insufficient basis for a general theory. But it occurred to Paterculus in confirmation of his doctrine that the very same tendency had reappeared in his native literature. The same phenomenon had manifested itself, and more than once, in the history of Roman intellect ; the same strong *nisus* of great wits to gather and crystallize about a common nucleus. That marked gregariousness in human genius had taken place amongst the poets and orators of Rome which had previously taken place amongst the poets, orators, and artists of Greece. What importance was attached by Paterculus to this interesting remark, what stress he laid upon its appreciation by the reader, is evident from the emphatic manner in which he introduces it, as well as from the conscious disturbance of the symmetry which he incurs rather than suppress it. These are his words :—" Notwithstanding that " this section of my work has considerably outrun the pro- " portions of that model which I had laid down for my " guidance, and although perfectly aware that, in circumstances " of hurry so unrelenting, which, like a revolving wheel or " the eddy of rapid waters, allows me no respite or pause, I " am summoned rather to omit what is necessary than to court " what is redundant: still, I cannot prevail on myself to

" forbear from uttering and giving a pointed expression to a " thought which I have often revolved in my mind, but " to this hour have not been able satisfactorily to account " for in theory (*nequeo tamen temperare mihi quin rem sæpe* " *agitatam animo meo, neque ad liquidum ratione perductam,* " *signem stylo*)." Having thus bespoke the reader's special attention, the writer goes on to ask if any man can sufficiently wonder on observing that eminent genius in almost every mode of its development (*eminentissima cujusque professionis ingenia*) had gathered itself into the same narrow ring-fence of a single generation. Intellects that in each several department of genius were capable of distinguished execution (*cujusque clari operis capacia ingenia*) had sequestrated themselves from the great stream and succession of their fellowmen into a close insulated community of time, and into a corresponding stage of proficiency measured on their several scales of merit [1] (*in similitudinem et temporum et profectuum semetipsa ab aliis separaverunt*). Without giving *all* the exemplifications by which Paterculus has supported this thesis, we shall cite two : *Una* (*neque multorum annorum spatio divisa*) *ætas per divini spiritus viros, Æschylum, Sophoclem, Euripidem, illustravit Tragœdiam.* Not that this trinity of poets was *so* contemporary as brothers are ; but they were contemporary as youthful uncles in relation to elderly nephews : Æschylus was viewed as a senior by Sophocles, Sophocles by Euripides ; but all might by possibility have met together (what a constellation !) at the same table. Again, says Paterculus, *Quid ante Isocratem,*

---

[1] Paterculus, it must be remembered, was composing a peculiar form of history, and, therefore, under a peculiar law of composition. It was designed for a rapid survey of many ages within a very narrow compass, and unavoidably pitched its scale of abstraction very high. This justified a rhetorical, almost a poetic, form of expression ; for in such a mode of writing, whether a writer seeks that effect or not, the abrupt and almost lyrical transitions, the startling leaps over vast gulfs of time and action, already have the effect of impassioned composition. Hence, by an instinct, he becomes rhetorical : and the natural character of his rhetoric, its pointed condensation, often makes him obscure at first sight. We, therefore, for the merely English reader, have a little expanded or at least brought out his meaning. But, for the Latin reader, who will enjoy his elliptical energy, we have sometimes added the original words.

quid post ejus auditores, clarum in oratoribus fuit ? Nothing
of any distinction in oratory *before* Isocrates, nothing *after*
his personal audience. So confined was that orbit within
which the perfection of Greek tragedy, within which the
perfection of Greek eloquence, revolved. The same law, the
same strong tendency, he insists, is illustrated in the different
schools of Greek comedy, and again of Greek philosophy.
Nay, it is more extensively illustrated amongst Greek artists
in general : *Hoc idem evenisse grammaticis, plastis, pictoribus,
scalptoribus, quisquis temporum institerit notis reperiet.*"

From Greece Paterculus translates the question to his
own country in the following pointed manner : summing up
the whole doctrine, and re-affirming it in a form almost
startling and questionable by its rigour : " *Adeo arctatum
angustiis temporum,*" so punctually concentrated was all merit
within the closest limits of time, " *ut nemo memoria dignus
alter ab altero videri nequiverint* " : no man of any consideration
but he might have had ocular cognisance of all others in his
own field who attained to distinction. He adds : " *Neque hoc
in Græcis quam in Romanis evenit magis.*"

His illustrations from the Roman Literature we do not
mean to follow : one only, as requisite for our purpose, we
cite :—" *Oratio, ac vis forensis, perfectumquæ prosæ eloquentiæ
decus (pace P. Crassi et Gracchorum dixerim) ita universa sub
principe operis sui erupit Tullio ut mirari neminem possis nisi
aut ab illo visum aut qui illum viderit.*" This is said with
epigrammatic point : the perfection of prose and the
brilliancy of style as an artificial accomplishment, was so
identified with Cicero's generation that no distinguished
artist, none whom you could greatly admire, but might be
called his contemporary : none so much his senior but Cicero
might have seen *him* ; none so much his junior but *he*
might have seen Cicero. It is true that Crassus, in Cicero's
infancy, and the two Gracchi, in the infancy of Crassus
(neither of whom, therefore, could have been seen by Cicero),
were memorably potent as orators, — in fact, for tragical
results to themselves (which, by the way, was the universal
destiny of great *Roman* orators) ; and nobody was more
sensible of their majestic pretensions, merely as orators, than
Cicero himself, who has accordingly made Crassus and

Antony predominant speakers in his splendid dialogues *De Oratore*. But they were merely demoniac powers, not artists. And, with respect to these early orators (as also with respect to some others, whose names we have omitted), Paterculus has made a special reservation. So that he had not at all overlooked the claims of these great men ; but he did not feel that any real exception to his general law was created by orators who were indeed wild organs of party rage or popular frenzy, but who wilfully disdained to connect themselves with the refinements of literature. Such orators did not regard themselves as intellectual, but as political, powers. Confining himself to oratory, and to the perfection of prose composition, written or spoken, in the sense of great literary accomplishments, beginning in natural power but perfected by art, Paterculus stands to his assertion that this mode of human genius had so crowded its development within the brief circuit of Cicero's life (threescore years and three) as that the total series of Roman Orators formed a sort of circle, centering in that supreme orator's person, such as in modern times we might call an electrical circle,—each link of the chain having been either electrified by Cicero or having elecrified *him.* Seneca, with great modesty, repeats the very same assertion in other words : " *Quicquid Romana facundia habuit quod insolenti Græciæ aut opponat aut præferat circa Ciceronem effloruit.*" A most ingenuous and self-forgetting homage in him ; for a nobler master of thinking than himself Paganism has not to show, nor, when the cant of criticism has done its worst, a more brilliant master of composition. And, were his rule construed literally, it would exclude the two Plinys, the two Senecas, Tacitus, Quintilian, and others, from the matricula of Roman eloquence. Not one of these men could have seen Cicero ; all were divided by more than one generation ; and yet, most unquestionably, though all were too reasonable to have fancied themselves any match for the almighty orator in public speaking, not one but was an equally accomplished artist in written composition, and under a law of artificial style far more difficult to manage.

However, with the proper allowances for too unmodified a form of expression, we must allow that the singular phenom-

enon first noticed by Paterculus, as connecting itself with
the manifestations of human genius, is sufficiently established
by so much of human history as even he had witnessed.
For, if it should be alleged that political changes accounted
for the extinction of oral eloquence concurrently with the
death of Cicero, still there are cases more than enough even
in the poetry of both Greece and Rome, to say nothing of the
arts, which bear out the general fact of human genius coming
forward by insulated groups and clusters ; or, if Pagan ages
had left that point doubtful, we have since witnessed
Christian repetitions of the truth on the very widest scale.
The Italian age of Leo X, in the fifteenth century, the
French age of Louis XIV, in the seventeenth century, the
German age commencing with Kant, Wieland, Goethe, in the
eighteenth and nineteenth centuries, all illustrate the tendency to these intermitting paroxysms of intellectual energy.
The lightning and the storm seem to have made the circuit
of the whole European heavens, to have formed vortices
successively in every civilized land, and to have discharged
themselves by turns from every quarter of the atmosphere.
In our own country there have been three such gatherings of
intellectual power : 1st, The age of Shakspere, Spenser, and
the great school of dramatists that were already dying out in
the latter days of Ben Jonson (1636), and were finally extinguished by the great civil commotions beginning in 1642 ;
2dly, The age of Queen Anne and George I. ; 3dly, The age
commencing with Cowper, partially roused perhaps by the
American War, and afterwards so powerfully stimulated (as
was the corresponding era of Kant and Wieland) by the
French Revolution.   This last volcanic eruption of the
British genius has displayed enormous power and splendour.
Let malice and the base detraction of contemporary jealousy
say what it will, greater originality of genius, more expansive
variety of talent, never was exhibited than in our own
country since the year 1793.   Every mode of excellence,
except only dramatic excellence (in which we have nothing
modern to place by the side of Schiller's *Wallenstein*), has
been revealed in dazzling lustre.   And he that denies it,
may he be suffocated by his own bilious envy !

But the point upon which we wish to fix the reader's

attention in citing this interesting observation of the Roman
officer, and the reason for which we have cited it at all, is
not so much for the mere fact of these spring-tides occurring
in the manifestations of human genius, intermitting pulses
(so to speak) in human energies, as the psychological peculiarity which seems to affect the cycle of their recurrences.
Paterculus occupies himself chiefly with the *causes* of such
phenomena ; and one main cause he suggests as lying in the
emulation which possesses men when once a specific direction
has been impressed upon the public competitions. This no
doubt is one of the causes. But a more powerful cause
perhaps lies in a principle of union than in any principle of
division amongst men,—viz. in the principle of sympathy.
The great Italian painters, for instance, were doubtless
evoked in such crowds by the action of this principle. To
hear the buzz of idolizing admiration settling for years upon
particular works of art and artists kindles something better
than merely the ambition and rivalship of men ; it kindles
feelings happier and more favourable to excellence, viz.
genial love and comprehension of the qualities fitted to stir
so profound and lasting an emotion. This contagion of
sympathy runs electrically through society, searches high and
low for congenial powers, and suffers none to lurk unknown
to the possessor. A vortex is created which draws into its
suction whatever is liable to a similar action. But, not to
linger upon this question of causes, what we wish to place
under the reader's eye is rather the peculiar type which
belongs to these revolutions of national intellect, according to
the place which each occupies in the order of succession.
Possibly it would seem an over-refinement if we were to
suggest that the odd terms in the series indicate creative
energies, and the even terms reflective energies ; and we are
far enough from affecting the honours of any puerile hypothesis. But, in a general way, it seems plausible and reasonable that there will be alternating successions of power in
the first place, and next of reaction upon that power from
the reflective faculties. It does seem natural that first of all
should blossom the energies of creative power, and in the
next era of the literature, when the consciousness has been
brightened to its own agencies, will be likely to come forward

the re-agencies of the national mind on what it has created
The period of meditation will succeed to the period of production.   Or, if the energies of creation are again partially
awake, finding themselves forestalled as regards the grander
passions, they will be likely to settle upon the feebler elements
of manners.   Social differences will now fix the attention by
way of substitute for the bolder differences of nature.   Should
a third period, after the swing of the pendulum through an
arch of centuries, succeed for the manifestation of the national
genius, it is possible that the long interval since the inaugural
era of creative art will have so changed all the elements of
society and the aspects of life as to restore the mind to much
of its infant freedom ; it may no longer feel the captivity of
an imitative spirit in dealing with the very same class of
creations as exercised its earliest powers.   The original
national genius may now come forward in perfectly new forms
without the sense of oppression from inimitable models.   The
hoar of ages may have withdrawn some of these models from
active competition.   And thus it may not be impossible that
oscillations between the creative and reflective energies of
the mind might go on through a cycle of many ages.

In our own literature we see this scheme of oscillations
illustrated.   In the Shakspere period we see the fulness of
life and the enormity of power throwing up a tropical
exuberance of vegetation.   A century afterwards we see a
generation of men lavishly endowed with genius, but partly
degraded by the injurious training of a most profligate era
growing out of great revolutionary convulsions, and partly
lowered in the tone of their aspirations by a despair of rival-
ling the great creations of their predecessors.   We see them
universally acquiescing in humbler modes of ambition ;
showing sometimes a corresponding merit to that of their
greatest forefathers, but merit (if sometimes equal) yet equal
upon a lower scale.   *Thirdly,* In the eighteenth and nineteenth centuries we see a new birth of original genius, of
which it is not lawful to affirm any absolute inferiority even
by comparison with the Shaksperian age of Titans.   For
whatsoever is strictly and thoroughly original, being *sui
generis,* cannot be better or worse than any other model of
excellence which is also original.   One animal structure

compared with another of a different class is equally good and perfect. One valley which is no copy of another, but has a separate and peculiar beauty, cannot be compared for any purpose of disadvantage with another. One poem which is composed upon a law of its own, and has a characteristic or separate beauty of its own, cannot be inferior to any other poem whatsoever. The class, the order, may be inferior ; the scale may be a lower one ; but the individual work, the degree of merit marked upon the scale must be equal, if only the poem is equally original. In all such cases understand, ye miserable snarlers at contemporary merit, that the puerile *goût de comparaison* (as La Bruyère calls it) is out of place ; universally you cannot affirm any *imparity* where the ground is preoccupied by *disparity*. Where there is no parity of principle there is no basis for comparison.

Now, passing, with the benefit of these explanations, to Grecian Literature, we may observe that there were in that field of human intellect no more than two developments of power from first to last. And, perhaps, the unlearned reader (for it is to the praise and honour of a powerful journal that it has the unlearned equally with the learned amongst its readers) will thank us for here giving him, in a very few words, such an account of the Grecian Literature in its periods of manifestation, and in the relations existing between these periods, that he shall not easily forget them.

There were, in illustration of the Roman aide-de-camp's [1]

[1] " *The Roman aide-de-camp's* " :—Excuse, reader, this modern phrase : by what other is it possible to express the relation to Tiberius, and the military office about his person, which Paterculus held on the German frontier ? In the 104th chapter of his second book he says— " *Hoc tempus me, functum ante tribunatu castrorum, Tib. Cæsaris militem fecit* " ; which in our version is—" This epoch placed me, who had previously discharged the duties of camp-marshal, upon the staff of Cæsar." And he goes on to say that, having been made a brigadier-general of cavalry (*alæ præfectus*) under a commission which dated from the very day of Cæsar's adoption into the Imperial house and the prospect of succession,—so that the two acts of grace ran concurrently, —thenceforwards "per annos continuos IX præfectus aut legatus, spectator, et pro captu mediocritatis meæ adjutor, fui " ; or, as I beg to translate, " through a period of nine consecutive years from this date, I acted either as military lieutenant to Cæsar, or as ministerial secretary" (such we hold to be the true virtual equivalent of *præfectus*;

doctrine, two groups or clusters of Grecian wits, two depositions or stratifications of the national genius ; and these were
about a century apart.   What makes them specially remem-
berable is the fact that each of these brilliant clusters had
gathered separately about that man as central pivot who,
even apart from this relation to the literature, was otherwise
the leading spirit of his age.   It is important for our purpose
—it will be interesting, even without that purpose, for the
reader—to notice the distinguishing character or marks by
which the two clusters are separately recognised ; the marks
both personal and chronological.   As to the personal distinctions, we have said that in each case severally the two men
who offered the nucleus to the gathering happened to be
otherwise the most eminent and splendid men of the period.
Who were they ?   The one was PERICLES, the other was
ALEXANDER OF MACEDON.   Except Themistocles, who may
be ranked as senior to Pericles by just one generation (or
thirty-three years),[1] in the whole deduction of Grecian annals

---

i.e., speaking fully, of *præfectus prætorio*), " acting simultaneously as
inspector of the public works " (bridges and vast fortifications on the
north-east German frontier), "and (to the best capacity of my slender
faculties) as his personal aide-de-camp."   Possibly the reader may
choose to give a less confined or professional meaning to the word
adjutor.   But, in apology, we must suggest two cautions to him : 1st,
That elsewhere Paterculus does certainly apply the term as a military
designation, bearing a known technical meaning ; and, 2d, That this
word *adjutor*, in other non-military uses, as for instance on the stage,
had none *but* a technical meaning.

[1] This is too much to allow for a generation in those days, when
the average duration of life was much less than at present ; but, as an
exceedingly convenient allowance (*since thrice 33⅓ is just equal to a
century*) it may be allowedly used in all cases not directly bearing on
technical questions of civil economy.   Meantime, as we love to suppose
ourselves in all cases as speaking *virginibus puerisque,*—who, though
reading no man's paper throughout, may yet often read a page or a
paragraph of every man's,—we, for the chance of catching their eye in
a case where they may really gain in two minutes an ineradicable
conspectus of the Greek Literature (and for the sake of ignorant
people universally, whose interests we hold sacred), add a brief explanation of what is meant by *a generation*.   Is it meant or imagined that
in so narrow a compass as 33 years + 4 months the whole population
of a city, or a people, could have died off ?   By no means : not under
the lowest value of human life.   What is meant is—that a number
equal to the whole population will have died : not X, the actual

no other public man, statesman, captain-general, administrator of the national resources, can be mentioned as approaching to these two men in splendour of reputation, or even in real merit. Pisistratus was too far back ; Alcibiades, who might (chronologically speaking) have been the son of Pericles, was too unsteady and (according to Mr. Coleridge's coinage) " unreliable," or, perhaps in more correct English, too " *unrelyuponable.*"

Thus far our purpose prospers. No man can pretend to forget two such centres as Pericles for the elder group, or Alexander of Macedon (the "strong he-goat" of Jewish prophecy) for the junior. Round these two *foci,* in two different but adjacent centuries, gathered the total starry heavens—the galaxy, the Pantheon—of Grecian intellect. All that Greece produced of awful solemnity in her tragic stage, of riotous mirth and fancy in her comic stage, of power in her eloquence, of wisdom in her philosophy ; all that has since tingled in the ears of twenty-four centuries of her prosperity in the arts, her sculpture, her architecture, her painting, her music ; everything, in short, excepting only her higher mathematics, which waited for a further development which required the incubation of the musing intellect for yet another century, revolved like two neighbouring planetary systems about these two solar orbs. Two mighty vortices, Pericles and Alexander the Great, drew into strong eddies about themselves all the glory and the pomp of Greek literature, Greek eloquence, Greek wisdom, Greek art. Next,

population, but a number equal to X. Suppose the population of Paris 900,000. Then, in the time allowed for one generation, 900,000 will have died : but then, to make up that number, there will be 300,000 furnished, not by the people now existing, but by the people who *will be born* in the course of the 33 years. And thus the balloting for death falls only upon two out of three whom at first sight it appears to hit. It falls not exclusively upon X, but upon X + Y : this latter quantity Y being a quantity flowing concurrently with the lapse of the generation. Obvious as this explanation is, and almost childish, to every man who has even a tincture of political arithmetic, it is so far from being generally obvious that, out of every thousand who will be interested in learning the earliest revolutions of literature, there will not be as many as ten who will know, even conjecturally, what is meant by a generation. Besides infinite other blunders and equivocations, many use an *age* and *a generation* as synonymous, whilst by *siècle* the French *uniformly* mean a *century.*

that we may still more severely search the relations in all
points between the two systems, let us assign the chronological
locus of each, because that will furnish another element
towards the exact distribution of the chart representing the
motion and the oscillations of human genius.   Pericles had
a very long administration.   He was Prime Minister of
Athens for upwards of one entire generation.   He died in
the year 429 before Christ, and in a very early stage of that
great Peloponnesian War which was the one sole intestine
war for Greece, affecting *every* nook and angle in the land.
Now, in this long public life of Pericles, we are at liberty to
fix on *any* year as his chronological *locus*.   On good reasons,
not called for in this place, we fix on the year 444 before
Christ.   This is too remarkable to be forgotten.   *Four, four,
four*, what at some games of cards is called a "*prial*" (we
presume, by an elision of the first vowel *a*, for *parial*), forms
an era which no man can forget.   It was the fifteenth year
before the death of Pericles, and not far from the bisecting
year of his political life.   Now, passing to the other system,
the *locus* of Alexander is quite as remarkable, as little liable
to be forgotten when once indicated, and more easily determined, because selected from a narrower range of choice.
The exact chronological *locus* of Alexander the Great is 333
years before Christ.   Everybody knows how brief was the
career of this great man : it terminated in the year 320 before
Christ.   But the *annus mirabilis* of his public life, the most
effective and productive year throughout his oriental anabasis,
was the year 333 before Christ.   Here we have another
"*prial*," a prial of threes, for the *locus* of Alexander, *if
properly corrected*.

Thus far the elements are settled, the chronological
longitude and latitude of the two great planetary systems
into which the Greek Literature breaks up and distributes
itself : 444 and 333 are the two central years for the two
systems ; allowing, therefore, an interspace of 111 years
between the *foci* of each.   It is thought by some people
that all those stars which you see glittering so restlessly on
a keen frosty night in a high latitude, and which seem to
have been sown broadcast with as much carelessness as
grain lies on a threshing-floor,—here showing vast zaarrahs

of desert blue sky, there again lying close and to some eyes presenting

"The beauteous semblance of a flock at rest,"—

are in fact all gathered into zones or *strata* ; that our own wicked little earth (with the whole of our peculiar solar system) is a part of such a zone, and that all this perfect geometry of the heavens, these radii in the mighty wheel, would become apparent if we, the spectators, could but survey it from the true centre,—which centre may be far too distant for any vision of man, naked or armed, to reach. However that may be, it is most instructive to see how many apparent scenes of confusion break up into orderly arrangement when you are able to apply an *a priori* principle of organization to their seeming chaos. The two vortices of the Greek Literature are now separated ; the chronological *loci* of their centres are settled. And next we request the reader thoughtfully to consider who *they* are of whom the elder system is composed.

In the centre, as we have already explained, is Pericles, the great practical statesman, and that orator of whom (amongst so many that vibrated thunderbolts) it was said peculiarly that he thundered and lightened as if he held this Jovian attribute by some individual title. We spare you Milton's magnificent description from the *Paradise Regained* of such an orator "wielding at will that fierce democracy," partly because the closing line in its reference "to *Macedon* and Artaxerxes' throne," too much points the homage to Demosthenes, but still more because by too trivial a repetition of splendid passages a serious injury is done to great poets.[1] Passages of great musical effect, metrical

---

[1] The passage, however, may be quoted here, if only for the recovery of the exact original form of one of the words in Milton's own text :—

"Thence to the famous Orators repair,
Those ancient whose resistless eloquence
Wielded at will that fierce democraty,
Shook the Arsenal, and fulmined over Greece
To Macedon and Artaxerxes' throne."

P. R., iv. 267-271.

De Quincey's insinuated doubt as to the merits of Demosthenes is characteristic.—M

bravuras, are absolutely vulgarized by too perpetual a
parroting; and the care of Augustus Cæsar *ne nomen suum
obsolefieret*,[1] that the majesty of his name should not be
vulgarized by bad poets, is more seriously needed in our
days on behalf of great poets, to protect them from trivial
or too parrot-like a citation.

Passing onwards from Pericles, you find that all the rest
in *his* system were men in the highest sense creative, absolutely setting the very first examples, each in his peculiar
walk of composition; themselves without previous models,
and yet destined every man of them to become models for
all after-generations; themselves without fathers or mothers,
and yet having all posterity for their children.   First come
the three men *divini spiritus*, under a heavenly afflatus,
Æschylus, Sophocles, Euripides, the creators of Tragedy out
of a village mummery; next comes Aristophanes, who
breathed the breath of life into Comedy; then comes the
great philosopher, Anaxagoras, who first theorised success-
fully upon man and the world.   Next come, whether great
or not, the still more *famous* philosophers, Socrates, Plato,
Xenophon; then comes, leaning upon Pericles, as sometimes
Pericles leaned upon *him*, the divine artist, Phidias[2]; and

---

[1] The oddest feature in so odd a business was that Augustus committed this castigation of bad poets to the police; but whence the police
were to draw the skill for distinguishing between good poets and bad
is not explained.   The poets must have found their weak minds somewhat astonished by the sentences of these reviewers—sitting like our
Justices in Quarter Sessions, and deciding perhaps very much in the
same terms; treating an Ode, if it were too martial, as a breach of the
peace; directing an Epic poet to find security for his good behaviour
during the next two years; and, for the writers of Epithalamia on
imperial marriages, ordering them "to be privately whipped and discharged."   The whole affair is the more singular as coming from one
who carried his *civilitas*, or show of popular manners, even to affectation.   Power, without the invidious exterior of power, was the object
of his life.   Ovid seems to have noticed his inconsistency in this
instance by reminding him that even Jupiter did not disdain to furnish
a theme for panegyric.

[2] "*Phidias*":—That he was as much of a creative power as the
rest of his great contemporaries, that he did not merely take up or
pursue a career already opened by others, is pretty clear from the
state of Athens, and of the forty marble quarries which he began to
lay under contribution.   The quarries were previously unopened; the
city was as yet without architectural splendour.

behind this immortal man walk Herodotus and Thucydides.
What a procession to Eleusis would these men have formed !
what a frieze, if some great artist could arrange it as
dramatically as Chaucer has arranged the *Pilgrimage to
Canterbury* !

It will be granted that this is unmasking a pretty strong
battery of great guns for the Athens of Pericles. Now, let
us step on a hundred years forward. We are now within
hail of Alexander ; and a brilliant consistory of Grecian men
that is by which *he* is surrounded. There are now exquisite
masters of the more refined comedy ; there are, again, great
philosophers, for all the great schools are represented by
able successors ; and, above all others, there is the one philosopher who played with men's minds (according to Lord
Bacon's comparison) as freely as ever his princely pupil
with their persons—there is Aristotle. There are great
orators, and, above all others, there is that orator whom
succeeding generations (wisely or not) have adopted as the
representative name for what is conceivable in oratorical
perfection—there is Demosthenes. Aristotle and Demosthenes are in themselves bulwarks of power ; many hosts lie
in those two names. For artists, again, to range against
Phidias, there is Lysippus the sculptor, and there is Apelles
the painter ; for great captains and masters of strategic art,
there is Alexander himself, with a glittering *cortége* of
general officers, well qualified to wear the crowns which
they will win, and to head the dynasties which they will
found. Historians there are now, as in that former age ;
and, upon the whole, it cannot be denied that the " turn-
out" is showy and imposing.

Before coming to that point,—that is, before comparing
the second "deposit" (geologically speaking) of Grecian
genius with the first,—let us consider what it was (if anything) that connected them. Here, reader, we would wish
to put a question. Saving your presence, Did you ever see
what is called a dumb-bell ? We have ; and know it by
more painful evidence than that of sight.

You, therefore, O reader ! if personally cognisant of dumb-
bells, we will remind,—if not, we will inform,—that it is a
cylindrical bar of iron or lead issuing at each end in a globe

of the same metal, and usually it is sheathed in green baize; but, perfidiously so, if that covering is meant to deny or to conceal the fact of those heart-rending thumps which it inflicts upon one's too confiding fingers every third *ictus*. By the way, we have a vague remembrance that the late Mr. Thurtell, the same who was generally censured for murdering the late Mr. Weare, once in a dark lobby attempted to murder a friend by means of a dumb-bell; in which he showed his judgment,—we mean in his choice of tools,—for otherwise, in attempting to murder his friend, he was to blame.[1] Now, reader, it is under this image of the dumb-bell we couch an allegory. Those globes at each end are the two systems or separate clusters of Greek Literature; and that cylinder which connects them is the long man that ran into each system, binding the two together. Who was that? It was Isocrates. *Great* we cannot call him in conscience; and, therefore, by way of compromise, we call him *long*,—which, in one sense, he certainly was; for he lived through four-and-twenty Olympiads, each containing four solar years. He narrowly escaped being a hundred years old; and, though that did not carry him from centre to centre, yet, as each system might be supposed to protend a radius each way of twenty years, he had, in fact, a full personal cognisance (and pretty equally) of the two systems, remote as they were, which composed the total world of Grecian Genius. Two circumstances have made this man interesting to all posterity; so that people the most remote and different in character (Cicero, for instance, and Milton) have taken a delight in his memory. One is, that the school of rhetoric in Athens, which did not finally go down till the reign of Justinian, and therefore lasted above 940 years without interruption, began with *him*. He was, says Cicero, *De Orat.*, "pater eloquentiæ"; and elsewhere he calls him "communis magister oratorum." True, he never practised himself, for which he had two reasons: "My lungs," he tells us himself, "are weak"; and, secondly, "I am naturally, as well as upon

[1] John Thurtell, hanged at Hertford in January 1824 for the murder of Mr. William Weare. De Quincey recurs to the story of this once famous murder more at large, and to the particular of the dumb-bell, in his *Murder considered as one of the Fine Arts.*—M.

principle, a coward." There he was right. A man would never have seen twenty-four Olympiads who had gone about brawling and giving "jaw" as Demosthenes and Cicero did. You see what *they* made of it. The other feature of interest in this long man is precisely that fact, viz. that he *was* long. Everybody looks with kindness upon the snowy-headed man who saw the young prince Alexander of Macedon within four years of his starting for Persia, and personally knew most of those that gave lustre to the levees of Pericles. Accordingly, it is for this quality of length that Milton honours him with a touching memorial; for Isocrates was "that old man eloquent" of Milton's sonnet whom the battle of Chæronea, "fatal to liberty, killed with report."[1] This battle, by which Philip overthrew the last struggles of dying independence in Greece, occurred in the year 338 before Christ. Philip was himself assassinated two years later. Consequently, had Isocrates pulled out, like caoutchouc or Indian rubber, a little longer, he might have seen the silver shields, or Macedonian life-guards, embarking for Persia. In less than five years from that same battle, "fatal to liberty," Alexander was taking fatal liberties with Persia, and "tickling the catastrophe" of Darius. There were just seventy good years between the two expeditions,—the Persian anabasis of Cyrus the younger, and the Persian anabasis of Alexander; but Isocrates knew personally many officers and *savans*[2] in both.

[1] "As that dishonest victory
At Chæronea, fatal to liberty,
Killed with report that old man eloquent."
MILTON—Sonnet X.—M.

[2] "Officers and *savans*":—Ctesias held the latter character, Xenophon united both, in the earlier expedition. These were friends of Isocrates. In the latter expedition, the difficulty would have been to find the man, whether officer or *savant*, who was *not* the friend of Isocrates. Old age such as his was a very rare thing in Greece; a fact which is evident from a Greek work surviving on the subject of Macrobiotics : few cases occur beyond seventy. This accident, therefore, of longevity in Isocrates must have made him already one of the standing lions in Athens for the last twenty-six years of his life; while, for the last seventy, his professorship of rhetoric must have brought him into connexion with every great family in Greece. One thing puzzles us,—what he did with his money : for he must have made a great deal. He had two prices ; for he charged high to those

Others, beside Cicero and Milton, have taken a deep interest in Isocrates,—and, for the very circumstance we have been noticing, his *length*, combined with the accident of position which made that length effective in connecting the twofold literature of Greece. Had he been " *long* " in any other situation than just in that dreary desert between the oasis of Pericles and the oasis of Alexander, what good would that have done us ? " A wounded snake " or an Alexandrine verse, that " drags its slow length along," would have been as useful. But he, feeling himself wanted, laid his length down like a railroad exactly where he could be useful — with his positive pole towards Pericles and his negative pole towards Alexander. Even Gibbon—even the frosty Gibbon—condescends to be pleased with this seasonable application of his two termini : " Our sense," says he, in his 40th chapter, " of the dignity of human nature is exalted [1] by the simple recollection that Isocrates was the companion of Plato and Xenophon,—that he assisted, perhaps

who could afford it ; and why not ? people are not to learn the art of prating for nothing, Yet, being a teetotaller and a coward, how could he spend his money ? That question is vexatious. However, this one possibility in the long man's life will for ever make him interesting : he might have seen, and it is even probable that he *did* see Xenophon *dis*mount from some horse which he had stolen at Trebizond on his return from the Cyrus expedition ; and he might also have seen Alexander mount for Chæronea. Alexander was present at that battle, and personally joined in a charge of cavalry. It is not impossible that he may have ridden Bucephalus.

[1] " *Is exalted* " :—The logic of Gibbon may seem rather cloudy. Why should it exalt our sense of human dignity that Isocrates was the youthful companion of Plato or Euripides and the aged companion of Demosthenes ? It ought, therefore, to be mentioned that, in the sentence preceding, he had spoken of Athens as a city that " condensed within the period of a single life the genius of ages and millions." The condensation is the measure of the dignity ; and Isocrates, as the " single life " alluded to, is the measure of the condensation. That is the logic. By the way, Gibbon ought always to be cited by the *chapter*. The page and volume of course evanesce with many forms of publication, whilst the chapter is *always* available ; and, in the commonest form of twelve volumes, becomes useful in a second function, as a guide to the particular volume ; for six chapters, with hardly any exception (*if* any) are thrown into each volume. Consequently, the 40th chapter, standing in the seventh series of sixes, indicates the seventh volume.

with the historian Thucydides, at the first representations of
the Œdipus of Sophocles and the Iphigenia of Euripides."
So far in relation to the upper terminus of the long man ;
next, with reference to the lower terminus, Gibbon goes on :
" And that his pupils, Æschines and Demosthenes, contended
for the *crown* of patriotism in the presence of Aristotle, the
master of Theophrastus, who taught at Athens with the
founders of the Stoic and Epicurean sects."

Now then, reader, you have arrived at that station from
which you overlook the whole of Greek Literature, as a few
explanations will soon convince you. Where is Homer,
where is Hesiod ? you ask ; where is Pindar ? Homer and
Hesiod lived a thousand years B.C., or, by the lowest com-
putations, near nine hundred. For anything that we know,
they may have lived with Tubal Cain. At all events, they
belong to no power or agency that set in motion the age of
Pericles, or that operated on that age. Pindar, again, was a
solitary emanation of some unknown influences at Thebes,
more than five hundred years before Christ. He may be
referred to the same era as Pythagoras. These are all that
can be cited *before* Pericles.

Next, for the ages *after* Alexander, it is certain that
Greece proper was so much broken in spirit by the loss of
her *autonomy* dating from that era as never again to have
rallied sufficiently to produce a single man of genius,—not
one solitary writer who acted as a power upon the national
mind. Callimachus was nobody, and not decidedly Grecian.
Theocritus, a man of real genius in a limited way, is a
Grecian in that sense only according to which an Anglo-
American is an Englishman. Besides that, one swallow
does not make a summer. Of any other writers, above all
others of Menander, apparently a man of divine genius,
we possess only a few wrecks ; and of Anacreon, who must
have been a poet of original power, we do not certainly know
that we have even any wrecks. Of those which pass under
his name, not merely the authorship, but the era, is very
questionable indeed. Plutarch and Lucian, the unlearned
reader must understand, both belong to *post*-Christian ages.
And, for all the Greek emigrants who may have written histories, such as we now value for their matter more than for

their execution, one and all they belong too much to Roman civilisation that we should ever think of connecting them with native Greek literature.[1] Polybius in the days of the second Scipio, Dion Cassius and Appian in the acme of Roman civility, are no more Grecian authors because they wrote in Greek than the Emperor Marcus Antoninus, or Julian, were other than Romans because, from monstrous coxcombry, they chose to write in Greek their barren memoranda. As well might Gibbon be thought not an Englishman, or Leibnitz not a German, because the former, in composing the first draft of his essay on literature, and the latter in composing his *Theodicée*, used the French language. The motive in all these cases was analogous : amongst the Greek writers it was the affectation of reaching a particular body of educated men, a learned class, to the exclusion of the uninstructed multitude. With the affectors of French the wish was to reach a particular body of thinkers, with whose feelings they had a special sympathy from

---

[1] Excepting fragmentary writers,—Sappho and Simonides, and the contributors to the Greek Anthologies (which, however, next after the scenic literature, offer the most interesting expressions of Greek household feeling),—we are not aware of having omitted in this rapid review any one name that could be fancied to be a weighty name, excepting that of Lycophron. Of him we will say a word or two :—The work by which he is known is a monologue or dramatic scene from the mouth of one single speaker ; this speaker is Cassandra the prophetic daughter of Priam. In about 1500 Iambic lines (the average length of a Greek tragedy) she pours forth a dark prophecy with respect to all the heroes engaged in the Trojan War, typifying their various unhappy catastrophes by symbolic images which should naturally be intelligible enough to us who know their several histories, but which (from the particular selection of accidents or circumstances used for the designation of the persons) read like riddles without the aid of a commentator. This prophetic gloom, and the impassioned character of the many woes arising notoriously to the conquerors as well as the conquered in the sequel of the memorable war, give a colouring of dark power to the Cassandra of Lycophron. Else we confess to the fact of not having been much impressed by the poem. We read it in the year 1809, having been told that it was the most difficult book in the Greek language. This is the popular impression, but a very false one. It is not difficult at all as respects the language (allowing for a few peculiar Lycophrontic words) ; the difficulty lies in the allusions, which are *intentionally* obscure. Lycophron did as we now do in eclipses—he *smoked* the glass through which he gazed.

personal habituation of their society, and to whose prejudices, literary or philosophic, they had adapted their train
of argument.

No ; the Greek Literature ends at the point we have
fixed, viz. with the era of Alexander. No power, no heart-
subduing agency, was ever again incarnated in any book,
system of philosophy, or other model of creative energy,
growing upon Grecian soil or from Grecian roots. Creation
was extinct ; the volcano was burnt out. What books
appeared at scattered intervals during the three centuries
still remaining before the Christian era lie under a reproach,
pretty general, which perhaps has not been perceived. From
the titles and passing notices of their objects, or mode of
dealing with their objects, such as we derive from Cicero and
many others, it is evident that they were merely professional
books, text-books for lectures addressed to students, or polemic
works addressed to competitors. Chairs of Rhetoric and
Philosophy had now been founded in Athens. A great
University, the resort of students from all nations, was established, and, in a sense sufficient to insure the perpetual
succession of these corporate bodies, was endowed. Books,
therefore, and labouring with the same two opposite defects
as are unjustly charged upon the schoolmen of the middle
ages,—viz. dulness from absolute monotony, and visionariness
from the aerial texture of the speculations,—continued to be
written in discharge of professional obligations, or in pursuit
of professional interest. The *summum bonum* was discussed
until it had become the capital affliction of human patience,
the *summum malum* of human life. Beyond these there was
no literature ; and these products of dreaming indolence,
which terminated in making the very name of Greek philosopher and Greek rhetorician a jest and byword amongst the
manlier Romans, no more constituted a literature than a
succession of academic studies from the pupils of a royal
institution can constitute a school of fine art.

Here, therefore, at this era of Alexander, 333 B.C.,—
when every Greek patriot had reason to say of his native
literature " *Venimus ad summum fortunœ*," We have seen the
best of our days,—we must look for the Greek ideas of style,
and the Greek theories of composition, in the uttermost

development that either *could* have received. In the earlier
system of Greek intellectual strength, in the era of Pericles,
the powers of style would be most comprehensively exercised.
In the second system, in the era of Alexander, the light of
conscious recognition and direct examination would be most
effectually applied. The first age furnished the power ; the
second furnished the science. The first brought the concrete
model, the second brought the abstracting skill ; and between
them the whole compass of Greek speculation upon this
point would be brought to a focus. Such being the state of
preparation, what was the result ?

Part IV

" *Such being the state of preparation, what was the result ?* "
These words concluded our last essay. There had been two
manifestations or bright epiphanies of the Grecian intellect,
revelations in two separate forms : the first having gathered
about Pericles in the year 444 B.C., the second about Alexander the Great in 333 B.C. ; the first being a pure literature
of creative power, the second in a great measure of reflective
power ; the first fitted to call out the differences of style, the
second to observe, classify, and discuss them. Under these
circumstances of favourable preparation, what had been the
result ? Where style exists in strong colouring as a practice
or art, we reasonably expect that style should soon follow as
a theory, as a science explaining that art, tracing its varieties,
and teaching its rules. To use ancient distinctions, where
the "*rhetorica utens*" has been cultivated with eminent success
(as in early Greece it had) it is but natural to expect many
consequent attempts at a "*rhetorica docens.*" And especially
it is natural to do so in a case where the theorizing intellect
had been powerfully awakened. What, therefore, we ask
again, had been in fact the result ?

We must acknowledge that it had fallen far below the
reasonable standard of our expectations. Greece, it is true,
produced a long series of works on rhetoric, many of which,
though not easily met with,[1] survive to this day ; and one

---

[1] "*Not easily met with*" :—From Germany we have seen reprints
of some eight or nine ; but once only, so far as our bibliography

which stands first in order of time, viz. the great work of
Aristotle, is of such distinguished merit that some eminent
moderns have not scrupled to rank it as the very foremost
legacy in point of psychological knowledge which Pagan
Literature has bequeathed to us. Without entering upon so
large a comparison as that, we readily admit the commanding
talent which this work displays. But it is under an equivocal
use of the word "rhetoric" that the *Rhetoric* of Aristotle
could ever have been classed with books treating of style.
There is in fact a complex distinction to which the word
Rhetoric is liable. 1st, it means the *rhetorica utens*, as when
we praise the rhetoric of Seneca or Sir Thomas Browne, not
meaning anything which they taught, but something which
they practised,—not a doctrine which they delivered, but a
machinery of composition which they employed. 2dly, it
means the *rhetorica docens*, as when we praise the Rhetoric of
Aristotle or Hermogenes, writers far enough from being
rhetorical by their own style of writing, but writers who
professedly taught others to be rhetorical. 3dly, the *rhetorica
utens* itself is subdivided into two meanings, so wide apart
that they have very little bearing on each other : one being
applied to the art of persuasion, the dexterous use of plausible
topics for recommending any opinion whatever to the favour
of an audience (this is the Grecian sense universally) ; the
other being applied to the art of composition, the art of
treating any subject ornamentally, gracefully, affectingly.
There is another use of the word rhetoric distinct from all
these, and hitherto, we believe, not consciously noticed ; of
which at some other time.[1]

Now, this last subdivision of the word rhetoric, viz.
"Rhetoric considered as a practising art, *rhetorica utens*,"—
which is the sense exclusively indicated by our modern use
of the term, — is not at all concerned in the Rhetoric of

extends, were the whole body published collectively. This was at the
Aldine press in Venice more than three centuries ago. Such an
interval, and so solitary a publication, sufficiently explain the non-
familiarity of modern scholars with this section of Greek Literature.
[The most complete account of the Rhetoric of the Greeks and Romans
even to this day is a product of German scholarship : viz. Volkmann's
Rhetorik der Griechen und Römer, published in 1872.—M.]

[1] See *ante*, pp. 82-85 and 92-93, footnotes.—M.

Aristotle. It is rhetoric as a mode of moral suasion, as a technical system for obtaining a readiness in giving to the false a colouring of plausibility, to the doubtful a colouring of probability, or in giving to the true, when it happens to be obscure, the benefit of a convincing exposition,—this it is which Aristotle undertakes to teach, and not at all the art of ornamental composition. In fact, it is the whole body of public *extempore* speakers whom he addresses, not the body of deliberate writers in any section whatever. And, therefore, whilst conceding readily all the honour which is claimed for that great man's Rhetoric, by this one distinction as to what it was that he meant by Rhetoric, we evade at once all necessity for modifying our general proposition,—viz. that style in our modern sense, as a theory of composition, as an art of constructing sentences and weaving them into coherent wholes, was not effectually cultivated amongst the Greeks. It was not so well understood, nor so distinctly contemplated in the light of a separate accomplishment, as afterwards among the Romans. And we repeat that this result from circumstances *prima facie* so favourable to the very opposite result is highly remarkable. It is *so* remarkable that we shall beg permission to linger a little upon those features in the Greek Literature which most of all might seem to have warranted our expecting from Greece the very consummation of this delicate art. For these same features, which would separately have justified that expectation, may happen, when taken in combination with others, to account for its disappointment.

There is, then, amongst the earliest phenomena of the Greek Literature, and during its very inaugural period, one which of itself and singly furnishes a presumption for expecting an exquisite investigation of style. It lies in the fact that two out of the three great tragic poets carried his own characteristic quality of style to a morbid excess,—to such an excess as should force itself, and in fact *did* force itself, into popular notice. Had these poets all alike exhibited that sustained and equable tenor of tragic style which we find in Sophocles, it is not probable that the vulgar attention would have been fixed by its character. Where a standard of splendour is much raised, provided all parts are simultaneously raised on the same uniform scale, we know by repeated experience in many modes of display, whether in dress, in architecture, in the embellishment of rooms, &c., that this raising of the standard is not perceived with much vivacity, and that the feelings of the spectator are soon reconciled to alterations that are harmonized. It is always by some want of uniformity, some defect in following out the scale, that we become roused to conscious observation of the difference between this and our former standards. We exaggerate these differences in such a case as much as we undervalue them in a case where all is symmetrical. We might expect, therefore, beforehand, that the opposite characteristics as to style of Æschylus and Euripides would force themselves upon the notice of the Athenian populace ; and, in fact, we learn from the Greek scholiasts on these poets that this effect did really follow. These scholiasts, indeed, belong to a later age. But we know by traditions which they have preserved, and we know from Aristotle himself, the immediate successor of the great tragic poets (indirectly we know also from the stormy ridicule of Aristophanes, who may be viewed as contemporary with those poets), that Æschylus was notorious to a proverb amongst the very mob for the stateliness, pomp, and towering character of his diction, whilst Euripides was equally notorious not merely for a diction in a lower key, more household, more natural, less elaborate, but also for cultivating such a diction by study and deliberate preference. Having such great models of contrasting style to begin with, having the attention converged upon these differences by the furious merriment of Aristophanes, less than a Grecian wit would have felt a challenge in all this to the investigation of style, as a great organ of difference between man and man, between poet and poet.

But there was a more enduring reason in the circumstances of Greece for entitling us to expect from her the perfect theory of style. It lay in those accidents of time and place which obliged Greece to spin most of her speculations, like a spider, out of her own bowels. Now, for such a kind of literature style is, generally speaking, paramount ; for a literature less self-evolved style is more liable to

neglect.   Modern nations have laboured under the very
opposite disadvantage.   The excess of external materials
has sometimes oppressed their creative power, and sometimes
their meditative power.   The exuberance of *objective* know
ledge—that knowledge which carries the mind to materials
existing *out* of itself, such as natural philosophy, chemistry,
physiology, astronomy, geology, where the mind of the
student goes for little and the external object for much—has
had the effect of weaning men from subjective speculation,
where the mind is all in all and the alien object next to
nothing, and in that degree has weaned them from the
culture of style.   Now, on the other hand, if you suppose a
man in the situation of Baron Trenck at Spandau, or Spinoza
in the situation of Robinson Crusoe at Juan Fernandez, or a
contemplative monk of the thirteenth century in his cell,
you will perceive that—unless he were a poor feeble-minded
creature like Cowper's Bastille prisoner, thrown by utter
want of energy upon counting the very nails of his dungeon
in all permutations and combinations—rather than quit the
external world, he must in his own defence, were it only as
a relief from gnawing thoughts, cultivate some *subjective*
science ; that is, some branch of knowledge which, drawing
everything from the mind itself, is independent of external
resources.   Such a science is found in the relations of man to
God,—that is in theology ; in the determinations of space,--
that is in geometry ; in the relations of existence or being
universally to the human mind,—otherwise called metaphysics or ontology ; in the relations of the mind to itself,—
otherwise called logic.   Hence it was that the scholastic
philosophy evolved itself, like a vast spider's loom, between
the years 1100 and 1400.   Men shut up in solitude, with
the education oftentimes of scholars, with a life of leisure,
but with hardly any books, and no means of observation,
were absolutely forced, if they would avoid lunacy from
energies unoccupied with any object, to create an object out
of those very energies : they were driven by mere pressure of
solitude, and sometimes of eternal silence, into raising vast
aerial Jacob's ladders of vapoury metaphysics, just as endless
as those meteorologic phenomena which technically bear that
name, just as sublime and aspiring in their tendency

upwards, and sometimes (but not always) just as unsub-
stantial. In this present world of the practical and the
ponderable, we so little understand or value such abstractions, though once our British schoolmen took the lead in
these subtleties, that we confound their very natures and
names. Most people with us mean by metaphysics what is
properly called psychology. Now, these two are so far from
being the same thing that the former could be pursued (and,
to say the truth, was, in fact, under Aristotle created) by the
monk in his unfurnished cell, where nothing ever entered
but moonbeams. Whereas psychology is but in part a
subjective science ; in some proportion it is also *objective*,
depending on multiplied experience, or on multiplied records
of experience. Psychology, therefore, *could* not have been
cultivated extensively by the schoolmen, and in fact would
not have been cultivated at all but for the precedent of
Aristotle. He, who laid the foundation of their metaphysics,
which have nothing to do with man, had also written a work
on man,—viz. on the human soul,—besides other smaller
works on particular psychological phenomena (such as dreaming). Hence, through mere imitation, arose the short
sketches of psychology amongst the schoolmen. Else *their*
vocation lay to metaphysics, as a science which can dance
upon moonbeams ; and that vocation arose entirely out of
their circumstances,—solitude, scholarship, and no books.
Total extinction there was for them of all objective materials,
and therefore, as a consequence inevitable, reliance on the
solitary energies of their own minds. Like Christabel's
chamber lamp, and the angels from which it was suspended,
all was the invention of the unprompted artist,—

" All made out of the carver's brain."

Models he had none before him, for printed books were yet
sleeping in futurity, and the gates of a grand asceticism were
closed upon the world of life. We moderns, indeed, fancy
that the necessities of the Romish Church—the mere
instincts of self-protection in Popery—were what offered
the bounty on this air-woven philosophy ; and partly that is
true ; but it is most certain that all the bounties in this
world would have failed to operate effectually, had they not

met with those circumstances in the silent life of monasteries
which favoured the growth of such a self-spun metaphysical
divinity.   Monastic life predisposed the restlessness of
human intellect to move in that direction.   It was one of
the few directions compatible with solitude and penury of
books.   It was the only one that opened an avenue at once
to novelty and to freedom of thought.   Now, then, precisely
what the monastic life of the schoolmen was in relation to
Philosophy, the Greece of Pericles had been in relation to
Literature.   What circumstances, what training, or predis-
posing influences existed for the monk in his cell, the same
(or such as were tantamount) existed for the Grecian wit in
the atmosphere of Athens.   Three great agencies were at
work, and unconsciously moulding the efforts of the earliest
schoolmen about the opening of the Crusades, and of the
latest some time after their close ;—three analogous agencies,
the same in virtue, though varied in circumstances, gave
impulse and guidance to the men of Greece, from Pericles, at
the opening of Greek literature, to Alexander of Macedon,
who witnessed its second harvest.   And these agencies were :
—1st, Leisure in excess, with a teeming intellect ; the
burden, under a new-born excitement, of having nothing to
do.   2d, Scarcity, without an absolute famine, of books ;
enough to awake the dormant cravings, but not enough to
gratify them without personal participation in the labours of
intellectual creation.   3d, A revolutionary restlessness, produced by the recent establishment of a new and growing
public interest.

The two first of these agencies for stimulating intellects
already roused by agitating changes are sufficiently obvious ;
though few perhaps are aware to what extent idleness prevailed in Pagan Greece, and even in Rome, under the system
of household slavery, and under the bigoted contempt of
commerce.   But, waiving that point, and for the moment
waiving also the degree of scarcity which affected books at
the era of Pericles, we must say one word as to the two great
analogous public interests which had formed themselves
separately, and with a sense of revolutionary power, for the
Greeks on the one hand, and for the Schoolmen on the other.
As respected the Grecians, and especially the Athenians, this

excitement lay in the sentiment of nationality which had been first powerfully organised by the Persian War. Previously to that war the sentiment no doubt smouldered obscurely ; but the oriental invasion it was which kindled it into a torrent of flame. And it is interesting to remark that the very same cause which fused and combined these scattered tribes into the unity of Hellas, viz. their common interest in making head against an awful invader, was also the cause which most of all separated them into local parties by individual rivalship and by characteristic services. The arrogant Spartan, mad with a French-like self-glorification, boasted for ever of his little Thermopylæ. Ten years earlier the far sublimer display of Athenian Marathon, to say nothing of after-services at Salamis or elsewhere, had placed Attica at the summit of the Greek family. No matter whether selfish jealousy would allow that pre-eminence to be recognised ; doubtless it was felt. With this civic pre-eminence arose concurrently for Athens the development of an intellectual pre-eminence. On this we need say nothing. But even here, although the pre-eminence was too dazzling to have been at any time overlooked, yet, with some injustice in every age to Athens, her light has been recognised, but not what gave it value,—the contrasting darkness of all around her. This did not escape Paterculus, whose understanding is always vigilant. " We talk," says he, " of *Grecian* eloquence " or *Grecian* poetry, when we should say *Attic* ; for who has " ever heard of Theban orators, of Lacedæmonian artists, or " Corinthian poets ? " [1] Æschylus, the first great author of Athens (for Herodotus was not Athenian), personally fought in the Persian War. Consequently the two modes of glory for Athens were almost of simultaneous emergence. And what we are now wishing to insist on is that precisely by

[1] People will here remind us that Aristotle was half a foreigner, being born at Stagira in Macedon. Ay, but amongst Athenian emigrants, and of an Athenian father ! His mother, we think, was Thracian. The crossing of races almost uniformly terminates in producing splendour, at any rate energy, of intellect. If the roll of great men, or at least of energetic men, in Christendom were carefully examined, it would astonish us to observe how many have been the children of mixed marriages,—*i.e.* of alliances between two bloods as to nation, although the races might originally have been the same.

and through this great unifying event, viz. the double inroad of Asia militant upon Greece, Greece first became generally and reciprocally known to Greece herself; that Greece was then first arranged and *cast*, as it were dramatically, according to her capacities, services, duties; that a general consciousness was then diffused of the prevailing relations in which each political family stood to the rest; and that in the leading states every intellectual citizen drew a most agitating excitement from the particular character of glory which had settled upon his own tribe, and the particular station which had devolved upon it amongst the champions of civilisation.

That was the *positive* force acting upon Athens. Now, reverting to the monkish schoolmen, in order to complete the parallel, what was the corresponding force acting upon *them*? Leisure and want of books were accidents common to both parties,—to the scholastic age and to the age of Pericles. These were the *negative* forces, concurring with others to sustain a movement once begun, but incapable of giving the original impulse. What was the active, the *affirmative*, force which effected for the scholastic monks that unity and sense of common purposes which had been effected for the Greeks by the sudden development of a Grecian interest opposed to a Persian,—of a civilized interest, under sudden peril, opposed to the barbarism of the universal planet? What was there, for the race of monkish schoolmen labouring through three centuries, in the nature of a known palpable interest, which could balance so grand a principle of union and of effort as this acknowledged guardianship of civilisation had suddenly unfolded, like a banner, for the Greeks during the infancy of Pericles?[1] What *could* there be of corresponding grandeur?

Beforehand, this should have seemed impossible: but, in reality, a far grander mode of interest had arisen for the

---

[1] It is well to give unity to our grandest remembrances by connecting them, as many as can be, with the same centre. Pericles died in the year 429 before Christ. Supposing his age to be fifty-six, he would then be born about 485 B.C.,—that is, five years after the first Persian invasion under Darius, five years before the second under Xerxes.

schoolmen : grander, because more indefinite; more indefinite, because spiritual.   It was this :—The Western or
Latin Church had slowly developed her earthly power.   As
an edifice of civil greatness throughout the western world,
she stood erect and towering.   In the eleventh century,
beyond all others, she had settled her deep foundations.
The work thus far was complete ; but blank civil power,
though indispensable, was the feeblest of her arms, and,
taken separately, was too frail to last, besides that it was
liable to revolutions.   The authority by which chiefly she
ruled, had ruled, and hoped to rule, was spiritual ; and, with
the growing institutions of the age, embodying so much of
future resistance, it was essential that this spiritual influence
should be founded on a subtle philosophy, difficult to learn,
difficult to refute ; as also that many dogmas already established, such as tradition by way of prop to infallibility,
should receive a far ampler development.   The Latin Church,
we must remember, was not yet that Church of Papal Rome,
in the maturity of its doctrines and its pretensions, which
it afterwards became.   And, when we consider how vast a
benefactress this Church had been to early Christendom
when moulding and settling her foundations, as also in what
light she must have appeared to her own pious children in
centuries where as yet only the first local breezes of opposition had begun to whisper amongst the Albigenses, &c., we
are bound in all candour to see that a sublimer interest could
not have existed for any series of philosophers than the profound persuasion that by marrying metaphysics to divinity,
two sciences even separately so grand, and by the pursuit of
labyrinthine truth, they were building up an edifice reaching
to the heavens,—the great spiritual fortress of the Catholic
Church.

Here let us retrace the course of our speculations, lest the
reader should suppose us to be wandering.

First, for the sake of illustrating more vividly the influences which acted on the Greece of Pericles, we bring
forward another case analogously circumstanced, as moulded
by the same causes :—1. The same condition of intellect
under revolutionary excitement ; 2. The same penury of
books ; 3. The same chilling gloom from the absence of

female charities,—the consequent reaction of that oppressive
ennui which Helvetius fancied, amongst all human agencies,
to be the most potent stimulant for the intellect ; 4. The
same (though far different) enthusiasm and elevation of thought
from disinterested participation in forwarding a great movement of the age : for the one side involving the glory of their
own brilliant country and concurrent with civilisation ; for
the other, co-extensive with all spiritual truth and all spiritual
power.

Next, we remark that men living permanently under such
influences must, of mere necessity, resort to that order of
intellectual pursuits which requires little aid *ab extra,*—that
order, in fact, which philosophically is called "subjective,"
as drawing much from our own proper selves, or little (if
anything) from extraneous objects.

And then, thirdly, we remark that such pursuits are
peculiarly favourable to the culture of style. In fact they
force that culture. A man who has absolute facts to communicate from some branch of study external to himself, as
physiology, suppose, or anatomy, or astronomy, is careless of
style ; or at least he may be so, because he is independent of
style, for what he has to communicate neither readily admits,
nor much needs, any graces in the mode of communication ;
the matter transcends and oppresses the manner. The
matter tells without any manner at all. But he who has to
treat a vague question, such as Cicero calls a *quæstio infinita,*
where everything is to be finished out of his own peculiar
feelings, or his own way of viewing things (in contradistinction to a *quæstio finita,* where determinate *data* from without
already furnish the main materials), soon finds that the
manner of treating it not only transcends the matter, but
very often, and in a very great proportion, *is* the matter.
In very many subjective exercises of the mind,—as, for
instance, in that class of poetry which has been formally
designated by this epithet (meditative poetry, we mean, in
opposition to the Homeric, which is intensely objective), the
problem before the writer is to project his own inner mind ;
to bring out consciously what yet lurks by involution in
many unanalysed feelings ; in short, to pass through a prism
and radiate into distinct elements what previously had been

even to himself but dim and confused ideas intermixed with each other. Now, in such cases, the skill with which detention or conscious arrest is given to the evanescent, external projection to what is internal, outline to what is fluxionary, and body to what is vague,—all this depends entirely on the command over language as the one sole means of embodying ideas ; and in such cases the style, or, in the largest sense, *manner*, is confluent with the matter. But, at all events, even by those who are most impatient of any subtleties, or what they consider " metaphysical " distinctions, thus much must be conceded : viz. that those who rest upon external facts, tangible realities, and circumstantial details,—in short, generally upon the *objective*, whether in a case of narration or of argument,—must for ever be less dependent upon style than those who have to draw upon their own understandings and their own peculiar feelings for the furniture and matter of their composition. A single illustration will make this plain. It is an old remark, and, in fact, a subject of continual experience, that lawyers fail as public speakers in the House of Commons. Even Erskine, the greatest of modern advocates, was nobody as a senator ; and the " fluent Murray," two generations before him, had found his fluency give way under that mode of trial. But why? How was it possible that a man's fluency in one chamber of public business should thus suddenly be defeated and confounded in another ? The reason is briefly expressed in Cicero's distinction between a *quæstio finita* and a *quæstio infinita*. In the courts of law, the orator was furnished with a brief, an abstract of facts, downright statements upon oath, circumstances of presumption, and, in short, a whole volume of topics external to his own mind. Sometimes, it is true, the advocate would venture a little out to sea *proprio marte* : in a case of *crim. con.*, for instance, he would attempt a little picture of domestic happiness drawn from his own funds. But he was emboldened to do this from his certain knowledge that in the facts of his brief he had always a hasty retreat in case of any danger that he should founder. If the little picture prospered, it was well : if not, if symptoms of weariness began to arise in the audience, or of hesitation in himself, it was but to cut the matter short, and return to the *terra firma* of his brief,

when all again was fluent motion.   Besides that, each separate
transition, and the distribution of the general subject, offered
themselves spontaneously in a law case ; the logic was given
as well as the method.   Very often the mere order of chron-
ology dictated the succession and arrangement of the topics.
Now, on the other hand, in a House of Commons oration,
although sometimes there may occur statements of fact and
operose calculations, still these are never more than a text,
at the very best, for the political discussion, but often no
more than a subsequent illustration or proof attached to
some one of its heads.   The main staple of any long speech
must always be some general view of national policy ; and,
in Cicero's language, such a view must always be *infinita* ;
that is, not determined *ab extra*, but shaped and drawn from
the funds of one's own understanding.   The facts are here
subordinate and ministerial ; in the case before a jury the
facts are all in all.   The forensic orator satisfies his duty if
he does but take the facts exactly as they stand in his brief,
and place them before his audience in that order, and even
(if he should choose it) in those words.   The parliamentary
orator has no opening for facts at all, but as he himself may
be able to create such an opening by some previous exposi-
tions of doctrine or opinion, of the probable or expedient.
The one is always creeping along shore ; the other is always
out at sea.   Accordingly, the degrees of anxiety which
severally affect the two cases are best brought to the test in
this one question—" *What shall I say next ?* "—an anxiety
besetting orators like that which besets poor men in respect
to their children's daily bread.   " This moment it is secured ;
but, alas for the next ! "   Now, the judicial orator finds an
instant relief : the very points of the case are numbered ;
and, if he cannot find more to say upon No. 7, he has only
to pass on and call up No. 8.   Whereas the deliberative
orator, in a senate or a literary meeting, finds himself always
in this situation,—that, having reached with difficulty that
topic which we have supposed to be No. 7, one of three
cases uniformly occurs : either he does not perceive any
No. 8 at all ; or, secondly, he sees a distracting choice of
No. 8's—the ideas to which he might next pass are many,
but he does not see whither they will lead him ; or, thirdly,

he sees a very fair and promising No. 8, but cannot in any way discover off-hand how he is to effect a transition to this new topic. He cannot, with the rapidity requisite, modulate out of the one key into the other. His anxiety increases, utter confusion masters him, and he breaks down.

We have made this digression by way of seeking, in a well-known case of public life, an illustration of the difference between a subjective and an objective exercise of the mind. It is the sudden translation from the one exercise to the other which, and which only, accounts for the failure of advocates when attempting senatorial efforts. Once used to depend on memorials or briefs of facts, or of evidence not self-derived, the advocate, like a child in leading-strings, loses that command over his own internal resources which otherwise he might have drawn from practice. In fact, the advocate, with his brief lying before him, is precisely in the condition of a parliamentary speaker who places a written speech or notes for a speech in his hat. This trick has sometimes been practised ; and the consternation which would befall the orator in the case of such a hat-speech being suddenly blown away precisely realizes the situation of a *nisi prius* orator when first getting on his legs in the House of Commons. He has swum with bladders all his life : suddenly he must swim without them.

This case explains why it is that all subjective branches of study favour the cultivation of style. Whatsoever is entirely independent of the mind, and external to it, is generally equal to its own enunciation. Ponderable facts and external realities are intelligible in almost any language : they are self-explained and self-sustained. But, the more closely any exercise of mind is connected with what is internal and individual in the sensibilities,—that is, with what is philosophically termed *subjective,*—precisely in that degree, and the more subtly, does the style or the embodying of the thoughts cease to be a mere separable ornament, and in fact the more does the manner, as we expressed it before, become confluent with the matter. In saying this, we do but vary the form of what we once heard delivered on this subject by Mr. Wordsworth. His remark was by far the weightiest thing we ever heard on the subject of style ; and it was this :

that it is in the highest degree unphilosophic to call language or diction " the *dress* of thoughts." And what was it then that he would substitute ? Why this : he would call it "the *incarnation* of thoughts." Never in one word was so profound a truth conveyed. Mr. Wordsworth was thinking, doubtless, of poetry like his own : viz. that which is eminently meditative. And the truth is apparent on consideration : for, if language were merely a dress, then you could separate the two ; you could lay the thoughts on the left hand, the language on the right. But, generally speaking, you can no more deal thus with poetic thoughts than you can with soul and body. The union is too subtle, the intertexture too ineffable,—each co-existing not merely *with* the other, but each *in* and *through* the other. An image, for instance, a single word, often enters into a thought as a constituent part. In short, the two elements are not united as a body with a separable dress, but as a mysterious incarnation. And thus, in what proportion the thoughts are subjective, in that same proportion does the very essence become identical with the expression, and the style become confluent with the matter.

The Greeks, by want of books, philosophical instruments, and innumerable other aids to all objective researches, being thrown more exclusively than we upon their own unaided minds, cultivated logic, ethics, metaphysics, psychology,—all thoroughly subjective studies. The schoolmen, in the very same situation, cultivated precisely the same field of knowledge. The Greeks, indeed, added to their studies that of geometry ; for the inscription over the gate of the Academy ("Let no one enter who is not instructed in geometry") sufficiently argues that this science must have made some progress in the days of Pericles, when it could thus be made a general qualification for admission to a learned establishment within thirty years after his death. But geometry is partly an objective, partly a subjective, study. With this exception, the Greeks and the Monastic Schoolmen trod the very same path.

Consequently, in agreement with our principle, both ought to have found themselves in circumstances favourable to the cultivation of style. And it is certain that they did.

As an *art*, as a practice, it was felicitously pursued in both cases. It is true that the harsh ascetic mode of treating philosophy by the schoolmen generated a corresponding barrenness, aridity, and repulsiveness, in the rigid forms of their technical language. But, however offensive to genial sensibilities, this diction was a perfect thing in its kind ; and, to do it justice, we ought rather to compare it with the exquisite language of algebra,—equally irreconcilable to all standards of æsthetic beauty ; but yet, for the three qualities of elliptical rapidity (that rapidity which constitutes very much of what is meant by *elegance* in mathematics), of absolute precision, and of simplicity, this algebraic language is unrivalled amongst human inventions. On the other hand, the Greeks, whose objects did not confine them to these austere studies, carried out their corresponding excellence in style upon a far wider, and indeed a comprehensive, scale. Almost all modes of style were exemplified amongst *them.* Thus we endeavour to show that the subjective pursuits of the Greeks and the Schoolmen ought to have favoured a command of appropriate diction ; and afterwards that it did.

But, *fourthly,* we are entitled to expect that, wherever style exists in great development as a practice, it will soon be investigated with corresponding success as a theory. If fine music is produced spontaneously in short snatches by the musical sensibility of a people, it is a matter of certainty that the science of composition, that counterpoint, that thorough-bass, will soon be cultivated with a commensurate zeal. This is matter of such obvious inference that in any case where it fails we look for some extraordinary cause to account for it. Now, in Greece, with respect to style, the inference *did* fail. Style, as an art, was in a high state of culture ; style, as a science, was nearly neglected. How is this to be accounted for ? It arose naturally enough out of one great phenomenon in the condition of ancient times, and the relation which that bore to literature and to all human exertion of the intellect.

Did the reader ever happen to reflect on the great idea of *publication* ? An idea we call it ; because even in our own times, with all the mechanic aids of steam-presses, &c., this object is most imperfectly approached, and is destined, perhaps, for ever to remain an unattainable ideal,—useful (like all ideals) in the way of regulating our aims, but also as a practicable object not reconcilable with the limitation of human power. For it is clear that, if books were multiplied by a thousandfold, and truths of all kinds were carried to the very fireside of every family,—nay, placed below the eyes of every individual,—still the purpose of any universal publication would be defeated and utterly confounded, were it only by the limited opportunities of readers. One condition of publication defeats another. Even so much as a general publication is a hopeless idea. Yet, on the other hand, publication in some degree, and by some mode, is a *sine qua non* condition for the generation of literature. Without a larger sympathy than that of his own personal circle, it is evident that no writer could have a motive for those exertions and previous preparations without which excellence is not attainable in any art whatsoever.

Now, in our own times, it is singular, and really philosophically curious, to remark the utter blindness of writers, readers, publishers, and all parties whatever interested in literature, as to the trivial fraction of publicity which settles upon each separate work. The very multiplication of books has continually defeated the object in growing progression. Readers have increased, the engines of publication have increased ; but books, increasing in a still greater proportion, have left as the practical result an average quotient of publicity for each book, taken apart, continually decreasing. And, if the whole world were readers, probably the average publicity for each separate work would reach a *minimum* ; such would be the concurrent increase of books. But even this view of the case keeps out of sight the most monstrous forms of this phenomenon. The inequality of the publication has the effect of keeping very many books absolutely without a reader. The majority of books are never opened ; five hundred copies may be printed, or half as many more ; of these it may happen that five are carelessly turned over. Popular journals, again, which carry a promiscuous miscellany of papers into the same number of hands, as a stage-coach must convey all its passengers at the same rate of speed, dupe the public with a notion that here at least all are read.

Not at all. One or two are read from the interest attached to their subjects. Occasionally one is read a little from the ability with which it treats a subject not otherwise attractive. The rest have a better chance certainly than books, because they are at any rate placed under the eye and in the hand of readers. But this is no more than a variety of the same case. A hasty glance may be taken by one in a hundred at the less attractive papers ; but reading is out of the question. Then, again, another delusion, by which all parties disguise the truth, is the absurd belief that, not being read at present, a book may, however, be revived hereafter. Believe it not ! This is possible only with regard to books that demand to be studied, where the merit is slowly discovered. Every month, every day indeed, produces its own novelties, with the additional zest that they *are* novelties. Every future year, which will assuredly fail in finding time for its own books, —how should it find time for defunct books ? No, no ; every year buries its own literature. Since Waterloo there have been added upwards of fifty thousand books and pamphlets to the shelves of our *native* literature, taking no account of foreign importations.[1] Of these fifty thousand possibly two hundred still survive ; possibly twenty will survive for a couple of centuries ; possibly five or six thousand may have been indifferently read ; the rest not so much as opened. In this hasty sketch of a calculation we assume a single copy to represent a whole edition. But, in order to have the total sum of copies numerically neglected since Waterloo, it will be requisite to multiply fourty-four thousand by five hundred at the least, but probably by a higher multiplier. At the very moment of writing this—by way of putting into a brighter light the inconceivable blunder as to publicity habitually committed by sensible men of the world—let us mention what we now see before us in a public journal. Speaking with disapprobation of a just but disparaging expression applied to the French war-mania by a London morning paper, the writer has described

[1] Only 50,000 in the twenty-five years between 1815 (the date of Waterloo) and 1840 (the date of De Quincey's paper) seems a very moderate computation, giving an average of only 2000 for every year, whereas our annual average now is between 5000 and 6000.—M.

it as likely to irritate the people of France. O genius of arithmetic ! The offending London journal has a circulation of four thousand copies daily ; and it is assumed that thirty-three millions, of whom assuredly not twenty-five individuals will ever see the English paper as a visible object, nor five ever read the passage in question, are to be maddened by one word in a colossal paper laid this morning on a table amongst fifty others, and to-morrow morning pushed off that table by fifty others of more recent date. How are such delusions possible ? Simply from the previous delusion, of ancient standing, connected with printed characters : what is printed seems to every man invested with some fatal character of publicity such as cannot belong to mere MS. ; whilst, in the meantime, out of every thousand printed pages, one at the most, but at all events a very small proportion indeed, is in any true sense more public when printed than previously as a manuscript ; and that one, even that thousandth part, perishes as effectually in a few days to each separate reader as the words perish in our daily conversation. Out of all that we talk, or hear others talk, through the course of a year, how much remains on the memory at the closing day of December ? Quite as little, we may be sure, survives from most people's reading. A book answers its purpose by sustaining the intellectual faculties in motion through the current act of reading, and a general deposition or settling takes effect from the sum of what we read ; even that, however, chiefly according to the previous condition in which the book finds us for understanding it, and referring them to heads under some existing arrangement of our knowledge. Publication is an idle term applied to what is not published ; and nothing is *published* which is not made known *publicly* to the understanding as well as the eye ; whereas, for the enormous majority of what is printed, we cannot say so much as that it is made known to the eyes.

For what reason have we insisted on this unpleasant view of a phenomenon incident to the limitation of our faculties, and apparently without remedy ? Upon another occasion it might have been useful to do so, were it only to impress upon every writer the vast importance of compression. Simply to retrench one word from each sentence, one superfluous epithet, for example, would probably increase the disposable time of the public by one twelfth part ; in other words, would add another month to the year, or raise any sum of volumes read from eleven to twelve hundred. A mechanic operation would effect *that* change ; but, by cultivating a closer logic and more severe habits of thinking, perhaps two sentences out of each three might be pruned away, and the amount of possible publication might thus be increased in a threefold degree. A most serious duty, therefore, and a duty which is annually growing in solemnity, appears to be connected with the culture of an unwordy diction ; much more, however, with the culture of clear thinking,—that being the main key to good writing, and consequently to fluent reading.

But all this, though not unconnected with our general theme, is wide of our immediate purpose. The course of our logic at this point runs in the following order. The Athenians, from causes assigned, ought to have consummated the whole science and theory of style. But they did *not*. Why ? Simply from a remarkable deflexion or bias given to their studies by a difficulty connected with *publication*. For some modes of literature the Greeks *had* a means of publication, for many they had *not*. That one difference, as we shall show, disturbed the just valuation of style.

Some mode of publication must have existed for Athens : that is evident. The mere *fact* of a literature proves it. For without public sympathy how can a literature arise ? or public sympathy without a regular organ of publication ? What poet would submit to the labours of his most difficult art, if he had no reasonable prospect of a large audience, and somewhat of a permanent audience, to welcome and adopt his productions ?

Now then, in the Athens of Pericles, what *was* the audience, how composed, and how insured, on which the literary composer might rely ? By what channel, in short, did the Athenian writer calculate on a *publication* ? This is a very interesting question, and, as regards much in the civilisation of Greece, both for what it caused and what it prevented, is an important question. In the elder days,—in fact we may

suppose through the five hundred years from the Trojan
expedition to Pisistratus and Solon,—all *publication* was
effected through two classes of men : the public reciters and
the public singers.   Thus, no doubt, it was that the Iliad and
Odyssey were sent down to the hands of Pisistratus, who
has the traditional reputation of having first arranged and
revised these poems.   These reciters or singers to the harp
would probably rehearse one entire book of the Iliad at
every splendid banquet.   Every book would be kept in
remembrance and currency by the peculiar local relations
of particular states or particular families to ancestors connected with Troy.   This mode of publication, however, had
the disadvantage that it was among the arts ministerial to
sensual enjoyment.   And it is some argument for the extensive diffusion of such a practice in the early times of
Greece that, both in the Greece of later times, and, by adoption from her, in the Rome of cultivated ages, we find the
ἀκροαματα as commonly established by way of a dinner
appurtenance—that is, exercises of display addressed to the
ear, recitations of any kind with and without music—not at
all less frequently than ὁραματα, or the corresponding display
to the eye (dances or combats of gladiators).   These were
doubtless inheritances from the ancient usages of Greece,—
modes of publication resorted to long before the Olympic
Games by the mere necessitous cravings for sympathy, and
kept up long after that institution, as in itself too brief and
rare in its recurrence to satisfy the necessity.

Such was the earliest effort of publication, and in its
feeble infancy ; for this, besides its limitation in point of
audience, was confined to narrative poetry.   But, when the
ideal of Greece was more and more exalted by nearer comparison with barbarous standards, after the sentiment of
patriotism had coalesced with vindictive sentiments, and
when towering cities began to reflect the grandeur of this
land as in a visual mirror, these cravings for publicity became more restless and irrepressible.   And at length, in the
time of Pericles, concurrently with the external magnificence
of the city, arose for Athens two modes of publication, each
upon a scale of gigantic magnitude.

What were these ?   The *Theatre* and the *Agora* or

Forum : publication by the Stage, and publication by the Hustings. These were the extraordinary modes of publication which arose for Athens : one by a sudden birth, like that of Minerva, in the very generation of Pericles ; the other slowly maturing itself from the generation of Pisistratus, which preceded that of Pericles by a hundred years. This double publication, scenic and forensic, was virtually, and for all the loftier purposes of publication, the press of Athens. And, however imperfect a representative this may seem of a typographical publication, certain it is that in some important features the Athenian publication had separate advantages of its own. It was a far more effective and correct publication in the first place, enjoying every aid of powerful accompaniment from voice, gesture, scenery, music, and suffering in no instance from false reading or careless reading. Then, secondly, it was a far wider publication : each drama being read (or heard, which is a far better thing) by 25,000 or 30,000 persons, counterbalancing at least forty editions such as we on an average publish ; each oration being delivered with just emphasis to perhaps 7000. But why, in this mention of a stage or hustings publication, as opposed to a publication by the printing-press, why was it, we are naturally admonished to ask, that the Greeks had no press ? The ready answer will be,—because the art of printing had not been discovered. But that is an error, the detection of which we owe to the present Archbishop of Dublin. The art of printing *was* discovered. It had been discovered repeatedly. The art which multiplied the legends upon a coin or medal (a work which the ancients performed by many degrees better than we moderns,—for we make it a mechanic art, they a fine art) had in effect anticipated the art of printing. It was an art, this typographic mystery, which awoke and went back to sleep many times over from mere defect of materials. Not the defect of typography as an art, but the defect of *paper* as a material for keeping this art in motion,—*there* lay the reason, as Dr. Whately most truly observes, why printed books had no existence amongst the Greeks of Pericles, or afterwards amongst the Romans of Cicero. And why was there no paper ? The common reason applying to both countries was the want of linen rags,

and that want arose from the universal habit of wearing
woollen garments.   In this respect Athens and Rome were
on the same level.   But for Athens the want was driven to
a further extremity by the slenderness of her commerce with
Egypt, whence only any substitute could have been drawn.

Even for Rome itself the scarcity of paper ran through
many degrees.   Horace, the poet, was amused with the
town of Equotuticum for two reasons : as incapable of
entering into hexameter verse from its prosodial quantity
(*versu quod dicere non est*) ; and because it purchased water
(*vœnit vilissima rerum aqua*),—a circumstance in which it
agrees with the well-known Clifton, above the hot wells of
Bristol, where water is bought by the shilling's worth.
But neither Horatian Equotuticum nor Bristolian Clifton
can ever have been as "hard up" for water as the Mecca
caravan.   And the differences were as great in respect to
the want of paper between the Athens of Pericles or
Alexander and the Rome of Augustus Cæsar.   Athens had
bad poets, whose names have come down to modern times ;
but Athens could no more have afforded to punish bad
authors by sending their works to grocers—

"in vicum vendentem pus et odores,
Et piper, et quicquid *chartis amicitur ineptis*"—

than London, because gorged with the wealth of two Indies,
can afford to pave her streets with silver.   This practice of
applying unsaleable authors to the ignoble uses of retail
dealers in petty articles must have existed in Rome for
some time before it could have attracted the notice of
Horace, and upon some considerable scale as a known
public usage before it could have roused any echoes of
public mirth as a satiric allusion, or have had any meaning
and sting.

In that one revelation of Horace we see a proof how
much paper had become more plentiful.   It is true that so
long as men dressed in woollen materials it was impossible
to look for a *cheap* paper.   Maga might have been printed
at Rome very well for ten guineas a copy.   Paper was dear,
undoubtedly, but it could be had.   On the other hand, how
desperate must have been the bankruptcy at Athens in all

materials for receiving the record of thoughts, when we find
a polished people having no better tickets or cards for con-
veying their sentiments to the public than shells ! Thence
came the very name for civil banishment, viz. *ostracism*,
because the votes were marked on an *ostracon*, or marine
shell. Again, in another great city, viz. Syracuse, you see
men reduced to *petalism*, or marking their votes by the
petals of shrubs. Elsewhere, as indeed many centuries
nearer to our own times in Constantinople, bull's hide was
used for the same purpose.

Well might the poor Greeks adopt the desperate expedient of white plastered walls as the best memorandum-
book for a man who had thoughts occurring to him in the
night-time. Brass only, or marble, could offer any lasting
memorial for thoughts ; and upon what material the parts
were written out for the actors on the Athenian stage, or
how the elaborate revisals of the text could be carried on, is
beyond our power of conjecture.

In this appalling state of embarrassment for the great
poet or prose writer, what consequences would naturally
arise ? A king's favourite and friend like Aristotle might
command the most costly materials. For instance, if you
look back, from this day to 1800, into the advertising records or catalogues of great Parisian publishers, you will
find more works of excessive luxury, costing from a thousand
francs for each copy all the way up to as many *guineas*, in
each separate period of fifteen years than in the whole forty
among the wealthier and more enterprising publishers of
Great Britain. What is the explanation ? Can the very
moderate incomes of the French gentry afford to patronize
works which are beyond the purses of our British aristocracy, who, besides, are so much more of a reading class ?
Not so : the patronage for these Parisian works of luxury
is not domestic, it is exotic : chiefly from emperors and
kings ; from great national libraries ; from rich universities ;
from the grandees of Russia, Hungary, or Great Britain ;
and generally from those who, living in splendid castles or
hotels, require corresponding furniture, and therefore corresponding books, because to such people books are necessarily
furniture,— since, upon the principles of good taste, they

must correspond with the splendour of all around them. And in the age of Alexander there were already purchasers enough among royal houses, or the imitators of such houses, to encourage costly copies of attractive works. Aristotle was a privileged man. But in other less favoured cases the strong yearnings for public sympathy were met by blank impossibilities. Much martyrdom, we feel assured, was then suffered by poets. Thousands, it is true, perish in our days, who have never had a solitary reader. But still the existence *in print* gives a delusive feeling that they *may* have been read. They are standing in the market all day, and somebody, unperceived by themselves, may have thrown an eye upon their wares. The thing is possible. But for the ancient writer there was a sheer physical impossibility that any man should sympathize with what he never could have seen, except under the two conditions we have mentioned.

These two cases there were of exemption from this dire physical resistance, — two conditions which made publication possible; and, under the horrible circumstances of sequestration for authors in general, need it be said that to benefit by either advantage was sought with such a zeal as, in effect, extinguished all other literature? If a man could be a poet for the stage, a *scriptor scenicus*, in that case he was published. If a man could be admitted as an orator, as a regular *demagogus*, upon the popular *bema* or hustings, in that case he was published. If his own thoughts were a torment to him, until they were reverberated from the hearts and flashing eyes and clamorous sympathy of a multitude, thus only an outlet was provided, a mouth was opened, for the volcano surging within his brain. The vast theatre was an organ of publication; the political forum was an organ of publication. And on this twofold arena a torch was applied to that inflammable gas which exhaled spontaneously from so excitable a mind as the mind of the Athenian.

Need we wonder, then, at the torrent-like determination with which Athenian literature, from the era 444 B.C. to the era 333 B.C., ran headlong into one or other channel, — the scenical poetry or the eloquence of the hustings? For an Athenian in search of popular applause or of sympathy there was no other avenue to either; unless, indeed, in the character of an artist, or of a leading soldier : but too often, in this latter class, it happened that mercenary foreigners had a preference. And thus it was that, during that period when the popular cast of government throughout Greece awakened patriotic emulation, scarcely anything is heard of in literature (allowing for the succession to philosophic chairs, which made it their pride to be private and exclusive) except dramatic poetry on the one hand, comic or tragic, and political oratory on the other.

As to this last avenue to the public ear, how it was abused, in what excess it became the nuisance and capital scourge of Athens, there needs only the testimony of all contemporary men who happened to stand aloof from that profession, or all subsequent men even of that very profession who were not blinded by some corresponding interest in some similar system of delusion. Euripides and Aristophanes, contemporary with the earliest practitioners of name and power on that stage of jugglers, are overrun with expressions of horror for these public pests. "You have every qualification," says Aristophanes to an aspirant, " that could be wished for a public orator : φωνη μιαρα—a voice like seven devils ; κακος γεγονας—you are by nature a scamp ; ἀγοραιος εἰ—you are up to snuff in the business of the forum." From Euripides might be gathered a small volume, relying merely upon so much of his works as yet survives, in illustration of the horror which possessed him for this gang of public misleaders :—

Τουτ᾽ ἐσθ᾽ ὁ θνητων εὐ πολεις οἰκουμενας
Δομους τ᾽ ἀπολλυτ᾽—οἱ καλοι λιαν λογοι.

"This is what overthrows cities admirably organized, and the households of men,—your superfine harangues." Cicero, full four centuries later, looking back to this very period from Pericles to Alexander, friendly as he was by the *esprit de corps* to the order of orators, and professionally biassed to uphold the civil uses of eloquence, yet, as an honest man, cannot deny that it was this gift of oratory, hideously abused, which led to the overthrow of Athens and the ruin of Grecian liberty : " Illa vetus Græcia, quæ quondam opibus, imperio, gloria floruit, hoc uno malo concidit,—*libertate*

immoderata ac licentia concionum."   Quintilian, standing on
the very same ground of professional prejudice, all in favour
of public orators, yet is forced into the same sorrowful con-
fession.   In one of the Declamations ascribed to him he
says, " Civitatum status scimus ab oratoribus esse conversos " ;
and in illustration he adds the example of Athens : "sive
illam Atheniensium civitatem (quondam late principem)
intueri placeat, accisas ejus vires animadvertemus *vitio con-
cionantium.*"   Root and branch, Athens was laid prostrate
by her wicked Radical orators ; for Radical, in the elliptic
phrase of modern politics, they were almost to a man ; and
in this feature above all others (a feature often scornfully
exposed by Euripides) those technically known as οἱ λεγοντες,
the speaking men, and as οἱ δημαγωγοι,[1] the misleaders of
the mob, offer a most suitable ancestry for the modern
leaders of Radicalism, — that with their base, fawning
flatteries of the people they mixed up the venom of vipers
against their opponents and against the aristocracy of the
land.

Ὑπογλυκαινειν ῥηματιοις μαγειρικοις—

"subtly to wheedle the people with honeyed words dressed
to its palate " : this had been the ironical advice of the
scoffing Aristophanes.   That practice made the mob orator
contemptible to manly tastes, rather than hateful.   But the
sacrifice of independence — the "pride which licks the
dust "—is the readiest training for all un charitableness and
falsehood towards those who seem either rivals for the
same base purposes, or open antagonists for nobler.   And,
accordingly, it is remarked by Euripides that these pestilent
abusers of the popular confidence would bring a mischief
upon Athens before they had finished, equally by their

[1] With respect to the word "demagogues," as a technical designation for the political orators and partisans at Athens (otherwise called
οἱ προσταται, those who headed any movement), it is singular that so
accurate a Greek scholar as Henry Stephens should have supposed
linguas promptas ad plebem concitandum (an expression of Livy's)
potius των δημαγωγων *fuisse quam* των ῥητορων ; as if the demagogues
were a separate class from the popular orators.   But, says Valckenaer,
the relation is soon stated : not all the Athenian orators were demagogues, but all the demagogues were in fact, and technically were
called, orators.

sycophancies to the mob and by their libels of foreign
princes.   Hundreds of years afterwards, a Greek writer,
upon reviewing this most interesting period of one hundred
and eleven years, from Pericles to Alexander, sums up and
repeats the opinion of Euripides in this general representative portrait of Attic oratory, with respect to which we wish
to ask, Can any better delineation be given of a Chartist, or
generically of a modern Jacobin ?—Ὁ δημαγωγος κακοδιδασ-
καλειτους πολλους, λεγων τα κεχαρισμενα—"The mob-leader
dupes the multitude with false doctrines, whilst delivering
things soothing to their credulous vanity."   This is one half
of his office,—sycophancy to the immediate purse-holders, and
poison to the sources of truth ; the other half is expressed
with the same spirit of prophecy as regards the British future,
και διαβολαις αυτους ἐξαλλοτριοι προς τους ἀριστους,—
"and by lying calumnies he utterly alienates them in relation to their own native aristocracy."

Now this was a base pursuit, though somewhat relieved
by the closing example of Demosthenes, who, amidst much
frailty, had a generous nature ; and he showed it chiefly by
his death, and in his lifetime, to use Milton's words, by
uttering many times "odious truth," which, with noble
courage, he compelled the mob to hear.   But one man could
not redeem a national dishonour.   It *was* such, and such it
was felt to be.   Men, therefore, of elevated natures, and men
of gentle pacific natures, equally revolted from a trade of
lies, as regarded the audience, and of strife, as regarded the
competitors.   There remained the one other pursuit of
scenical poetry ; and it hardly needs to be said what crowd-
ing there was amongst all the energetic minds of Athens into
one or other of these pursuits : the one for the unworldly
and idealizing, the other for the coarsely ambitious.   These,
therefore, became the two *quasi* professions of Athens, and at
the same time, in a sense more exclusive than can now be
true of *our* professions, became the sole means of publication
for truth of any class, and a publication by many degrees
more certain, more extensive, and more immediate, than ours
by the press.

The Athenian theatre published an edition of thirty
thousand copies in one day, enabling, in effect, every male

citizen capable of attending, from the age of twenty to sixty, together with many thousands of domiciled aliens, to read the drama, with the fullest understanding of its sense and poetic force that could be effected by natural powers of voice and action, combined with all possible auxiliaries of art, of music, of pantomimic dancing, and the whole carried home to the heart by visible and audible sympathy in excess. This, but in a very inferior form as regarded the adjuncts of art, and the scale of the theatre, and the *mise en scène*, was precisely the advantage of Charles I. for appreciating Shakspere.

It was a standing reproach of the Puritans, adopted even by Milton, a leaden shaft feathered and made buoyant by *his* wit, that the King had adopted that stage poet as the companion of his closet retirements. So it would have been a pity if these malignant persecutors of the royal solitude should have been liars as well as fanatics. Doubtless, even when king, and in his afflictions, this storm-vexed man did read Shakspere. But that was not the original way in which he acquired his acquaintance with the poet. A Prince of Wales, what between public claims and social claims, finds little time for reading after the period of childhood,—that is, at any period when he can comprehend a great poet. And it was as Prince of Wales that Charles prosecuted his studies of Shakspere. He saw continually at Whitehall, personated by the best actors of the time, illustrated by the stage management, and assisted by the mechanic displays of Inigo Jones, all the principal dramas of Shakspere actually performed.[1] That was publication with an Athenian advantage. A thousand copies of a book may be brought into public libraries, and not one of them opened. But the three thousand copies of a play which Drury Lane used to publish in one night were in the most literal sense as well as in spirit read,—properly punctuated by the speakers, made intelligible by voice and action endowed with life and emphasis : in short, on each successive performance, a very

---

[1] An exaggeration ! There were frequent theatrical performances in Whitehall in the later part of James's reign and the earlier of Charles's, but nothing like such a run on Shakespeare in Whitehall Palace as this sentence would suggest.—M.

large edition of a fine tragedy was published in the most impressive sense of publication,—not merely with accuracy, but with a mimic reality that forbade all forgetting, and was liable to no inattention.

Now, if Drury Lane published a drama for Shakspere by three thousand copies in one night,[1] the Athenian theatre published ten times that amount for Sophocles. And this mode of publication in Athens, not co-operating (as in modern times) with other modes, but standing out in solitary conspicuous relief, gave an artificial bounty upon that one mode of poetic composition, as the hustings did upon one mode of prose composition. And those two modes, being thus cultivated to the utter exclusion of others which did not benefit by that bounty of publication, gave an unnatural bias to the national style, determined in effect upon too narrow a scale the operative ideal of composition, and finally made the dramatic artist and the mob orator the two sole intellectual professions for Athens. Hence came a great limitation of style in practice; and hence, secondly, for reasons connected with these two modes of composition, a general neglect of style as a didactic theory.[2]

---

[1] An anachronism! *Drury Lane* was not the great theatrical centre of the metropolis till after the Restoration. There were, indeed, stage-performances at the *Cockpit Theatre* in Drury Lane from about the year 1616 (the year of Shakespeare's death); but the *Drury Lane Theatre* of famous memory, which De Quincey seems to have had in his mind, dates from 1663 only; and it was at the *Blackfriars* and the *Globe*, on opposite banks of the river, that Shakespeare's plays were first published in his own lifetime.—M.

[2] In the Preface to the volume of De Quincey's Collective Edition containing his reprint of this paper on Style there was this note of correction by way of Postscript:—" Amongst the vicarious modes of " Publication resorted to by the Ancients in default of the Printing- " Press I have forgotten to mention the Roman Recitations in the " Porticos of Baths, &c."—M.

LANGUAGE[1]

No language is stationary, except in rude and early periods of society. The languages of nations like the English and French, walking in the van of civilization, having popular institutions, and taking part in the business of the earth with morbid energy, are placed under the action of causes that will not allow them any respite from change. Neologism, in revolutionary times, is not an infirmity of caprice, seeking (to use the proverb of Cervantes) "for better bread than is made of wheat," but is a mere necessity of the unresting intellect. New ideas, new aspects of old ideas, new relations of objects to each other, or to man—the subject who contemplates those objects,—absolutely insist on new words. And it would not be a more idle misconception to find a disease in the pains of growth than to fancy a decay of vernacular purity in the multitude of verbal coinages which modern necessities of thought and action are annually calling forth on the banks of the Thames and the Seine.

Such coinages, however, do not all stand upon the same basis of justification. Some are regularly formed from known roots upon known analogies; others are formed licentiously. Some again meet a real and clamorous necessity of the intellect; others are fitted to gratify the mere appetite for innovation. They take their rise in various sources, and are moulded with various degrees of skill. Let us throw a hasty glance on the leading classes of these coinages, and of the laws which appear to govern them, or of the anomalies

[1] Place of original not ascertained : reprinted by De Quincey in 1858 in vol. ix of his Collective Edition of his Writings. —M.

with which they are sometimes associated. There are also large cases of innovation in which no process of coinage whatever is manifested, but perhaps a simple restoration of old words, long since obsolete in literature and good society, yet surviving to this hour in provincial usage, or, again, an extension and emancipation of terms heretofore narrowly restricted to a technical or a professional use—as we see exemplified in the word *ignore* ; which, until very lately, was so sacred to the sole use of grand juries that a man would have been obscurely suspected by a policeman, and would indeed have suspected himself, of something like petty larceny in forcing it into any general and philosophic meaning,—which, however, it has now assumed, with little offence to good taste, and with *yeoman* service to the intellect. Other cases, again, there are, and at present far too abundant, in which the necessities of social intercourse, and not unfrequently the necessities of philosophic speculation, are provisionally supplied by *slang*, and the phraseology that is born and bred in the streets. The market-place and the highway, the *forum* and the *trivium*, are rich seed-plots for the sowing and the reaping of many indispensable ideas. That a phrase belongs to the slang dictionary is certainly no absolute recommendation ; sometimes such a phrase may be simply disgusting from its vulgarity, without adding anything to the meaning or to the rhetorical force. How shocking to hear an official dignitary saying (as but yesterday *was* heard) " What *on earth* could the clause mean ? " Yet neither is it any safe ground of absolute excommunication even from the sanctities of literature that a phrase is entirely a growth of the street. The word *humbug*, for instance, rests upon a rich and comprehensive basis : it cannot be rendered adequately either by German or by Greek, the two richest of human languages ; and without this expressive word we should all be disarmed for one great case, continually recurrent, of social enormity. A vast mass of villainy, that cannot otherwise be reached by legal penalties, or brought within the rhetoric of scorn, would go at large with absolute impunity, were it not through the stern Rhadamanthian aid of this virtuous and inexorable word.

Meantime, as it would not suit the purposes of a sketch

to be too systematic in the treatment of a subject so inexhaustible as language and style, neither would it be within the limits of just proportion that I should be too elaborate in rehearsing beforehand the several avenues and classes of cases through which an opening is made for new words amongst ourselves or the French. I will select such cases for separate notice as seem most interesting or most seasonable. But, previously, as a proper mode of awakening the reader into giving relief and just prominence to the subject, I will point attention to the varying scale of appreciation applied to the diction and the national language, as a ground of national distinction and honour, by the five great intellectual nations of ancient and modern history : viz. the Greeks, the Romans, the French, the English, and the Germans. In no country, except one, is such a preface more requisite than in England, where it is strange enough that, whilst the finest models of style exist, and sub-consciously operate effectively as sources of delight, the *conscious* valuation of style is least perfectly developed.

Every nation has reason to feel interested in the pretensions of its own native language, in the original quality of that language or characteristic *kind* of its powers, and in the particular *degree* of its expansions at the period in question. Even semi-barbarous tribes sometimes talk grandiloquently on this head, and ascribe to uncultivated jargons a fertility or a range of expressiveness quite incompatible with the particular stage of social development which the national capacities have reached. Not only in spite of its barbarism, but oftentimes in mere virtue of its barbarism, we find a language claiming, by its eulogists, to possess more than ordinary powers of picturesque expression. Such a claim is continually put forward on behalf of the Celtic languages,— as, for instance, the Armoric, the Welsh, the Irish, the Manx, the Gaelic. Such a claim is put forward also for many oriental languages. Yet in most of these cases there is a profound mistake committed, and generally the same mistake. Without being strictly barbarous, all these languages are uncultured and rude in a degree corresponding to the narrow social development of the races who speak them. These races are precisely in that state of imperfect expansion,

both civilly and intellectually, under which the separation
has not fully taken place between poetry and prose. Their
social condition is too simple and elementary to require
much cultivation of intellectual topics. Little motive exists
for writing, unless on occasions of poetic excitement. The
subdued colouring, therefore, of prose has not yet been (to
speak physiologically) secreted. And the national diction
has the appearance of being more energetic and sparkling
simply because it is more inflated,—the chastities of good
taste not having yet been called forth by social necessities to
disentangle the separate forms of impassioned and non-
impassioned composition. The Kalmuck Tartars, according
to a German traveller, viz. Bergmann, long resident amongst
them, speak in rapturous terms of their own language [1];
but it is probable that the particular modes of phraseology
which fascinate their admiration are precisely those which a
more advanced civilisation, and a corresponding development
of taste, would reject as spurious. Certainly, in the case of
a language and a literature likely to be much in advance of
the Kalmuck,—viz. the Arabic at the era of Mahomet,—we
find this conjecture realized. The Koran is held by the
devout Mahommedan to be the most admirable model of
composition ; but exactly those ornaments of diction or of
imagery which he regards as the jewels of the whole are
most entirely in the childish taste of imperfect civilisation.
That which attracts the Arab critic or the Persian is
most of all repulsive to the masculine judgment of the
European.

Barbarism, in short, through all degrees, generates its
own barbaresque standards of taste, and nowhere so much as
in the great field of diction and ornamental composition. A
high civilisation is an indispensable condition for developing
the full powers of a language ; and it is equally a condition
for developing the taste which must preside over the appreciation of diction and style. The elder civilisations of Egypt
and of Asiatic empires are too imperfectly known at this day
to furnish any suggestions upon the subject. The earliest

---

[1] For Bergmann and his acquaintance with the Kalmuck Tartars,
and De Quincey's acquaintance with his book about them, see *ante*,
Vol. VII, pp. 8-10.—M.

civilisation that offers a practical field of study to our own age is the superb one of Greece.

It cannot be necessary to say that from that memorable centre of intellectual activity have emanated the great models in art and literature which, to Christendom, when recasting her mediæval forms, became chiefly operative in controlling her luxuriance, and in other negative services, though not so powerful for positive impulse and inspiration. Greece was, in fact, *too* ebullient with intellectual activity—an activity too palestric and purely human—so that the opposite pole of the mind, which points to the mysterious and the spiritual, was, in the agile Greek, too intensely a child of the earth, starved and palsied; whilst in the Hebrew, dull and inert intellectually, but in his spiritual organs awake and sublime, the case was precisely reversed. Yet, after all, the result was immeasurably in favour of the Hebrew. Speaking in the deep sincerities of the solitary and musing heart, which refuses to be duped by the whistling of names, we must say of the Greek—*laudatur et alget*: he has won the admiration of the human race, he is numbered amongst the chief brilliancies of earth, but on the deeper and more abiding nature of man he has no hold. He will perish when any deluge of calamity overtakes the libraries of our planet, or if any great revolution of thought remoulds them, and will be remembered only as a generation of flowers is remembered; with the same tenderness of feeling, and with the same pathetic sense of a natural predestination to evanescence. Whereas the Hebrew, by introducing himself to the secret places of the human heart, and sitting there as incubator over the awful germs of the spiritualities that connect man with the unseen worlds, has perpetuated himself as a power in the human system: he is co-enduring with man's race, and careless of all revolutions in literature or in the composition of society. The very languages of these two races repeat the same expression of their intellectual differences, and of the differences in their missions. The Hebrew, meagre and sterile as regards the numerical wealth of its ideas, is infinite as regards their power; the Greek, on the other hand, rich as tropic forests in the polymorphous life, the life of the dividing and distinguishing intellect, is weak only in the supreme region of thought. The Hebrew has scarcely any individuated words. Ask a Hebrew scholar if he has a word for a *ball* (as a tennis ball, *pila lusoria*) ; he says, " O yes." What is it then ? Why, he gives you the word for *globe*. Ask for *orb*, for *sphere*, &c., still you have the same answer ; the individual circumstantiations are swallowed up in the generic outline. But the Greek has a parity of wealth alike in the abstract and the concrete. Even as *vocal* languages, the Hebrew and the Greek obey the same prevailing law of difference. The Hebrew is a sublime monochord, uttering vague vowel sounds as indistinct and shy as the breathings of an Æolian harp when exposed to a fitful breeze. The Greek is more firmly articulated by consonants, and the succession of its syllables runs through a more extensive compass of sonorous variety than can be matched in any other known language. The Spanish and the Italian, with all the stateliness of their modulation, make no approach to the canorous *variety* of the sounds of the Greek.[1] Read a passage from almost any Greek poet, and each syllable seems to have been placed in its present position as a relief, and by way of contrast, to the syllable which follows and precedes.

Of a language thus and otherwise so divinely endowed the Greeks had a natural right to be proud. Yet *were* they so ? There is no appearance of it : and the reason, no doubt, lay in their insulated position. Having no *intellectual* inter-

---

[1] The Romans discover something apparently of the same tendency to a vague economy of abstraction. But in *them* it is merely casual, and dependent on accidental ignorance. Thus, for instance, it is ridiculous to render the Catullian *Passer meœ puellœ* by *sparrow*. As well suppose Lesbia to have fondled a pet hedgehog. *Passer*, or *passerculus*, means *any* little bird whatever. The sternness of the Roman mind disdained to linger upon petty distinctions ; or at least until the ages of luxurious refinement had paved the way for intellectual refinements. So, again, *malum*, or even *pomum*, does not mean an apple, but any whatever of the larger spherical or spheroidical fruits. A peach, indeed, was described differentially as *malum Persicum* ; an apricot, had the Romans known it, would have been rendered by *malum apricum*, or *malum apricatum* ; but an apple also, had it been mentioned with any stress of opposition or pointed distinction attached to it, would have been described differentially as *malum vulgare* or *malum domesticum*.

course with foreign nations, they had virtually no intercourse at all—none which could affect the feelings of the literary class, or generally of those who would be likely to contemplate language as a subject of æsthetic admiration.   Each Hellenic author might be compared with others of his compatriot authors in respect to his management of their common language, but not the language itself compared as to structure or capacities with other languages ; since these other languages (one and all) were in any practical sense hardly assumed to exist.   In this there was no arrogance.   Aliens, as to country and civil polity, being objects of jealousy in the circumstances of Greece, there could be no reason for abstaining from any designation, however hostile, which might seem appropriate to the relation between the parties.   But, in reality, the term *barbarians* [1] seems, for many ages, to have implied nothing either hostile or disrespectful.   By a natural *onomatopœia*, the Greeks used the iterated syllables *barbar* to denote that a man was unintelligible in his talk ; and by the word *barbarian* originally it is probable that no sort of reproach was intended, but simply the fact that the people so called spoke a language not intelligible to Greeks.   Latterly, the term seems to have been often used as one of mere convenience for classification, indicating the *non-Hellenes* in opposition to the *Hellenes* ; and it was not meant to express any qualities whatever of the aliens — simply they were described as *being* aliens.   But in the earliest times it was meant, by the word *barbarians*, to describe them under the idea of men who were ἑτερογλωττοι, men who, speaking in a tongue different from the Grecian, spoke unintelligibly ; and at this day it is not impossible that the Chinese mean nothing more by the seemingly offensive term *outside barbarians*. The mis-translations must be many between ourselves and the Chinese ; and the probability is that this reputedly arrogant expression means only " the aliens, or external people, who speak in tongues foreign to China." Arrogant or not arrogant, however, in the mouth of the Greeks, the word *barbarians* included the whole human race not living

---

[1] There is a short note by Gibbon upon this word ; but it adds nothing to the suggestions which every thoughtful person will furnish to himself.

in Hellas, or in colonies thrown off from Hellas.[1] Having no temptation or facilities for holding any intellectual intercourse with those who could not communicate through the channel of the Greek language, it followed that the Greeks had no means or opportunity for comparing their own language with the languages of other nations ; and together with this power of mutual comparison fell away the call and excitement to vanity upon that particular subject. Greece was in the absolute insulation of the phœnix, the unique of birds, that dies without having felt a throb of exultation or a pang of jealousy, because it has exposed its gorgeous plumage and the mysterious solemnities of its beauty only to the dusky recesses of Thebaic deserts.

Not thus were the Romans situated. The Greeks, so profound and immovable was their self-conceit, never in any generation came to regard the Romans with the slightest tremor of jealousy, as though they were or ever could be rivals in literature. The Roman nobles, as all Greece knew, resorted in youth to Athens as to the eternal well-head of learning and eloquence ; and the literary or the forensic efforts of such persons were never viewed as by possibility efforts of competition with their masters, but simply as graceful expressions of homage to the inimitable by men whose rank gave a value to this homage. Cicero and other Romans of his day were egregiously duped by their own vanity when they received as sincere the sycophantic praises of mercenary Greek rhetoricians. No Greek ever in good faith admired a Roman upon intellectual grounds, except indeed as Polybius did, whose admiration was fixed upon the Roman institutions,

[1] In the later periods of Greek Literature, viz. at and after the era of Pericles, when the attention had been long pointed to language, and a more fastidious apprehension had been directed to its slighter shades of difference, the term "*barbarous*" was applied apparently to uncouth dialects of the Greek language itself. Thus, in the Ajax of Sophocles, Teucer (though certainly talking Greek) is described as speaking barbarously. Perhaps, however, the expression might bear a different construction. But in elder periods it seems hardly possible that the term *barbarous* could ever have been so used. Sir Edward B. Lytton, in his "Athens," supposes Homer, when describing the Carians by this term, to have meant no more than that they spoke some provincial variety of the Ionic Greek ; but, applied to an age of so little refinement as the Homeric, I should scarcely think this interpretation admissible.

not upon their literature : though even in *his* day the Roman literature had already put forth a masculine promise, and in Plautus at least a promise of *unborrowed* excellence. The Greeks were wrong : the Romans had some things in their literature which a Greek could neither have rivalled nor even understood. They had a peculiar rhetoric for example, such as Ovid's in the contest for the arms of Achilles—such as Seneca's, which, to this hour, has never been properly examined, and which not only has no parallel in Grecian literature, but which, strangely enough, loses its whole effect and sense when translated into Greek : so entirely is it Roman by incommunicable privilege of genius.

But, if the Greeks did no justice to their Roman pupils, on the other hand, the Roman pupils never ceased to regard the Greeks with veneration, or to acknowledge them for their masters in literature : *they* had a foreign literature before their eyes challenging continual comparison ; and this foreign literature was in a language which also challenged comparison with their own. Every Roman of distinction, after Sylla and Marius, understood Greek, — often talked it fluently, declaimed in it, and wrote books in it. But there is no language without its own peculiar genius, and therefore none without its separate powers and advantages. That the Latin language has in excess such an original character, and consequently such separate powers, Romans were not slow to discover. Studying the Greek so closely, they found by continual collation in what quarter lay the peculiar strength of the Latin. And, amongst others, Cicero did himself the greatest honour, and almost redeems the baseness of his political conduct, by the patriotic fervour which he now and then exhibits in defending the claims of his native language and native literature. He maintains, also, more than once, and perhaps with good reason, the native superiority of the Roman mind to the Grecian in certain qualities of racy humour, &c.[1]

---

[1] Where, by the way, the vocabulary of æsthetic terms, after all the labours of Ernesti and other German editors, is still far from being understood. In particular, the word *facetus* is so far from answering to its usual interpretation that *nostro periculo* let the reader understand it as precisely what the French mean by *naïve*.

Here, viz. in the case of Cicero, we have the first eminent
example (though he himself records some elder examples
amongst his own countrymen) of a man's standing up manfully to support the pretensions of his mother-tongue.   And
this might be done in a mere spirit of pugnacious defiance to
the arrogance of another nation,—a spirit which finds matter
of quarrel in a straw.   But here also we find the first example
of a statesman's seriously regarding a language in the light
of a foremost jewel amongst the trophies of nationality.

Coming forward to our own times, we find sovereign
rulers, on behalf of great nations, occasionally raising disputes
which presume some weak sense of the value and dignity
attached to a language.   Cromwell, for instance, insisted
upon Cardinal Mazarin's surrendering his pretension to have
the French language used in a particular negotiation ; and
accordingly Latin was substituted.[1]   But this did not argue
in Cromwell any *real* estimation of the English language.
He had been weak enough to wish that his own life and
annals should be written in Latin rather than in English.
The motive, it is true, might be to facilitate the circulation
of the work amongst the literati of the Continent.   But
vernacular translations would more certainly have been
executed all over the Continent in the absence of a Latin
original ; for this, by meeting the demand of foreigners in
part (viz. of *learned* foreigners), would *pro tanto* have lessened
the motives to such translations.   And, apart from this
preference of a Latin to a domestic portraiture addressing
itself originally to his own countrymen, or, if Latin were
otherwise the preferable language, apart from Cromwell's
preference of a Latin Casaubon [2] to a Latin Milton, in no
instance did Cromwell testify any sense of the commanding
rank due to English Literature amongst the contemporary [3]

[1] Latin had been adopted as the language for the foreign correspondence of the English Commonwealth from its institution in 1649 ;
and Milton, as secretary for the foreign correspondence of the Commonwealth Government, and then of Cromwell, was known indifferently as
the Foreign Secretary or the Latin Secretary.—M.

[2] Meric Casaubon (1599-1671), though by birth a Genevese, was for
most of his life resident in England.—M.

[3] At this era, when Chaucer, Spenser, Shakspere, and the contemporary dramatists, when Lord Bacon, Selden, Milton, and many of

Literatures of Christendom, nor any concern for its extension.

In the case of resisting the French arrogance, Cromwell had seemed to express homage to the language of his country, but in reality he had only regarded the political dignity of his country. A pretension may be lighter than a feather ; and yet in behalf of our country we do right to suffer no insolent aggression upon it by an enemy. But this argues no sincere regard for that feather on its own account. We have known a sailor to knock an Italian down for speaking disrespectfully of English tenor voices. The true and appropriate expression of reverence to a language is not by fighting for it as a subject of national rivalry, but, by taking earnest pains to write it with accuracy, practically to display its beauty, and to make its powers available for commensurate ends. Tried by this test, which of the three peoples that walk at the head of civilization—French, Germans, or English —have best fulfilled the duties of their position ?

To answer that the French only have been fully awake to these duties is painful, but too manifestly it is true. The French language possesses the very highest degree of merit, though not in the very highest mode of merit ; it is the unique language of the planet as an instrument for giving effect to the powers, and for meeting the necessities, of social gaiety and colloquial intercourse. This is partly the effect, and partly the cause, of the social temperament which distinguishes the French : partly follows the national disposition, and partly leads to it. The adaptation of the language to the people, not perhaps more really prominent in this case

---

the leading English theologians (Jewel, Hooker, Chillingworth, and Jeremy Taylor), had appeared—in fact, all the *optimates* of the English Literature—it must be remembered that the French Literature was barely beginning. Montaigne was the only *deceased* author of eminence ; Corneille was the only living author in general credit. The reader may urge that already, in the times of Catherine de Medici, there were eminent poets. In the reign of her son Charles IX were several ; and in the reign of her husband there was even a celebrated *Pleiad* of poets. But these were merely *court* poets ; they had no national name or life, and were already forgotten in the days of Louis XIII. As to German Literature, *that* was a blank. Germany had then but one tolerable poet, viz. Opitz, whom some people (chiefly his countrymen) honour with the title of the German Dryden !

than in others, is more conspicuously so ; and it may be in
a spirit of gratitude for this genial co-operation in their
language that the French are in a memorable degree anxious
to write it with elegance and correctness. They take a pride
in doing so ; and it is remarkable that grammatical inaccuracies, so common amongst ourselves, and common even
amongst our literary people, are almost unknown amongst
the educated French.[1]

But mere fidelity to grammar would leave a *negative*
impression : the respect which the French show to their
language expresses itself chiefly in their way of managing
it,—that is, in their attention to style and diction. It is
the rarest thing possible to find a French writer erring by
sentences too long, too intricate and loaded with clauses, or
too clumsy in their structure. The very highest qualities of
style are not much within the ideal of French composition ;
but in the executive results French prose composition usually
reveals an air of finish, of self-restraint under any possible
temptation to *des longueurs*, and of graceful adroitness in the
transitions.

Precisely the reverse of all this is found in the compositions of the German ; who is the greatest nuisance, in what
concerns the treatment of language, that the mind of man
is capable of conceiving. Of his language the German is
proud, and with reason, for it is redundantly rich. Even in

---

[1] This the reader might be apt to doubt, if he were to judge of
French grammar by French orthography. Until recently—that is,
through the last thirty years—very few people in France, even of the
educated classes, could spell. They spelt by procuration. The compositors of the press held a general power-of-attorney to spell for
universal France. A *facsimile* of the spelling which prevailed amongst
the royal family of France at the time of the elder Revolution is given
in Cléry's Journal: it is terrific. Such forms occur, for instance, as
J'avoient (J'avois) for *I had* : *J'été* (étois) for *I was*. But, in publish-
ing such facts, the reader is not to imagine that Cléry meant to expose
anything needing concealment. All people of distinction spelled in
that lawless way ; and the loyal valet doubtless no more thought it
decorous for a man of rank to spell his own spelling than to clean his
own shoes or to wash his own linen. "Base is the man that pays,"
says Ancient Pistol ; "Base is the man that spells," said the French
of that century. It would have been vulgar to spell decently ; and it
was not illiterate to spell abominably ; for literary men spelled not at
all better ; they also spelled by proxy, and by grace of compositors.

its Teutonic section, it is *so* rich as to be self-sufficing, and capable, though awkwardly, of dispensing with the Greek and Latin counter-section. This independence of alien resources has sometimes been even practically adopted as the basis of a dictionary, and officially patronized by adoption in the public *bureaus*. Some thirty years ago the Prussian government was said to have introduced into the public service a dictionary[1] which rejected all words not purely vernacular. Such a word, for instance, as *philosophie* was not admissible ; the indigenous word *weltweisheit* was held to be not only sufficient, which it really *is*, but exclusively legitimate. Yet, with all this scrupulosity and purism of veneration for his native language,—to which he ascribes *every* quality of power and beauty, and amongst others—*credite posteri !*—sometimes even *vocal* beauty[2] and euphony,—the true German has no sense of grace or deformity in the management of his language. Style, diction, the construction of sentences, are ideas perfectly without meaning to the German writer. If a whole book were made up of a single sentence, all collateral or subordinate ideas being packed into it as parenthetical intercalations,—if this single sentence should even cover an acre of ground,—the true German would see in all *that* no want of art, would recognise no opportunities thrown away for the display of beauty. The temple would in *his* eyes exist, because the materials of the temple—the stone, the lime, the iron, the timber—had been carted to the ground. A sentence, even when insulated and viewed apart for itself, is a subject for complex art : even *so* far it is capable of multiform beauty, and liable to a whole *nosology* of malconformations. But it is in the *relation* of sentences, in what Horace terms their "*junctura*," that the true life of composition resides. The

---

[1] By Heinze, if I recollect ; and founded partly on that of Wolf.

[2] Foreigners do not often go so far as this ; and yet an American, in his "Sketches of Turkey" (New York, 1833), characterizes the German (p. 478) not only as a soft and melodious language, but absolutely as "the *softest* of all European languages." Schiller and Goethe had a notion that it was capable of being hammered into euphony, that it was by possibility malleable in that respect, but then only by great labour of selection, and as a trick of rope-dancing ingenuity.

mode of their *nexus*, the way in which one sentence is made to arise out of another, and to prepare the opening for a third : this is the great loom in which the textile process of the moving intellect reveals itself and prospers. Here the separate clauses of a period become architectural parts, aiding, relieving, supporting each other. But how can any approach to that effect, or any suggestion of it, exist for him who hides and buries all openings for parts and graceful correspondences in one monotonous continuity of period, stretching over three octavo pages ? Kant was a great man, but he was obtuse and deaf as an antediluvian boulder with regard to language and its capacities. He has sentences which have been measured by a carpenter, and some of them run two feet eight by six inches. Now, a sentence with that enormous span is fit only for the use of a megatherium or a pre-Adamite. Parts so remote as the beginning and the end of such a sentence can have no sensible relation to each other : not much as regards their logic, but none at all as regards their more *sensuous* qualities—rhythmus, for instance, or the continuity of metaphor. And it is clear that, if the internal relations of a sentence fade under the extravagant mispro-portion of its scale, *a fortiori* must the outer relations. If two figures, or other objects, are meant to modify each other visually by means of colour, of outline, or of expression, they must be brought into juxtaposition, or at least into neigh-bourhood. A chasm between them, so vast as to prevent the synthesis of the two objects in one co-existing field of vision, interrupts the play of all genial comparison. Periods, and clauses of periods, modify each other, and build up a whole then only when the parts are shown *as* parts, cohering and conspiring to a common result. But, if each part is separately so vast as to eclipse the disc of the adjacent parts, then substantially they are separate wholes, and do not coalesce to any joint or complex impression.

We English in this matter occupy a middle position between the French and the Germans. Agreeably to the general cast of the national character, our tendency is to degrade the value of the ornamental, whenever it is brought before us under any suggestion of comparison or rivalry with the substantial or grossly useful. Viewing the thoughts as the substantial objects in a book, we are apt to regard the manner of presenting these thoughts as a secondary or even trivial concern. The one we typify as the metallic substance, the silver or gold, which constitutes the true value that cannot perish in a service of plate ; whereas the style too generally, in *our* estimate, represents the mere casual fashion given to the plate by the artist—an adjunct that any change of public taste may degrade into a positive disadvantage. But in this we English err greatly ; and by these three capital oversights :—

1. It is certain that style, or (to speak by the most general expression) the management of language, ranks amongst the fine arts, and is able therefore to yield a separate intellectual pleasure quite apart from the interest of the subject treated. So far it is already one error to rate the value of style as if it were necessarily a secondary or subordinate thing. On the contrary, style has an *absolute* value, like the product of any other exquisite art, quite distinct from the value of the subject about which it is employed, and irrelatively to the subject ; precisely as the fine workmanship of Scopas the Greek, or of Cellini the Florentine, is equally valued by the connoisseur, whether embodied in bronze or marble, in an ivory or a golden vase. But

2. If we *do* submit to this narrow valuation of style, founded on the interest of the subject to which it is ministerial, still, even on that basis, we English commit a capital blunder which the French earnestly and sincerely escape ; for, assuming that the thoughts involve the primary interest, still it must make all the difference in the world to the success of those thoughts whether they are treated in the way best fitted to expel the doubts or darkness that may have settled upon them, and, secondly, in cases where the business is not to establish new convictions, but to carry old convictions into operative life and power, whether they are treated in the way best fitted to rekindle in the mind a practical sense of their value. Style has two separate functions : first, to brighten the *intelligibility* of a subject which is obscure to the understanding ; secondly, to regenerate the normal *power* and impressiveness of a subject which has

become dormant to the sensibilities. Darkness gathers upon many a theme, sometimes from previous mistreatment, but oftener from original perplexities investing its very nature. Upon the style it is, if we take that word in its largest sense,—upon the skill and art of the developer,—that these perplexities greatly depend for their illumination. Look, again, at the other class of cases, when the difficulties are not for the understanding but for the practical sensibilities as applicable to the services of life. The subject, suppose, is already understood sufficiently; but it is lifeless as a motive. It is not new light that is to be communicated, but old torpor that is to be dispersed. The writer is not summoned to convince, but to persuade. Decaying lineaments are to be retraced, and faded colouring to be refreshed. Now, these offices of style are really not essentially below the level of those other offices attached to the original *discovery* of truth. He that to an old conviction, long since inoperative and dead, gives the regeneration that carries it back into the heart as a vital power of action—he, again, that by new light, or by light trained to flow through a new channel, reconciles to the understanding a truth which hitherto had seemed dark or doubtful—both these men are really, *quoad* us that benefit by their services, the *discoverers* of the truth. Yet these results are amongst the possible gifts of style. Light to *see* the road, power to *advance along* it—such being amongst the promises and proper functions of style, it is a capital error, under the idea of its ministeriality, to undervalue this great organ of the advancing intellect—an organ which is equally important considered as a tool for the culture and *populariza-tion* of truth and also (if it had no use at all in that way) as a mode *per se* of the beautiful and a fountain of intellectual pleasure. The vice of that appreciation which we English apply to style lies in representing it as a mere ornamental accident of written composition—a trivial embellishment, like the mouldings of furniture, the cornices of ceilings, or the arabesques of tea-urns. On the contrary, it is a product of art the rarest, subtlest, and most intellectual ; and, like other products of the fine arts, it is then finest when it is most eminently disinterested—that is, most conspicuously detached from gross palpable uses. Yet, in very many cases, it really *has* the obvious uses of that gross palpable order ; as in the cases just noticed, when it gives light to the understanding, or power to the will, removing obscurities from one set of truths, and into another circulating the life-blood of sensibility.   In these cases, meantime, the style is contemplated as a thing separable from the thoughts ; in fact, as the *dress* of the thoughts—a robe that may be laid aside at pleasure.   But

3. There arises a case entirely different, where style cannot be regarded as a *dress* or alien covering, but where style becomes the *incarnation* of the thoughts.   The human body is not the dress or apparel of the human spirit : far more mysterious is the mode of their union.   Call the two elements A and B ; then it is impossible to point out A as existing aloof from B, or *vice versa*.   A exists in and through B ; B exists in and through A.   No profound observer can have failed to observe this illustrated in the capacities of style.   Imagery is sometimes not the mere alien apparelling of a thought, and of a nature to be detached from the thought, but is the coefficient that, being superadded to something else, absolutely *makes* the thought as a *third* and separate existence.

In this third case, our English tendency to undervalue style goes more deeply into error than in the other two. In those two we simply underrate the enormous services that are or might be rendered by style to the interests of truth and human thinking ; but in the third case we go near to abolish a mode of existence.   This is not so impossible an offence as might be supposed.   There are many ideas in Leibnitz, in Kant, in the schoolmen, in Plato at times, and certainly in Aristotle (as the ideas of antiperistasis, entelecheia, &c.), which are only to be arrested and realized by a signal *effort*—by a struggle and a *nisus* both of reflection and of large combination.   Now, where so much depends upon an effort—on a spasmodic strain,—to fail by a hair's breadth is to collapse.   For instance, the idea involved in the word transcendental,[1] as used in the critical philosophy, illustrates the metaphysical relations of style.

[1] " *Transcendental* " :—Kant, who was the most sincere, honourable, and truthful of human beings, always understood himself.   He

hated tricks, disguises, or mystifications, simulation equally with dissimulation ; and his love of the English was built avowedly on their *veracity*. So far he has an extra chance of intelligibility. On the other hand, of all men, he had the least talent for explaining himself, or communicating his views to others. Whenever Kant undertakes to render into popular language the secrets of metaphysics, one inevitably thinks of Bardolph's attempt to analyse and justify the word *accommodation* :—"*Accommodation*—that is, when a man is (as they say) accommodated ; or when a man is being whereby he may be thought to be accommodated, which is an excellent thing." There are sometimes Eleusinian mysteries, sealed by nature herself, the mighty mother, as *aporreta*, things essentially ineffable and unutterable in vulgar ears. Long, for instance, he laboured, but vainly he laboured, to render intelligible the scholastic idea of the transcendental. This should have been easy to deal with ; for, on the one side lay the *transcendent*, on the other the *immanent*, two buoys to map out the channel ; and yet did Kant, throughout his long life, fail to satisfy any one man who was not previously and independently in possession of the idea. Difficulties of this nature should seem as little related to artifice of style and diction as geometrical difficulties ; and yet it is certain that, by throwing the stress and emphasis of the perplexity upon the exact verbal *nodus* of the problem, a better structure of his sentences would have guided Kant to a readier apprehension of the real shape which the difficulty assumed to the ordinary student.

CONVERSATION [1]

AMONGST the arts connected with the *elegancies* of social life in a degree which nobody denies is the Art of Conversation ; but in a degree which almost everybody denies, if one may judge by their neglect of its simple rules, this same art is not less connected with the *uses* of social life. Neither the luxury of conversation, nor the possible benefit of conversation, is to be found under that rude administration of it which generally prevails. Without an art, without some simple system of rules, gathered from experience of such contingencies as are most likely to mislead the practice when left to its own guidance, no act of man nor effort accomplishes its purposes in perfection. The sagacious Greek would not so much as drink a glass of wine amongst a few friends without a systematic art to guide him, and a regular form of polity to control him,—which art and which polity (begging Plato's pardon) were better than any of more ambitious aim in his Republic. Every *symposium* had its set of rules, and rigorous they were ; had its own *symposiarch* to govern it, and a tyrant he was. Elected democratically, he became, when once installed, an autocrat not less despotic than the King of Persia. Purposes still more slight and fugitive have been organized into arts. Taking soup gracefully, under the difficulties opposed to it by a dinner dress at that time fashionable, was reared into an art about forty-

---

[1] First published in *Tait's Magazine* for October 1847 : reprinted, with considerable enlargements, in 1860, in the fourteenth or posthumous volume of De Quincey's Edition of his Collective Writings. —M.

five years ago by a Frenchman who lectured upon it to
ladies in London ; and the most brilliant duchess of that
day, viz. the Duchess of Devonshire, was amongst his best
pupils.   Spitting, if the reader will pardon the mention of
so gross a fact, was shown to be a very difficult art, and
publicly prelected upon, about the same time in the same
great capital.   The professors in this faculty were the
hackney-coachmen ; the pupils were gentlemen, who paid a
guinea each for three lessons ; the chief problem in this
system of hydraulics being to throw the salivating column in
a parabolic curve from the centre of Parliament Street, when
driving four-in-hand, to the foot pavements, right and left,
so as to alarm the consciences of guilty peripatetics on either
side.   The ultimate problem, which closed the *curriculum* of
study, was held to lie in spitting round a corner ; when *that*
was mastered, the pupil was entitled to his doctor's degree.
Endless are the purposes of man, merely festal or merely
comic, and aiming but at the momentary life of a cloud,
which have earned for themselves the distinction and
apparatus of a separate art.   Yet for conversation, the great
paramount purpose of social meetings, no art exists or has
been attempted.

That seems strange, but is not really so.   A limited
process submits readily to the limits of a technical system ;
but a process so unlimited as the interchange of thought
seems to reject them.   And, even if an art of conversation
were less unlimited, the means of carrying such an art into
practical effect amongst so vast a variety of minds seems
wanting.   Yet again, perhaps, after all, this may rest on a
mistake.   What we begin by misjudging is the particular
phasis of conversation which brings it under the control of
art and discipline.   It is not in its relation to the intellect
that conversation ever has been improved or *will* be improved primarily, but in its relation to manners.   Has a
man ever mixed with what in technical phrase is called
"good company," meaning company in the highest degree
polished,—company which (being or *not* being aristocratic as
respects its composition) is aristocratic as respects the standard of its manners and usages ?   If he really *has*, and does
not deceive himself from vanity or from pure inacquaintance

with the world, in that case he must have remarked the
large effect impressed upon the grace and upon the freedom
of conversation by a few simple instincts of real good breeding. Good breeding—what is it? There is no need in
this place to answer that question comprehensively ; it is sufficient to say that it is made up chiefly of *negative* elements,—
that it shows itself far less in what it prescribes than in what
it forbids. Now, even under this limitation of the idea, the
truth is that more will be done for the benefit of conversation
by the simple magic of good manners (that is, chiefly by a
system of forbearances), applied to the besetting vices of
social intercourse, than ever *was* or *can* be done by all
varieties of intellectual power assembled upon the same arena.
Intellectual graces of the highest order may perish and confound each other when exercised in a spirit of ill-temper, or
under the licence of bad manners ; whereas very humble
powers, when allowed to expand themselves colloquially in
that genial freedom which is possible only under the most
absolute confidence in the self-restraint of your collocutors,
accomplish their purpose to a certainty if it be the ordinary
purpose of liberal amusement, and have a chance of accom-
plishing it even when this purpose is the more ambitious one
of communicating knowledge or exchanging new views upon
truth.

In my own early years, having been formed by nature
too exclusively and morbidly for solitary thinking, I observed nothing. Seeming to have eyes, in reality I saw
nothing. But it is a matter of no very uncommon experience that, whilst the mere observers never became meditators, the mere meditators, on the other hand, may finally
ripen into close observers. Strength of thinking, through
long years, upon innumerable themes, will have the effect
of disclosing a vast variety of questions, to which it soon
becomes apparent that answers are lurking up and down
the whole field of daily experience ; and thus an external
experience which was slighted in youth, because it was a
dark cipher that could be read into no meaning, a key that
answered to no lock, gradually becomes interesting as it is
found to yield one solution after another to problems that
have independently matured in the mind. Thus, for in-

stance, upon the special functions of conversation, upon its powers, its laws, its ordinary diseases, and their appropriate remedies, in youth I never bestowed a thought or a care. I viewed it not as one amongst the gay ornamental arts of the intellect, but as one amongst the dull necessities of business.   Loving solitude too much, I understood the capacities of colloquial intercourse too little.   And thus it is, though not for *my* reason, that most people estimate the intellectual relations of conversation.   Let these, however, be what they may, one thing seemed undeniable—that this world talked a great deal too much.   It would be better for all parties if nine in every ten of the *winged words* flying about in this world (Homer's *epea pteroenta*) had their feathers clipped amongst men,—or even amongst women, who have a right to a larger allowance of words.   Yet, as it was quite out of my power to persuade the world into any such self-denying reformation, it seemed equally out of the line of my duties to nourish any moral anxiety in that direction.   *To talk* seemed to me at that time in the same category as *to sleep,*—not an accomplishment, but a base physical infirmity.   As a moralist, I really was culpably careless upon the whole subject.   I cared as little what absurdities men practised in their vast tennis-courts of conversation, where the ball is flying backwards and forwards to no purpose for ever, as what tricks Englishmen might play with their monstrous national debt.   Yet at length what I disregarded on any principle of moral usefulness I came to make an object of the profoundest interest on principles of art.   *Betting*, in like manner, and *wagering,*—which apparently had no moral value, and for that reason had been always slighted as inconsiderable arts (though, by the way, they always had one valuable use, viz. that of evading quarrels, since a bet summarily intercepts an altercation),— rose suddenly into a philosophic rank when, successively, Huygens, the Bernoullis, and De Moivre were led by the suggestion of these trivial practices amongst men to throw the light of a high mathematical analysis upon the whole doctrine of Chances.[1]   Lord Bacon had been led to remark

---

[1] Huygens, 1629-1695 ; James Bernoulli, 1654-1705 ; John Bernoulli, 1667-1748 ; De Moivre, 1667-1754.

the capacities of conversation as an organ for sharpening one particular mode of intellectual power.[1] Circumstances, on the other hand, led me into remarking the special capacities of conversation as an organ for absolutely creating another mode of power. Let a man have read, thought, studied, as much as he may, rarely will he reach his possible advantages as a *ready* man, unless he has exercised his powers much in conversation : that, I think, was Lord Bacon's idea. Now, this wise and useful remark points in a direction not objective, but subjective ; that is, it does not promise any absolute extension to truth itself, but only some greater facilities to the man who expounds or diffuses the truth. Nothing will be done for truth objectively that would not at any rate be done ; but subjectively it will be done with more fluency, and at less cost of exertion to the doer. On the contrary, my own growing reveries on the latent powers of conversation (which, though a thing that then I hated, yet challenged at times unavoidably my attention) pointed to an absolute birth of new insight into the truth itself as inseparable from the finer and more scientific exercise of the talking art. It would not be the brilliancy, the ease, or the adroitness of the expounder that would benefit, but the absolute interests of the thing expounded. A feeling dawned on me of a secret magic lurking in the peculiar life, velocities, and contagious ardour of conversation, quite separate from any which belonged to books,—arming a man with new forces, and not merely with a new dexterity in wielding the old ones. I felt (and in this I could not be mistaken, as too certainly it was a fact of my own experience) that in the electric kindling of life between two minds,—and far less

[1] "Reading maketh a full man ; conference a ready man ; and " writing an exact man,"—is Bacon's well-known saying in his essay *Of Studies* ; but in his essay *Of Friendship* he discusses the benefits of "conference" or conversation more at large, thus :—"Certain it " is that, whosoever hath his mind fraught with many thoughts, his " wits and understanding do clarify and break up in the communicating " and discussing with another : he tosseth his thoughts more easily ; " he marshalleth them more orderly ; he seeth how they look when " they are turned into words ; finally, he waxeth wiser than himself, " and that more by an hour's discourse than by a day's meditation. " . . . In a word, a man were better relate himself to a statua or " picture than to suffer his thoughts to pass in smother."—M.

from the kindling natural to conflict (though *that* also is something) than from the kindling through sympathy with the object discussed in its momentary coruscation of shifting phases,—there sometimes arise glimpses and shy revelations of affinity, suggestion, relation, analogy, that could not have been approached through any avenues of methodical study. Great organists find the same effect of inspiration, the same result of power creative and revealing, in the mere movement and velocity of their own voluntaries. Like the heavenly wheels of Milton, throwing off fiery flakes and bickering flames, these *impromptu* torrents of music create rapturous *fioriture*, beyond all capacity in the artist to register, or afterwards to imitate. The reader must be well aware that many philosophic instances exist where a change in the degree makes a change in the kind. Usually this is otherwise ; the prevailing rule is that the principle subsists unaffected by any possible variation in the amount or degree of the force. But a large class of exceptions must have met the reader,—though, from want of a pencil, he has improperly omitted to write them down in his pocket-book,—cases, viz., where, upon passing beyond a certain point in the graduation, an alteration takes place suddenly in the *kind* of effect, a new direction is given to the power. Some illustration of this truth occurs in conversation, where a velocity in the movement of thought is made possible (and often natural) greater than ever can arise in methodical books, and where, 2*dly*, approximations are more obvious and easily effected between things too remote for a steadier contemplation.

One remarkable evidence of a *specific* power lying hid in conversation may be seen in such writings as have moved by impulses most nearly resembling those of conversation,—for instance, in those of Edmund Burke. For one moment, reader, pause upon the spectacle of two contrasted intellects, Burke's and Johnson's : one an intellect essentially going forward, governed by the very necessity of growth, by the law of motion in advance ; the latter essentially an intellect retrogressive, retrospective, and throwing itself back on its own steps. This original difference was aided accidentally in Burke by the tendencies of political partisanship,—which, both from moving amongst moving things and uncertainties, as compared with the more stationary aspects of moral philosophy, and also from its more fluctuating and fiery passions, must unavoidably reflect in greater life the tumultuary character of conversation. The result from these original differences of intellectual constitution, aided by these secondary differences of pursuit, is, that Dr. Johnson never, in any instance, GROWS a truth before your eyes whilst in the act of delivering it or moving towards it. All that he offers up to the end of the chapter he had when he began. But to Burke, such was the prodigious elasticity of his thinking, equally in his conversation and in his writings, the mere act of movement became the principle or cause of movement. Motion propagated motion, and life threw off life. The very violence of a projectile as thrown by *him* caused it to rebound in fresh forms, fresh angles, splintering, coruscating, which gave out thoughts as new (and as startling) to himself as they are to his reader. In this power, which might be illustrated largely from the writings of Burke, is seen something allied to the powers of a prophetic seer, who is compelled oftentimes into seeing things as unexpected by himself as by others. Now, in conversation, considered as to its *tendencies* and capacities, there sleeps an intermitting spring of such sudden revelation, showing much of the same general character,—a power putting on a character *essentially* differing from the character worn by the power of books.

If, then, in the *colloquial* commerce of thought there lurked a power not shared by other modes of that great commerce, a power separate and *sui generis*, next it was apparent that a great art must exist somewhere applicable to this power,—not in the Pyramids, or in the tombs of Thebes, but in the unwrought quarries of men's minds, so many and so dark. There was an art missing. If an art, then an artist was missing. If the art (as we say of foreign mails) were "due," then the artist was "due." How happened it that this great man never made his appearance ? But perhaps he *had*. Many persons think Dr. Johnson the *exemplar* of conversational power. I think otherwise, for reasons which I shall soon explain ; and far sooner I should look for such an *exemplar* in Burke. But neither Johnson nor Burke, however they might rank as *powers*, was the *artist* that I demanded. Burke valued not at all the reputation of a great performer in conversation ; he scarcely contemplated the skill as having a real existence ; and a man will never be an artist who does not value his art, or even recognise it as an object distinctly defined. Johnson, again, relied sturdily upon his natural powers for carrying him aggressively through all conversational occasions or difficulties that English society, from its known character and composition, could be supposed likely to bring forward, without caring for any art or system of rules that might give further effect to that power. If a man is strong enough to knock down ninety-nine in a hundred of all antagonists in spite of any advantages as to pugilistic science which they may possess over himself, he is not likely to care for the improbable case of a hundredth man appearing with strength equal to his own superadded to the utmost excess of that artificial skill which is wanting in himself. Against such a contingency it is not worth while going to the cost of a regular pugilistic training. Half a century might not bring up a case of actual call for its application. Or, if it did, for a single *extra* case of that nature there would always be a resource in the *extra* (and, strictly speaking, foul) arts of kicking, scratching, pinching, and tearing hair.

The conversational powers of Johnson were narrow in compass, however strong within their own essential limits. As a *conditio sine qua non*, he did not absolutely demand a *personal* contradictor by way of " stoker " to supply fuel and keep up his steam ; but he demanded at least a *subject* teeming with elements of known contradictory opinion, whether linked to partisanship or not. His views of all things tended to negation, never to the positive and the creative. Hence may be explained a fact which cannot have escaped any keen observer of those huge Johnsonian *memorabilia* which we possess,—viz. that the gyration of his flight upon any one question that ever came before him was so exceedingly brief. There was no process, no evolution, no movement of self-conflict or preparation : a word, a distinction, a pointed antithesis, and, above all, a new abstraction of the logic involved in some popular fallacy, or doubt, or prejudice, or

problem, formed the utmost of his efforts. He dissipated
some casual perplexity that had gathered in the eddies of
conversation, but he contributed nothing to any weightier
interest; he unchoked a strangulated sewer in some blind
alley, but what river is there that felt his cleansing power?
There is no man that can cite any single error which Dr.
Johnson unmasked, or any important truth which he expanded. Nor is this extraordinary. Dr. Johnson had not
within himself the fountain of such power, having not a
brooding or naturally philosophic intellect. Philosophy in
any acquired sense he had none. How else could it have
happened that upon David Hartley, upon David Hume, upon
Voltaire, upon Rousseau,—the true or the false philosophy
of his own day,—beyond a personal sneer, founded on some
popular slander, he had nothing to say and said nothing?
A new world was moulding itself in Dr. Johnson's meridian
hours; new generations were ascending, and "other palms
were won." Yet of all this the Doctor suspected nothing.
Countrymen and contemporaries of the Doctor's, brilliant
men, but (as many think) trifling men, such as Horace
Walpole and Lord Chesterfield, already in the middle of
that eighteenth century could read the signs of the great
changes advancing. Already they started in horror from
the portents which rose before them in Paris like the procession of regal phantoms before Macbeth, and have left
in their letters records undeniable (such as now read like
Cassandra prophecies) that already they had noticed tremors
in the ground below their feet, and sounds in the air,
running before the great convulsions under which Europe
was destined to rock full thirty years later. Many instances
during the last war showed us that in the frivolous dandy
might often lurk the most fiery and accomplished of *aides-de-
camp*; and these cases show that men in whom the world
sees only elegant *roués*, sometimes from carelessness, sometimes from want of opening for display, conceal qualities of
penetrating sagacity, and a learned spirit of observation, such
as may be looked for vainly in persons of more solemn and
academic pretension. But there was a greater defect in Dr.
Johnson for purposes of conversation than merely want of
eye for the social phenomena rising around him. He had

no eye for such phenomena, because he had a somnolent want of interest in them ; and why ? Because he had little interest in man. Having no sympathy with human nature in its struggles, or faith in the progress of man, he could not be supposed to regard with much interest any forerunning symptoms of changes that to him were themselves indifferent. And the reason that he felt thus careless was the desponding taint in his blood. It is good to be of a melancholic temperament, as all the ancient physiologists held, but only if the melancholy is balanced by fiery aspiring qualities,— not when it gravitates essentially to the earth. Hence the drooping, desponding character, and the monotony, of the estimate which Dr. Johnson applied to life. We are all, in *his* view, miserable, scrofulous wretches ; the "strumous diathesis " was developed in our flesh, or soon would be ; and, but for his piety,— which was the best indication of some greatness latent within him,—he would have suggested to all mankind a nobler use for garters than any which regarded knees. In fact I believe that, but for his piety, he would not only have counselled hanging in general, but hanged himself in particular. Now, this gloomy temperament, not as an occasional but as a permanent state, is fatal to the power of brilliant conversation, in so far as that power rests upon raising a continual succession of topics, and not merely using with lifeless talent the topics offered by others. Man is the central interest about which revolve all the fleeting phenomena of life ; these secondary interests demand the first ; and, with the little knowledge about them which must follow from little care about them, there can be no salient fountain of conversational themes. "*Pectus*," says Quintilian, "*id est quod disertum facit*":—*The* heart (and not the brain) *is that which makes a man eloquent*. From the heart, from an interest of love or hatred, of hope or care, springs all permanent eloquence ; and the elastic spring of conversation is gone if the talker is a mere showy man of talent, pulling at an oar which he detests.

What an index might be drawn up of subjects interesting to human nature, and suggested by the events of the Johnsonian period, upon which the Doctor ought to have talked, and must have talked if his interest in man had been catholic, but on which the Doctor is not recorded to have uttered one word! Visiting Paris once in his whole life, he applied himself diligently to the measuring of—what? Of gilt mouldings and diapered panels! Yet books, it will be said, suggest topics as well as life and the moving sceneries of life; and surely Dr. Johnson had *this* fund to draw upon? No; for, though he had read much in a desultory way, he had studied nothing[1]; and without that sort of systematic reading, it is but a rare chance that books can be brought to bear effectually, and yet indirectly, upon conversation; whilst to make them directly and formally the subjects of discussion, presupposes either a learned audience, or, if the audience is not so, much pedantry and much arrogance in the talker.[2]

The flight of our human hours, not really more rapid at any one moment than another, yet oftentimes to our feelings *seems* more rapid; and this flight startles us like guilty things with a more affecting *sense* of its rapidity when a distant church-clock strikes in the night-time, or when, upon some solemn summer evening, the sun's disc, after settling for a minute with farewell horizontal rays, suddenly drops out of sight. The record of our loss in such a case seems to us the first intimation of its possibility,—as if we could not be made sensible that the hours were perishable until it is announced to us that already they have perished. We feel a perplexity of distress when that which seems to us the cruellest of injuries, a robbery committed upon our dearest possession by the conspiracy of the world outside, seems also as in part a robbery sanctioned by our own collusion.

---

[1] "*Had studied nothing*":—It may be doubted whether Dr. Johnson understood any one thing thoroughly except Latin: not that he understood even *that* with the elaborate and circumstantial accuracy required for the editing critically of a Latin classic. But, if he had less than *that*, he also had more: he *possessed* that language in a way that no extent of mere critical knowledge could confer. He wrote it genially, not as one translating into it painfully from English, but as one using it for his original organ of thinking. And in Latin verse he expressed himself at times with the energy and freedom of a Roman. With Greek his acquaintance was far more slender.

[2] The original article in *Tait's Magazine* for October 1847 stopped here: what follows is subsequent addition.—M.

The world, and the customs of the world, never cease to
levy taxes upon our time : that is true, and so far the blame
is not ours ; but the particular *degree* in which we suffer by
this robbery depends much upon the weakness with which
we ourselves become parties to the wrong, or the energy
with which we resist it. Resisting or not, however, we are
doomed to suffer a bitter pang as often as the irrecoverable
flight of our time is brought home with keenness to our
hearts. The spectacle of a lady floating over the sea in a
boat, and waking suddenly from sleep to find her magnificent
ropes of pearl-necklace by some accident detached at one end
from its fastenings, the loose string hanging down into the
water, and pearl after pearl slipping off for ever into the
abyss, brings before us the sadness of the case. That particular pearl which at the very moment is rolling off into the
unsearchable deeps carries its own separate reproach to the
lady's heart. But it is more deeply reproachful as the representative of so many others, uncounted pearls, that have
already been swallowed up irrecoverably whilst she was yet
sleeping, and of many beside that must follow before any
remedy can be applied to what we may call this jewelly
hæmorrhage. A constant hæmorrhage of the same kind is
wasting our jewelly hours. A day has perished from our
brief calendar of days : and *that* we could endure ; but this
day is no more than the reiteration of many other days,—
days counted by thousands,—that have perished to the same
extent and by the same unhappy means, viz. the evil usages
of the world made effectual and ratified by our own *lâcheté*.
Bitter is the upbraiding which we seem to hear from a secret
monitor—" My friend, you make very free with your days :
pray, how many do you expect to have ? What is your
rental, as regards the total harvest of days which this life is
likely to yield ? " Let us consider. Threescore years and
ten produce a total sum of 25,550 days,—to say nothing of
some seventeen or eighteen more that will be payable to you
as a *bonus* on account of leap years. Now, out of this total,
one-third must be deducted at a blow for a single item, viz.
sleep. Next, on account of illness, of recreation, and the
serious occupations spread over the surface of life, it will be
little enough to deduct another third. Recollect also that

twenty years will have gone from the earlier end of your
life (viz. above seven thousand days) before you can have
attained any skill or system, or any definite purpose in the
distribution of your time. Lastly, for that single item
which amongst the Roman armies was indicated by the
technical phrase "*corpus curare*,"—tendance on the animal
necessities, viz. eating, drinking, washing, bathing, and
exercise, — deduct the smallest allowance consistent with
propriety ; and, upon summing up all these appropriations,
you will not find so much as four thousand days left disposable for direct intellectual culture. Four thousand, or
forty hundreds, will be a hundred forties : that is, according
to the lax Hebrew method of indicating six weeks by the
phrase of "forty days," you will have a hundred bills or
drafts on Father Time, value six weeks each, as the whole
period available for intellectual labour. A solid block of
about eleven and a half continuous years is all that a long
life will furnish for the development of what is most august
in man's nature. After *that*, the night comes when no man
can work ; brain and arm will be alike unserviceable ; or, if
the life should be unusually extended, the vital powers will
be drooping as regards all motions in advance.

Limited thus severely in his *direct* approaches to knowledge, and in his approaches to that which is a thousand
times more important than knowledge, viz. the conduct and
discipline of the knowing faculty, the more clamorous is the
necessity that a wise man should turn to account any
INDIRECT and supplementary means towards the same ends ;
and amongst these means a chief one by right and potentially
is CONVERSATION. Even the primary means,—books, study,
and meditation,—through errors from without and errors
from within, are not *that* which they might be made. Too
constantly, when reviewing his own efforts for improvement,
a man has reason to say (indignantly, as one injured by
others ; penitentially, as contributing to this injury himself)
"Much of my studies has been thrown away ; many books
which were useless, or worse than useless, I have read ;
many books which ought to have been read I have left
unread : such is the sad necessity under the absence of all
preconceived plan ; and the proper road is first ascertained

when the journey is drawing to its close." In a wilderness
so vast as that of books, to go astray often and widely is
pardonable, because it is inevitable ; and, in proportion as
the errors on this primary field of study have been great, it
is important to have reaped some compensatory benefits on
the secondary field of conversation. Books teach by one
machinery, conversation by another ; and, if these resources
were trained into correspondence to their own separate ideals,
they might become reciprocally the complements of each
other. The false selection of books, for instance, might
often be rectified at once by the frank collation of experiences
which takes place in miscellaneous colloquial intercourse.
But other and greater advantages belong to conversation for
the effectual promotion of intellectual culture. Social discussion supplies the natural integration for the deficiencies of
private and sequestered study. Simply to rehearse, simply
to express in words amongst familiar friends, one's own
intellectual perplexities, is oftentimes to clear them up. It
is well known that the best means of learning is by teaching.
The effort that is made for others is made eventually for
ourselves ; and the readiest method of illuminating obscure
conceptions, or maturing such as are crude, lies in an earnest
effort to make them apprehensible by others. Even this is
but one amongst the functions fulfilled by conversation.
Each separate individual in a company is likely to see any
problem or idea under some difference of angle. Each may
have some difference of views to contribute, derived either
from a different course of reading, or a different tenor of
reflection, or perhaps a different train of experience. The
advantages of colloquial discussion are not only often commensurate in *degree* to those of study, but they recommend
themselves also as being different in *kind* ; they are special
and *sui generis*. It, must, therefore, be important that so
great an organ of intellectual development should not be
neutralized by mismanagement, as generally it is, or neglected
through insensibility to its latent capacities. The importance
of the subject should be measured by its relation to the
interests of the intellect ; and on this principle we do not
scruple to think that, in reviewing our own experience of
the causes most commonly at war with the free movement of

conversation as it ought to be, we are in effect contributing hints for a new chapter in any future " Essay on the Improvement of the Mind." Watts's book under that title is really of little practical use ; nor would it ever have been thought so had it not been patronized, in a spirit of partisanship, by a particular section of religious dissenters.[1] Wherever *that* happens, the fortune of a book is made ; for the sectarian impulse creates a sensible current in favour of the book, and the general or neutral reader yields passively to the motion of the current without knowing or caring to know whence it is derived.

Our remarks must of necessity be cursory here, so that they will not need or permit much preparation ; but one distinction which is likely to strike on some minds as to the two different purposes of conversation ought to be noticed, since otherwise it will seem doubtful whether we have not confounded them, or, secondly, if we have *not* confounded them, which of the two it is that our remarks contemplate.   In speaking above of conversation, we have fixed our view on those uses of conversation which are ministerial to intellectual culture ; but, in relation to the majority of men, conversation is far less valuable as an organ of intellectual culture than of social enjoyment.   For one man interested in conversation as a means of advancing his studies, there are fifty men whose interest in conversation points exclusively to convivial pleasure.   This, as being a more extensive function of conversation, is so far the more dignified function ; whilst, on the other hand, such a purpose as direct mental improvement seems by its superior gravity to challenge the higher rank.   Yet, in fact, even here the more general purpose of conversation takes precedency ; for, when dedicated to the objects of festal delight, conversation rises by its tendency to the rank of a fine art.   It is true that not one man in a million rises to any distinction in this art ; nor, whatever France may conceit of herself, has any one nation, amongst other nations, a real precedency in

---

[1] A repetition of De Quincey's opinion of Watts as given *ante*, pp. 28-29.   But the sentence is of blundered structure :—"*of little practical use* ; nor would it ever have been *thought so*" ! &c.—M.

this art. The artists are rare indeed ; but still the art, as distinguished from the artist, may, by its difficulties, by the quality of its graces, and by the range of its possible brilliances, take rank as a *fine* art ; or, at all events, according to its powers of execution, it tends to that rank ; whereas the best order of conversation that is simply ministerial to a purpose of use cannot pretend to a higher name than that of a *mechanic* art. But these distinctions, though they would form the grounds of a separate treatment in a regular treatise on Conversation, may be practically neglected on this occasion, because the hints offered, by the generality of the terms in which they express themselves, may be applied indifferently to either class of conversation. The main diseases, indeed, which obstruct the healthy movement of conversation recur everywhere ; and, alike whether the object be pleasure or profit in the free interchange of thought, almost universally that free interchange is obstructed in the very same way,— by the very same defect of any controlling principle for sustaining the general rights and interests of the company, and by the same vices of self-indulgent indolence, or of callous selfishness, or of insolent vanity, in the individual talkers.

Let us fall back on the recollections of our own experience. In the course of our life we have heard much of what was reputed to be the select conversation of the day, and we have heard many of those who figured at the moment as effective talkers ; yet, in mere sincerity, and without a vestige of misanthropic retrospect, we must say that never once has it happened to us to come away from any display of that nature without intense disappointment ; and it always appeared to us that this failure (which soon ceased to be a *disappointment*) was inevitable by a necessity of the case. For here lay the stress of the difficulty : almost all depends in most trials of skill upon the parity of those who are matched against each other. An ignorant person supposes that to an able disputant it must be an advantage to have a feeble opponent ; whereas, on the contrary, it is ruin to him ; for he cannot display his own powers but through something of a corresponding power in the resistance of his antagonist. A brilliant fencer is lost and confounded in playing with a novice ; and the same thing takes place in playing at ball, or battledore, or in dancing, where a powerless partner does not enable you to shine the more, but reduces you to mere helplessness, and takes the wind altogether out of your sails. Now, if by some rare good luck the great talker, the protagonist, of the evening has been provided with a commensurate second, it is just possible that something like a brilliant "passage of arms" may be the result,—though much even in that case will depend on the chances of the moment for furnishing a fortunate theme, and even then, amongst the superior part of the company, a feeling of deep vulgarity and of mountebank display is inseparable from such an ostentatious duel of wit. On the other hand, supposing your great talker to be received like any other visitor, and turned loose upon the company, then he must do one of two things : either he will talk upon *outré* subjects specially tabooed to his own private use,—in which case the great man has the air of a quack-doctor addressing a mob from a street stage ; or else he will talk like ordinary people upon popular topics,—in which case the company, out of natural politeness, that they may not seem to be staring at him as a lion, will hasten to meet him in the same style, the conversation will become general, the great man will seem reasonable and well-bred, but at the same time, we grieve to say it, the great man will have been extinguished by being drawn off from his exclusive ground.   The dilemma, in short, is this :—If the great talker attempts the plan of showing off by firing cannon-shot when everybody else is content with musketry, then undoubtedly he produces an impression, but at the expense of insulating himself from the sympathies of the company, and standing aloof as a sort of monster hired to play tricks of funambulism for the night.   Yet, again, if he contents himself with a musket like other people, then for *us*, from whom he modestly hides his talent under a bushel, in what respect is he different from the man who *has* no such talent ?

> " If she be not fair to me,
> What care I how fair she be ? "

The reader, therefore, may take it, upon the *a priori* logic of this dilemma, or upon the evidence of our own experience, that all reputation for brilliant talking is a visionary thing, and rests upon a sheer impossibility : viz. upon such a histrionic performance in a state of insulation from the rest of the company as could not be effected, even for a single time, without a rare and difficult collusion, and could not, even for that single time, be endurable to a man of delicate and honourable sensibilities.

Yet surely Coleridge *had* such a reputation, and without needing any collusion at all; for Coleridge, unless he could have all the talk, would have none. But then this was not conversation. It was not *colloquium*, or talking *with* the company, but *alloquium*, or talking *to* the company. As Madame de Staël observed, Coleridge talked, and *could* talk, only by monologue. Such a mode of systematic trespass upon the conversational rights of a whole party gathered together under pretence of amusement is fatal to every purpose of social intercourse, whether that purpose be connected with direct use and the service of the intellect, or with the general graces and amenities of life. The result is the same under whatever impulse such an outrage is practised ; but the impulse is not always the same ; it varies, and so far the criminal intention varies. In some people this gross excess takes its rise in pure arrogance. They are fully aware of their own intrusion upon the general privileges of the company ; they are aware of the temper in which it is likely to be received ; but they persist wilfully in the wrong, as a sort of homage levied compulsorily upon those who may wish to resist it, but hardly *can* do so without a violent interruption, wearing the same shape of indecorum as that which they resent. In most people, however, it is not arrogance which prompts this capital offence against social rights, but a blind selfishness, yielding passively to its own instincts, without being distinctly aware of the degree in which this self-indulgence trespasses on the rights of others. We see the same temper illustrated at times in travelling. A brutal person, as we are disposed at first to pronounce him, but more frequently one who yields unconsciously to a lethargy of selfishness, plants himself at the public fireplace, so as to exclude his fellow-travellers from all but a fraction of the warmth. Yet he does not do this in a spirit of wilful aggression upon others; he has but a glimmering suspicion of the odious shape which his own act assumes to others, for the luxurious torpor of self-indulgence has extended its mists to the energy and clearness of his perceptions. Meantime, Coleridge's habit of soliloquizing through a whole evening of four or five hours had its origin neither in arrogance nor in absolute selfishness. The fact was that he *could* not talk unless he were uninterrupted, and unless he were able to count upon this concession from the company. It was a silent contract between him and his hearers that nobody should speak but himself. If any man objected to this arrangement, why did he come? For, the custom of the place, the *lex loci*, being notorious, by coming at all he was understood to profess his allegiance to the autocrat who presided. It was not, therefore, by an insolent usurpation that Coleridge persisted in monology through his whole life, but in virtue of a concession from the kindness and respect of his friends. You could not be angry with him for using his privilege, for it was a privilege conferred by others, and a privilege which he was ready to resign as soon as any man demurred to it. But, though reconciled to it by these considerations, and by the ability with which he used it, you could not but feel that it worked ill for all parties. Himself it tempted oftentimes into pure garrulity of egotism, and the listeners it reduced to a state of debilitated sympathy or of absolute torpor. Prevented by the custom from putting questions, from proposing doubts, from asking for explanations, reacting by no mode of mental activity, and condemned also to the mental distress of hearing opinions or doctrines stream past them by flights which they must not arrest for a moment so as even to take a note of them, and which yet they could not often understand, or, seeming to understand, could not always approve, the audience sank at times into a listless condition of inanimate vacuity. To be acted upon for ever, but never to react, is fatal to the very powers by which sympathy must grow, or by which intelligent admiration can be evoked. For his own sake, it was Coleridge's interest to have forced his hearers into the active commerce of question and answer, of objection and demur. Not otherwise was it possible that even the attention could be kept from drooping, or the coherency and dependency of the arguments be forced into light.

The French rarely make a mistake of this nature. The graceful levity of the nation could not easily err in this direction, nor tolerate such deliration in the greatest of men. Not the gay temperament only of the French people, but the particular qualities of the French language,—which (however poor for the higher purposes of passion) is rich beyond all others for purposes of social intercourse,—prompt them to rapid and vivacious exchange of thought. Tediousness, therefore, above all other vices, finds no countenance or indulgence amongst the French, excepting always in two memorable cases : viz., first, the case of tragic dialogue on the stage, which is privileged to be tedious by usage and tradition ; and, secondly, the case (authorised by the best usages in living society) of narrators or *raconteurs*. This is a shocking anomaly in the code of French good taste as applied to conversation. Of all the bores whom man in his folly hesitates to hang, and Heaven in its mysterious wisdom suffers to propagate their species, the most insufferable is the teller of "good stories,"—a nuisance that should be put down by cudgelling, a submersion in horse-ponds, or any mode of abatement, as summarily as men would combine to suffocate a vampire or a mad dog. This case excepted, however, the French have the keenest possible sense of all that is odious and all that is ludicrous in prosing, and universally have a horror of *des longueurs*. It is not strange, therefore, that Madame de Staël noticed little as extraordinary in Coleridge beyond this one capital monstrosity of unlimited soliloquy, —that being a peculiarity which she never could have witnessed in France ; and, considering the burnish of her French tastes in all that concerned colloquial characteristics, it is creditable to her forbearance that she noticed even this rather as a memorable fact than as the inhuman fault which it was. On the other hand, Coleridge was not so forbearing as regarded the brilliant French lady. He spoke of her to ourselves as a very frivolous person, and in short summary terms that disdained to linger on a subject so inconsiderable. It is remarkable that Goethe and Schiller both conversed with Madame de Staël, like Coleridge, and both spoke of her

afterwards in the same disparaging terms as Coleridge.   But
it is equally remarkable that Baron *William* Humboldt, who
was personally acquainted with all the four parties—Madame
de Staël, Goethe, Schiller, and Coleridge—gave it as his
opinion (in letters subsequently published) that the lady had
been calumniated through a very ignoble cause,—viz. mere
ignorance of the French language, or at least non-familiarity
with the fluencies of *oral* French.   Neither Goethe nor
Schiller, though well acquainted with written French, had
any command of it for purposes of *rapid* conversation ; and
Humboldt supposes that mere spite at the trouble which they
found in limping after the lady so as to catch one thought
that she uttered had been the true cause of their unfavourable sentence upon her.   Not malice aforethought, so much
as vindictive fury for the sufferings they had endured,
accounted for their severity in the opinion of the diplomatic
baron.   He did not extend the same explanation to Coleridge's case,—because, though even then in habits of intercourse with Coleridge, he had not heard of *his* interview
with the lady, nor of the results from that interview ; else
what was true of the two German wits was true *a fortiori* of
Coleridge.   The Germans at least *read* French, and talked it
slowly, and occasionally understood it when talked by others ;
but Coleridge did none of these things.   We are all of us
well aware that Madame de Staël was *not* a trifler : nay,
that she gave utterance at times to truths as worthy to be
held oracular as any that were uttered by the three inspired
wits,—all philosophers, and bound to truth, but all poets,
and privileged to be wayward.   Thus we may collect from
these anecdotes that people accustomed to colloquial des-
potism, and who wield a sceptre within a circle of their own,
are no longer capable of impartial judgments, and do not
accommodate themselves with patience, or even with justice,
to the pretensions of rivals ; and, were it only for this result
of conversational tyranny, it calls clamorously for extinction
by some combined action upon the part of society.

Is such a combination on the part of society possible as a
sustained effort ?   We imagine that it *is* in these times, and
will be more so in the times which are coming.   Formerly
the social meetings of men and women, except only in capital

cities, were few ; and even in such cities the infusion of female influence was not broad and powerful enough for the correction of those great aberrations from just ideals which disfigured social intercourse. But great changes are proceeding : were it only by the vast revolution in our *means* of intercourse, laying open every village to the contagion of social temptations, the world of Western Europe is tending more and more to a mode of living in public. Under such a law of life, conversation becomes a vital interest of every hour, that can no more suffer interruption from individual caprice or arrogance than the animal process of respiration from transient disturbances of health. Once, when travelling was rare, there was no fixed law for the usages of public rooms in inns or coffee-houses ; the courtesy of individuals was the tenure by which men held their rights. If a morose person detained the newspaper for hours, there was no remedy. At present, according to the circumstances of the case, there are strict regulations which secure to each individual his own share of the common rights.

A corresponding change will gradually take place in the usages which regulate conversation. It will come to be considered an infringement of the general rights for any man to detain the conversation, or arrest its movement, for more than a short space of time,—which gradually will be more and more defined. This one curtailment of arrogant pretensions will lead to others. Egotism will no longer freeze the openings to intellectual discussions ; and conversation will then become, what it never *has* been before, a powerful ally of education and generally of self-culture. The main diseases that besiege conversation at present are—1*st*, The want of *timing*. Those who are not recalled by a sense of courtesy and equity to the continual remembrance that, in appropriating too large a share of the conversation, they are committing a fraud upon their companions, are beyond all control of monitory hints or of reproof which does not take a direct and open shape of personal remonstrance ; but this, where the purpose of the assembly is festive and convivial, bears too harsh an expression for most people's feelings. That objection, however, would not apply to any mode of admonition that was universally established. A public memento carries with it no personality. For instance, in the Roman law - courts, no advocate complained of the *clepsydra*, or water time-piece, which regulated the duration of his pleadings. Now, such a contrivance would not be impracticable at an after-dinner talk. To invert the clepsydra, when all the water had run out, would be an act open to any one of the guests, and liable to no misconstruction when this check was generally applied, and understood to be a simple expression of public defence, not of private rudeness or personality. The clepsydra ought to be filled with some brilliantly-coloured fluid, to be placed in the centre of the table, and with the capacity, at the very most, of the little minute-glasses used for regulating the boiling of eggs. It would obviously be insupportably tedious to turn the glass every two or three minutes ; but to do so occasionally would avail as a sufficient memento to the company. 2*d*, Conversation suffers from the want of some discretional power lodged in an individual for controlling its movements. Very often it sinks into flats of insipidity through mere accident. Some trifle has turned its current upon ground where few of the company have anything to say : the commerce of thought languishes ; and the consciousness that it *is* languishing about a narrow circle, " unde pedem proferre pudor vetat," operates for a general refrigeration of the company. Now, the ancient Greeks had an officer appointed over every convivial meeting, whose functions applied to all cases of doubt or interruption that could threaten the genial harmony, or, perhaps, the genial movement intellectually, of the company. We also have such officers,—presidents, vice-presidents, &c. ; and we need only to extend their powers so that they may exercise over the movement of the conversation the beneficial influence of the Athenian *symposiarch*. At present the evil is that conversation has no authorized originator ; it is servile to the accidents of the moment, and generally these accidents are merely verbal. Some word or some name is dropped casually in the course of an illustration ; and *that* is allowed to suggest a topic, though neither interesting to the majority of the persons present, nor leading naturally into other collateral topics that are more so. Now, in such cases it will be the business of the symposiarch to restore the interest of the conversation, and to rekindle its animation, by recalling it from any tracks of dulness or sterility into which it may have rambled. The natural *excursiveness* of colloquial intercourse, its tendency to advance by subtle links of association, is one of its advantages ; but mere *vagrancy* from positive acquiescence in the direction given to it by chance or by any verbal accident is amongst its worst diseases. The business of the symposiarch will be to watch these morbid tendencies, which are not the deviations of graceful freedom, but the distortions of imbecility and collapse. His business it will also be to derive occasions of discussion bearing a general and permanent interest from the fleeting events or the casual disputes of the day. His business again it will be to bring back a subject that has been imperfectly discussed, and has yielded but half of the interest which it promises, under the interruption of any accident which may have carried the thoughts of the company into less attractive channels. Lastly, it should be an express office of education to form a particular style, cleansed from *verbiage,* from elaborate parenthesis, and from circumlocution,[1] as the only style fitted for a purpose which is one of pure enjoyment, and where every moment used by the speaker is deducted from a public stock.

Many other suggestions for the improvement of conversation might be brought forward within ampler limits ; and especially for that class of conversation which moves by discussion a whole code of regulations might be proposed that would equally promote the interests of the individual speakers and the public interests of the truth involved in the question discussed. Meantime nobody is more aware than we are that no style of conversation is more essentially vulgar than that which moves by disputation. This is the vice of the young and the inexperienced, but especially of those amongst them who are fresh from academic life. But discussion is not necessarily disputation ; and the two orders of conversation—*that,* on the one hand, which contemplates an interest of knowledge and of the self-developing intellect ;

---

[1] *Circumlocution* and *parenthesis* agree in this — that they keep the attention in a painful condition of suspense. But suspense is anxiety.

that, on the other hand, which forms one and the widest amongst the gay embellishments of life — will always advance together. Whatever there may remain of illiberal in the first (for, according to the remark of Burke, there is always something illiberal in the severer aspects of study until balanced by the influence of social amenities) will correct itself, or will tend to correct itself, by the model held up in the second ; and thus the great organ of social intercourse by means of speech, which hitherto has done little for man, except through the channel of its ministrations to the direct *business* of daily necessities, will at length rise into a rivalship with books, and become fixed amongst the alliances of intellectual progress, not less than amongst the ornamental accomplishments of convivial life.

A BRIEF APPRAISAL OF THE GREEK LITERATURE
IN ITS FOREMOST PRETENSIONS [1]

Part I.—The Greek Poets and Prose-Writers
GENERALLY

No question has been coming up at intervals for reconsideration more frequently than that which respects the comparative pretensions of Pagan (viz. Greek and Roman) Literature on the one side, and Modern (that is, the Literature of Christendom) on the other. Being brought uniformly before unjust tribunals—that is, tribunals corrupted and bribed by their own vanity—it is not wonderful that this great question should have been stifled and overlaid with peremptory decrees, dogmatically cutting the knot rather than skilfully untying it, as often as it has been moved afresh and put upon the roll for a re-hearing. It is no mystery to those who are in the secret, and who can lay A and B together, why it should have happened that the most interesting of all literary questions, and the most comprehensive (for it includes most others, and some special to itself), has, in the first place, never been pleaded in a style of dignity, of philosophic precision, of feeling, or of research, proportioned

---

[1] Published in *Tait's Magazine* for December 1838 and June 1839, with this for the full title :—" A Brief Appraisal of the Greek Litera-" ture in its Foremost Pretensions : By way of Counsel to Adults who " are hesitating as to the Propriety of Studying the Greek Language " with a view to the Literature ; and by way of consolation to those " whom circumstances have obliged to lay aside that plan. By Thomas " De Quincey." The paper was not reprinted in De Quincey's Collective Edition ; nor is it in the American Collective Edition. See remarks in Editor's Preface to this volume.—M.

to its own merits, and to the numerous "issues" (forensically speaking) depending upon it ; nor, in the second place, has ever received such an adjudication as was satisfactory *even at the moment*. For, be it remembered, after all, that any provisional adjudication—one growing out of the fashion or taste of a single era—could not, at any rate, be binding for a different era. A judgment which met the approbation of Spenser could hardly have satisfied Dryden, nor another which satisfied Pope have been recognised as authentic by us of the year 1838. It is the normal or exemplary condition of the human mind, its ideal condition, not its abnormal condition as seen in the transitory modes and fashions of its taste or its opinions, which only

"Can lay great bases for eternity",

or give even a colourable permanence to any decision in a matter so large, so perplexed, so profound, as this great pending suit between antiquity and ourselves—between the junior men of this earth and ourselves, the seniors, as Lord Bacon reasonably calls us. Appeals will be brought *ad infinitum*—we ourselves shall bring appeals—to set aside any judgment that may be given, until something more is consulted than individual taste ; better evidence brought forward than the result of individual reading ; something higher laid down as the *grounds* of judgment, as the very principles of the jurisprudence which controls the court, than those vague *responsa prudentum*, countersigned by the great name, perhaps, of Aristotle, but still too often mere products of local convenience, of inexperience, of experience too limited and exclusively Grecian, or of absolute caprice— rules, in short, which are themselves not less truly *sub judice* and liable to appeal than that very appeal cause to which they are applied as decisive.

We have remarked that it is no mystery why the decision should have gone pretty uniformly in favour of the ancients; for here is the dilemma :—A man, attempting this problem, *is* or *is not* a classical scholar. If he *is*, then he has already received a bias in his judgment ; he is a bribed man, bribed by his vanity ; and is liable to be challenged as one of the judges. If he is *not*, then he is but imperfectly qualified—

imperfectly as respects his knowledge and powers; whilst, even as respects his will and affections, it may be alleged that he also is under a bias and a corrupt influence; his interest being no less obvious to undervalue a literature which, as to *him*, is tabooed and under lock and key than his opponent's is to put a preposterous value upon that knowledge which very probably is the one sole advantageous distinction between him and his neighbours.

We might cite an illustration from the French literary history on this very point. Every nation in turn has had its rows in this great quarrel; which is, in fact, coextensive with the controversies upon human nature itself. The French, of course, have had *theirs*—solemn tournaments, single duels, casual "turn-ups," and regular "stand-up" fights. The most celebrated of these was in the beginning of the last century, when, amongst others who acted as bottle-holders, umpires, &c., two champions in particular "peeled" and fought a considerable number of rounds, mutually administering severe punishment, and both coming out of the ring disfigured: these were M. la Motte and Madame Dacier.[1]   But Motte was the favourite at first; and once he got Dacier "into chancery," and "fibbed" her twice round the ropes, so that she became a truly pitiable and delightful spectacle to the connoisseurs in fibbing and bloodshed. But here lay the difference: Motte was a hard hitter; he was a clever man, and (which all clever men are not) a man of sense; but, like Shakspere, he had no Greek. On the other hand, Dacier had nothing *but* Greek. A certain abbé at that time amused all Paris with his caricatures of this Madame Dacier; "who," said he, "ought to be cooking her husband's dinner, and darning his stockings, instead of skirmishing and tilting with Grecian spears; for be it known that, after all her *not cooking* and her *not darning*, she is as poor a scholar as her injured husband is a good one." And *there* the abbé was right; witness the husband's Horace, in 9 vols., against the wife's Homer. However, this was not generally understood. The lady, it was believed, waded

---

[1] Anthony Houdart de la Motte, French critic, 1672-1731; Anne Dacier, French critic and scholar, 1654-1720 (wife of André Dacier, also scholar and critic).—M.

petticoat-deep in Greek clover ; and in any Grecian field of dispute, naturally she must be in the right as against one who barely knew his own language and a little Latin. Motte was, therefore, thought by most people to have come off second best. For, as soon as ever he opened thus— " Madame, it seems to me that, agreeably to all common sense or common decorum, the Greek poet should here ————," instantly, without listening to his argument, the intrepid Amazon replied (ὑπόδρα ἰδοῦσα), " You foolish man ! you remarkably silly man !—*that* is because you know no better ; and the reason you know no better, is because you do not understand *ton d'apameibomenos* as I do." *Ton d'apameibomenos* fell like a hand-grenade amongst Motte's papers, and blew him up effectually in the opinion of the multitude. No matter what he might say in reply—no matter how reasonable, how unanswerable—that one spell of " No Greek ! no Greek ! " availed as a talisman to the lady both for offence and defence, and refuted all syllogisms and all eloquence as effectually as the cry of *A la lanterne !* in the same country some fourscore years after.

So it will always be. Those who (like Madame Dacier) possess no accomplishment *but* Greek will, of necessity, set a superhuman value upon that literature in all its parts to which their own narrow skill becomes an available key. Besides that, over and above this coarse and conscious motive for overrating that which reacts with an equal and answerable overrating upon their own little philological attainments, there is another agency at work, and quite unconsciously to the subjects of that agency, in disturbing the sanity of any estimate they may make of a foreign literature. It is the habit (well known to psychologists) of transferring to anything created by our own skill, or which reflects our own skill, as if it lay causatively and objectively [1] in the reflecting thing itself, that pleasurable power which in very truth belongs subjectively [1] to the mind of him who surveys it, from conscious success in the

---

[1] *Objectively* and *subjectively* are terms somewhat too metaphysical ; but they are so indispensable to accurate thinking that we are inclined to show them some indulgence ; and the more so in cases where the mere position and connexion of the words are half sufficient to explain their application.

exercise of his own energies.   Hence it is that we see daily
without surprise young ladies hanging enamoured over the
pages of an Italian author, and calling attention to trivial
commonplaces, such as, clothed in plain mother-English,
would have been more repulsive to them than the distinctions of a theologian or the counsels of a great-grandmother.
They mistake for a pleasure yielded by the author what is
in fact the pleasure attending their own success in mastering
what was lately an insuperable difficulty.

It is indeed a pitiable spectacle to any man of sense and
feeling who happens to be really familiar with the golden
treasures of his own ancestral literature, and a spectacle
which moves alternately scorn and sorrow, to see young
people squandering their time and painful study upon
writers not fit to unloose the shoes' latchets of many amongst
their own compatriots ; making painful and remote voyages
after the drossy refuse, when the pure gold lies neglected at
their feet.   Too often he is reminded of a case which is still
sometimes to be witnessed in London.   Now and then it
will happen that a lover of art, modern or antique alike,
according to its excellence, will find himself honoured by an
invitation from some *millionaire*, or some towering grandee,
to "assist," as the phrase is, at the opening of a case newly
landed from the Tiber or the Arno, and fraught (as he is
assured) with the very gems of Italian art, intermingled
besides with many genuine antiques.   He goes : the cases are
solemnly disgorged; adulatory hangers-on, calling themselves
artists, and, at all events, so much so as to appreciate the
solemn farce enacted, stand by uttering hollow applauses of
my Lord's taste, and endeavouring to play upon the tinkling
cymbals of spurious enthusiasm : whilst every man of real
discernment perceives at a glance the mere refuse and sweep-
ing of a third-rate *studio*, such as many a native artist would
disdain to turn out of his hands, and antiques such as could
be produced, with a month's notice, by cart-loads in many
an obscure corner of London.   Yet for this rubbish has the
great man taken a painful tour ; compassed land and sea ;
paid away in exchange a king's ransom ; and now claims on
their behalf the very humblest homage of artists who are
taxed with the basest envy if they refuse it, and who, mean-

time, cannot in sincerity look upon the trumpery with other
feelings than such as the potter's wheel, if (like Ezekiel's
wheels) it were instinct with spirit, would entertain for the
vilest of its own creations—culinary or "post-culinary"
mugs and jugs. We, the writers of this paper, are not artists,
are not connected with artists. God knows it, as well as
Mr. Tait.[1] And yet, upon the general principle of sympathy
with native merit, and of disgust towards all affectation, we
cannot but .recall such anecdotes with scorn ; and often we
recollect the stories recorded by poor Benvenuto Cellini, that
dissolute but brilliant vagabond,[2] who (like our own British
artists) was sometimes upbraided with the degeneracy of
modern art, and, upon his humbly requesting some evidence,
received, by way of practical answer, a sculptured gem or
vase, perhaps with a scornful demand of—when would *he* be
able to produce anything like that. "Eh, Master Ben ?
Fancy we must wait a few centuries or so before *you'll* be
ready with the fellow of this." And, lo ! on looking into
some hidden angle of the beautiful production, poor Cellini
discovered his own private mark, the supposed antique having
been a pure forgery of his own. Such cases remind one too
forcibly of the pretty Horatian tale where, in a contest
between two men who undertake to mimic a pig's grunting,
he who happens to be the favourite of the audience is
applauded to the echo for his felicitous execution, and
repeatedly *encored*, whilst the other man is hissed off the
stage, and well kicked by a band of amateurs and cogno-
scenti, as a poor miserable copyist and impostor ; but, unfortunately for the credit of his exploders, he has just time,
before they have quite kicked him off, for exposing to view
the real pig concealed under his cloak, which pig it was, and
not himself, that had been the artist—forced by pinches into
"mimicry" of his own porcine music. Of all baffled connoisseurs, surely these Roman pig-fanciers must have looked
the most confounded. Yet there is no knowing : and we
ourselves have a clever friend, but rather too given to
subtilising, who contends, upon some argument not perfectly

---

[1] The proprietor and main editor of *Tait's Magazine.*—M.
[2] Benvenuto Cellini, Italian artist (1500-1570) ; whose autobiography is one of the most curious and interesting of books.—M.

intelligible to us, that Horace was not so conclusive in his logic as he fancied ; that the real pig might not have an "ideal" or normal squeak, but a peculiar and non-representative squeak ; and that, after all, the man might deserve the "threshing" he got. Well, it may be so ; but, however, the Roman audience, wrong or not, for once fancied themselves in the wrong ; and we cannot but regret that our own ungenerous disparagers of native merit, and *exclusive* eulogisers of the dead or the alien—of those only " *quos Libitina sacravit,*" or whom oceans divide from us—are not now and then open to the same *palpable* refutation, as they are certainly guilty of the same mean error, in prejudging the whole question, and refusing to listen even to the plain evidence of their own feelings, or, in some cases, to the voice of their own senses.

From this preface it is already abundantly clear what side *we* take in this dispute about modern literature and the antique.[1]   And we now propose to justify our leaning by a general review of the Pagan authors in their elder section— that is, the Grecians. These will be enough in all conscience for one essay ; and even for them we meditate a very cursory inquest ; not such as would suffice in a grand ceremonial day of battle—a *justum prælium,* as a Roman would call it—but in a mere perfunctory skirmish, or (if the reader objects to that word as pedantic, though, really, it is a highly favoured word amongst ancient divines, and with many a

---

[1] In general usage "*the antique*" is a phrase limited to the expression of art ; but improperly so. It is quite as legitimately used to denote the *literature* of ancient times, in contradistinction to the modern. As to the term *classical,* though generally employed as equivalent to Greek and Roman, the reader must not forget that this is quite a false limitation, contradicting the very reason for applying the word in *any* sense to literature. For the application arose thus :— The social body of Rome being divided into six classes, of which the lowest was the sixth, it followed that the highest was the first. Thence, by a natural process common to most languages, those who belonged to this highest had no number at all assigned to them. The very absence of a number, the calling them *classici,* implied that they belonged to *the* class emphatically, or *par excellence. The classics* meant, therefore, the grandees in social consideration ; and thence by analogy in literature. But, if this analogy be transferred from Rome to Greece, where it had no corresponding root in civic arrangement,—then, by parity of reason, to all nations.

"philosopher
Who has read Alexander Ross over ")[1]—

why, in that case, let us indulge his fastidious taste by call
ing it an autoschediastic combat,—to which, surely, there can
be no such objection.   And,. as the manner of the combat is
autoschediastic or extemporaneous, and to meet a hurried
occasion, so is the reader to understand that the object of our
disputation is not the learned, but the unlearned student,
and our purpose not so much to discontent the one with
his painful acquisitions as to console the other under what,
upon the old principle of *omne ignotum pro magnifico*, he is
too apt to imagine his irreparable disadvantages.   We set
before us as our especial auditor the reasonable man of plain
sense but strong feeling, who wishes to know how much he
has lost, and what injury the gods did him when, though
making him perhaps poetical, they cut short his allowance
of Latin, and, as to Greek, gave him not a jot more than a
cow has in her side pocket.

Let us begin at the beginning,—and that, as everybody knows, is Homer.   He is, indeed, so much at the
beginning that for that very reason (if even there were no
other) he is, and will be evermore, supremely interesting.
Is the unlearned reader aware of his age ?   Upon that point
there are more hypotheses than one or even two.   Some
there are among the chronologers who make him eleven hundred years anterior to Christ.   But those who allow him
least place him more than nine—that is, about two centuries
before the establishment of the Grecian Olympiads, and
(which is pretty nearly the same thing as regards time) before
Romulus and Remus.   Such an antiquity as this, even on its
own account, is a reasonable object of interest.   A poet to
whom the great-grandfather of old Ancus Martius (his grand-
father, did we say—that is, *avus*?—nay, his *abavus*, his
atavus, his *tritavus*) looked back as to one in a line with his
remote ancestor,—a poet who, if he travelled about as extensively as some have supposed him to do, or even as his
own countryman Herodotus most certainly did five or six

---

[1] The immortal rhyme in *Hudibras* which conserves the memory
of the voluminous seventeenth-century divine and author Alexander
Ross (1590-1654), Scottish by birth, but naturalised in England.—M.

hundred years afterwards, might have conversed with the
very workmen who laid the foundations of the first temple
at Jerusalem—might have bent the knee before Solomon in
all his glory :—such a poet, were he no better than the
worst of our own old metrical romancers, would, merely for
his antiquity, merely for the sublime fact of having been
coeval with the eldest of those whom the eldest of histories
presents to our knowledge, coeval with the earliest kings of
Judah, older than the greatest of the Judean prophets, older
than the separation of the two Jewish crowns and the revolt
of Israel, and, even with regard to Moses and to Joshua, not
in any larger sense junior than as we ourselves are junior to
Chaucer,—purely and exclusively with regard to these pretensions backed and supported by an antique form of an
antique language, the most comprehensive and the most
melodious in the world,—would, could, should, ought to,
merit a filial attention, and perhaps, with those who had
waggon-loads of time to spare, might plead the benefit, beyond most of those in whose favour it was enacted, of that
Horatian rule—

> " vos exemplaria Græca
> Nocturna versate manu, versate diurna."

In fact, when we recollect that, in round numbers, we ourselves may be considered as two thousand years in advance
of Christ, and that (by assuming less even than a mean between the different dates assigned to Homer) he stands a
thousand years before Christ, we find between Homer and
ourselves a gulf of three thousand years, or about one clear
half of the total extent which we grant to the present
duration of our planet.   This in itself is so sublime a circumstance in the relations of Homer to our era, and the
sense of power is so delightfully titillated to that man's
feeling who, by means of Greek, and a very moderate skill
in this fine language, is able to grasp the awful span, the
vast arch of which one foot rests upon 1838 and the other
almost upon the War of Troy,—the mighty rainbow which,
like the Archangel in the Revelation, plants its western limb
amongst the carnage and the magnificence of Waterloo, and the
other amidst the vanishing gleams and the dusty clouds of Agamemnon's rearguard,—that we may pardon a little exultation

to the man who can actually mutter to himself, as he rides home of a summer evening, the very words and vocal music of the old blind man at whose command

> " the Iliad and the Odyssey
> Rose to the murmurs of the voiceful sea."

But pleasures in this world fortunately are without end. And every man, after all, has many pleasures peculiar to himself—pleasures which no man shares with him, even as he is shut out from many of other men.   To renounce one in particular is no subject for sorrow, so long as many remain in that very class equal or superior.   Ellwood the Quaker had a luxury which none of us will ever have, in hearing the very voice and utterance of a poet quite as blind as Homer, and by many a thousand times more sublime.[1] And yet Ellwood was not perhaps much happier for *that*. For (now to proceed, reader) abstract from his *sublime* anti-quity, and his being the very earliest of authors—allowance made for one or two Hebrew writers (who, being inspired, are scarcely to be viewed as human competitors),—how much is there in Homer, *intrinsically* in Homer, stripped of his fine draperies of time and circumstance,—in the naked Homer, dis-apparelled of the pride, pomp, and circumstance of glorious antiquity,—to remunerate a man for his labour in acquiring Greek ?   Men think very differently about what *will* re-munerate any given labour.   A fool (professional *fool*) in Shakspere ascertains, by a natural process of logic, that a " remuneration " means a *testern*, which is just sixpence, and two remunerations, therefore, a testoon, or one shilling. But many men will consider the same service ill paid by a thousand pounds.   So of the reimbursement for learning a language.   Lord Camden is said to have learned Spanish merely to enjoy Don Quixote more racily.   Cato, the elder Cato, after abusing Greek throughout his life, sat down in extreme old age to study it ; and wherefore ?   Mr. Coleridge

---

[1] Thomas Ellwood, the young Quaker who knew Milton in his later years and blindness, visited him at the cottage in Chalfont-St.-Giles's, Buckinghamshire, where he spent some months of 1665-6 to avoid the Great Plague in London, and had the honour of being then allowed to read *Paradise Lost* while it was still in manuscript.—M.

mentions an author in whom, upon opening his pages with
other expectations, he stumbled upon the following fragrant
passage :—" But from this frivolous digression upon philosophy and the fine arts let us return to a subject too little
understood or appreciated in these sceptical days—the subject of *dung*." Now, *that* was precisely the course of thought
with this old censorious Cato.   So long as Greek offered, or
seemed to offer, nothing but philosophy or poetry, he was
clamorous against Greek ; but he began to thaw and melt a
little upon the charms of Greek,—he " owned the soft
impeachment,"—when he heard of some Grecian treatises
upon *beans* and *turnips* ; and, finally, he sank under its
voluptuous seductions when he heard of others upon DUNG.
There are, therefore, as different notions about a " remuneration ' in this case as the poor fool had met with in *his* case.
We, however, unappalled by the bad names of " Goth,"
" Vandal," and so forth, shall honestly lay before the reader
our notions.

When Dryden wrote his famous, indeed matchless, epigram upon the three great masters (or reputed masters) of the
Epopee,[1] he found himself at no loss to characterise the last
of the triad : no matter what qualities he imputed to the
first and the second, he knew himself safe in imputing them
all to the third.   The mighty modern had everything that
his predecessors were ever *thought* to have, as well as something beside.[2]   So he expressed the surpassing grandeur of

---

[1] Dryden's famous lines on Homer, Virgil, and Milton, first printed
under the portrait of Milton prefixed to Tonson's illustrated folio edition of *Paradise Lost* in 1688 :—

> "Three poets, in three distant ages born,
> Greece, Italy, and England did adorn.
> The first in loftiness of thought surpassed ;
> The next in majesty ; in both the last.
> The force of Nature could no farther go :
> To make a third, she joined the former two."—M.

[2] The beauty of this famous epigram lies in the *form* of the conception.   The first had A ; the second had B ; and, when Nature, to
furnish out a third, should have given him C, she found that A and
B had already exhausted her cycle, and that she could distinguish her
third great favourite only by giving him both A and B in combination.
But the filling up of this outline is imperfect ; for the A (*loftiness*)
and the B (*majesty*) are one and the same quality under different
names.

Milton by saying that in him Nature had embodied, by concentration as in one focus, whatever excellencies she had
scattered separately amongst her earlier favourites. But, in
strict regard to the facts, this is far from being a faithful
statement of the relations between Milton and his elder
brothers of the *Epos*. In sublimity, if that is what Dryden
meant by "loftiness of thought," it is not so fair to class
Milton with the greatest of poets as to class him apart, re-
tired from all others, sequestered, "sole-sitting by the shores
of old romance." In other poets,—in Dante, for example,—
there may be rays, gleams, sudden coruscations, casual scintillations, of the sublime ; but, for any continuous and sustained blaze of the sublime, it is in vain to look for it
except in Milton, making allowances (as before) for the inspired sublimities of Isaiah, Ezekiel, and of the great
Evangelist's Revelations. As to Homer, no critic who writes
from personal and *direct* knowledge on the one hand, or who
understands the value of words on the other, ever contended
in any critical sense for sublimity as a quality to which he
had the slightest pretensions. What ! not Longinus ?[1] If
he did, it would have been of little consequence ; for he had
no field of comparison, as we,—knowing no literature but one,
whereas *we* have a range of seven or eight. But he did
not. Τὸ ὑψηλον,[2] or the elevated, in the Longinian sense,

---

[1] Dionysius Cassius Longinus, Greek philosopher and rhetorician
of the third century (213-273), best remembered now for his treatise
Περὶ ὕψους, generally translated "Of the Sublime."—M.

[2] Because the Latin word *sublimis* is applied to objects soaring upwards, or floating aloft, or at an aerial altitude, and because the word
does *sometimes* correspond to our idea of the sublime (in which the
notion of height is united with the notion of moral grandeur), and because, in the excessive vagueness and lawless latitudinarianism of our
common Greek Lexicons, the word ὕψος is translated, *inter alia*, by
τὸ *sublime*, *sublimitas*, &c.—hence it has happened that the title of
the little essay ascribed to Longinus, Περὶ ὕψους, is usually rendered
into English *Concerning the Sublime*. But the idea of the Sublime, as
defined, circumscribed, and circumstantiated, in English literature—
an idea altogether of English growth—the *Sublime by way of polar
antithesis to the Beautiful*, had no existence amongst ancient critics ;
consequently it could have no expression. It is a great thought, a
true thought, a demonstrable thought, that the Sublime, as thus
ascertained, and in contraposition to the Beautiful, grew up on the
basis of *sexual* distinctions,—the Sublime corresponding to the male,

expressed all, no matter of what origin, of what tendency, which gives a character of life and animation to composition —whatever raises it above the dead level of flat prosaic style. Emphasis, or what in an artist's sense gives *relief* to a passage, causing it to stand forward and in advance of what surrounds it —*that* is the predominating idea in the "sublime" of Longinus. And this explains what otherwise has perplexed his modern interpreters—viz. that amongst the elements of his sublime he ranks even the pathetic, *i.e.* (say they) what by connecting itself with the depressing passion of grief is the very counter-agent to the elevating affection of the sublime.   True, most sapient sirs, my very worthy and approved good masters ; but that very consideration should have taught you to look back, and reconsider your translation of the capital word ὕψος.   It was rather too late in the day, when you had waded half-seas over in your translation, to find out either that you yourselves were ignoramuses, or that your principal was an ass.   " Returning were as tedious as go o'er " ; and any man might guess how you would settle such a dilemma.   It is, according to you, a little oversight of your principal : " *humanum aliquid passus est.*"   We, on the other hand, affirm that, if an error at all on the part of Longinus, it is too monstrous for any man to have " overlooked."   As long as he could see a pike-staff, he must have seen that.   And, therefore, we revert to *our* view of the case—viz. that it is yourselves who have committed the blunder, in translating by the Latin word *sublimis* [1] at all, but still more after it had received new determinations under modern usage.

and the Beautiful, its anti-pole, corresponding to the female.   Behold ! we show you a mystery !

[1] No word has ever given so much trouble to modern critics as this very word (now under discussion) of the *sublime*.   To those who have little Greek and *no* Latin it is necessary in the first place that we should state what are the most obvious elements of the word. According to the noble army of etymologists, they are these two Latin words—*sub*, under, and *limus*, mud.   Oh ! gemini ! who would have thought of groping for the sublime in such a situation as that ?— unless indeed, it were that writer cited by Mr. Coleridge, and just now referred to by ourselves, who complains of frivolous modern readers, as not being able to raise and sequester their thoughts to the abstract consideration of dung.   Hence it has followed that most people have quarrelled with the etymology.   Whereupon the late Dr.

Now, therefore, after this explanation, recurring to the Longinian critiques upon Homer, it will avail any idolater of Homer but little, it will affect *us* not much, to mention that Longinus makes frequent reference to the Iliad as the great source of the sublime—

> " A quo, ceu fonte perenni,
> Vatum Pieriis ora rigantur aquis " ;

for, as respected Grecian poets, and as respected *his* sense of the word, it cannot be denied that Homer was such. He was the great well-head of inspiration to the Pagan poets of after times; who, however (*as a body*), moved in the narrowest circle that has ever yet confined the natural freedom of the poetic mind. But, in conceding this, let it not be forgotten how much we concede. We concede as much as Longinus demanded,—that is, that Homer furnished an ideal or model of fluent narration, picturesque description, and the first outlines of what could be called characteristic delineations of persons. Accordingly, uninventive Greece,—for we maintain loudly that Greece, in her poets, *was* uninventive and sterile beyond the example of other nations,—received as a tradi-

---

Parr, of pedantic memory, wrote a huge letter to Mr. Dugald Stewart, but the marrow of which lies in a nutshell, especially being rather hollow within. The learned doctor, in the first folio, grapples with the word *sub*, which, says he, comes from the Greek : so much is clear —but from what Greek, Bezonian ? The thoughtless world, says he, trace it to ὑπὸ (hypo) sub, *i.e.* under ; but I, Ego, Samuel Parr, the Birmingham doctor, trace it to ὑπερ (hyper), super, *i.e.* above ; between which the difference is not less than between a chestnut horse and a horse-chestnut. To this learned Parrian dissertation on mud there cannot be much reasonably to object, except its length in the first place, and, secondly, that we ourselves exceedingly doubt the common interpretation of *limus*. Most unquestionably, if the sublime is to be brought into any relation at all to mud, we shall all be of one mind—that it must be found *above*. But to us it appears that, when the true modern idea of mud was in view, *limus* was not the word used. Cicero, for instance, when he wishes to call Piso " filth, mud," &c. calls him *Cœnum* : and, in general, *limus* seems to have involved the notion of something adhesive, and rather to express *plaister*, or artificially prepared cement, &c., than filth or impure depositions. Accordingly, our own definition differs from the Parrian or Birmingham definition, and may, nevertheless, be a Birmingham definition also. Not having room to defend it, for the present we forbear to state it.

tional inheritance the characters of the Paladins of the Troad.[1] Achilles is always the all-accomplished and supreme amongst these Paladins, the Orlando of ancient romance ; Agamemnon, for ever the Charlemagne ; Ajax, for ever the sullen, imperturbable, columnar champion, the Mandricardo, the *Bergen-op-Zoom* of his faction, and corresponding to our modern " Chicken " in the pugilistic ring, who was so called (as the books of the Fancy say) because he was a "glutton," and a "glutton" in this sense—that he would take any amount of cramming (*i.e.* any possible quantum of "milling," or "punishment ").   Ulysses, again, is uniformly, no matter whether in the solemnities of the tragic scene or the festivities of the Ovidian romance, the same shy cock, but also sly cock, with the least thought of a white feather in his plumage ; Diomed is the same unmeaning double of every other hero, just as Rinaldo is with respect to his greater cousin, Orlando ; and so of Teucer, Meriones, Idomeneus, and the other less marked characters.   The Greek Drama took up these traditional characters, and sometimes deepened, saddened, exalted the features : as Sophocles, for instance, does with his "Ajax Flagellifer," Ajax the knouter of sheep,— where, by the way, the remorse and penitential grief of Ajax for his own self-degradation, and the depth of his affliction for the triumph which he had afforded to his enemies, taken in connexion with the tender fears of his wife Tecmessa for the fate to which his gloomy despair was too manifestly driving him ; her own conscious desolation, and the orphan weakness of her son, in the event which she too fearfully anticipates—the final suicide of Ajax ; the brotherly affection of Teucer to the widow and the young son of the hero, together with the unlooked-for sympathy of Ulysses, who, instead of exulting in the ruin of his antagonist, mourns over it with generous tears,—compose a situation, and a suc-

[1] There is a difficulty in assigning any term as comprehensive enough to describe the Grecian heroes and their antagonists who fought at Troy.   The Seven Chieftains against Thebes are described sufficiently as Theban captains ; but to say *Trojan* chieftains would express only the heroes of one side ; *Grecian*, again, would be liable to that fault equally, and to another far greater,—of being under no limitation as to time.   This difficulty must explain and (if it can) justify our collective phrase of the Paladins of the Troad.

cession of situations, not equalled in the Greek Tragedy ; and, in that instance, we see an effort, rare in Grecian poetry, of conquest achieved by idealization over a mean incident— viz. the hallucination of brain in Ajax, by which he mistakes the sheep for his Grecian enemies, ties them up for flagellation, and scourges them as periodically as if he were a critical reviewer. But, really, in one extremity of this madness, where he fixes upon an old ram for Agamemnon as the leader of the flock, the ἄναξ ἀνδρῶν Ἀγαμεμνων, there is an extravagance of the ludicrous against which, though not exhibited scenically, but simply narrated, no solemnity of pathos could avail. Even in narration the violation of tragical dignity is insufferable, and is as much worse than the hyper-tragic horrors of " Titus Andronicus " (a play which is usually printed without reason amongst those of Shakspere) as absolute farce or contradiction of all pathos must inevitably be a worse indecorum than physical horrors which simply outrage it by excess. Let us not, therefore, hear of the judgment displayed upon the Grecian stage, when even Sophocles, the chief master of dramatic economy and scenical propriety, could thus err by an aberration so far transcending the most memorable violation of stage decorum which has ever been charged upon the English Drama.

From Homer, therefore, were left, as a bequest to all future poets, the romantic adventures which grow, as so many collateral dependencies,

" From the tale of Troy divine " ;

and from Homer was derived also the discrimination of the leading characters : which, after all, were but coarsely and rudely discriminated,—at least, for the majority. In one instance only we acknowledge an exception. We have heard a great modern poet dwelling with real and not counterfeit enthusiasm upon the character (or rather upon the general picture, as made up both of character and position) which the course of the Iliad assigns gradually to Achilles. The view which he took of this impersonation of human grandeur, combining all gifts of intellect and of body,—matchless speed, strength, inevitable eye, courage, and the immortal beauty of a god,—being also, by his birth-right, half-divine, and conse-

crated to the imagination by his fatal interweaving with the
destinies of Troy, and to the heart by the early death which
to *his own knowledge* [1] impended over his magnificent career,
and so abruptly shut up its vista—the view, we say, which
our friend took of the presiding character throughout the
" Iliad," who is introduced to us in the very first line, and
who is only eclipsed for seventeen books to emerge upon us
with more awful lustre ;—the view which he took was that
Achilles, and Achilles only, in the Grecian poetry, was a
great idea—an idealized creation ; and we remember that in
this respect he compared the Homeric Achilles with the
Angelica of Ariosto.   Her only be regarded as an idealization
in the " Orlando Furioso."   And certainly in the luxury and
excess of her all-conquering beauty, which drew after her
from " ultimate Cathay " to the camps of the baptized in
France, and back again from the palace of Charlemagne
drew half the Paladins and " half Spain militant " to the
portals of the rising sun,—that sovereign beauty which (to
say nothing of kings and princes withered by her frowns)
ruined for a time the most princely of all the Paladins, the
supreme Orlando, crazed him with scorn,

"And robbed him of his noble wits outright,"—

in all this we must acknowledge a glorification of power not
unlike that of Achilles :—

"Irresistible Pelides, whom, unarmed,
No strength of man or fiercest wild beast could withstand ;
Who tore the lion as the lion tears the kid ;
Ran on embattled armies clad in iron,
And, weaponless himself,
Made arms ridiculous, useless the forgery
Of brazen shield and spear, the hammered cuirass,
Chalybean-tempered steel, and frock of mail,
Adamantean proof :
But safest he who stood aloof,

---

[1] " *To his own knowledge* " :—See, for proof of this, the gloomy
serenity of his answer to his dying victim, when predicting his
approaching end :—

"Enough ; I know my fate ; to die—to see no more
My much-loved parents, and my native shore," &c. &c.

> When insupportably his foot advanced,
> In scorn of their proud arms and their warlike tools,
> Spurned them to death by troops.   The bold Priamides
> Fled from his lion ramp ; old warriors turned
> Their plated backs under his heel,
> Or grovelling soiled their crested helmets in the dust." [1]

These are the words of Milton in describing that "heroic Nazarite," God's champion

> "Promised by heavenly message twice descending " ;

heralded, like Pelides,

> "By an angel of his birth,
> Who from his father's field
> Rode up in flames after his message told " :

these are the celestial words which describe the celestial prowess of the Hebrew monomachist, the irresistible Samson, and are hardly less applicable to the "champion paramount" of Greece confederate.

This, therefore, this unique conception, with what power they might, later Greek poets adopted ; and the other Homeric characters they transplanted somewhat monotonously, but at times, we are willing to admit and have already admitted, improving and solemnizing the original epic portraits when brought upon the stage.   But all this extent of obligation amongst later poets of Greece to Homer serves less to argue *his* opulence than *their* penury.   And, if, quitting the one great blazing jewel, the Urim and Thummim of the "Iliad," you descend to individual passages of poetic effect, and if amongst these a fancy should seize you of asking for a specimen of the *sublime* in particular, what is it that you are offered by the critics?   Nothing that we remember beyond one single passage, in which the god Neptune is described in a steeplechase, and "making play" at a terrific pace.   And, certainly, enough is exhibited of the old boy's hoofs, and their spanking qualities, to warrant our backing him against a railroad for a rump and dozen ; but, after all, there is nothing to grow frisky about, as Longinus does,—who gets up the steam of a blue-stocking

---

[1] Transferred, with somewhat forced adaptation to Achilles, from Milton's *Samson Agonistes*, 125-141.—M.

enthusiasm, and boils us a regular gallop of ranting, in which, like the conceited snipe [1] upon the Liverpool railroad, he thinks himself to run a match with Samson, and, whilst affecting to admire Homer, is manifestly squinting at the reader to see how far he admires his own flourish of admiration, and in the very agony of his frosty raptures is quite at leisure to look out for a little private traffic of rapture on his own account. But it won't do ; this old critical posture-master (whom if Aurelian hanged, surely he knew what he was about) may as well put up his rapture pipes, and (as Lear says) "not squiny" at us ; for let us ask Master Longinus, in what earthly respect do these great strides of Neptune exceed Jack with his seven-league boots ? Let him answer that, if he can. We hold that Jack has the advantage. Or, again, look at the Koran ! Does any man but a foolish Oriental think that passage sublime where Mahomet describes the divine pen ? It is, says he, made of mother-of-pearl : so much for the "raw material," as the economists say. But now for the size : it can hardly be called a "portable" pen at all events, for we are told that it is so tall of its age that an Arabian thoroughbred horse would require 500 years for galloping down the slit to the nib. Now, this Arabic sublime is *in this instance* quite a kin brother to the Homeric.

However, it is likely that we shall here be reminded of our own challenge to the Longinian word $\dot{v}\psi\eta\lambda ov$ as not at all corresponding, or even alluding, to the modern word *sublime*. But in this instance the distinction will not much avail that critic ; for, no matter by what particular *word* he may convey his sense of its quality, clear it is, by his way of illustrating its peculiar merit, that in his opinion these huge strides of Neptune's have something supernaturally grand about them. But, waiving this solitary instance in Homer of the sublime according to his idolatrous critics—of the pseudo-sublime according to ourselves—in all other cases

---

[1] On the memorable inaugural day of the Liverpool railroad, when Mr. Huskisson met with so sad a fate, a snipe or a plover tried a race with Samson, one of the engines. The race continued neck and neck for about six miles ; after which the snipe, finding itself likely to come off second best, found it convenient to wheel off at a turn of the road, into the solitudes of Chat Moss.

where Longinus or any other Greek writer has cited Homer
as the great exemplary model of ὕψος in composition, we are
to understand him according to the Grecian sense of that
word. He must then be supposed to praise Homer not so
much for any ideal grandeur either of thought, image, or situation, as in a general sense for his animated style of narration,
for the variety and spirited effect with which he relieves
the direct formal narration in his own person by dialogue
between the subjects of his narration,—thus ventriloquising,
and throwing his own voice as often as he can into the surrounding objects,—or again for the similes and allusive pic-
tures by which he points emphasis to a situation or interest
to a person.

Now then we have it. When you describe Homer, or
when you hear him described, as a lively picturesque old boy
(by the way, why does everybody speak of Homer as old ?),
full of life, and animation, and movement, then you say (or
you hear say) what is true, and not much more than what is
true.   Only about that word *picturesque* we demur a little.
As a chirurgeon, he certainly *is* picturesque ; for Howship
upon Gunshot Wounds is a joke to him when he lectures
upon *traumacy*,—if we may presume to coin that word,—
or upon traumatic philosophy (as Mr. MacCulloch says so
grandly "Economic Science").   But, apart from this, we cannot allow that simply to say Ζακυνθος νεμοεσσα, woody
Zacynthus, is any better argument of picturesqueness than
Stony Stratford or Harrow on the Hill.   Be assured, reader,
that the Homeric age was not ripe for the picturesque.
" Price on the Picturesque " or " Gilpin on Forest Scenery "
would both have been sent post-haste to bedlam in those
days ; or perhaps Homer himself would have tied a mill-
stone about their necks, and have sunk them as public
nuisances by woody Zante.   Besides, it puts almost an
extinguisher on any little twinkling of the picturesque that
might have flared up at times from this or that suggestion,
when each individual had his own regular epithet stereo-
typed to his name like a brass plate upon a door : Hector,
the tamer of horses ; Achilles, the swift of foot; the ox-eyed
respectable Juno.   Some of the "big uns," it is true, had a
dress and an undress suit of epithets : as, for instance, Hector

was also κορυθαιολος, Hector with the tossing or the varie-
gated plumes. Achilles again was διος or divine. But still
the range was small, and the monotony was dire.

And now, if you come in good earnest to picturesqueness,
let us mention a poet in sober truth worth five hundred of
Homer; and that is Chaucer. Show us a piece of Homer's
handiwork that comes within a hundred leagues of that
divine prologue to the Canterbury Tales, or of " The
Knight's Tale," of the " Man of Law's Tale," or of the
" Tale of the Patient Griseldis," or, for intense life of narration and festive wit, of the " Wife of Bath's Tale." Or,
passing out of the Canterbury Tales for the picturesque
in human manner and gesture and play of countenance
never equalled as yet by Pagan or Christian, go to the
Troilus and Cresseid, and, for instance, to the conversation
between Troilus and Pandarus, or, again, between Pandarus
and Cresseid. Rightly did a critic of the 17th century pronounce Chaucer a miracle of natural genius, as having
" taken into the compass of his Canterbury Tales the
various manners and humours of the whole English nation
in his age: not a single character has escaped him." And
this critic then proceeds thus :—" The matter and manner of
" these tales, and of their telling, are so suited to their different
" educations, humours, and calling, that each of them would be
" improper in any other mouth. Even the grave and serious
" characters are distinguished by their several sorts of gravity.
" Even the ribaldry of the low characters is different. But
" there is such a variety of game springing up before me that
" I am distracted in my choice, and know not which to follow.
" It is sufficient to say, according to the proverb, that here is
" God's plenty." And soon after he goes on to assert (though
Heaven knows in terms far below the whole truth) the
superiority of Chaucer to Boccaccio. And, in the meantime,
who was this eulogist of Chaucer ? Why, the man who himself was never equalled upon this earth, unless by Chaucer,
in the art of fine narration. It is John Dryden whom we
have been quoting.

Between Chaucer and Homer—as to the main art of
narration, as to the picturesque life of the manners, and as to
the exquisite delineation of character—the interval is as

wide as between Shakspere, in dramatic power, and Nic.
Rowe. And we might wind up this main chapter of the comparison between Grecian and English literature,—viz. the
chapter on Homer,—by this tight dilemma :—You do or you
do not use the Longinian word ὕψος in the modern sense of
the sublime. If you do not, then of course you translate it
in the Grecian sense as explained above ; and in that sense
we engage to produce many scores of passages from Chaucer,
not exceeding 50 to 80 lines, which contain more of picturesque simplicity, more tenderness, more fidelity to nature,
more felicity of sentiment, more animation of narrative, and
more truth of character, than can be matched in all the
Iliad or the Odyssey. On the other hand, if by ὕψος
you choose absurdly to mean sublimity in the modern sense,
then it will suffice for us that we challenge *you* to the production of one instance which truly and incontestably
embodies that quality.[1] The burthen of proof rests upon
you who affirm, not upon us who deny. Meantime, as a kind
of choke-pear, we leave with the Homeric adorer this one
brace of portraits, or hints for such a brace, which we commend to his comparison, as Hamlet did the portraits of the
two brothers to his besotted mother.—We are talking of the
sublime : that is our thesis. Now, observe : there is a
catalogue in the Iliad — there is a catalogue in the
Paradise Lost ; and, like the river of Macedon and of
Monmouth, the two catalogues agree in that one fact—
viz. that they *are* such. But, as to the rest, we are willing
to abide by the issue of that one comparison, left to the very
dullest sensibility, for the decision of the total question at
issue. And what is that ? Not, Heaven preserve us ! as to
the comparative claims of Milton and Homer in this point of
sublimity—for surely it would be absurd to compare him

---

[1] The description of Apollo in wrath as νυκτι ἐοικως, like night, is a
doubtful case. With respect to the shield of Achilles, it cannot be
denied that the general conception has, in common with all abstractions (as *e.g.* the abstractions of dreams, of prophetic visions, such as
that in the 6th Æneid, that to Macbeth, that shown by the angel
Michael to Adam), something fine, and, in its own nature, let the
execution be what it may, sublime. But this part of the Iliad we
firmly believe to be an interpolation of times long posterior to that of
Homer.

who has most with him whom we affirm to have none at all
—but whether Homer has the very smallest pretensions in
that point.   The result, as we state it, is this :—The catalogue of the ruined angels in Milton is, in itself taken
separately, a perfect poem, with the beauty, and the felicity,
and the glory, of a dream.   The Homeric catalogue of ships
is exactly on a level with the muster-roll of a regiment, the
register of a tax-gatherer, the catalogue of an auctioneer.
Nay, some catalogues are far more interesting, and more
alive with meaning.   " But him followed fifty black ships " !
—" But him follow seventy black ships " !   Faugh !   We
could make a more readable poem out of an Insolvent's
Balance Sheet.

One other little suggestion we could wish to offer.
Those who would contend against the vast superiority of
Chaucer (and him we mention chiefly because he really has
in excess those very qualities of life, motion, and picturesque
simplicity to which the Homeric characteristics chiefly tend)
ought to bear in mind one startling fact evidently at war
with the *degree* of what is claimed for Homer.   It is this :—
Chaucer is carried naturally by the very course of his tales
into the heart of domestic life and of the scenery most
favourable to the movements of human sensibility.   Homer,
on the other hand, is kept out of that sphere, and is
imprisoned in the monotonies of a camp or a battle-field,
equally by the necessities of his story, and by the proprieties
of Grecian life (which in fact are pretty nearly those of
Turkish life at this day).   Men and women meet only
under rare, hurried, and exclusive circumstances.   Hence
it is that throughout the entire Iliad we have but one
scene in which the finest affections of the human heart can
find an opening for display : of course, everybody knows
at once that we are speaking of the scene between Hector,
Andromache, and the young Astyanax.   No need for question here ; it is Hobson's choice in Greek Literature when
you are seeking for the poetry of human sensibilities.   One
such scene there is, and no more ; which, of itself, is some
reason for suspecting its authenticity.   And, by the way, at
this point, it is worth while remarking that a late excellent
critic always pronounced the words applied to Andromache,

δακρυοεν γελασασα (*tearfully smiling*, or *smiling through her tears*), a mere Alexandrian interpolation. And why ? Now mark the reason. Was it because the circumstance is in itself vicious, or out of nature ? Not at all : nothing more probable or more interesting under the general situation of peril combined with the little incident of the infant's alarm at the plumed helmet. But any just taste feels it to be out of the Homeric key. The barbarism of the age, not mitigated (as in Chaucer's far less barbarous age) by the tenderness of Christian sentiment, turned a deaf ear and a repulsive aspect to such beautiful traits of domestic feeling ; to Homer himself the whole circumstance would have been one of pure effeminacy. Now, we recommend it to the reader's reflection ; and let him weigh well the condition under which that poetry moves that cannot indulge a tender sentiment without being justly suspected of adulterous commerce with some after age. This remark, however, is by the bye,—having grown out of the δακρυοεν γελασασα, itself a digression. But, returning from that to our previous theme, we desire every candid reader to ask himself what must be the character, what the circumscription, of that poetry which is limited by its very subject [1] to a scene of such intense uniformity as a battle or a camp, and by the prevailing spirit of manners to the exclusive society of men. To make bricks without straw was the excess even of Egyptian bondage ; Homer could not fight up against the necessities of his age, and the defects of its manners. And the very apologies which will be urged for him, drawn as they must be from the spirit of manners prevalent in his era, are reciprocally but so many reasons for not seeking in him the kind of poetry which has been ascribed to him by ignorance, or by defective sensibility, or by the mere self-interest of pedantry.

From Homer the route stretches thus :—The Grecian Drama lies about six hundred years nearer to the Christian era, and Pindar lies in the interval. These—*i.e.* the Dramatic

---

[1] But the Odyssey at least, it will be said, is not thus limited. No, not by its subject, because it carries us amongst cities and princes in a state of peace ; but it is equally limited by the spirit of manners ; we are never admitted amongst women, except by accident (Nausicaa) —by necessity (Penelope)—or by romance (Circe).

and Lyric—are the important chapters of the Greek Poetry ;
for, as to Pastoral poetry, having only Theocritus surviving,
and a very little of Bion and Moschus, and of these one
only being of the least separate importance, we cannot hold
that department entitled to any notice in so cursory a review
of the literature : else we have much to say on this also.
Besides that, Theocritus was not a natural poet indigenous to
Sicily, but an artificial blue-stocking ; as was Callimachus in
a different class.[1]

The Drama we may place loosely in the generation next
before that of Alexander the Great. And his era may be
best remembered by noting it as 333 years B.C. Add thirty
years to this era—that will be the era of the Drama. Add
a little more than a century, and that will be the era of
Pindar.   Him, therefore, we will notice first.

Now, the chief thing to say as to Pindar is to show
cause, good and reasonable, why no man of sense should
trouble his head about him.   There was in the seventeenth
century a notion prevalent about Pindar the very contradiction to the truth.   It was imagined that he " had a demon " ;
that he was under a burthen of prophetic inspiration ; that
he was possessed, like a Hebrew prophet or a Delphic
priestess, with divine fury. Why was this thought ? Simply
because no mortal read him.   Laughable it is to mention
that Pope, when a very young man, and writing his " Temple
of Fame " (partly on the model of Chaucer's), when he came
to the great columns and their bas-reliefs in that temple, each
of which is sacred to one honoured name, having but room
in all for six, chose Pindar for one [2] of the six.   And the
first bas-relief on Pindar's column is so pretty that we shall
quote it,—especially as it suggested Gray's car for Dryden's
" less presumptuous flight ! "

> " Four swans sustain a car of silver bright,
>   With heads advanc'd, and pinions stretch'd for flight :
>   Here, *like some furious prophet*, Pindar rode,
>   And seem'd to *labour with th' inspiring God.*"

---

[1] Pindar, Theban lyric poet, B.C. 518-442 ; Theocritus, Bion, and
Moschus, pastoral poets of the third century B.C. ; Callimachus, Alexandrian poet of the same century.—M.

[2] The other five were Homer, Virgil, Horace, Aristotle, Cicero

Then follow eight lines describing other bas-reliefs containing "the figured games of Greece" (Olympic, Nemean,
&c.)   But what we spoke of as laughable in the whole affair
is that Master Pope neither had then read one line of
Pindar, nor ever read one line of Pindar : and reason good ;
for at that time he could not read the simple Homeric
Greek, while the Greek of Pindar exceeds all other Greek
in difficulty, excepting perhaps a few amongst the tragic
choruses, which are difficult for the very same reason—
lyric abruptness, lyric involution, and lyric obscurity of
transition.   Not having read Homer, no wonder that Pope
should place amongst the bas-reliefs illustrating the " Iliad "
an incident which does not exist in the " Iliad." [1]   Not having
read Pindar, no wonder that Pope should ascribe to Pindar
qualities which are not only imaginary, but in absolute contradiction to his true ones.   A more sober old gentleman
does not exist : his demoniac possession is a mere fable.
But there are two sufficient arguments for not reading him,
so long as innumerable books of greater interest remain unread.   First, he writes upon subjects that, to us, are mean
and extinct—racehorses that have been defunct for twenty-
five centuries, chariots that were crazy in his own day, and
contests with which it is impossible for us to sympathise.
Then his digressions about old genealogies are no whit better
than his main theme, nor more amusing than a Welshman's
pedigree.   The best translator of any age, Mr. Cary, who
translated Dante, has done what human skill could effect to
make the old Theban readable [2] ; but, after all, the man is
yet to come who *has* read Pindar, *will* read Pindar, or *can*
read Pindar,—except, indeed, a translator in the way of duty.
And the son of Philip himself, though he bade " spare the
house of Pindarus," we vehemently suspect, never read the
works of Pindarus ; that labour he left to some future

[1] Viz. the supposed dragging of Hector three times round Troy by
Achilles—a mere post-Homeric fable.   But it is ludicrous to add
that in after years—nay, when nearly at the end of his translation of
the " Iliad " in 1718—Pope took part in a discussion upon Homer's
reasons for ascribing such conduct to his hero, seriously arguing the
pro and *con* upon a pure fiction.
[2] The Rev. Henry Francis Cary, 1772-1844, scholar, poet, and
translator of Dante and Pindar.—M.

Hercules. So much for his subjects ; but a second objection is — his metre. The hexameter, or heroic metre of the ancient Greeks is delightful to our modern ears ; so is the Iambic metre, fortunately, of the stage : but the lyric metres generally, and those of Pindar without one exception, are as utterly without meaning to us, as merely chaotic labyrinths of sound, as Chinese music or Dutch concertos. Need we say more ?

Next comes the Drama. But this is too weighty a theme to be discussed slightly ; and the more so because here only we willingly concede a strong motive for learning Greek, here only we hold the want of a ready introduction to be a serious misfortune. Our general argument, therefore, which had for its drift to depreciate Greek, dispenses in this case with our saying anything,—since every word we *could* say would be hostile to our own purpose. However, we shall, even upon this field of the Greek Literature, deliver one oracular sentence, tending neither to praise nor dispraise it, but simply to state its relations to the Modern, or, at least, the English, Drama. In the ancient drama, to represent it justly, the unlearned reader must imagine grand situations, impressive groups ; in the modern tumultuous movement, a grand stream of action. In the Greek drama, he must conceive the presiding power to be *Death* ; in the English, *Life*. What Death ?—What Life ? That sort of death, or of life locked up and frozen into everlasting slumber, which we see in sculpture ; that sort of life, of tumult, of agitation, of tendency to something beyond, which we see in painting. The picturesque, in short, domineers over English tragedy ; the sculpturesque, or the statuesque, over the Grecian.

The moralists, such as Theognis, the miscellaneous or didactic poets, such as Hesiod, are all alike below any notice in a sketch like this.[1] The epigrammatists, or writers of monumental inscriptions, &c., remain ; and they, next after the dramatic poets, present the most interesting field by far in the Greek Literature ; but these are too various to be treated otherwise than *viritim* and in detail.

There remains the Prose Literature ; and, with the excep-

[1] Theognis, elegiac poet, about B.C. 570-490 ; Hesiod, in ninth century B.C.—M.

tion of those critical writers who have written on Rhetoric
(such as Hermogenes, Dionysius of Halicarnassus, Demetrius
Phalereus, &c. &c.,[1] some of whom are the best writers
extant on the mere art of constructing sentences, but could
not interest the general reader), the Prose Writers may be
thus distributed : 1st, the Orators ; 2d, the Historians ; 3d,
the Philosophers ; 4th, the Litterateurs (such as Plutarch,
Lucian, &c.)

As to the Philosophers : of course there are only two who
can present any general interest—Plato and Aristotle ; for
Xenophon is no more a philosophic writer than our own
Addison.[2] Now, in this department, it is evident that the
matter altogether transcends the manner. No man will wish
to study a profound philosopher but for some previous
interest in his doctrines ; and, if by any means a man has
obtained this, he may pursue this study sufficiently through
translations. It is true that neither Sydenham nor Taylor
has done justice to Plato, for example, as respects the
colloquial graces of his style ; but, when the object is purely
to pursue a certain course of principles and inferences, the
student cannot complain much that he has lost the dramatic
beauties of the dialogue, or the luxuriance of the style.
These he was not then seeking, by the supposition—what he
did seek, is still left ; whereas in poetry, if the golden
apparel is lost, if the music has melted away from the
thoughts, all, in fact, is lost. Old Hobbes, or Ogilby, is no
more Homer than the score of Mozart's " Don Giovanni " is
Mozart's " Don Giovanni." [3]

If, however, Grecian Philosophy presents no absolute
temptations to the attainment of Greek, far less does Grecian
History. If you except later historians—such as Diodorus,
Plutarch, and those (like Appian, Dionysius, Dion Cassius)
who wrote of Roman things and Roman persons in Greek,

[1] Hermogenes, second century after Christ ; Dionysius of Halicarnassus, about A.D. 18 ; Demetrius Phalereus, about B.C. 345-282.
—M.

[2] Plato, B.C. 428-347 ; Aristotle, B.C. 384-322.—M.

[3] Hobbes's translation of the Iliad and Odyssey was completed in
1675 ; and a translation of the Iliad was one of the works of the indefatigable bookmaker John Ogilby (1600-1676).—M.

and Polybius,[1] who comes under the same class at a much
earlier period—none of whom have any interest of style,
excepting only Plutarch :—these dismissed, there are but
three who can rank as classical Greek historians,—*three who
can lose by translation.* Of these the eldest, Herodotus,[2]
is perhaps of real value. Some call him the Father of History ; some call him the father of lies. Time and Major
Rennel have done him ample justice. Yet here, again, see
how little need of Greek for the amplest use of a Greek
author. Twenty-two centuries and more have passed since
the fine old man read his history at the Grecian games of
Olympia. One man only has done him right, and put his
enemies under his footstool ; *and yet this man had no Greek.*
Major Rennel read Herodotus only in the translation of
Beloe. He has told us so himself. Here, then, is a little
fact, my Grecian boys, that you won't easily get over. The
Father of History, the eldest of prose writers, has been first
explained, illustrated, justified, liberated from scandal and
disgrace, first had his geography set to rights, first been
translated from the region of fabulous romance, and installed
in his cathedral chair as Dean (or eldest) of Historians, by a
military man who had no more Greek than Shakspere, or
than we (perhaps you, reader) have of the Kalmuck.

Next comes Thucydides.[3] He is the second in order of
time amongst the Grecian historians who survive, and the
first of those (a class which Mr. Southey, the laureate, always
speaks of as the corrupters of genuine history) who affect to
treat it philosophically. If the philosophic historians are
not always so faithless as Mr. Southey alleges, they are, however, always guilty of dulness. Commend us to one
picturesque, garrulous old fellow, like Froissart, or Philip de
Comines, or Bishop Burnet, before all the philosophic prosers
that ever prosed. These picturesque men will lie a little

---

[1] Diodorus Siculus, contemporary with Augustus Cæsar ; Plutarch,
about A.D. 46-120 ; Appian, about A.D. 98-160 ; Dionysius, about
B.C. 18 ; Dion Cassius, about A.D. 155-229 ; Polybius, about B.C. 204-
122.—M.

[2] Herodotus, B.C. 484-408. For De Quincey's fuller and better
appreciation of Herodotus, see his paper "Philosophy of Herodotus"
ante, Vol. VI.—M.

[3] B.C. 471-401.—M.

now and then, for the sake of effect—but so will the philosophers.   Even Bishop Burnet, who, by the way, was hardly
so much a picturesque as an anecdotal historian, was famous
for his gift of lying ; so diligently had he cultivated it.   And
the Duchess of Portsmouth told a noble lord, when inquiring
into the truth of a particular fact stated by the very reverend
historian, that he was notorious in Charles the Second's
court, and that no man believed a word he said.   But now
Thucydides, though writing about his own time, and doubtless embellishing by fictions not less than his more amusing
brethren, is as dull as if he prided himself on veracity.
Nay, he tells us no secret anecdotes of the times,—surely
there must have been many ; and this proves to us that he
was a low fellow without political connexions, and that he
never had been behind the curtain.   Now, what business
had such a man to set himself up for a writer of history and
a speculator on politics ?   Besides, his history is imperfect ;
and, suppose it were not, what is its subject ?   Why simply
one single war : a war which lasted twenty-seven years, but
which, after all, through its whole course was enlivened by
only two events worthy to enter into General History—viz.
the plague of Athens, and the miserable licking which the
Athenian invaders received in Sicily.   This dire overthrow
dished Athens out and out ; for one generation to come, there
was an end of Athenian domination ; and that arrogant
state, under the yoke of their still baser enemies of Sparta,
learned experimentally what were the evils of a foreign conquest.   There was, therefore, in the domination of the
Thirty Tyrants, something to "point a moral" in the Peloponnesian War: it was the judicial reaction of martial
tyranny and foreign oppression, such as we of this generation
have beheld in the double conquest of Paris by insulted and
outraged Christendom.   But nothing of all this will be found
in Thucydides : he is as cool as a cucumber upon every act
of atrocity, whether it be the bloody abuse of power, or
the bloody retribution from the worm that, being trampled
on too long, turns at last to sting and to exterminate ;
all alike he enters in his day-book and his ledger, posts them
up to the account of brutal Spartan or polished Athenian
with no more expression of his feelings (if he had any) than

a merchant making out an invoice of puncheons that are to
steal away men's wits, or of frankincense and myrrh that are
to ascend in devotion to the saints.   Herodotus is a fine old
genial boy, that, like Froissart or some of .the crusading historians, kept himself in health and jovial spirits by travelling
about ; nor did he confine himself to Greece or the Grecian
islands ; but he went to Egypt, got bousy in the Pyramid of
Cheops, ate a beef-steak in the hanging-gardens of Babylon,
and listened to no sailors' yarns at the Piræus, which doubtless before his time had been the sole authority for Grecian
legends concerning foreign lands.   But, as to Thucydides,
our own belief is that he lived like a monk shut up in his
museum or study, and that at the very utmost he may
have gone in the steamboat[1] to Corfu (*i.e.* Corcyra) because
that was the island which occasioned the row of the Peloponnesian War.

Xenophon now is quite another sort of man.[2]   He could
use his pen ; but also he could use his sword, and (when
need was) his heels in running away.   His Grecian history
of course is a mere fraction of the General History ; and,
moreover, our own belief, founded upon the differences of
the style, is that the work now received for his must be
spurious.   But in this place the question is not worth discussing.   Two works remain, professedly historical, which,
beyond a doubt, *are* his ; and one of them the most interesting prose work by much which Athens has bequeathed us ;
though, by the way, Xenophon was living in a sort of elegant
exile at a chateau in Thessaly, and not under Athenian pro-
tection, when he wrote it.   Both of his great works relate
to a Persian Cyrus, but to a Cyrus of different centuries.
The " Cyropædia " is a romance, pretty much on the plan of
Fenelon's " Telemaque," only (Heaven be praised !) not so
furiously apoplectic.   It pursues the great Cyrus, the founder
of the Persian Empire, the Cyrus of the Jewish prophets,
from his infancy to his death-bed, and describes evidently

[1] " In the steamboat ! "   Yes, reader, the steamboat.   It is clear
that there *was* one in Homer's time.   See the art. *Phæacian* in the
" Odyssey " : if it paid then, *a fortiori* six hundred years after.   The
only point unknown about it is the captain's name and the state- cabin
fares.

[2] Xenophon, B.C. 444-359.—M.

not any real prince according to any authentic record of his
life, but, upon some basis of hints and vague traditions, im-
proves the actual Cyrus into an ideal fiction of a sovereign
and a military conqueror as he *ought* to be.   One thing only
we shall say of this work, though no admirers ourselves of
the twaddle which Xenophon elsewhere gives us as philosophic memorabilia,—that the episode of Abradates and
Panthea (especially the behaviour of Panthea after the death
of her beloved hero, and the incident of the dead man's hand
coming away on Cyrus grasping it) exceeds for pathos everything in Grecian Literature, always excepting the Greek
Drama, and comes nearest of anything throughout Pagan
Literature to the impassioned simplicity of Scripture in its
tale of Joseph and his brethren.   The other historical work
of Xenophon is the "Anabasis."   The meaning of the title
is *the going up* or *ascent*—viz. of Cyrus the younger.   This
prince was the younger brother of the reigning king
Artaxerxes, nearly two centuries from Cyrus the Great ; and,
from opportunity rather than a better title, and because his
mother and his vast provincial government furnished him
with royal treasures able to hire an army,—most of all, because he was richly endowed by nature with personal gifts—
took it into his head that he would dethrone his brother,
and the more so because he was only his half-brother.   His
chance was a good one : he had a Grecian army, and one
from the very *élite* of Greece ; whilst the Persian king had
but a small corps of Grecian auxiliaries, long enfeebled by
Persian effeminacy and Persian intermarriages.   Xenophon
was personally present in this expedition.   And the catastrophe was most singular, such as does not occur once in a
thousand years.   The cavalry of the great King retreated
before the Greeks continually, no doubt from policy and
secret orders ; so that, when a pitched battle became inevitable, the foreign invaders found themselves in the very heart
of the land, and close upon the Euphrates.   The battle was
fought : the foreigners were victorious : they were actually
singing *Te Deum* or *Io Pæan* for their victory, when it was
discovered that their leader, the native prince in whose
behalf they had conquered, was missing, and, soon after, that
he was dead.   What was to be done ?   The man who should

have improved their victory, and placed them at his own
right hand when on the throne of Persia, was no more ; key
they had none to unlock the great fortresses of the empire,
none to unloose the enthusiasm of the native population.
Yet such was the desperation of their circumstances that a
coup-de-main on the capital seemed their best chance.   The
whole army was and felt itself a forlorn hope.   To go forward was desperate, but to go back much more so ; for they
had a thousand rivers without bridges in their rear ; and, if
they set their faces in that direction, they would have
300,000 light cavalry upon their flanks, besides nations
innumerable—

"Dusk faces with white silken turbants wreathed "—

fierce fellows who understood no Greek, and, what was worse,
no joking, but well understood the use of the scimitar.   Bad
as things were, they soon became worse ; for the chiefs of
the Grecian army, being foolish enough to accept a dinner
invitation from the Persian commander-in-chief, were assassinated ; and the words of Milton became intelligible—that in
the lowest deep a lower deep had opened to destroy them.
In this dilemma, Xenophon, the historian of the expedition,
was raised to a principal command ; and by admirable skill
he led back the army by a different route to the Black Sea,
on the coast of which he knew that there were Grecian
colonies : and from one of these he obtained shipping, in
which he coasted along (when he did not march by land) to
the mouth of the Bosporus and the Dardanelles.   This was
the famous Retreat of the Ten Thousand ; and it shows how
much defect of literary skill there was in those days amongst
Grecian authors that the title of the book, " *The Going Up*,"
does not apply to the latter and more interesting seven-
eighths of the account.   The Going Up is but the preparation or preface to the Going Down, the *Anabasis* to the
Katabasis, in which latter part it is that Xenophon plays any
conspicuous part.   A great political interest, however, over
and above the personal interest, attaches to this expedition :
for there can be no doubt that to this proof of weakness in
the Persian Empire, and perhaps to this *as recorded by Xeno-*

phon, was due the expedition of Alexander in the next generation, which changed the face of the world.

The Litterateurs, as we have styled Plutarch and Lucian, though far removed from the true classical era, being both posterior to Christianity, are truly interesting. And, for Lucian in particular,[1] though he is known by reputation only as a humorous and sneering writer, we can say, upon our personal knowledge, that there are passages of more terrific effect, more German and approaching to the sublime, than anywhere else in Greek literature, out of the tragic poets. Of Plutarch we need hardly speak ; one part of his voluminous works—viz. his biographies of Greek and Roman leaders in arts [2] and arms—being so familiar to all nations, and having been selected by Rousseau as the book for him who should be limited (or, like Collins the poet, should limit himself) to one book only : a foolish choice un-doubtedly, but still arguing great range of resources in Plutarch, that he should be thought of after so many myriads of modern books had widened the range of selection. Meantime, the reader is not to forget that, whatever may be his powers of amusement, a more inaccurate or faithless author as to dates, and, indeed, in all matters of research, does not exist than Plutarch. We make it a rule, whenever we see *Plut.* at the-bottom of a dictionary article as the authority on which it rests, to put the better half down as a bouncer. And, in fact, Joe Miller is quite as good authority for English History as Plutarch for Roman.

Now remain the Orators ; and of these we have a right to speak, for we have read them ; and, believe us, reader, not above one or two men in a generation have. If the Editor would allow us room, we would gladly contrast them with modern orators ; and we could easily show how prodigious are the advantages of modern orators in every point which can enter into a comparison. But to what purpose ? Even modern orators, with all the benefit of modern interest, and

---

[1] Lucian, about A.D. 120-200.—M.

[2] " In arts," we say, because great orators are amongst his heroes ; but, after all, it is very questionable whether, simply as orators, Plutarch would have noticed them. They were also statesmen ; and Mitford always treats Demosthenes as first lord of the treasury and premier. Plutarch records no poet, no artist, however brilliant.

of allusions everywhere intelligible, are not read in any
generation after their own, pulpit orators only being excepted.
So that, if the gods *had* made our reader a Grecian, surely he
would never so far misspend his precious time, and squander
his precious intellect upon old dusty quarrels, never of
more value to a philosopher than a tempest in a wash-hand
basin, but now stuffed with obscurities which no man can
explain, and with lies to which no man can bring the counter-
statement.   But this would furnish matter for a separate
paper.

Part II—The Greek Orators

Now let us come to the Orators.   Isocrates, the eldest of
those who have survived, is a mere scholastic rhetorician :
for he was a timid man, and did not dare to confront the
terrors of a stormy political audience ; and hence, though he
lived about an entire century, he never once addressed the
Athenian citizens.[1]   It is true that, although no *bona fide*
orator—for he never *spoke* in any usual acceptation of that
word, and, as a consequence, never had an opportunity of
replying, which only can bring forward a man's talents as a
debater—still he employed his pen upon real and upon existing questions of public policy, and did not, as so many
generations of chamber rhetoricians continued to do in Greece,
confine his powers to imaginary cases of political difficulty,
or (what were tantamount to imaginary) cases fetched up
from the long-past era of King Priam, or the still earlier era
of the Seven Chiefs warring against the Seven-gated Thebes
of Bœotia, or the half-fabulous era of the Argonauts.   Isocrates was a man of sense—a patriot in a temperate way—
and with something of a feeling for Greece generally, not
merely a champion of Athens.   His heart was given to
politics ; and, in an age when heavy clouds were gathering
over the independence and the civil grandeur of his country,
he had a disinterested anxiety for drawing off the lightning
of the approaching storms by pacific counsels.   Compared,
therefore, with the common mercenary orators of the Athenian

[1] About Isocrates see *ante*, pp. 209-213.—M.

forum—who made a regular trade of promoting mischief by inflaming the pride, jealousy, vengeance, or the martial instincts of a "fierce democracy," and, generally speaking, with no views, high or low, sound or unsound, that looked beyond the momentary profit to themselves from thus pandering to the thoughtless nationality of a most sensitive people —Isocrates is entitled to our respect. His writings have also a separate value, as memorials of political transactions from which the historian has gathered many useful hints; and, perhaps, to a diligent search, they might yield more. But, considered as an orator—if that title can be with any propriety allowed to one who declaimed only in his closet—one who, in relation to public affairs, was what, in England, when speaking of practical jurisprudence, we call a Chamber Counsel—Isocrates is languid, and with little of anything characteristic in his manner to justify a separate consideration. It is remarkable that he, beyond all other rhetoricians of that era, cultivated the *rhythmus* of his periods. And to this object he sacrificed not only an enormity of time, but, I have no doubt, in many cases, the freedom and natural movement of the thoughts. My reason, however, for noticing this peculiarity in Isocrates is by way of fixing the attention upon the superiority, even for artificial ornaments, of downright practical business and the realities of political strife over the torpid atmosphere of a study or a school. Cicero, long after, had the same passion for *numerositas*, and the full, pompous rotundity of cadence. But in Cicero all habits and all faculties were nursed by the daily practice of life and its impassioned realities in the forum or in the senate. What is the consequence ? Why this—that, whereas in the most laboured performance of Isocrates (which cost him, I think, one whole *decennium*, or period of ten years) few modern ears are sensible of any striking art, or any great result of harmony, in Cicero, on the other hand, the fine, sonorous modulations of his periodic style are delightful to the dullest ear of any European. Such are the advantages from real campaigns, from the unsimulated strife of actual stormy life, over the torpid dreams of what the Romans called an *umbratic* [1] experience.

[1] " *Umbratic* " :—I have perhaps elsewhere drawn the attention of

Isocrates I have noticed as the oldest of the surviving Greek orators : Demosthenes, of course, claims a notice more emphatically, as, by universal consent of Athens, and afterwards of Rhodes, of Rome, and other impartial judges, the greatest, or, at least, the most comprehensively great.   For, by the way, it must not be forgotten—though modern critics *do* forget this rather important fact in weighing the reputation of Demosthenes—he was not esteemed in his own day as the greatest in that particular quality of energy and demoniac power (δεινοτης) which is generally assumed to have been his leading characteristic and his *forte*, not only by comparison with his own compatriots, but even with Cicero and the greatest men of the Roman bar.   It was not of Demosthenes that the Athenians were accustomed to say " he thunders and lightens," but of Pericles, an elder orator ; and even amongst the written oratory of Greece which still survives (for, as to the speeches ascribed to Pericles by Thucydides, I take it for granted that, as usual, these were mere forgeries of the historian) there is a portion which perhaps exceeds Demosthenes in the naked quality of vehemence. But this, I admit, will not impeach his supremacy ; for it is probable that, wherever an orator is characterised exclusively by turbulent power, or at least remembered chiefly for that quality, all the other numerous graces of eloquence were wanting to that man, or existed only in a degree which made no equipoise to his insulated gift of Jovian terror.   The Gracchi, amongst the Roman orators, were probably more properly "sons of thunder" than Crassus or Cicero, or even than Cæsar himself,—whose oratory, by the way, was in this respect like his own character and infinite accomplishments, so that even by Cicero it is rarely cited without the epithet of splendid, magnificent, &c.   We must suppose, therefore, that neither Cicero nor Demosthenes was held to be at the

readers to the peculiar effects of climate in shaping the modes of our thinking and imaging.   A life of *inertia*, which retreats from the dust and toil of actual experience, we (who represent the idea of effeminacy more naturally by the image of shrinking from cold) call a chimney-corner or a fireside experience ; but the Romans, to whom the same effeminacy more easily fell under the idea of shrinking from the heat of the sun, called it an experience won in the shade, and a mere scholastic student they called an *umbraticus doctor*.

head of their respective fields in Rome and Athens in right of any absolute pre-eminence in the one leading power of an orator—viz. native and fervent vigour—but in right of a large comprehensive harmony of gifts, leaving possibly to some other orators, elder or rival to themselves, a superiority in each of an orator's talents taken apart, but claiming the supremacy, nevertheless, upon the whole, by the systematic union of many qualities tending to one result: pleasing the taste by the harmonious *coup d'œil* from the total assemblage, and also adapting itself to a far larger variety of situations ; for, after all, the *mere* son of thunder is disarmed, and apt to become ridiculous, if you strip him of a passionate cause, of a theme saturated with human strife, and of an excitable or tempestuous audience.[1]

Such an audience, however, it will be said that Demosthenes had, and sometimes (but not very often in those orations which survive) such a theme. As to his audience, certainly it was all that could be wished in point of violence and combustible passion ; but also it was something more. A mighty advantage it is, doubtless, to an orator, when he sees and hears his own kindling passions instantaneously reflected in the blazing eyes and fiery shouts (the *fremitus*) of his audience—when he sees a whole people, personally or by deputation, swayed backwards and forwards, like a field of corn in a breeze, by the movements of his own appeals. But, unfortunately, in the Athenian audience, the ignorance, the headstrong violence of prejudice, the arrogance, and, above all, the levity of the national mind, presented, to an orator the most favourite, a scene like that of an ocean always rocking with storms ; like a wasp always angry ; like a

---

[1] In spite of all that De Quincey here says, δεινοτης or "tremendousness" was the quality noted as specially characterising the eloquence of Demosthenes. Περὶ τῆς τοῦ Δημοσθὲνους δεινότητος, "Of the tremendousness of Demosthenes," is the title of a criticism on him by the rhetorician Dionysius of Halicarnassus ; and it was said of him that he was a man "whose food was shields and steel." No one can now read, even in translation, such a passage as that on the distinction between the real statesman and the sycophant in the speech "Concerning the Crown"—a passage as noble intellectually as it is morally, and the very perfection of Attic density and fineness in expression—without feeling the reasons for the tradition of the supreme greatness of Demosthenes among the orators of the world.—M.

lunatic, always coming out of a passion or preparing to go into one. Well might Demosthenes prepare himself by sea-shore practice ; in which I conceive that his purpose must have been, not so much (according to the common notion) to overcrow the noise of the forum as to *stand fire* (if I may so express it) against the uproarious demonstrations of mob fury.

This quality of an Athenian audience must very seriously have interfered with the intellectual display of an orator. Not a word could he venture to say in the way of censure towards the public will—not even hypothetically to insinuate a fault ; not a syllable could he utter even in the way of dissent from the favourite speculations of the moment. If he did, instantly a roar of menaces recalled him to a sense even of personal danger. And, again, the mere vivacity of his audience, requiring perpetual amusement and variety, compelled a man, as great even as Demosthenes, to curtail his arguments, and rarely indeed to pursue a theme with the requisite fulness of development or illustration,—a point in which the superior dignity and the far less fluctuating mobility of the Roman mind gave an immense advantage to Cicero.

Demosthenes, in spite of all the weaknesses which have been arrayed against his memory by the hatred of his con-temporaries, or by the anti-republican feelings of such men as Mitford, was a great man and an honest man. He rose above his countrymen. He despised, in some measure, his audience ; and, at length, in the palmy days of his influence, he would insist on being heard ; he would insist on telling the truth, however unacceptable ; he would not, like the great rout of venal haranguers, lay any flattering unction to the capital distempers of the public mind ; he would point out their errors, and warn them of their perils. But this upright character of the man, victorious over his constitutional timidity, does but the more brightly illustrate the local law and the tyranny of the public feeling. How often do we find him, when on the brink of uttering "odious truth," obliged to pause, and to propitiate his audience with depre-catory phrases, entreating them to give him time for utter-ance, not to yell him down before they had heard his sentence to the end. Μη θορυβειτε—" Gentlemen of Athens ! for the love of God, do not make an uproar at what I am going to say! Gentlemen of Athens! humbly I beseech you to let me finish my sentence!" Such are his continual appeals to the better feelings of his audience. Now, it is very evident that, in such circumstances, no man could do justice to any subject. At least, when speaking not before a tribunal of justice, but before the people in council assembled—that is, in effect, on his greatest stage of all—Demosthenes (however bold at times and restive in a matter which he held to be paramount) was required to bend, and did bend, to the local genius of democracy, reinforced by a most mercurial temperament. The very air of Attica, combined with great political power, kept its natives in a state of habitual intoxication; and even wise men would have had some difficulty in mastering, as it affected themselves, the permanent bias towards caprice and insolence.

Is this state of things at all taken into account in our modern critiques upon Demosthenes? The upshot of what I can find in most modern lecturers upon rhetoric and style, French or English, when speaking of Demosthenes, is this notable simile, by way of representing the final effect of his eloquence,— "that, like a mountain torrent, swollen by melting snow, or by rain, it carries all things before it." Prodigiously original! and exceedingly discriminative! As if such an illustration would not equally represent the effect of a lyrical poem, of Mozart's music, of a stormy chorus, or any other form whatever of impassioned vehemence! Meantime, I suspect grievously that not one of these critics has ever read a paragraph of Demosthenes. Nothing do you ever find quoted but a few notorious passages about Philip of Macedon, and the too-famous oath by the manes of those that died at Marathon.[1] I call it too famous, because (like Addison's comparison of Marlborough at Blenheim to the angel in the storm—of which a schoolmaster then living said that nine out of every ten boys would have hit upon it

---

[1] " Never, never, can ye have done wrong, O men of Athens, in undertaking the battle for the freedom and safety of all,—no: I swear it by your forefathers : those that met the peril at Marathon, those that took the field at Plataea, those in the sea-fight at Salamis, and those at Artemisium ! "—*Speech concerning the Crown.*—M.

in a school exercise [1]) it has no peculiar boldness, and must have occurred to every Athenian of any sensibility every day of his life. Hear, on the other hand, a modern oath, and (what is most remarkable) an oath sworn in the pulpit. A dissenting clergyman (I believe, a Baptist), preaching at Cambridge, and having ocasion to affirm or to deny something or other, upon his general confidence in the grandeur of man's nature, the magnificence of his conceptions, the immensity of his aspirations, &c., delivered himself thus :—" By the greatness of human ideals—by the greatness of human aspirations —by the immortality of human creations—*by the Iliad —by the Odyssey* ! "——Now, that *was* bold, startling, sublime. But, in the other case, neither was the oath invested with any great pomp of imagery or expression ; nor, if it had— which is more to the purpose—was such an oath at all representative of the peculiar manner belonging to Demosthenes. It is always a rude and inartificial style of criticism to cite from an author that which, whether fine or not in itself, is no fair specimen of his ordinary style.

What, then, *is* the characteristic style of Demosthenes ? It is one which grew naturally, as did his defects (by which I mean faults of *omission*, in contradiction to such as are positive), from the composition of his audience. His audience, comprehending so much ignorance, and, above all, so much high-spirited impatience,—being, in fact, always on the fret,—kept the orator always on the fret. Hence arose short sentences ; hence the impossibility of the long, voluminous

[1] " 'Twas then great Marlborough's mighty soul was proved.
    That, in the shock of charging hosts unmoved,
    Amidst confusion, horror, and despair,
    Examined all the dreadful scenes of war ;
    In peaceful thought the field of death surveyed,
    To fainting squadrons sent the timely aid,
    Suffered repulsed battalions to engage,
    And taught the doubtful battle where to rage.
    So, when an angel by divine command
    With rising tempests shakes a guilty land,
    Such as of late o'er pale Britannia passed,
    Calm and serene he drives the furious blast,
    And, pleased the Almighty's orders to perform,
    Rides on the whirlwind, and directs the storm."
                                        The Campaign. —M.

sweeps of beautiful rhythmus which we find in Cicero ; hence the animated form of apostrophe and crowded interro gations addressed to the audience. This gives, undoubtedly, a spirited and animated character to the style of Demosthenes ; but it robs him of a large variety of structure applied to the logic, or the embellishment, or the music of his composition. His style is full of life, but not (like Cicero's) full of pomp and continuous grandeur. On the contrary, as the necessity of rousing attention, or of sustaining it, obliged the Attic orator to rely too much on the *personality* of direct question to the audience, and to use brief sentences, so also the same impatient and fretful irritability forbade him to linger much upon an idea—to theorize, to speculate, or, generally, to quit the direct business path of the question then under considera- tion—no matter for what purpose of beauty, dignity, instruc- tion, or even of *ultimate* effect. In all things, the *immediate* —the instant—the *præsens præsentissimum*, was kept steadily before the eye of the Athenian orator by the mere coercion of self-interest.

And hence, by the way, arises one most important feature of distinction between Grecian oratory (political oratory at least) on the one hand, and Roman (to which, in this point, we may add British) on the other. A Roman lawyer, senator,, or demagogue even, under proper restrictions—a British member of parliament, or even a candidate from the hustings—but, most assuredly, and by the evidence of many a splendid example, an advocate addressing a jury—may embellish his oration with a wide circuit of historical, or of antiquarian, nay, even speculative, discussion. Every Latin scholar will remember the leisurely and most facetious, the good-natured and respectful, yet keenly satiric, picture which the great Roman barrister draws of the Stoic philosophy, by way of *rowing* old Cato, who professed that philosophy with too little indulgence for venial human errors. The *judices*— that is, in effect, the jury—were tickled to the soul by seeing the grave Marcus Cato badgered with this fine razor-like raillery ; and there can be no doubt that, by flattering the self-respect of the jury in presuming them susceptible of so much wit from a liberal kind of knowledge, and by really delighting them with such a display of adroit teasing applied

to a man of scenical gravity, this whole scene, though quite
extrajudicial and travelling out of the record, was highly
useful in conciliating the good-will of Cicero's audience.[1]
The same style of liberal *excursus* from the more thorny path
of the absolute business before the court has been often and
memorably practised by great English barristers : as in the
trial of Sacheverell by many of the managers for the Commons ; by "the fluent Murray" on various occasions ; in the
great cause of impeachment against our English Verres (or,
at least, Verres as to the situation, though not the guilt), Mr.
Hastings ; in many of Mr. Erskine's addresses to juries,
where political rights were at stake ; in Sir James Mackin-
tosh's defence of Peltier for a libel upon Napoleon, when he
went into a history of the press as applied to politics (a
liberal inquiry, but which, except in the remotest manner,
could not possibly bear upon the mere question of fact before
the jury) ; and in many other splendid instances which have
really made *our* trials and the annals of *our* criminal jurisprudence one great fund of information and authority to the
historian.   In the senate I need not say how much farther,
and more frequently, this habit of large generalisation, and
of liberal excursion from perhaps a lifeless theme, has been
carried by great masters : in particular, by Edmund Burke,
who carried it, in fact, to such excess, and to a point which
threatened so much to disturb the movement of public
business, that, from that cause more perhaps than from rude
insensibility to the value of his speculations, he put his
audience sometimes in motion for dinner, and acquired (as is
well known) the surname of the Dinner Bell.[2]

Now, in the Athenian audience all this was impossible.
Neither in political nor in forensic harangues was there any
licence by rule, or any indulgence by usage, or any special
privilege by personal favour, to the least effort at improving
an individual case of law or politics into general views of
jurisprudence, of statesmanship, of diplomacy ; no collateral

[1] The reference is to Cicero's speech *Pro L. Murena.*—M.

[2] Yet this story has been exaggerated ; and, I believe, in strict
truth, the whole case arose out of some fretful expressions of ill-temper
on the part of Burke, and that the name was a retort from a man of
wit who had been personally stung by a sarcasm of the offended
orator.

discussions were tolerated—no illustrative details—no historical parallelisms—still less any philosophical moralisations.
The slightest show of any tendency in these directions was
summarily nipped in the bud : the Athenian gentlemen
began to θορυβεῖν in good earnest if a man showed symptoms
of entering upon any discussion whatever that was not
intensely needful and pertinent in the first place, or which,
in the second place, was not of a nature to be wound up in
two sentences when a summons should arise either to dinner,
or to the theatre, or to the succession of some variety anticipated from another orator.

Hence, therefore, finally arises one great peculiarity of
Greek eloquence, and a most unfortunate one for its chance
of ever influencing a remote posterity, or, in any substantial
sense, of its ever surviving in the real unaffected admiration
of us moderns,— that it embodies no alien, no collateral
information as to manners, usages, modes of feeling, no
extrinsic ornament, no side glimpses into Grecian life, no
casual historical details. The cause and nothing but the
cause, the political question and nothing but the question,
pealed for ever in the ears of the terrified orator,—always
on sufferance, always on his good behaviour, always afraid,
for the sake of his party or of his client, lest his auditors
should become angry, or become impatient, or become weary.
And from that intense fear, trammelling the freedom of his
steps at every turn, and overruling every motion to the right
or to the left, in pure servile anxiety for the mood and disposition of his tyrannical master, arose the very opposite
result for us of this day,—that we, by the very means
adopted to prevent weariness in the immediate auditors, find
nothing surviving in Grecian orations but what *does* weary
us insupportably through its want of all general interest,
and, even amongst private or instant details of politics or
law, presenting us with none that throw light upon the
spirit of manners, or the Grecian peculiarities of feeling.
Probably an Athenian mob would not have cared much at
the prospect of such a result to posterity, and, at any rate,
would not have sacrificed one atom of their ease or pleasure
to obviate such a result ; but to an Athenian orator this
result would have been a sad one to contemplate.   The final

consequence is that, whilst all men find, or may find, infinite amusement, and instruction of the most liberal kind, in that most accomplished of statesmen and orators, the Roman Cicero—nay, would doubtless, from the causes assigned, have found, in their proportion, the same attractions in the speeches of the elder Antony, of Hortensius, of Crassus, and other contemporaries or immediate predecessors of Cicero— no person ever reads Demosthenes, still less any other Athenian orator, with the slightest interest beyond that which inevitably attaches to the words of one who wrote his own divine language with probably very superior skill.

But from all this results a further inference—viz. the dire affectation of those who pretend an enthusiasm in the oratory of Demosthenes, and also a plenary consolation to all who are obliged, from ignorance of Greek, to dispense with that novelty.   If it be a luxury at all, it is and can be one for those only who cultivate verbal researches and the pleasures of philology.

Even in the oratory of our own times, which oftentimes discusses questions to the whole growth and motion of which we have been ourselves parties present or even accessary, questions which we have followed in their first emersion and separation from the clouds of general politics,—their advance, slow or rapid, towards a domineering interest in the public passions ; their meridian altitude ; and perhaps their precipitous descent downwards, whether from the consummation of their objects (as in the questions of the Slave Trade, of Catholic Emancipation, of East India Monopoly), or from a partial victory and compromise with the abuse (as in the purification of that Augean stable, prisons, and, still more, private houses for the insane), or from the accomplishment of one stage or so in a progress which by its nature is infinite (as in the various steps taken towards the improvement and towards the extension of education) :—even in cases like these, when the primary and ostensible object of the speaker already on its own account possesses a commanding attraction, yet will it often happen that the secondary questions growing out of the leading one, the great elementary themes suggested to the speaker by the concrete case before him— as, for instance, the general question of Test Laws, or the

still higher and transcendent question of Religious Toleration and the relations between the State and religious
opinions, or the general history of Slavery and the commerce
in the human species, the general principles of Economy as
applied to monopolies, the past usages of mankind in their
treatment of prisoners or of lunatics—these comprehensive
and transcendent themes are continually allowed to absorb
and throw into the shade for a time the minor but more
urgent question· of the moment through which they have
gained their interest. The capital and primary interest
gives way for a time to the derivative interest ; and it does
so by a silent understanding between the orator and his
audience. The orator is well assured that he will not be
taxed with wandering ; the audience are satisfied that, eventually, they will not have lost their time ; and the final result
is to elevate and liberalise the province of oratory, by exalting mere business (growing originally, perhaps, out of contingencies of finance, or trade, or local police) into a field for
the higher understanding, and giving to the mere necessities
of our position as a nation the dignity of great problems for
civilising wisdom or philosophic philanthropy. Look back
to the superb orations of Edmund Burke on questions limited
enough in themselves, sometimes merely personal,—for instance,
that on American Taxation, on the Reforms in our Household
or Official Expenditure, or at that from the Bristol hustings
(by its *prima facie* subject, therefore, a mere electioneering
harangue to a mob) ! With what marvellous skill does he
enrich what is meagre, elevate what is humble, intellectualise
what is purely technical, delocalise what is local, generalise
what is personal ! And with what result ? Doubtless, to the
absolute contemporaries of those speeches, steeped to the very
lips in the passions besetting their topics, even to those whose
attention was sufficiently secured by the domineering interest,
friendly or hostile, to the views of the speaker—even to these
I say that, in so far as they were at all capable of an intellectual pleasure, those parts would be most attractive which
were least occupied with the present business and the
momentary details. This order of precedency in the interests
of the speech held even for them ; but to us, removing at
every annual step we take in the century to a greater distance

from the mere business and partisan interests of the several cases, this secondary attraction is not merely the greater of the two : to us it has become pretty nearly the sole one, pretty nearly the exclusive attraction.

As to religious oratory, *that* stands upon a different footing, —the questions afloat in that province of human speculation being eternal, or at least essentially the same under new forms.   This receives a strong illustration from the annals of the English Senate, to which also it *gives* a strong and useful illustration.   Up to the era of James I. the eloquence of either House could not, for political reasons, be very striking, on the very principle which we have been enforcing.   Parliament met only for dispatch of business ; and that business was purely fiscal, or (as at times it happened) judicial.   The constitutional functions of Parliament were narrow ; and they were narrowed still more severely by the jealousy of the executive government.   With the expansion, or rather first growth and development, of a gentry, or third estate, expanded, *pari passu*, the political field of their jurisdiction and their deliberative functions.   This widening field, as a birth out of new existences unknown to former laws or usages, was, of course, not contemplated by those laws or usages.   Constitutional law could not provide for the exercise of rights by a body of citizens when as yet that body had itself no existence.   A gentry, as the depository of a vast overbalance of property, real as well as personal, had not matured itself till the latter years of James I.   Consequently the new functions which the instinct of their new situation prompted them to assume were looked upon by the Crown, most sincerely, as unlawful usurpations.   This led, as we know, to a most fervent and impassioned struggle, the most so of any struggle which has ever armed the hands of men with the sword. For the passions take a far profounder sweep when they are supported by deep thought and high principles.

This element of fervid strife was already, for itself, an atmosphere most favourable to political eloquence.   Accordingly, the speeches of that day, though generally too short to attain that large compass and sweep of movement without which it is difficult to kindle or to sustain any conscious enthusiasm in an audience, were of a high quality as to thought and energy of expression, as high as their circumstantial disadvantages allowed. Lord Strafford's great effort is deservedly admired to this day, and the latter part of it has been often pronounced a *chef-d'œuvre*.[1] A few years before that era, all the orators of note were, and must have been, judicial orators ; and, amongst these, Lord Bacon, to whom every reader's thoughts will point as the most memorable, attained the chief object of all oratory, if what Ben Jonson reports of him be true,—that he had his audience passive to the motions of his will.[2] But Jonson was, perhaps, too scholastic a judge to be a fair representative judge ; and, whatever he might choose to say or to think, Lord Bacon was certainly too weighty—too massy with the bullion of original thought—ever to have realized the idea of a great popular orator, one who

"Wielded at will a fierce democracy,"

and ploughed up the great deeps of sentiment, or party strife, or national animosities, like a Levanter or a monsoon. In the schools of Plato, in the *palæstra Stoicorum*, such an orator might be potent ; not *in fœce Romuli*. If he had laboured with no other defect, had he the gift of tautology ? Could he say the same thing three times over in direct sequence ? For, without this talent of iteration—of repeating the same thought in diversified forms—a man may utter good heads of an oration, but not an oration. Just as the same illustrious man's Essays are good hints, useful topics, for essays, but no approximation to what we, in modern days, understand by *essays* : they are, as an eminent author once happily

---

[1] The reference is to the peroration of the Earl of Strafford's speech on his impeachment before the House of Lords for high treason, 13th April 1641.—M.

[2] "There happened in my time one noble speaker, who was full of gravity in his speaking. His language (where he could spare or pass by a jest) was nobly censorious. No man ever spake more neatly, more pressly, more weightily, or suffered less emptiness, less idleness, in what he uttered. No member of his speech but consisted of his own graces. His hearers could not cough, or look aside from him, without loss. He commanded when he spoke, and had his judges angry and pleased at his devotion. No man had these affections more in his power. The fear of every man that heard him was lest he should make an end."—Ben Jonson's *Discoveries*.—M.

expressed it to myself, "*seeds, not plants or shrubs; acorns, that is, oaks in embryo, but not oaks.*"

Reverting, however, to the oratory of the Senate, from the era of its proper birth, which we may date from the opening of our memorable Long Parliament, brought together in November of 1640,[1] our Parliamentary eloquence has now, within four years, travelled through a period of two centuries. A most admirable subject for an essay, or a magazine article, as it strikes me, would be a bird's-eye view —or rather a bird's-wing flight—pursuing rapidly the revolutions of that memorable Oracle (for such it really was to the rest of civilized Europe), which, through so long a course of years, like the Delphic Oracle to the nations of old, delivered counsels of civil prudence and of national grandeur that kept alive for Christendom the recollections of freedom, and refreshed to the enslaved Continent the old ideas of Roman patriotism, which, but for our Parliament, would have uttered themselves by no voices on earth. That this account of the position occupied by our British Parliament in relation to the rest of Europe, at least after the publication of the Debates had been commenced by Cave with the aid of Dr. Johnson,[2] is, in no respect, romantic or overcharged, may be learned from the German novels of the last century, in which we find the British debates as uniformly the morning accompaniment of breakfast at the houses of the rural gentry, &c., as in any English or Scottish county. Such a

[1] There was another Parliament of this same year 1640, which met in the spring (April, I think), but was summarily dissolved. A small quarto volume, of not unfrequent occurrence, I believe, contains some good specimens of the eloquence then prevalent. It was rich in thought, never wordy—in fact, too parsimonious in words and illustrations; and it breathed a high tone of religious principle as well as of pureminded patriotism ; but, for the reason stated above—its narrow circuit and very limited duration—the general character of the Parliamentary eloquence was ineffective. [I have changed "1642" in the original in *Tait* into 1640 ; which is the correct date. Specimens of the speeches in the Long Parliament will be found in the *Parliamentary History.* —M.]

[2] It was in 1738 that Johnson became a regular coadjutor to Edward Cave, proprietor of the *Gentleman's Magazine,* and began to furnish for that periodical in disguised form what might pass for reports or summaries of the debates in both Houses of Parliament.—M.

sketch would, of course, collect the characteristics of each
age, show in what connexion these characteristics stood with
the political aspects of the time, or with the modes of managing public business (a fatal rock to our public eloquence in
England !), and illustrate the whole by interesting specimens
from the leading orators in each generation : from Hampden
to Pulteney, amongst oppositionists or patriots ; from Pulteney
to O'Connell ; or, again, amongst Ministers, from Hyde to
Somers, from Lord Sunderland to Lords Oxford and Bolingbroke ; and from the plain, downright Sir Robert Walpole,
to the plain, downright Sir Robert Peel.

Throughout the whole of this review the same "moral,"
if one might so call it, would be apparent—viz. that in proportion as the oratory was high and intellectual did it travel
out into the collateral questions of less instant necessity, but
more durable interest, and that, in proportion as the Grecian
necessity *was* or was *not* enforced by the temper of the House
or by the pressure of public business—the necessity which
cripples the orator by confining him within the severe limits
of the case before him—in that proportion had or had not
the oratory of past generations a surviving interest for modern
posterity.   Nothing, in fact, so utterly effete—not even old
law, or old pharmacy, or old erroneous chemistry—nothing
so insufferably dull, as political orations, unless when powerfully animated by that spirit of generalization which only
gives the breath of life and the salt which preserves from
decay through every age alike.   The very strongest proof,
as well as exemplification, of all which has been said on
Grecian oratory may thus be found in the records of the
British Senate.

And this, by the way, brings us round to an aspect of
Grecian Oratory which has been rendered memorable, and
forced upon our notice, in the shape of a problem, by the
most popular of our native historians—the aspect, I mean, of
Greek Oratory in comparison with English.   Hume has an
essay upon the subject [1] ; and the true answer to that essay
will open a wide field of truth to us.   In this little paper
Hume assumes the superiority of Grecian eloquence, as a
thing admitted on all hands, and requiring no proof.   Not

---

[1] "*Of Eloquence*" is the title of the essay.—M,

the proof of this point did he propose to himself as his object; not even the illustration of it.   No.   All *that* Hume held to be superfluous.   His object was to investigate the causes of this Grecian superiority ; or, if *investigate* is too pompous a word for so slight a discussion, more properly, he inquired for the cause as something that must naturally lie upon the surface.

What is the answer ?   First of all, before looking for causes, a man should be sure of his facts.   Now, as to the main fact at issue, I utterly deny the superiority of Grecian eloquence.   And, first of all, I change the whole field of inquiry by shifting the comparison.   The Greek oratory is all political or judicial :   we have those also ; but the best of our eloquence, by immeasurable degrees the noblest and richest, is our religious eloquence.   Here, of course, all comparison ceases ; for classical Grecian religious eloquence, in Grecian attire, there is none until three centuries after the Christian era, when we have three great orators : Gregory Nazianzen, Basil—of which two I have a very fixed opinion, having read large portions of both—and a third, of whom I know nothing.   To our Jeremy Taylor, to our Sir Thomas Browne, there is no approach made in the Greek eloquence.[1] The inaugural chapter of the " Holy Dying," to say nothing of many another golden passage ; or the famous passage in the " Urn Burial," beginning —" Now, since these bones have rested under the drums and tramplings of three conquests "—have no parallel in literature.   The winding-up of the former is more, in its effect, like a great tempestuous chorus from the Judas Maccabeus, or from Spohr's St. Paul, than like human eloquence.

But, grant that this transfer of the comparison is unfair, still, it is no less unfair to confine the comparison on our part to the weakest part of our oratory.   But no matter—let issue be joined even here.   Then we may say at once that, for the intellectual qualities of eloquence,—in fineness of understanding, in depth and in large compass of thought,— Burke far surpasses any orator, ancient or modern.   But, if the comparison were pushed more widely, very certain I am

[1] For De Quincey more at large on Jeremy Taylor and Sir Thomas Browne, see *ante*, pp. 104-109.—M.

that, apart from classical prejudice, no qualities of just thinking, or fine expression, or even of artificial ornament, could
have been assigned by Hume in which the great body of our
deliberative and forensic orators fall short of Grecian models ;
though I will admit that, by comparison with the Roman
model of Cicero, there is seldom the same artful prefigura-
tion of the oration throughout its future course, or the same
sustained rhythmus and oratorial tone.   The qualities of art
are nowhere so prominently expressed, nowhere aid the effect
so much, as in the great Roman master.

But, as to Greece, let us now, in one word, unveil the
sole advantage which the eloquence of the Athenian assembly
has over that of the English senate.   It is this :—*the public
business of Athens was as yet simple and unencumbered by
details ;* the dignity of the occasion was scenically sustained.
But, in England, the vast intricacy and complex interweaving
of property, of commerce, of commercial interests, of details
infinite in number and infinite in littleness, break down and
fritter away into fractions and petty minutiæ the whole huge
labyrinth of our public affairs.   It is scarcely necessary to
explain my meaning.   In Athens, the question before the
public assembly was, peace or war—before our House of
Commons, perhaps the Exchequer Bills Bill ; at Athens, a
league or no league—in England, the Tithe of Agistment
Commutation-Bills Renewal Bill ; in Athens — shall we
forgive a ruined enemy ? in England—shall we cancel the
tax on farthing rushlights ?   In short, with us, the infinity
of details overlays the simplicity and grandeur of our public
deliberations.

Such was the advantage—a mighty advantage—for Greece.
Now, finally, for the use made of this advantage !   To that
point I have already spoken.   By the clamorous and unde-
liberative qualities of the Athenian political audience, by its
fitful impatience, and vehement arrogance, and fervid partisanship, all wide and general discussion was barred *in limine.*
And thus occurred this singular inversion of positions :—The
greatest of Greek orators was obliged to treat these catholic
questions as mere Athenian questions of business.   On the
other hand, the least eloquent of British senators, whether
from the immense advance in knowledge, or from the custom

and usage of Parliament, seldom fails, more or less, to elevate his intense details of pure technical business into something dignified, either by the necessities of pursuing the *historical* relations of the matter in discussion, or of arguing its merits as a case of general finance, or as connected with general political economy, or perhaps in its bearings on peace or war. The Grecian was forced, by the composition of his headstrong auditory, to degrade and personalise his grand themes ; the Englishman is forced, by the difference of his audience, by old prescription, and by the opposition of a well - informed hostile party, into elevating his merely technical and petty themes into great national questions, involving honour and benefit to tens of millions.

SELECTED BIBLIOGRAPHY

Aristotle. *The Basic Works of Aristotle,* ed. Richard McKeon. New York, 1941.

Baldwin, Charles Sears. *Ancient Rhetoric and Poetic.* New York, 1924.

Bate, Walter Jackson. *From Classic to Romantic, Premises of Taste in Eighteenth Century England.* New York, 1961.

Beattie, James. "An Essay on Poetry and Music, as they Affect the Mind," *Essays.* London, 1779.

————. *An Essay on the Nature and Immutability of Truth, in opposition to Sophistry and Scepticism.* Edinburgh, 1771.

Blair, Hugh. *Lectures on Rhetoric and Belles Lettres,* ed. Harold F. Harding. 2 vols. Carbondale, Ill., 1965.

Brown, Calvin S. "De Quincey and the Participles in Mallarmé's *Coup de dés,*" *CL,* XVI (Winter, 1964), 65–69.

Campbell, George. *The Philosophy of Rhetoric,* ed. Lloyd F. Bitzer. Carbondale, Ill., 1963.

Christoph, Friedrich. *Über den Einflub Jean Paul Friedrich Richters auf Thomas De Quincey.* Programm des königlichen humanistischen Gymnasiums in Hof. Hof, 1899.

Cicero. *De Inventione,* trans. H. M. Hubbell. London, 1949.

Cooper, Lane. *The Prose Poetry of Thomas De Quincey.* Leipzig, 1902.

De Quincey, Thomas. *The Collected Writings of Thomas De Quincey,* ed. David Masson. 14 vols. Edinburgh, 1889-1890.

————. *De Quincey at Work: As Seen in One Hundred Thirty New and Newly Edited Letters,* ed. Willard H. Bonner. Buffalo, 1936.

————. *De Quincey's Essays on Style, Rhetoric, and Language,* ed. Fred Newton Scott. Boston, 1893.

————. *De Quincey Memorials. Being Letters and Other Records, Here First Published. With Communications from Coleridge, the Wordsworths, Hannah More, Professor Wilson, and Others,* ed. Alexander H. Japp. London, 1891.

De Quincey, Thomas. *De Quincey's Literary Criticism*, ed. Helen Darbishire. London, 1909.

———. *De Quincey's Writings*, ed. Ticknor, Reed, and Fields. 12 vols. Boston, 1851-59.

———. *A Diary of Thomas De Quincey, 1803*, ed. Horace A. Eaton, London, 1927.

———. *The Posthumous Works of Thomas De Quincey*, ed. Alexander H. Japp ["H. A. Page"]. 2 vols. London, 1891-1893.

———. *Selections Grave and Gay*, ed. Thomas De Quincey. 14 vols. Edinburgh, 1853-1860.

———. *The Uncollected Writings of Thomas De Quincey*, ed. James Hogg. 2 vols. London, 1892.

Dowden, Edward. "How De Quincey Worked," *Saturday Review*, LXXXIX (1895), 246-48.

Dunn, William. *Thomas De Quincey's Relation to German Literature and Philosophy*. Strassburg, 1900.

Durand, Walter Y. "De Quincey and Carlyle in Their Relation to the Germans," *PMLA*, XXII, new series, XV (1907), 521-30.

Eaton, Horace Ainsworth. "De Quincey's Love of Music," *JEGP*, XIII (1914), 247-58.

———. *Thomas De Quincey, A Biography*. New York, 1936.

Essig, Erhardt Herbert. "Thomas De Quincey and Robert Pearse Gillies as Champions of German Literature and Thought," unpublished diss. Northwestern University, 1951.

Fowler, John Henry. "De Quincey as Literary Critic," *The English Association Pamphlets*, No. 52. London, 1922.

Gay, Frank R. "De Quincey as a Student of Greek, and a writer on Greek Literature and History," unpublished diss. University of Chicago, 1917.

Goldman, Albert. *The Mine and The Mint, Sources for the Writings of Thomas De Quincey*. Carbondale, Ill., 1965.

Green, J. A. *Thomas De Quincey. A Bibliography Based upon the De Quincey Collection in the Moss Side Library*. Manchester, 1908.

Hogg, James, ed. *De Quincey and His Friends: Personal Recollections, Souvenirs and Anecdotes of Thomas De Quincey, His Friends and Associates*. London, 1895.

Howell, Wilbur Samuel. "De Quincey on Science, Rhetoric, and Poetry," *Speech Monographs*, XIII, i (1946), 1-13.

Hudson, Hoyt. "De Quincey on Rhetoric and Public Speaking," in *Historical Studies of Rhetoric, and Rhetoricians*, ed. Raymond F. Howes. Ithaca, N. Y., 1961. Reprinted from *Studies in Rhetoric and Public Speaking in Honor of James Albert Winans*. New York, 1925.

Japp, Alexander H. *Thomas De Quincey: His Life and Writings, With Unpublished Correspondence*. 2 vols. New York, 1877.

Jolles, Matthijs. "Toter Buchstabe and lebendiger Geist, Schillers Stellung zur Sprache," *Deutsche Beiträge zur geistigen Überlieferung*, IV (1961), 65–108.

Jordan, John. "De Quincey on Wordsworth's Theory of Diction," *PMLA*, LXVIII (September, 1953), 764–78.

———. *De Quincey to Wordsworth. A Biography of a Relationship*. Berkeley, 1963.

———. *Thomas De Quincey, Literary Critic. His Method and Achievement*. Berkeley, 1952.

Kames, Henry Home, Lord. *Elements of Criticism*. 2 vols. 7th ed. Edinburgh, 1788.

Masson, David. *Thomas De Quincey*. London, 1881.

McBurney, James H. "Some Recent Interpretations of the Aristotelian Enthymeme," *Papers of the Michigan Aceadmy of Science, Arts, and Letters*, XXI (1935), 485–500.

Metcalf, J. C. *De Quincey: A Portrait*. Cambridge, Mass., 1940.

Michelsen, Peter. "Thomas De Quincey and Schiller," *German Life and Letters, A Quarterly Review*, new series IX (January, 1956), 91–99.

Miller, J. Hillis. *The Disappearance of God, Five Nineteenth-Century Writers*. Cambridge, Mass., 1963.

Paull, H. M. "De Quincey–and Style," *Fortnightly Review*, CLXVII (1922), 152–62.

Priestley, Joseph. *A Course of Lectures on Oratory and Criticism*, ed. Vincent Bevilacqua and Richard Murphy. Carbondale, Ill., 1965.

Proctor, Sigmund. *Thomas De Quincey's Theory of Literature*. Ann Arbor, 1943.

Sackville-West, Edward. *A Flame in Sunlight, The Life and Work of Thomas De Quincey*. London, 1936.

Saintsbury, George. *A History of English Prose Rhythm*. London, 1912.

———. *Essays in English Literature, 1780-1860*. London, 1896.

Salt, Henry S. *De Quincey*. London, 1904.

Schiller, Friedrich. *Friedrich Schiller, Sämtliche Werke*, ed. Gerhard Fricke and Herbert G. Göpfert. 5 vols. Munich, 1960.

———. *Schillers Briefe. Kritische Gesamtausgabe*, ed. Fritz Jonas. 7 vols. Stuttgart, 1892-1896.

Sehrt, Ernst Theodor. *Geschichtliches und religiöses Denken bei Thomas De Quincey*. Berlin, 1936.

Smith, Adam. *Lectures on Rhetoric and Belles Lettres*, ed. John M. Lothia. London, 1963.

Stockley, Violet. *German Literature as Known in England, 1750 - 1830*. London, 1929.

Talley, Paul M. "De Quincey On Persuasion, Invention, and Style," *Central States Speech Journal*, XVI (November, 1965), 243–54.

Thorpe, Clarence D. "Addenda, and a Comment on De Quincey's Relation to German Literature," in *Thomas De Quincey's Theory of Literature* by Sigmund Proctor. Ann Arbor, 1943.

Wellek, René. "De Quincey's Status in the History of Ideas," PQ XXIII (July, 1944), 248–72.

————. *Confrontations, Studies in the intellectual and literary relations between Germany, England, and the United States during the nineteenth Century*. Princeton, 1965.

————. *Immanuel Kant in England, 1793-1838*. Princeton, 1931.

Whately, Richard. *Elements of Rhetoric*, ed. Douglas Ehninger. Carbondale, Ill., 1963.

Wilson, John. *Noctes Ambrosianae*, ed. R. Shelton Mackenzie. 5 vols. New York, 1875.

Woolf, Virginia. "Impassioned Prose" (from *TLS*, 10 Sept., 1926), *Granite and Rainbow*. New York, 1958.

Zimmern, Helen. "Thomas De Quincey. Eine biographische Skizze," *Deutsche Monatsblätter*, I (April-Sept., 1878), 335–61.

INDEX

Addison, Joseph, 316, 328
Aeschylus; 197, 208, 219, 223
Agricola, Rodolphus, 91 n
Alexander of Macedon: the Age of Alexander in comparison with the Age of Pericles, 204–16; the Age of Alexander, 313
Anacreon, 213
Anaxagoras, 186
Apelles (the painter), 209
Aphrodisiensis, Alexander, 91 n
Appian, 214, 216
Ariosto, Lodovico: *Orlando Furioso*, 303, 305
Aristophanes, 208, 219; satire on oratorical manner, 241–42
Aristotle: probability and enthymemic reasoning, 83–92, 218; his *Rhetoric*, 83, 217–18; his *Poetic*, 168; Socratic school, 181; teacher of philosophy, 209, 213, 221; privilege of publication, 239–40; expression of ideas, 262; *responsa prudentum*, 292; mentioned, 316
Arnobius, 95
Augustine, St. (Aurelius Augustinus) 95–96

Bacon, Francis, 109 n, 132, 141, 209, 255 n, 267–68, 290, 336
Barbarian: meaning, 252
Barrow, Isaac: as dialectician, 109
Basil, 96, 339
Batteux, Charles, 192
Bergmann, Benjamin, 249
Bernoulli, James, 267
Birmingham, meaning spurious or of poor quality, 96, 114, 171, 302 n

Blair, Hugh, 192
Bolingbroke, Henry St. John: as rhetorician, 111, 338
Bossuet, Jacques Benigne, 157
Bouhours, Dominique, 192
Bourdaloue, Louis, 157
British character: failure to appreciate countrymen, music, and prose style, 134–38
Browne, Sir Thomas: rhetoric and eloquence, 104, 217; *Hydrotaphia, or Urne-Buriall*, 105, 339; *Religio Medici*, 109
Buffon, George Louis, 157
Burgersdyk, Francis, 88–89
Burke, Edmund: his colloquial talents contrasted with Samuel Johnson's, 125 n, 269–70; his use of tautology, 128–29; his oratory, 137, 165, 288; "supreme writer of his century," 192, 194–97; "far surpasses any orator, ancient or modern," 331, 334, 339
Burnet, Gilbert, 317–18
Burton, Robert: *Anatomy of Melancholy*, 102
Byron, George Gordon, Lord: theatrical manner, 135

Caesar, Augustus, 148, 208, 238
Caesar, Julius, 147, 325
Caesar, Tiberius, 194
Callimachus (the poet), 213, 313
Campbell, George: *The Philosophy of Rhetoric*, 82, 92, 133
Canning, George, 120
Casaubon, Florence Estienne Meric, 255

Shakespeare, William (*Continued*)
"Remuneration . . . the Latin
word for three farthings" (*Love's
Labour's Lost*: III, i, 143), 298;
Titus Andronicus, 304; dramatic
power, 310; comparison in *Hamlet*, 310
Sheridan, Richard Brinsley: a charlatan not a rhetorician, 112–14
Sidney, Sir Philip, 100
Simonides, 214 n
Slang, 247
Smigletius, Martin, 88–89
Socrates: *Comus Socratica*, 180–87;
the dialogues, 183, 208
Somers, John, 338
Sophistry, 81
Sophocles, 197, 208, 213, 218–19,
245, 253 n, 303–4
South, Robert: as dialectician, 109
Southey, Robert, 317
Spanish rhetoric, 123–24
Spenser, Edmund, 200, 255 n, 290
Staël, Madame de, 155, 281, 283–84
Sternhold, Thomas, 159
Style: natural and artificial, 144–53,
193; brief, aphoristic, curt, 157–
58, 181–82; as *synthesis onomation*, 163; as all possible relationships between thoughts and
words, 163; organic and mechanic, 163–67; *style coupé* and
style soutenu, 166; *form of style*
considered apart from *form of
logic*, 185; artificial, 199; defense
of brevity, 235; as the management of language, 260; intelligibility and power as ends of, 260–
62; natural, in conversation, 287;
elevated, 301
Sublime, 300–301 n, 306, 310, 322,
329
Sunderland, Robert Spencer, Lord,
348
Sympathy: of audience, 120, 138,
232, 236; binds the elaborate and
the fanciful, 121; with society,
215, 240; "electric kindling,"
268–69, 280; with human nature,
273; with native merit, 294
Symposiarch, Athenian, 264, 286

Tacitus, 175, 199
Talk, 267
Taylor, Jeremy: facility of play,
104–5, 108; florid Corinthian
style, 106; *Holy Living and Holy
Dying*, 106–7, 125, 339; mechanical defects of style, 108; rhetorical fancy, 115; theologian, 256 n
Tertullian, 95–96
Thales, 172
Theater, 236, 243
Theocritus, 213, 313
Theognis, 172, 315
Thucydides: compared to Herodotus and Tacitus, 174–75, 209, 213,
317–19, 325
Tillotson, John: sermons and ecclesiastical rhetoric, 109
Time, 274
Transcendentalism, 262–63
Transition. *See* Connectives
Troil, Unno von: *Iceland*, 122

Vaugelas, Claude Favre, 127
Virgil, 95 n
Voltaire, Francois Marie, 157, 272

Wallis, John, 127
Walpole, Horace, 148, 272
Walpole, Sir Robert, 112, 348
Watts, Isaac: *Improvement of the
Mind*, 278
Whately, Richard: *Elements of
Rhetoric*, 81 n, 93, 126, 128–33,
237
Wieland, Christoph Martin, 200
Woman: purity of language, 144
Wordsworth, William: paraphrased,
92, 115, 229–30; meditative,
philosophic poetry, 123, 136;
purity and accuracy of his English, 127; the Alpine hound, 182–
83; mentioned, 99
Writing: as compared with speaking, 139

Xenophon: as compared with Plato,
181–85, 208, 212, 316; *Cyropaedia*
and *Anabasis*, 319–22
Yankee: meaning, 143 n
Young, Edward: his meditative,
philosophic poetry, 123, 136